Y0-EHC-632

WITHDRAWN

John W. Brister Library
Memphis State University
Memphis, Tennessee 38152

INDEX TO POETRY IN PERIODICALS

1915-1919

INDEX TO POETRY
IN
PERIODICALS

American Poetic Renaissance
1915-1919

An Index of Poets and Poems
Published in American Magazines and Newspapers

Prepared By
The Editorial Board
Granger Book Co., Inc.

GRANGER BOOK CO., INC.
Great Neck, New York

Copyright © Granger Book Co., Inc. 1981
All rights reserved

International Standard Book Number 0-89609-212-7
Library of Congress Catalog Card Number 81-80120

Printed in the United States of America

CONTENTS

Reference
PS
324
I44x

INTRODUCTION

The Index to Poetry in Periodicals, 1915-1919, is an index of poets and poems published in 122 American magazines and newspapers during one of the most important periods of American poetic history.

The advent of the "new poetry" in 1913 heralded the beginning of the American poetic renaissance which was to continue through the decade. Louis Untermeyer indicates that the inaugural edition of Harriet Monroe's POETRY: A MAGAZINE OF VERSE at the end of 1912 came at the "very moment of the breaking of the storm...a few months later came the deluge" (Untermeyer, MODERN AMERICAN POETRY, New & enl. ed., 1962).

Dozens of new magazines devoted to poetry were founded at this seminal time, including Margaret Anderson's LITTLE REVIEW (1914), Alfred Kreymborg's OTHERS (1915), and Herbert Bruncken's MINARET (1915). Existing periodicals, such as AINSLEE'S MAGAZINE, CENTURY MAGAZINE, THE DIAL, THE FORUM, and THE YOUTH'S COMPANION published great amounts of poetry, particularly by new poets (T.S. Eliot's "The Waste Land" was first published in a periodical, THE DIAL, in 1922). Moreover, newspapers, daily and weekly, metropolitan and rural, printed more poetry than ever before (or since). The public appetite for the "new poetry" was almost insatiable. Untermeyer states that by 1917 it "ranked as America's first national art; its success was sweeping, its sales unprecedented."

This Index is intended to provide access to the great body of work published in this period which is not otherwise retrievable. As much of this poetry has never been anthologized in book form, it is not accessible through standard poetry indexes.

While every magazine devoted to poetry and almost every general magazine and newspaper which regularly published verse is indexed here, this work is not and cannot be encyclopedic or all-inclusive; it is believed, however, that there are no significant omissions.

EXPLANATORY NOTES

LIST OF PERIODICALS INDEXED

Each of the 122 periodicals indexed is listed at the front of the book together with a short alphabetical abbreviation or symbol which refers to it.

Magazines which are not extant have been annotated with dates of publication and other historical data where possible. Every effort consistent with an index of this type has been made to provide such material; more exhaustive labor to this end must be left to histories of American magazines.

Alternative titles of periodicals are shown in brackets when known.

INDEX TO POETS & POEMS

Each poem in the Index is listed under its author, or translator if the author is unknown. Under the full name of the author, the entry provides:

(1) Title of poem(s)
(2) Translator (if any)
(3) Symbol which refers to the periodical in which the poem appears
(4) Date of issue of the periodical.

Anonymous authors are not included in the Index. Authors identified by initials are listed under such initials which are enclosed in quotation marks and which are included at the beginning of the alphabetical sequence for each letter. The last initial is used as the "sur-initial" for alphabeting purposes; thus, for example, an attribution given as C.A.D. is listed as "D.,C.A."

Authors names beginning with "Mac" and "Mc" are filed together under "Mac." Various forms of an author's name as they may appear in two or more periodicals have been reconciled and are shown only in the most usual or readily identifiable form. Cross-references from pseudonyms to full legal names are given when known.

Articles at the beginning of titles are retained but disregarded in the alphabeting. Thus, each poem beginning with an article is alphabeted by the word following the article and is capitalized.

The date of issue of the periodical in which the poem appears follows the symbol and is given in the short numerical mode (e.g. November 22, 1915 is given as 11/22/15). If the precise issue of the periodical cannot be determined, a question mark is used for the uncertain factor (e.g. if the particular week in which a poem appeared in a weekly publication is unknown, the entry will read 11/?/15; if the particular month of a monthly periodical is uncertain, the citation will be given as ?/15).

LIST OF PERIODICALS INDEXED
AND
KEY TO SYMBOLS

Ain	Ainslee's Magazine. 1898-1926, then merged in True Western Stories
All	All Story Weekly [Magazine]. 1905-1920, then merged in Golden Argosy
AmH	American Hebrew. 1879-?
AmP	American Poetry Magazine. 1919-1933
AQ	Amherst Graduate Quarterly
ArW	Art World. 1916-1918, then united with Palette & Bench; absorbed Craftsman [see Cra], 1901-1916
AtM	Atlantic Monthly
Ave	Ave Maria. 1865-?
BaA	Baltimore American
Ban	Bang
Bea	Beacon
Bel	Bellman
Boo	Bookman. 1895-1933, then American Review
BosH	Boston Herald
BoT	Boston [Evening] Transcript
Bro	Broadside
CaW	Catholic World
Cen	Century Magazine
ChDN	Chicago Daily News
ChH	Chicago Herald [and Examiner]
ChT	Chicago Tribune
CnR	Christian Register. 1821-?
Coll	Collier's [Weekly]
Colo	Colonnade. 1907-?
CoV	Contemporary Verse. 1916-1929
Cra	Craftsman. 1901-1916, then merged in Art World [see ArW]
Cri	Crisis. 1910-?
Del	Delineator. 1873-1937
DenP	Denver Post
DetN	Detroit News
DetS	Detroit Sunday News
Dia	Dial. 1880-1929
ELM	Eliot Literary Magazine
Ene	Enemy
EvM	Everybody's Magazine. 1899-1929, then united with Romance
Ext	Extension Magazine

For	Forge
Foru	Forum. 1886-1930
Fra	Fra. 1908-1917, then Roycrafter
GoH	Good Housekeeping
GosD	Goshen Democrat
Har	Harper's Magazine
HarW	Harper's Weekly. 1857-1916
HoG	House and Garden
IlS	Illustrated Sunday Magazine
Ind	Independent. 1848-1928
Int	International. 1908 [as Moods]-1918
KSC	Kansas City Star
Kis	Kismet
Lib	Liberator. 1918-1924, superseded Masses [see Mas]
Lif	Life. 1883-1936
LiR	Little Review. 1914-1929
Liv	Live Stories
LivC	Living Church
LoAG	Los Angeles Graphic
Lyr	Lyric. 1917-1919, 1921-?
McCa	McCall's Magazine
McCl	McClure's Magazine. 1893-1929
Mad	Madrigal. 1917-1918
Mag	Magnificat
Mas	Masses. 1911-1917, then merged in Liberator [see Lib]
Men	Menorah Journal. 1915-?
Mid	Midland. 1915-1933, then merged with Frontier
Min	Minaret. 1915-?
Nat	Nation
NeO	New Opinion
NeR	New Republic
NeW	New World
New	Newarker
NYH	New York Herald
NYS	New York [Evening] Sun
NYSB	New York Sun Books and Book World
NYTi	New York Times
NYTM	New York Times Magazine
NYTr	New York Tribune
NYWM	New York World Magazine
NoAR	North American Review. 1815-1940
OSB	Omaha Sunday Bee
Oth	Others. 1915-1919
Out	Outlook. 1870-1935
OvM	Overland Monthly. 1868-1935
Pag	Pagan. 1916-1922
Par	Parisienne Monthly Magazine. 1915-1921

Pas	Pasadena Library and Civic Magazine
PatW	Patience Worth's Magazine
Pea	Pearson's Magazine. 1899-1925
PeHJ	People's Home Journal. 1889-1929
PhPL	Philadelphia [Evening] Public Ledger
PiR	Pictorial Review. 1899-1939
PoeL	Poet Lore. 1901-?
Poet	Poetry: A Magazine of Verse. 1912-1971
PoJ	Poetry Journal. 1912-1918
PoR	Poetry Review of America. 1916-1917
PpM	Popular Magazine [for Boys]. 1903-1931
Puc	Puck. 1877-1918
QW	Queen's Work
ReM	Reedy's Mirror. 1891-1920
REJ	Richmond Evening Journal
SanC	San Francisco Call & Post
SatE	Saturday Evening Post
ScM	Scribner's Magazine. 1887-1939, then united with Commentator
SeA	Seven Arts. 1916-1917, absorbed by Dia [see Dia]
SmS	Smart Set. 1900-1930
SnaS	Snappy Stories. 1916-?
Son	Sonnet. 1917-1921
SoW	Southern Woman's Magazine. 1904-1918
Sta	Stars & Stripes
StJ	Stratford Journal. 1916-1920, 1926-1932
Sun	Sunset
Sur	Survey. 1909-1937
Tea	Teachers' Monographs
TeR	Texas Review. 1915-1924, then Southwest Review
Tou	Touchstone
Tri	Trimmed Lamp
WaGA	Wadsworth Gas Attack
WiG	Williamsport [Pa.] Gazette and Bulletin
WoW	Woman's World. 1865-1940
WrM	Writer's Monthly
YaR	Yale Review
YoCh	Young Churchman. 1870-1922
You	Youth: Poetry of Today. 1918-1919
YouC	Youth's Companion. 1827-1929

A

"A." To a little boy. For 11/16
  To a little girl. For 11/16
  The Wind and rain. For 11/16

"A.,H.N." Augusta. For 11/16

"A.,M." Triumverate. For 11/16

"ABBOT, HELEN L. Pictures. BoT 1/26/18

ABER, LOUREINE. The Fallen. Poet 7/19
  Farewell. Poet 7/19
  My friend. Poet 7/19
  The Soldier to Helen. Poet 7/19

ABEY, STANLEY G. Nursery versery. LoAG 1/16/15

ACKERMAN, ZÖE. My canary's rhapsody. PoR

ACUNA, MANUEL. To the martyred poet, Juan Diaz Covarrubias (tr. Alice
  Stone Blackwell). StJ 9/18

ADAMS, FRANKLIN P. The Last laugh, Horace: epode 15. Har 12/19
  To an indifferent Desdemona. EvM 6/19
  Verse unshackled. Har 8/17

ADAMS, GEORGE MATTHEW. This "me" of mine. GoH 2/19

ADAMS, HENRY. Buddha and Brahma. YaR 10/15

ADAMS, J. DONALD. Pines. Bel 5/13/16

ADAMS, KATHARINE. Le Cygne. BoT 4/20/18

  La foi. Lyr 4/19
  Life. BoT 12/22/17
  Longing. CoV 8/17

ADAMS, ROBERT N. Who plants a tree. YouC 5/4/16

ADLER, MORTIMER J. Over here. NYSB 9/15/18

AGG, JAY. At the fountain bay. NYS 1/19/19

AGNEW, EDITH J. The Best place. WoW 4/19

AIKEN, CONRAD. Aerial Dodds. PoJ 12/15
  Amorosa and company. PoJ 12/15
  Bain's cats and rats. PoJ 12/15
  The Bitter love-song. NoAr 9/18
  Boardman and Coffin. PoJ 12/15
  Conversation: undertones. You 6/19
  Counterpoints Priapus and the pool. You 2/19
  Dancing Adairs. PoJ 12/15
  Discordants. Poet 9/15
  Duval's birds. PoJ 12/15
  Gabriel de Ford. PoJ 12/15
  Innocence. PoJ 6/15
  Meretrix: ironic. Oth 6/16

Miracles. PoJ 6/16
Movement from a symphony. Cen 9/16
Musical Cleggs. DetS 3/13/18
Portait of one dead. Oth 2/19
Rose and Murray. PoJ 12/15
Sonata in pathos. PoJ 11/17
Variations, I-XVIII. CoV 6/17
Violet Moore and Bert Moore. PoJ 12/15
Will you step into my grave, sir? Dia 11/30/18
Zudora. PoJ 12/15

AIKINS, CARROLL. Carpentry. ScM 10/16
Good to walk to world with. ScM 2/16
To a child. ScM 3/17

AKINS, ZÖE. Covenant: an ode, July 4, 1918, NYSB 8/25/18
Driftwood burning. Poet 9/18
Indifference. Cen 9/19
The Return. Cen 2/15
Rose and Narcissus. NYSB 2/23/19
Seventeen. Cen 3/19
The Stagnant pool. ReM 2/18/16
The Wanderer. Poet 1/15

ALDEN, BAXTER. In ink of India and gold. Oth 12/17
To an old Korean painting Avalakitesvara, goddess of compassion. Oth 3-4/19

ALDINGTON, RICHARD. At night. PoJ 11/15
Beauty unpraised. Poet 7/19
Blue, a conceit. LiR 6-7/15
Christine. LiR 6-7/15
Compensation. Poet 7/19
Dawn. PoJ 11/15
Fatigues. Dia 9/27/17
Images. PoR 10/15
In the trenches. Dia 12/6/17
Inarticulate grief. PoR 8/16
Insouciance. Poet 7/19
Interlude. Poet 2/15
Leave-taking. SeA 8/17
Loss. Poet 7/19
Night place. PoJ 11/15
Palace music hall (Les sylhides). Poet 2/15
Poems of Myrrhine, Mitylene, and Konallis. LiR 8/15
Prayers and fantasies. Poet 11/18
The Retort discorteous. LiR 6-7/15
Stream. LiR 4/17
To Nijinsky. Poet 2/15
Two impressions. Poet 7/19

ALDINGTON, MRS. RICHARD Hilda Doolittle] ("H.D.").
  The Garden. Poet 3/15
  Hymen. Poet 12/19
  Late spring. LiR 1-2/16
  Moonrise. Poet 3/15
  Night. LiR 1-2/16
  Sea iris. LiR 5/15
  Sea poppies. LiR 4/17
  Storm. Poet 3/15
  The Wind sleepers. Poet 3/15
ALDIS, MARY. The Barber shop. Mas 4/16
  Barberries. LoAG 3/25/16
  The Beginning of the journey. LoAG 6/10/16
  Embarcation. Poet 10/18
  Flames. CoV 1/19
  Forward singing. LoAG 4/1/16
  Go from me. Poet 10/18
  I cursed a woman. Mas 6/17
  A Little girl. Poet 5/16
  Looking toward O'Connell bridge. Mas 6/17
  O bitter day. Poet 10/18
  Thoroughly pagan. Mas 6/17
  Thrones. Poet 10/18
  Watchers. LoAG 5/6/16
  Words. Mas 10/16
ALEXANDER, HARTLEY B. A la belle France. Mid 3/17
  All Hallows eve. Mid 10/16
  Dies irae. Mid 8/18
  Enhallowed. Mid 12/17
  The Flower of love. Mid 6/16
  For delight. Mid 11-12/18
  The Trenches. Mid 3/16
ALLAN, MARGUERITE B. Deliverance. SmS 1/17
  Indecision. SmS 5/16
ALLEN, ALICE E. The Signal torch. GoH 9/18
ALLEN, GRACE COOK. The Heart of things. SoW 6/15
  To—lines written on the fly leaf... SoW 7/17
  A Valentine (to my mother). SoW 2/15
ALLEN, HERVEY. The Blindman. NoAR 11/19
ALLEN, JAMES LANE. On the mantlepiece. Boo 9/19
ALLEN, PERCIVAL. "Father." CoV 6/16
  Friends. CoV 11/16
  My brother. CoV 11/16
  The Statute of Liberty. CoV 7/16
  Those who mourn. CoV 9/16
  Ultimate grief. CoV 9/17

The Wind-gods. CoV 2/16

ALLEN, WILLIS BOYD. A vision. Nat 10/5/18
  The War Christmas, 1916. Nat 12/21/16

ALLEN, DeFORD MIRIAM. Faun. Poet 5/19
  Wisdom through tears. Poet 5/19

ALLNUTT, PHOEBE CROSBY. April nights. NeR 9/14/18
  Colors. NeR 4/12/19
  The Crazy pine tree. NeR 9/14/18
  Kings. NeR 9/14/18
  Morning. NeR 9/14/18
  My friends. NeR 9/14/18
  My house. NeR 9/14/18
  Nature study. NeR 9/14/18
  Old thoughts. NeR 9/14/18
  Seedman's store. NeR 9/14/18
  A Visit to Haverstown. NeR 9/14/18
  Weaving. NeR 9/14/18
  Windows. NeR 9/14/18

ALNODRA, A. The Trenches. Poet 10/18

ALTROOL, RUDOLPH. Summons to youth. Poet 7/17

ALVORD, JAMES CHURCH. An American ace. EvM 10/18
  The Bald eagle. Cen 11/17
  The Carpenter. Poet 8/18
  Drum taps to heaven. Nat ?/19
  Easter evening. Poet 4/17
  The Peal of peace. CoV 2/19
  Woonsocket, city of mills. YaR 7/19

ALWOOD, LISTER R. The Canary. SetN 12/22/18

AMID, JOHN. The Burning pompano. Bel 9/14/15
  The Tail of the world. Mas 2/15

AMIDON, BEULAH. The Dead. Mas 2/17
  In a southern garden. Lib 4/18
  The Night court. Sur ?/17
  To an aviator. Lib 5/18

ANDERSON, DOROTHY. Dust. CoV 11/19
  Elegy. CoV 11/18
  Grief. CoV 11/18
  Motley. CoV 11/19
  My soul is a moth CoV 6/18
  A Revenant. CoV 11/19

ANDERSON, FRANCES T. The Kite. Mas 6/17

ANDERSON, JESSIE ANNIE. My shepherd. Lyr 10/17
  The Royal. Lyr 3/19

ANDERSON, LILIAN M. The Christmas roses. PoeL Vacation #/17

ANDERSON, MAXWELL. Autumn again. Mid 3-4/19

Bacchanal. You 2/19
Despair. Mid 3-4/19
Epigram. You 10/18
Immortality. SmS 2/18
In an afternoon. SmS 1/18
Sic semper. NeR 9/8/17
A Slave prays to the wind. CoV 9/18
Welcome to earth. CoV 10/19

ANDERSON, ROBIN. A Song of the southern moon. PeHJ 1/18

ANDERSON, SHERWOOD. American spring song. Poet 9/17
Evening song. Poet 9/17
Song of industrial America. Poet 9/17
Song of the drunken business man. Poet 9/17
Song of Stephen the westerner. Poet 9/17
A Visit. Poet 9/17

ANDERSON, W.H. At the golden gate: morning. LoAG 5/29/19
Ephemeral marvel of light. LoAG 12/4/15
Midsummer night storm. LoAG 1/29/16
Mud lemon cullerd queen. LoAG 6/17/16
The plaything. LoAG 4/29/16
Race-gendered hate. LoAG 2/12/16
Sympathy. LoAG 5/8/15
To a kindly critic (myself). LoAG 2/12/16
Words. LoAG 2/20/15

ANDREWS, CHARLTON. A Ballad of little romance. Boo 3/15

ANDREWS, JESSIE. The Land that Uncle Sam built. YouC 5/31/17

ANDREWS, LORRAINE. When the mustard's all a-quiver. OVM 2/18

ANDREWS, MARY R.S. The Baby and the baby. ScM 8/18
The Boy in France. ScM 11/18
A Call to arms. ScM 7/18
The Flowering. ScM 5/18
A Godspeed. ScM 12/17
Night of the mountains. ScM 10/16
The Oldest angel. ScM 11/19
Playmates. GoH 7/18
Say, three months. ScM 8/17

ANDREYEV, LEONID. Belgium (tr. Lo Pasrolsky). NYTM 4/25/15

ANGLEMAN, IRENE C. The Pilgrim's land. NYS 3/9/19

ANSPACHER, LOUIS K. The Song of the shipbuilder. Tou 10/18

ANTHOLO, LYDIA BRADT. Filling the cup. PoR 7/16
Heavy rain. PoR 7/16
Nuno scio quid sit amor. PoR 8/16

APOTHEKER, NAN. A Gentleman. SeA 6/17
A Lonely one speaks. SmS 1/18
May. CoV 5/18

Morning-after thought. Mas 1/17
Negation. CoV 5/18
Parting. Par 8/18
Question. CoV 5/18
Words. Cen 2/18
ARATA, OLIVER S. The iris. Colo 8/15
To a Japanese nightingale. Colo 8/15
ARDEN, HOPE. Hunting for spring. YouC 3/15/17
ARENS, EGMONT HEGEL. In Petrograd. Mas 7/17
ARENSBERG, WALTER CONRAD. For forms that are free. Oth 9/15
June. Oth 9/15
The Voice of one dead. Oth 9/15
Voyage a l'infini. Oth 9/15
ARMSTRONG, HAMILTON FISH. The College, 1917. ScM 11/17
Complainte de Renaud. ScM 8/16
On Sargent mountain. ScM 7/18
Passing Princeton junction. Har 7/18
ARMSTRONG, MARGARET. Half-loaves. Har 10/17
Mutations. Cen 8/17
ARMSTRONG, NELCHEN. "El Camino Real." LoAG 11/4/16
Pacific ocean. Loag 4/14/17
ARNOLD, ANNE. April. Mas 6/17
Courage. Mas 4/17
I know. Mas 6/17
Spring. Mas 9/17
ARRABIN, ANNE. The Shulamite. Cen 6/17
Verses for a guest-room. Cen 5/17
ASHFIELD, FRED R. The Father. Mas 5/16
ASHLEIGH, CHARLES. Night in prison. Lib 5/18
Once more-the road. LiR 4/17
ATKINS, ELIZABETH. Ad astra. Mid 11-12/18
My madonna. Mid 11/16
Night-waking. Mid 11/16
Winter night. Mid 11/16
ATWOOD, CLARA E. A Japanese tale. YouC 3/22/17
AUERBACH, JOSEPH S. The Abiding questions. NoAR 4/19
Abode of justice. NoAr 4/19
The Battle of Neuve Chapelle. NoAR 5/15
Her life. NoAR 11/18
Invocation of reason. NoAR 11/19
AURINGER, O.C. Starlight song. Colo 9/15
AUSTIN, MARY. Neither spirit nor bird. Poet 2/17
Prayer to the mountain spirit, from the Navajo. Poet 2/17
AYRES, MALCOLM B. In June. Colo 6/15

AYSCOUGH, FLORENCE (with Amy Lowell).
  After how many years. Poet 2/19
  Autumn. Poet 2/19
  Calligraphy. Poet 2/19
  The Emperor's return from a journey to the south. Poet 2/19
  An Evening meeting. Poet 2/19
  From the straw hut among the seven peaks. Poet 2/19
  The Inn at the western lake. Poet 2/19
  On seeing the portrait of a beautiful concubine. Poet 2/19
  On the classic of the hills and the sea. Poet 2/19
  One goes on a journey. Poet 2/19
  The Palace blossoms. Poet 2/19
  A Recluse. Poet 2/19
  Summer. Poet 2/19
  Winter. Poet 2/19

B

"B.,A." In memoriam. For 2/17

"B.,D." The Debt. For 2/17

"B.,E.F.A." When dreams come true. Par 8/17

"B.,F.B." Mt. Desert. For 2/17

"B.,J.B." Song of Pierre. For 2/17
  The Trail boss. For 2/17

"B., J.Y." L'envoi. For 11/16

"B.,M.S." To one who laughs with the wind. For 2/17

"B., W.L." Prayer when the war is near. LoAG 7/8/16

BACHELLER, IRVING. The Carefullest man in the world. NYT: 6/30/18
  Git out o' my medder, bobolink. EvM 11/18

BACON, LEONARD. An Afternoon in artillery walk. CoV 3/16
  The Hard road. CoV 4/16
  The Maunderings of Momus: or lectures of the unlearned. Cen 1/18

BACON, VIRGINIA CLEAVER. The Mermaid. LoAG 6/8/15

BAIRD, GEORGE M.P. Old Walt drops in. ReM 2/1/18

BAKELESS, JOHN. Mountain tops. Poet 2/19

BAKER, HELBA. Without beginning. Ain 10/19

BAKER, KARLE WILSON. ACORNS. YaR 10/19
  Apple and rose. YaR 10/16
  At the picture show. YaR 10/16
  Beach play. EvM9/18
  A Clear night. YaR 10/16
  Eagle youth. YaR 10/18
  Fairy fires. YaR 10/19
  The Family. YaR 10/16

Good company. PoR 6/16
Graves in France. YaR 1/19
Gray days. YaR 10/19
The House mother. Poet 11/15
Leaves. YaR 10/19
A Little boy's bath. YaR 10/16
Overhead travellers. YaR 10/19
The Ploughman. YaR 1/18
A Simple song for America, 1917. Poet 9/17
The Small town celebrates. BoT 11/23/18
Stillness. YaR 10/16
Street doves. YaR 10/16
Vanity. YaR 1/18
W.V.M., 1910. Son #2/17
Wild geese. YaR 10/16
Winter streets. EvM 12/17

BAKER, LOUISE R. April fool. YouC 3/28/18

BAKER, MARY LOUISE. The Polka dot pup and the geese. YouC 4/19/17

BALDWIN, ANITA M. To Mars. LoAG 4/10/18

BALDWIN, FAITH. False dawn. Min 6/17
In a garden. CoV 7/19
Joyce Kilmer. CoV 12/18
The Novice. Min 5/17

BALDWIN, MARY. La Scala Santa, Rome. ScM 1/18

BALLAD, ADELE M. The Troubadour. Mid 5/17

BALMONT, KONSTANTIN. Evening fields. CoV 11/19
On the heights. Poet 8/18
The Secret of being (tr. Luba Wies). PoJ 12/16
With the wind. Poet 8/18

BALLOU, ADIN. After reading "Lavendro." ScM 7/17

BANGS, JANET NORRIS. The Sand dunes. Poet 9/18

BANGS, JOHN KENDRICK. To Columbia's sons. Out 12/12/17

BANKS, M.B. A Rime of raisins. YouC 5/10/17
What o'clock. YouC 9/13/17

BANKS, THEODORE HOWARD, JR. The Return. EvM 4/19

BANNING, GEORGE HUGH. The Calm. LoAG 3/18/16
The Flying merman. LoAG 1/22/16
Forget-me-not. LoAG 7/29/16
Life in darkness. LoAG 9/2/16
Little things. LoAg 5/20/16
My song. LoAG 1/22/16
Off the reef. LoAG 1/22/16
Pilot of the night watch. LoAG 2/5/16
Premonition. LoAG 2/19/16
Sad waves. LoAG 9/2/16

Soul by the sea of time. LoAG 8/5/16
Sunrise on the ocean. LoAG 8/5/16
To Walt Whitman. LoAG 4/1/16
Ukelele. LoAG 2/5/16
"You." LoAG 3/25/16

BARBER, FRANCES. The True concord. YaR 4/15

BARKER, ELSA. The Questioner. McCl ?/17

BARKER, PERCEVAL M. On hearing the carillon of Antwerp cathedral.
   Cent 6/18

BARLOW, JANE. A Knell and a chime. ReM 1/22/15

BARNARD, SEYMOUR. On a workman asleep in a subway train. Mas 7/17
   Philanthropy: a comic opera. Mas 3/15
   To a girl on a magazine cover. Mas 1/17

BARNES, DJUNA. Antique. Har 8/18
   Lines to a lady. All 6/1/18

BARNETT, HENRY. The Blind poet. CoV 12/18

BARNEY, DANFORD. Beauty. Lyr 8/17
   By a Tuscan ruin. Lyr 6/17
   The Dead awake. PoJ 9/17
   Diametrics. PoJ 9/17
   Finale. ScM 12/19
   Music (from a hill). ScM 4/19

BARONTI, GERVE. A Bouquet. PoJ 7/17
   Sahara. PoJ 7/17
   Seasons. PoJ 7/17
   Vocta. PoJ 2/18

BARR, NANN CLARK. The Marsh. Lib 3/18

BARR, SIMON. In the office. Ind ?/15

BARRETT, WILTON AGNEW. Adam. CoV 3/16
   The Adventurer, I-III. Poet 8/17
   An Awakening. Poet 12/19
   Beyond the bounds. Har 5/15
   The Children. EvM 2/19
   A Dead man. CoV 4/16
   The Dwellers. Foru 12/15
   John Cord. Mas 5/16
   A New England church. Poet 10/15
   Pictures. Poet 10/15
   Soldiers, behold your beauty. BoT 11/23/18
   Songs from the journey. CoV 8/17
   That night I danced. Foru 2/16
   There is a stream I know. CoV 7/17
   The Wash. Mas 4/16
   When I heard you were dead. Poet 8/17

BARRINGTON, PAULINE B. After. LoAG 12/2/16

At the symphony concert. LoAG 12/18/15
But for you. LoAG 9/30/16
California. LoAG 11/4/16
Carnival. LoAG 1/1/16
The Casement door. LoAG 3/4/16
Cubes and cones. LoAG 1/15/80
A Day of trees. LoAG 2/19/16
A Fire star. LoAG 12/25/15
The Hand of God. LoAG 1/9/15
I did not know. CoV 7/17
Ice skaters. LoAG 7/18/16
Impressions. LoAG 4/8/16
On hearing an etude by Bartkiewicz. LoAG 2/5/16
Outside. LoAG 1/29/16
The Pomegranate bush. Poet 9/18
Song. LoAG 12/20/17
Sonnet. LoAG 11/10/17
Spring. LoAG 3/18/16
Sunset at Santa Barbara. Poet 9/18
Sunday afternoon. LoAG 4/21/17
To a dancer. LoAG 6/26/15
Toy guns. Mas 5/16
Verse. LoAG 5/1/18
Vignettes. LoAG 5/27/16
A White iris. LoAG 6/10/16

BARRY, BEATRICE. The Coasters. NYTM 1/28/17

BARRY, IRIS. Domestic. Poet 7/16
Double. Poet 7/16
Enough has been said of sunset. Poet 7/16
The Fledgling. Poet 7/16
Impression. Poet 7/16
Study. Poet 7/16
Town-mouse. Poet 7/16

BARTLETT, BERTHA BURNHAM. Sealed orders. BoT 2/8/19

BARTLETT, RANDOLPH. Builders of a world. LoAG 3/13/15
An Outrageous sonnet. Ain 5/19

BATAILLE, FREDERIC. It is cold to-night (tr. Celia Louise Crittenton).
PoeL New Year's #/17

BATCHELDER, ANN. The Ancient one. SmS 4/15

BATCHELOR, JEAN M. Consecration. SmS 12/16
Song. CoV 8/17
BATES, EDITH C. The Haunting road. PoeL Vacation#/17
The Vagabond. PoeL Vacation#/17

BATES, ESTHER WILLARD. A Little song of her. Mid 9-10/18

BATES, KATHARINE LEE. America the beautiful. WoW 7/19
Apollo laughs. Min 10/16

Change. You 4/18
Darby and Joan keep their golden wedding. BoT 5/4/18
The Dead of the Tuscania. Bel 4/6/18
The Death of Olaf Tryggvison. StJ 4/18
A Frosted bush in the sun. CoV 2/19
The Lighthouse. YaR 7/16
Out of Sibera. Out 5/23/17
Playmates. YouC 9/13/17
The Purple thread. Out 9/5/17
The Roll of honor. GoH 1/19
Soldiers of Freedom. GoH 12/17
Starlight at sea. YaH 7/16
This tattered catechism. Son#3/17
To Sigurd. ScM 5/16
Wild weather. BoT 11/23/18
Wings. YaR 7/16
White moments. ScM 1/18
The World war, CoV 2/19
Yellow clover. PoR 2/17
Yellow warblers. AtM 5/17
BAUDERLAIRE, CHARLES PIERRE. Hymn (tr. Charlotte Prentis
Hardin). PoeL New Year's#/17
BAXTER, SYLVESTER. Service-flags. BoT 2/21/18
BAY, LILLIAN. The Secret. Lyr 4/19
BEACH, JOSEPH WARREN. The Black land. Poet 12/16
Cave talk. Poet 5/15
The Dance in the steerage. Bel 12/15
Jenny's dancing. Poet 5/15
Lynch law. Bel 1/8/16
The Masseur. Poet 5/15
Nostalgia. Oth 1/16
The Point of view. Poet 5/15
The Red land. Poet 12/16
Succession. Poet 12/16
The View at Gunderson's. Poet 5/15
BEALL, DOROTHY. At the Metropolitan. Foru 10/15
The Pharisee. Foru 4/15
BEALL, LAURA. Tribute. Out 6/17
BEARD. THERESA VIRGINIA. The Christ-child. Bel 12/22/17
Daughters of Rachel. Bel 12/23/16
The Flag goes by. Bel 5/4/18
Heritage. Bel 5/15/15
In a garden. Bel 1/1/16
October. Bel 10/19/18
A Song for marching men. Bel 5/4/18

BECKER, CHARLOTTE. Echo. Poet 6/16
  A Garden on the Bosporus. NYS 1/19/19
  The Lindens. NYS 3/23/19
  Nocture. Mid 1-2/19
  The Outsider. WoW 11/19
  Pierrot goes. EvM 7/18
  Song. EvM 5/19
  Sufficiency. WoW 1/19

BEEBE, FRANCES. After life. Oth 1/19
  Death. Oth 1/19
  Unclothed. Oth 1/19
  The Wife. Oth 1/19

BEECHER-GITTINGS, ELLA. The Price. CoV 12/19

BEER, MORRIS ABEL. The Chorus man. CoV 4/19
  Moses. Poet 7/17
  Old China. Poet 7/17
  "Though the rose is dust." CoV 4/19

BEERS, HENRY A. On Granby hill. YaR 1/19
  The Pasture bars. YaR 1/16
  The Remainder. YaR 7/15

BELFIELD, JANE. At Eshol. SoW 2/15
  Bid the night pass. SoW 7/15

BELL, JESSICA. Dreams. CoV 12/18
  The First snow. CoV 12/19

BELL, JOSEPHINE. The Happy rain. Mas 6/17
  Mighty fires. Mas 6/17
  A Tribute. Mas 8/17
  Weariness. Mas 7/17

BELL, RALEY HUSTED. Her new lovers. Lyr 2/19
  Life and death. Lyr 4/19

BELL, W.J.D. Salut d'amour. SmS 4/18
  We outgrow love. SmS 10/17

BELLOWS, HENRY ADAMS. After sunset in the Rockies. Bel 10/9/15
  Beggars in America. PoR 11/16
  On the train-March. Bel 4/8/16

BELZ, IRMA. The Moonlight. DetN 1/26/19

BENDER, JESSIE HUNGERFORD. How great a love. WoW 5/19

BENEDICT, BERTRAM. Stealing the Kaiser's stuff. Nat 12/27/19

BENÉT, LAURA. Adventrue. Lyr 5/17
  The Elf-boy. CoV 2/16
  The Goose girl's going. CoV 1/17
  Loosed. Lyr 10/17
  Old women picking dandelion greens. CoV 4/17
  Peter: philosopher and gooseboy. CoV 2/16
  The Quest. CoV 2/16

The Sea child. Lyr 7/17
To a parrot in a farm house. EvM 3/16
BENÉT, STEPHEN VINCENT. After Pharsalia. PoJ 10/15
Come back! You 12/18
The Hemp: a Virginia legend. Cen 1/16
Jaufre Rudel beholds the lady of Tripoli. Ain 5/18
Last song of the Trojan light infantry. Ain 8/19
Portrait of a boy. Cen 1/17
Queen's gambit declined. CoV 9/18
Rain after a vauderville show. SeA 1/17
Roads and hills. SeA 5/17
BENÉT, WILLIAM ROSE. Accosted. YaR 10/19
Aristeas relates his youth. Lyr 1-2/18
The Asylum. ReM 5/4/17
A Ballad of Fountainebleu. CoV 5/16
Birth. ReM 2/11/16
The Case of Jacques Ribaut. PoR 1/17
Christmas interior. ReM 12/22/16
Danae. Cen 2/15
The Emotionalist. Mas 7/15
Fairyland. Cen 1/19
Forecast. Cen 8/18
Front line. Cen 1/18
The Furnace. Cen 3/15
The Golden gull. SmS 5/17
Gray. Poet 5/19
The Haunted wood. Cen 1/15
Her way. YaR 10/19
The Heretic. Har 11/15
The Horse thief. Poet 4/16
House at evening. YaR 10/19
Human touch. NYSB 1/26/19
I am the rebel. PoJ 7/16
Information. Poet 5/19
Kites. Poet 8/17
The Long absence (in memory of T.F.B.). YaR 10/19
Mad Blake. ReM 10/1/15
"Man with pigeons." Cen 4/16
Michelangelo in the fish market. CoV 1/16
Miniature. EvM 2/18
The Mysterious ones. Cen 17/15
Night-motoring. Cen 2/16
On the decay of the Toy theatre. CoV 6/16
On Edward Webbe, English gunner. YaR 10/17
On Sunday. Cen 5/16
On a window display. Poet 8/15
The Pale dancer. NYSB 2/9/19

The Price. Poet 10/17
The Push cart. CoV 9/16
The Race. SeA 3/17
Recognition. Lyr 6/17
The Red country. ReM 3/24/16
The Relinquary. CoV 3/16
The sensible convict. SmS 12/17
The Silver wind. Mad 8/17
Smoke. Cen 3/16
Solid earth. Poet 5/19
The Soldiers' say. BoT 11/23/18
The Star. Cen 12/19
Steeplechase. Lyr 8/17
Suffering Poland. Mas 3/17
A Taper of incense. ReM 4/14/16
The Telephone booth. ReM 3/17/16
Travel. YaR 10/19
Tricksters. YaR 10/17
Urania in ambush. SmS 11/15
The Variety house. PoJ 7/16
Veteran. Lyr 10/19
War and death. YaR 10/19
Wish-horses. Cen 5/15
The Words of an elephant. PoJ 5/15

BENJAMIN, PAUL LYMAN. The Dead poet. Mid 1-2/19
Love. Lyr 4/19
The Mute singer. Mid 1-2/18
A Wreath for a soldier poet. BoT 4/27/18

BENNETT, GEORGIA E. Apart. Lib 7/19

BENNETT, HENRY HOLCOMB. The Flag goes by. WoW 7/19

BENNETT, JOY. The Good Samaritan. LoAG 11/18/16
The Inca Bride. LoAG 10/28/16

BENSEL, ANNA B. Slumber song. REJ 2/23/18

BENTON, RITA. Our daily bread. Poet 4/15

BERANGER, PIERRE JEAN DE. The Holy alliance of the nations
(tr. Margarete Munsterberg). Nat 11/2/18

BERNARD, R. If that rose be broken. EvM 9/18
Lest we forget. EvM 5/18

BERNARD, SEYMOUR. The Boy who refused to go to church. Mas 7/16
Education: a community masque. Mas 9/16
Journalism: an unbelievable fantasy. Mas 4/16

BERNHARDT, LYSIANE. La neige a Poughkeepsie. Poet 12/18

BERRINGTON, EMILIA. The Song. CoV 4/19
Sorrow. Mas 10/17

BETTS, THOMAS JEFFERIES. Cuirassiers of France. ScM 8/17

BEZIAT, GEORGES. La reve. SmS 11/17

BICKFORD, G.M. Slumber boats. YouC 3/21/18

BIDDLE, LIVINGSTON LUDLOW. In a garden. ScM 1/16
   To a loved one. Boo 7/15

BIDDLE, VIRGINIA. Silence. Tou 7/18

BILL, K.H. Lend the way they fight! NYSB 10/6/18

BINNS, HENRY BRYAN. The Blacksmith. Boo 1/18
   The Peacemaker—August, 1914. Boo 2/18

BINYON, LAURENCE. La patrie. Out 12/20/16

BIRCH, HELEN LOUISE. And so the days go by. Poet 11/18
   Artist. Poet 10/17
   Can this be all? Poet 10/17
   Forewarned. Poet 10/17
   Laughing in the moonlight. Poet 11/18
   Mid-October. Poet 10/17
   Music. Poet 10/17
   Prophets. Poet 10/17
   Up in the hills. Poet 10/17
   Vertigo. Poet 11/18
   A Voice breaks in upon the silence. Poet 10/17

BIRD, REMSEN D. The Men of the navy. Out 8/28/18

BIRD, STEPHEN MOYLAN. The Cornish sea. CoV 6/18
   The Dying seasons. CoV 2/19
   Evening dreams. CoV 2/19
   Forget me not. CoV 6/18
   In the sky garden. CoV 11/18
   May. CoV 2/19
   Maxfield Parrish. CoV 2/19
   The Red Cross nurse. CoV 12/19
   The Silent ranges. CoV 11/18
   What if the lapse of ages were a dream? CoV 2/19
   Wildness. CoV 6/18

BISHOP, JOHN M. The Liberty loan. NYSB 10/6/18

BISHOP, JOHN PEALE. The Birds of paradise. Lyr 10/17
   The Nassau inn. ScM 6/17

BISHOP, MORRIS. An Atlas. Colo 11/15
   Before my fire in a French village. Poet 3/19
   Fleurs de feu. Colo 12/15
   For a book by Francis Thompson. Colo 6/16
   From "Les hurleurs." Colo 10/15
   Inconstant indignation. Colo 2/17
   Le Pere Segret. Poet 3/19
   On a fallen airman. Colo 5/16
   The Piker. Poet 3/19
   Senecae fragmentum. Colo 3/16

A Timorous shepherd. Cen 3/17
With the A.E.F. Poet 3/19

BISPHAM, G. TUCKER. Charm. Poet 2/16
Failure. Poet 2/16
The Lacemaker of Ypres. Poet 2/16
Mountain song. NeR 11/11/16
Nocturne. Poet 2/16

BIXBY, FANNY. Life. StJ 7/18

BJORKMAN, EDWIN. To Diana. Cen 6/18

BLACK, JOHN. A Poet's epitaph. Poet 11/17

BLACK, MacKNIGHT. Moods. CoV 12/19
The West. CoV 12/19

BLAIR, ANNIE. Wedded to a shrew. Oth 5-6/16

BLAIR, ETHEL. Copy! Cen 10/18

BLANDEN, CHARLES G. The Dream that still remains. LoAG 4/1/16
An English daisy. Mid 10/16
Liberation. Mid 10/16
Light and shade. Mid 9-10/18
The River of thought. LoAG 1/29/16
Shamrocks. LoAG 6/17/16
The Skylark. LoAG 6/16/16
Song. LoAG 2/26/16; LoAG 3/4/16
The Unseen singer. LoAG 3/18/16

BLOCK, RALPH J. Escape. PoJ 12/15
The Game. PoJ 12/15
A Man named Irving Killigrew. PoJ 3/17
The Sea's urge. PoJ 12/15
To Amburn hill. PoJ 12/15

BLOOD, BENJAMIN PAUL. Belgium. ScM 3/15
Resurgere. ScM 1/19

BLOOM, MARION L. Disillusion. SmS 7/17
In the garden. PoJ 3/17

BLOSSOM, ALMINA. Circus time. YouC 7/20/16
A Morning walk. YouC 1/17/18
The Three pigs. YouC 4/4/18

BLUNT, HUGH F. His way. CaW 11/17

BODENHEIM, MAXWELL. An Abandoned amusement park. NeR 8/7/15
After writing poetry. Oth 9/15
The Cafeteria. Oth 4/16
The Cloud descends. Poet 9/19
Columns of evening. Poet 5/16
Comparison. Lib 6/19
The Crucifixion. Poet 11/15
A Day. Oth 4/16
Death. Oth 4/16; Cen 11/17

The Department store. Poet 5/16
East side children playing. Oth 12/17
East side moving picture theatre-Sunday. Boo 1/18
Factory-girl. Oth 12/17; Boo 1/18
First meeting. Oth 4/16
Happiness. Poet 5/16
A Head. LiR 5/15
Images of emotion. Oth 4/16
Images of friendship. LiR 4/17
Impression of a woman. Oth 4/16
In the park. Oth 4/16
Just after the middle age. Oth 4/16
A man to a dead woman. Poet 11/15; Poet 5/16
Meeting. SMS 11/17; Oth 12/17; Tou 10/18

An Old Negro asleep. Oth 4/16
An Old poet to his love. Cen 1/18
The Operation. LiR 5/15
Our heaven. PoR 7/16
Parade of conscripted soldiers. Oth 12/17
The Rear-porches of an apartment building. Oth 9/15
Silence. LiR 5/15
Songs to a woman. Poet 5/19
South State Street, Chicago. ReM 4/11/19
The Steam-shovel. Poet 11/15
Streets. Poet 11/15
Suffering. Poet 5/16
Sunday in a certain city suburb. Oth 9/15
Thoughts while walking. Poet 11/15
To A.K. Oth 4/16
To Dorothy. Dia 3/28/18; Oth 12/17
To a woman. Oth 4/16
The Vagabond in the park. Oth 9/15
While walking. SmS 12/17
Whimsy. Oth 12/17
The Window washer. Poet 5/16
Women. SmS 10/15
BOGAN, LOUISE. The Bethrothal of King Cophetua. StJ Autumn/16
Bethrothed. Oth 12/17
Morning glories. StJ Autumn/16
Sunset at Amador. StJ 9/18
To a young poet singing of war. StJ Autumn/16
With queens. StJ 9/18
The Young wife. Oth 12/17
BOGART, GUY. Blue canyon. StJ 7/18
Jesus and Siddartha. StJ 6/19
BOHANAN, OTTO LELAND. To give the world! Cri 3/19
BOLLING, BERTHA. I heard bird. SmS 11/17

If hearts were stars. SmS 6/18
No. 3 C. SmS 6/17
Vigil. SmS 8/18
The Yellow curtains of Rome. ScM 6/18
Youth. SmS 3/18

BONHAM, L.R. The Flower smeller. LiR 4/17

BOOGHER, SUSAN M. Alchemy. Poet 3/18
Beatrice: daughter of Dante. ReM 4/12/18
Dams. Mid 11-12/18
The Harlot's child. Poet 3/18
Silence. Mid 11-12/18
Touching reality. Cen 10/16
Troy. Mid 11-12/18

BOORMAN, CHARLOTTE SAYRE. Buy a Liberty Bond. Out 4/17/18

BOOTH, EDWARD TOWNSEND. The Ploughman. SeA 6/17

BOOTH, ELEANOR DIXON. Spring. BoT 1/30/18

BORDEN, LUCILLE. When there was peace. CaW 3/18

BORST, RICHARD WARNER. April showers. Mid 5-6/19
In a cathedral. Mid 5-6/19
To the memory of Buffalo Bill. Mid 3-4/19

BORTON, FRANCIS S. Mt. Rubidoux at dawn. LoAG 4/22/16

BOSSCHERE, JEAN DE. L'offre de plebs. LiR 11/16

BOSTWICK, GRACE G. Barren. Boo 6/18
Remorse. CoV 5/19
Understanding. SmS 3/18

BOSWELL, ARTHUR. Roughchin the pirate. CoV 9/17

BOTTOMLEY, GORDON, The Ploughman. Poet 1/17

BOUTELLE, GRACE HODSON. Spring at the British Museum.
Bel 3/10/15

BOUTWELL, MARY STANTON. The Pine tree. BoT 3/15/19
Spring. BoT 3/15/19
The Thrush. BoT 3/15/19
Two graves. BoT 3/15/19
A White rose. BoT 3/15/19

BOUVÉ, PAULINE CARRINGTON. Little Betty Buttermilk. YouC
12/27/17
Minding the baby. YouC 8/3/16

BOWDOIN, VIRGINIA. Afraid? YouC 6/8/16
Going on a journey. YouC 3/1/17
Jack and his hobbyhorse. YouC 8/16/17
Little Molly Meader. YouC 10/18/17
Little Dannie Durkee. YouC 11/22/17
May-basket time. YouC 5/2/18
A Summer morning. YouC 7/20/16

The Trials of Thomas and his friends. YouC 5/30/18
BOWEN, HELEN HICKS. A lquid lay. SmS 2/16
BOWEN, STIRLING. At the bedside. DetN 7/7/18
  Autumnal. DetS 12/8/18
  The City. DetN 1/25/19
  Home from Arras. Lib 6/18
  June nocturne. DetS 9/1/18
  The Last laugh. DetS 8/4/18
  Monochrome. DetN 1/1/18
  Octave. Lib 6/19
  On prose poems from the French decadents. DetS 3/16/19
  On a volume of verse. DetS 2/24/18
  Romance. DetS 9/1/18
  Russia. DetS 4/14/18
  Sonnet. DetS 12/21/19
  Summer pools. Lib 8/18
  War bride. DetS 5/26/18
BOWKER, KATHLEEN K. To the baby that died. GoH 1/19
BOWLES, JOSEPH P. Facts. Lyr 6/17
BOWMAN, BETTY. A Portrait. Mas 6/17
  Transition. Mas 6/17
BOWMAN, FORREST. Lyrics. DetN 1/5/19
BOWMAN, LOUISE MOREY. And forbid them not. Poet 3/19
BOYDEN, GEOFFREY. The Doctor. YouC 9/6/17
BOYESEN, BAYARD. Over the ultimate. Oth 1/16
BOYLAN, E.E. Friendship. SmS 1/18
BOYLE, VIRGINIA FRAZER. Henry Mills Alden. Har 12/19
BOYTON, W.G. British half and half. Mas 7/15
BRACKETT, CHARLES WILLIAM. Benediction. EvM 9/18
  In winter. Mas 5/17
  Once. EvM 2/19
  Remembrance. Lyr 4/19
  A Threnody. Mas 5/17
BRADFORD, GAMALIEL. Anacreon's apology. CoV 3/18
  Ardor. CoV 3/18
  The Clock. CoV 11/19
  The Congregation. Bel 2/8/19
  The Divagator. CoV 3/18
  Exit God. CoV 3/18
  Fear. CoV 3/18
  God. CoV 3/18
  Heinelet. StJ 5/19; StJ 10-12/19
  Heinelet, I-II. CoV 3/18
  Hereafter. StJ 5/19
  Hunger. CoV 9/17

The Idle wind. CoV 3/18
Immortality. CoV 11/19
Ineluctahilis. CoV 9/17
Napoleon. Nat 8/10/18
Nil extra te. CoV 11/19
The Pursuit. CoV 3/18
The Riot. CoV 3/18
Robert E. Lee. CoV 3/18
Seals. CoV 3/18
Shreds. Min 5/17
Things of clay. CoV 3/18
A Thousand years. CoV 3/18
The Tissue. CoV 11/18
The Topmost bough. CoV 11/18
The Touch. StJ 10-12/19
Vicissitudes. StJ 5/19
Who. CoV 11/18
Why? CoV 3/18

BRADLEY, MARY. A Stranger in the city. Mas 3/17

BRADLEY, MARY LINDA. The Threshold. NoAR 4/17

BRADLEY, WILLIAM ASPENWALL. Autumn. PoR 1/17
Eglon and Ehoud (Judges I, 12-). PoJ 11/17
Greek epigram for a Parisian paper doll. Cen 2/17
Mortal beauty. Lyr 2/19
Sancta Ursula. Cen 7/17
Summer. PoR 1/17

BRAITWAITE, WILLIAM STANLEY. A Chronicle. Boo 11/17
The Mystery. ScM 10/15
Twenty stars to match his face. Boo 12/17
The Wet woods. Boo 11/17

BRALEY, BERTON. The Hopeless passion. Cen 12/16
The lonesomest time. NYTM 5/13/17
The Migration. AIN 11/18
No flowers, please. PpM 1/20/19
This way out. Har 11/19

BRANCH, ANNA HEMPSTEAD. The Name. Boo 12/17

BRAND, MAX. The Ballad of St. Christopher. All ?/19

BRANDT, CARL. The Fountain. Cen 3/16
Portrait. Min 6/16

BRANDT, IRVING. Shakespeare. Mid 4/16

BARSTOW, VIRGINIA. A House with green blinds. Mas 1/17
Nocturne. Mas 9/16
The Returning. PoJ 1/18

BRAZIER, STEFAN. Dreams. LiR 11/16
Fear. LiR 11/16

Hate. LiR 11/16
Memory. LiR 11/16
Yen Shee. LiR 11/16
The Voice of my fathers. ChT 10/31/16

BRETHERTON, CYRIL H. At Point Pinos. LoAG 2/20/15

BREWSTER, CORA COLBERT. Morning glories. SoW 5/15

BREWSTER, MARGARET CABLE. The Chase. StJ 3/19
"In the valley of the shadow." ScM 1/17
Love's silence. ScM 10/17
Promise. ScM 5/17
Sacraments. ScM 12/18

BRIDGES, ROBERT. The Philosopher to his mistress. ScM 9/15

BRIDGHAM, LILIAN CLISBY. Halloween witches. YouC 10/25/17

BRIDGMAN, AMY SHERMAN. "And women must weep." LoAG 8/20/17
The Christening. PoR 11/16
Colors. StJ 5/18
John Masefield. StJ 2/19
The Roadside symphony. StJ 3/17

BRIDGMAN, L.J. Advice to kings. YouC 5/9/18
The Keys. YouC 2/22/17
Off to the south. YouC 11/9/16
Why not? Youc 2/8/17

BRIDGMAN, L.S. The Animal baby show. YouC 3/30/16
Hasty hair dressing. YouC 2/17/16
Trials. YouC 4/13/16

BRIGGS, CAREY C.D. Alpha and omega. Colo 7/15
Sidney Lanier. Colo 9/15
Sunset. Colo 2/17
To Milton - blind. Colo 6/16

BRIGGS, GEORGE. Eloise. Par 12/17
Evelyn. SmS 8/17
Love lingered for a while. Par 11/17
The Reason. SmS 5/16

BRISTOL, F.O. "Justice." LoAG 10/23/15

BRITON, ELOISE. To my friend, grown famous. ReM 3/2/17

BRODY, ALTER. The Ballad of the Iron Cross. Out 6/2/15
Faces. Mad 9/17
I am war. Out 6/23/15
Long ago: a rondeau. Mad 7/17
Ma. McCa 10/18
The Old courtesan (after the bronze by Auguste Rodin). SeA 8/17
A Row of poplars, Central Park. EvM 9/18

BRONTË, CHARLOTTE, EMILY, ANNE, & BRAUWELL. Poems.
NYTM 4/15

BROOK, REEVES. Shrouds. Poet 7/19

BROOKE, RUPERT, The Dead. Poet 4/15
Peace. Poet 4/15
The Soldier. Poet 4/15

BROOKS, WALTER R. Haunted. Cen 4/15

BROOKS, WILLIAM E. My garden with walls. Out 7/10/18

BROWER, PAULINE FLORENCE. Central Park in spring. PoR 1/17

BROWN, ABBIE FAREWELL. But there are wings. CoV 12/19
The Carpenter. BoT 6/19/18
Concerning Haloes. Har 6/17
The Cross-current. Bel 12/15/17
Fairy-foot. CoV 4/19
Fairy ring. Bel 9/7/18
Garden thoughts. YouC 4/26/16
John Townsend Trowbridge, Feb. 12, 1916. YouC 4/27/16
Knights. Har. 9/18
Maids and mushrooms. Boo 5/18
Peace with a sword. BoT 3/29/17
The Plume. Boo 1/18
The Statue. YouC 8/2/17
Tanager. CoV 4/18
To certain Irish-Americans. BoT 4/13/18
The Whole truth. YouC 1/6/16
Winter song. CoV 1/19
The Woodsy ones. YouC 9/27/17

BROWN, ALICE. The Deserted garden. Har 1/17
France. BoT 3/15/19
The Knitter. BoT 8/4/17
West wind. Har 5/17

BROWN, ELMER ELLSWORTH. Confidence. Colo 7/16
One May day. Colo 5/15
Victory. StJ 3/17

BROWN, HARRIET G. The Message. YouC 3/23/16

BROWN, MARION. The Garden gate. LoAG 4/20/18
In Japan. Colo 1/17
Loneliness. LoAG 4/10/18
Souvenir. LoAG 5/20/18

BROWN, MARION F. In March. CoV 3/17
Rosemary. Colo 2/16

BROWN, MATT. Old Indian. ReM 11/3/16
Rain. ReM 12/29/16
Travellers. ReM 12/29/16
Two prisons. ReM 12/29/16

BROWN, ROBERT CARLTON. Cob-webs. Mas 6/15
Dumb., but well-dressed. Mas 6/15

Girl. SmS 8/15
I am Aladin. Oth 8/15
I am hungry. Mas 6/15
A Nice affectionate girl. SmS 7/15
These things I love. SmS 5/15
A Thing need be high-sound. Mas 6/15
You turned. Mas 2/15

BROWN, WILLIAM LAIRD. Two thirds. Min 6/17

BROWNE, GEORGIANA. Give me my dreams. WoW 7/19

BROWNE, MAURICE. Love is more cruel than death. Poet 10/19
Night-fall. Poet 5/15
Silence of the night. Poet 2/18
To her who passes. Poet 10/19
To my heart. Poet 10/19

BROWNE, PORTER EMERSON. "Won't you work a little faster?" Out 2/13/18

BROWNE, WALDO R. The New crusaders. Nat 8/30/19

BROWNELL, BAKER. After word. Poet 2/19
Departure. Poet 3/18
En masse. Poet 2/19
Freebourne's rifle. Poet 3/18
The Hurricane. Poet 3/18
Major Fitzpatrick. Poet 3/18
The Number. Poet 3/18
On the road. Poet 3/18
Private Rausch. Poet 3/18
Reveille. Poet 3/18
Southward. Poet 3/18
Stones for Russia. Poet 10/19
Taps. Poet 3/18

BRUCE, CLARA BURRILL. We who are dark. Cri 12/18

BRUMBAUGH, ROSCOE. Interlopers. NYSB 2/23/19

BRUNCKEN, HERBERT. Ad finem. Min 3/17
At night. Min 4/16
Friendship. CoV 3/17
Ghosts. Min 10/16
Gray rain. PoJ 7/17
I saw two meadow-larks at dawn. Min 6/17
Last night. Min 2/16
Lilacs in the rain. Mad 7/17
Minuet. Min 4/17
My soul. Min 3/16
My temple. Min 6/16
Night song. Lyr 5/17
Song. Min 1/17

Through the cool damp grasses. Min 5/17
The Tide. Mid 3-4/18
The Wind above the forest tops. Min 12/16
A wind from Spain. CoV 10/18

BRYANT, LOUISE. As it. Mas 10/16
Beach grass. Mas 10/16
Dark eyes. Mas 7/17
Empty. Mas 10/16
From the tower. Mas 7/16
Lost music. Mas 1/17
Mountains. Mas 10/16
O thou. Mas 10/16
Sensations. Mas 4/17
To a swimmer. Mas 10/16
A Wish. Mas 9/16

BRYHER, WINIFRED. Adventure. Boo 2/19
March adventure. NoAR 3/19

BRYNING, W.L. Thy friends. BoT 2/2/18

BRYSON, LYMAN, The Garment. Poet 6/15
Moon-wraith. Colo 2/16
A Nameless bird. Mid 8/16
The Poppy. Colo 1/15
Some April evening. Mid 4/16

Sonnet. Colo 12/15
To a certain fair lady. Poet 7/16
Vengeance. Colo 11/15

BUCHANAN, JEAN. Camouflage. CoV 7/18
Recognition. CoV 10/18

BUCK, HOWARD. The Courier. CoV 4/17
Of a night. Mas 8/17
The Shattering. PoJ 6/17
Their strange eyes hold no vision. Poet 10/18

BUCK, MITCHELL S. Lotus blooms. CoV 10/16
Sands. CoV 10/16
Sin. CoV 10/16

BUELL, HESTER. A Tryst. WoW 7/19

BÜHLER, M.E. In a colonial churchyard. Bel 5/18/18
In the hall of mirrors. NYS 3/2/19
The Inscrutable gods. Mas 7/16
Lossovo: "the field of black-birds." CaW 2/19
Mona Lisa's smile. Bel 1/23/15
The Poet in Bryant Park. Nat 9/7/18
A Puritan exhortation. Out 11/7/17
The Scourge of God. ReM 8/18/16
The Song makers. CaW 8/17

BULL, MARY. The Daisy month. Youc 6/7/17
  The Ocean. YouC 5/17/17
BULL, NINA. Advent. Mas 4/17
  The Bath. Mas 5/17
  Shells. Mas 1/17
  Timeless. Tou 10/18
BULLARD, HAROLD. Of a great crowd of people. BoT 10/11/18
BUNKER, JOHN. Ballade of faces fair. CoV 10/19
  The Flute-player. CoV 6/18
  On bidding farewell to a poet, gone to the wars. Boo 8/18
  Saint's gold. CaW 2/18
  Sonnet to a boy. CaW 6/16
  To a little girl who died. ScM 8/18
  Twilight. CoV 10/19
BUNNER, ALICE L. Hic jacet. EvM 6/19
  Ordered to France. ScM 11/17
BUNNER, ANNE. Mothers of France. EvM 10/18
BURGAN, LUCRETIA H. The futuristic river (after Leo Ornstein).
  SmS 5/17
BURGESS, KATHERINE STANBERRY. The Bookshelves. Boo 12/17
BURKE, KENNETH. Adam's song and mine. Oth 3/16
BURLEIGH, ALSTON W. The Brave soldier. Cri 3/19
BURLINGAME, W.R. The Hall of infamy. Cen 7/17
  The Lady who always appears with a game of letters where two or
    three are gathered together. Cen 9/17
  The Man who dresses in the aisle. Cen 8/17
  The Man who is awfully cheery early in the morning. Cen 9/17
  The Successful dentist who sings. Cen 8/17
BURNET, DANA Aspiration Har 10/15
  Confession. Har 4/18
  Dedication. Har 7/15
  Gay heart, a story of defeat. NoAR 1/15
  Harvest. Har 4/15
  Hunger. Har 3/15
  In a garret. Mas 2/15
  Sisters of the cross of shame. Mas 2/15
  Song in the dusk. Har 2/15
  To a logician. Har 6/17
BURNETT, FRANCES HODGSON. From leaf to leaf. Har 11/18
BURNSTEAD, EUDORA S. To a boy. YouC 2/10/16
BURR, AMELIA JOSEPHINE. America arms. Boo 7/17
  America to Europe. Nat 2/22/17
  And the cock crew. EvM 8/18
  The Angel with the sword. Out 1/27/15

Artemis on Latmos. ScM 2/17
Beatrice speaks from heaven. Bel 11/11/16
Calypso. Boo 10/17
Carey's men. Out 5/8/18
Certainty enough. Out 9/24/19
Children of Abraham. Out 3/7/17
Dante, Paolo, and Francesca. Colo 11/16/17
Deliver us from. Out 7/26/16
End and beginning. Bel 11/20/15
The Enemy. Bel 6/9/17
The Engineers. NYSB 6/23/19
Father O'Shea. Out 11/21/18
The Fiery cross (to Harry Lauder). Out 11/21/17
For us, the living. Bel 6/7/19
Free. Foru 4/16
The Gain. EvM 1/18
Gifts. Boo 7/19
God's challenge. ReM 10/5/17
Herb of grace. Har 7/15
Holy Russia. Out 3/28/17
In a Polish garret. Bel 7/7/17
In amber. Cen 5/17
In the dark days. EvM 3/18
The Interpreters. Bel 8/18/17
It might have been. Out 5/24/16
Joyce Kilmer. Out 9/4/18
Kitchener's march. Out 6/21/16
La morte d'Arthur. Bel 12/1/16
Magdalen to Christ. ScM 1/15
A Man's prayer. Out 7/4/17
The March of the Tenth Siberian Rifles. Out 9/19/17
A Masque of women poets. StJ 3/17
The Meeting. Bel 3/9/18
Missed. Out 8/9/16
Mother moon. CoV 5/18
Mothers. Out 4/25/17
Night magic (a lie-awake song). Bel 7/21/17
Nocturne. Har 8/16
On the way of the cross. Bel 11/24/17
Out of jail. Foru 4/16
Pleads guilty. Bel 4/7/17
A Poet enlists. Out 10/24/17
A Point of honor. Cen 5/15
The Poppies. Bel 4/15/16
A Prayer for the year's beginning. EvM 1/18
The Prayer (the real experience of a French gunner). Out 11/21/17
A Prayer in the time of war. Bel 4/28/17

A Prayer of to-day. Bel 4/29/16
The Price. Out 5/24/16
A Priest of France. Bel 11/2/18
Rain in the night (a lie-awake song). Bel 4/28/17
A Record. Mad 7/17
Remembering. Out 2/24/17
Rest. Cen 11/17
The Romany sign. Out 12/27/16
A Rose for France. Bel 10/5/18
Saint Clare to the Virgin. Bel 7/15
Sentry-go. Out 2/13/18
Shadow friend (a lie-awake song). Bel 1/13/17
A Shadowy third. Cen 9/16
A Sheltered life. CoV 1/19
Singers in the service. Boo 9/18
Slaves. Har 4/15
"Soixante-dix" pau at Neuilly. Bel 1/12/18
Spring in Russia - 1917. Nat 3/29/17
A Spring symphony. Bel 5/1/15
Stay-at-home stars. Out 2/13/18
Surrender. Cen 5/16
Syrinx. Colo 1/16
To General Pershing. BoT 11/23/18
To God's fools everywhere. ReM 9/7/17
To a lilac-bush. PoJ 11/17
The Troop-train. EvM 7/18
Ulysses in Ithaca. Bel 7/17/15
Under the fig tree. Bel 6/28/19
Unpublished. Out 3/21/17
Vengeance. PoR 5/16
The Victims, November, 1916. Out 12/13/16
Vita nuova. Bel 6/19/15
When the transports sail. Out 2/27/18
Who is my neighbor? Bel 5/24/19
Windflowers. PoJ 11/17
The Woman at home. Bel 9/15/17

BURR, JANE. Incredibles. Mas 3/17
  "Nigger Tilly." Mas 4/16

BURR, LOUIS. Portrait. CoV 11/19

BURT, JEAN BROOKE. Ad finem. Out 1/23/18
  Escandido. Out 4/17/18
  The Fires. Out 1/16/18
  The Heralds of spring. Out 3/13/18
  The Things devine. Out 8/25/15

BURT, MAXWELL STRUTHERS. All night through. CoV 9/19
  Crepuscule. Poet 7/18

BYNNER, WITTER. Acknowledgment. PoJ 1/17
  Across the ferry. ReM 2/23/17
  After midnight. CoV 3/19
  Annunciation, song of the voices of the unknown. SmS 4/15
  Anthropophagi. ReM 10/11/18
  At heaven's gate. ReM 3/29/18
  At the touch of you. Poet 9/16
  Autumn. ReM 8/20/18
  The Bell. ReM 11/29/18
  The Beloved stranger. ReM 8/30/18; 11/8/18
  The Blue jay. ReM 9/6/18
  The Boatmen. Rem 9/27/18
  Bound. ReM 10/11/18
  Bounty. ReM 9/27/18
  The Camel. ReM 10/18/18
  The Cataract. ReM 9/27/18
  Certainty. ReM 11/8/18
  Chinese drawings. Nat 9/20/19
  Clan. CoV 3/19
  Climbing. ReM 9/20/18
  Coins. ReM 9/27/18
  The Conquerors. CoV 3/19
  The Corner. ReM 9/20/18
  The Crest. ReM 8/30/18
  The Crown. ReM 9/27/18
  Darkness. ReM 9/13/18
  Dawn. ReM 9/27/18
  The Dead-loon. Poet 9/16
  Death. ReM 10/11/18
  Dedication. ReM 8/30/18
  Dice. ReM 10/11/18
  A Dinner table. NeR 8/7/15
  The Dusk. ReM 9/27/18
  The Earth-clasp. Poet 9/16
  Ecco homo. Poet 9/16
  An End. ReM 9/27/18
  The End. ReM 11/29/18
  Epitaph. ReM 10/11/18
  Exile. ReM 11/15/18
  The Eyes of dawn. Foru 8/16
  The Farewell. Poet 2/19
  February; the feast. ReM 10/11/18
  Fire. ReM 11/22/18
  Fire music. Bel 9/28/18
  A Garden. CoV 3/19
  Gates. ReM 11/15/18
  A Ghost. ReM 11/15/18

The God. ReM 11/29/18
Gold. ReM 10/18/18
The Golden heart. Bel 5/12/17
A Great man. SmS 4/15
Grenstone. Bel 3/31/17
A Halo. ReM 10/25/18
He brought us clover leaves. Poet 9/16
He pleads with the gentry to permit. Mas 4/15
Heart's content. Bel 3/20/15
Hemispheres. ReM 9/13/18
The Hour. ReM 9/27/18
How can I know you all? Bel 3/11/16
The Hunter. ReM 10/18/18
I come and go. Boo 1/18
I have had the night. SmS 2/16
I heard her sing. Bel 8/21/15
Idiocy. ReM 9/20/18
In Havana. Nat 5/3/19
In love. Bel 11/6/15
In many streets. PoJ 4/16
In memory of a night. DetS 6/23/18
Invective. CoV 3/19
It is not strange. CoV 3/19
The Jewel. Bel 4/5/19
Jews. CoV 3/19
A Justice remembers Lincoln. ReM 9/7/17
Kilauea. ReM 11/22/18
The Knife. ReM 10/25/18
Lament. ReM 9/27/18
A Lane in Grenstone. SmS 1/15
Laughter. ReM 9/27/18
Laurel. ReM 11/8/18
Legacy. ReM 11/15/18
Lightning. ReM 9/6/18
Magic. ReM 9/6/18
The Mask. CoV 3/19
Meanings. ReM 9/6/18
Mice. ReM 10/25/18
Mirth. ReM 9/6/18
A Mocking-bird. Poet 9/16
Nakedness. ReM 9/13/18
The Net. ReM 10/18/18
Niagara on the lake. Har 1/1/16
The Niche. ReM 11/29/18
No ease. ReM 11/8/18
The Oldest house in Grenstone. CoV 3/16
On the street. Foru 3/15

The Vine. ReM 10/18/18
The Voice. ReM 8/30/18
The Wall ReM 9/6/18
Waves. ReM 10/25/18
What are the rules of the new poetry? Bel 2/19/16
Wilson. ReM 11/17/16
The Wind at the door. Bel 9/22/17
Wisdom. Poet 9/16
Words. ReM 10/18/18
World's end. Mas 9/16
The Wound. ReM 11/8/18
You told me of your mother. Mid 11-12/18
Youth sings to the sea. You 10/18
BYRNE, DONN. The Kingdom of Thule. SmS 12/15
Reveil. SmS 10/15

C

"C.,A.H." Anaesthesia. For 11/16
Delight. For 2/17
Geraniums and lilies. For 2/17
"Hard a-lee." For 11/16
Revelation. For 11/16
"C.,C." A Sonnet. For 11/16
"C.,J.W." The Poet man. For 11/16
"C.,K." A Movaiyat. For 2/17
Twilight. For 11/16
"C.,M." Fourteen points. NeR 6/14/19
Report of the committee. NeR 7/2/19
"C.,W.J." The Disciples of Midas. For 2/17
CABELL, JAMES BRANCH. Post annos. Poet 8/15
CALDWELL, ADELBERT. The Winds. YouC 5/3/17
CAMMAERTS, EMILE. Meditation sur la nuit du trois aout (1914-1917)
[tr. Madame Cammaerts]. YaR 10/17
CAMP, PAULINE FRANCES. A New year's bank. YouC 1/1/17
The Secret. Out 3/13/18
CAMPBELL, ALICE ORMOND. Modern music. Poet 1/15
CAMPBELL, GRAHAM. Consumer. Out 11/26/19
CAMPBELL, JOSEPH. At harvest. Poet 3/16
On walking. Poet 3/16
CAMPBELL, LAURA. A Fragment. Foru 8/15
CAMPBELL, NANCY. The Apple-tree. Poet 8/15
The Magic. Poet 12/15

The Monkey. Poet 8/15

CANN, LOUISE GEBHARD. Croquis. PoJ 9/17
Immortality. PoJ 9/17
Love sharing and further destiny. PoJ 9/17
Man and nature. PoJ 9/17
The Moon. PoJ 9/17
Sonnet, Nora May French, in memoriam. Ain 11/19

CANNELL, KATHLEEN. Elusion. Oth 1/16

CANNELL, SKIPWITH. The Coming of night. Oth 8/15
The Crown, the plate, and the bowl. Poet 6/15
The Dance. LiR 4/15
The Deeper scorn. LiR 6-7/16
The Flood tide. LiR 4/15
Ikons. Oth 2/16
In the forest. LiR 4/15
A Riddle. Poet 6/15
Scorn. LiR 6-7/16
The Temple of hunger. Poet 6/15
To England. Oth 8/15
Wonder-song. LiR 6-7/16

CAPRON, LOUIS B. Finis. SmS 5/17

CARDUCCI, GIOSUE. Ca Ira Sinnata (tr. Laura Fullerton Gilbert).
PoeL Summer#/16
Congedo (tr. Anne Simon). PoeL New Year#/15

CAREW, HAROLD D. The Guns o'Christmas morning, 1917. BoT 2/1/19

CARLIN, FRANCIS. Beyond Rathkelly. NYWM 3/17/18
The Booted hens. NYWM 3/17/18
By Clodagh's stream. NYWM 3/17/18
The Deaf-mute sermon. MYWM 3/17/18
The Market town. NYSB 2/16/19
Maureen Oge. NYWM 3/17/18
My Ireland. NYWM 3/17/18
The Silent clock. NYWM 3/17/18
The Two riddles. NYSB 2/16/19
We both set out. NYWM 3/17/18

CARLISLE, MABEL L. My daddy. DetN 1/26/19

CARLTON, AUGUSTUS. Beware the first kiss, young man. Par 8/17

CARMAN, BLISS. After parting. Bel 9/1/17
At twilight. SmS 12/15
A Fantasy. SmS 4/17
Fireflies. EvM 10/15
The Heart of the night. EvM 8/18
The Homestead. Cen 2/16
Lord of the morning. Poet 6/15
Lyric. SmS 9/15

A Measure of heaven. EvM 12/15
Noon. Poet 6/15
Off Monomoy. ScM 6/15
Spoon river anthology. Foru 1/16
A Threnody. ScM 1/16
The Winter scene. Nat 1/18/17
Winter twilight. YouC 12/30/15
The World voices. Har 11/15

CARMAN, MIRIAM C. CHARITY. ScM 3/16
The Singing heart. ScM 4/19

CARMICHAEL, WAVERLY TURNER. 'Taint no need o' women worrin'.
Cri 1/18

CARNEVALI, EMMANUEL. The Day of summer. Poet 9/19
Drolatique-serieux. Poet 3/18
His majesty the letter-carrier. Poet 3/18
In this hotel. Poet 3/18
Italian song.. Lyr 2/19
"Last day." Lyr 2/19
Marche funebre. Lyr 2/19
Nocturne. You 2/19
Sentimental dirge. Poet 3/18
Serenade. Oth 7/19
To the poets. Poet 3/18
Walt Whitman. Poet 5/19
When it has passed. Poet 3/19

CARPENTER, RHYS. A Marching song for England in the east. Scm 6/19

CARR, DAPHNE. After writing poetry. Kis 2/19
Amour feminine. Oth 12/18
Insomnia. Kis 2/19
Realities. PoJ 7/17
Steel town. Oth 4-5-/19
Trifles. Oth 12/18

CARR, MRS. M.C. Cost. Mas 4/17

CARRALL, GODWIN TREZEVANT. Your voice. Poet 11/19

CARREL, MORTON. Protest. Mas 3/17
The Scullion. Mas 10/17

CARRICK, ALICE V. Twilight. YouC 5/4/16

CARRUTH, GORTON V. The Home-to-be. YouC 12/6/17
Together. YouC 9/20/17

CARRUTH, WILLIAM H. Donald singing in the dark. YouC 11/15/17

CARRY, MABEL D. A Spring song. Poet 5/15

CARSON, NORMA BRIGHT. Sonnet. Colo 1/15

CARSTAIRS, CARROLL. For the piano. PoJ 2/18

CARTER, ELIZABETH. Mnemonian wind. Mas 10/17

CARTER, LOUISE ADELE. One listens. Poet 8/15

CARUTHERS, MAZIE V. A Protest. Par 10/17

CARVEL, JOHN, Gifts. Sms 2/18

CASHEL, ALICE M. "The Road to come." CaW 3/17

CASSEL, MIRIAM. You are lilac blossoms. Mid 7-8/18

CATHER, WILLA SIBERT. Street in Packington. Cen 5/15

CAVALOTTI, FELICE. Thou shalt not (tr. Margaret E. N. Fraser).
  PoeL New Year#16
  Quel che so (tr. Anne Simon). PoeL New Year#/15

CAWEIN, MADISON. Adversity. NoAR 2/15
  At the day's close. Boo 4/15
  The Child in the house. ScM 6/18
  The Dead child. Poet 6/16
  Happiness. NoAR 2/15
  In a train. NoAR 2/15
  The Lonely land. ScM 12/15
  Love. NoAR 2/15
  Matins. Bel 8/12/16
  On the road. Bel 2/27/15
  The Sound of rain. ScM 6/16
  The Troubadours. Poet 1/15
  What the flowers saw. SmS 3/15
  The Wood brook. Poet 6/16

CECH, SVATOPLUK. Songs of the slave (tr. Otto Kotone).
  PoeL New Year#/16

CHADWICK, J.C. November sun. Poet 11/15

CHAFEE, ZECHARIAH, JR. To our elders and betters. CoV 11/16

CHAMBERLAIN, BEULAH. Barter. CoV 5/19
  Civilized. Nat 1/18/19
  An Insane girl. CoV. 12/18

CHAMBERLAYNE, LEWIS PARKE. Leaves from an anthology. Cen 1/16

CHANDLER, ANNA C. Wafting wishes. YouC 4/25/18

CHANNING, GEORGE C. Aut omnis aut nihil. DetS 7/28/18

CHANNING, GRACE ELLERY. A Field cemetery in France. SmS 9/18

CHAPIN, ANNA ALICE. In Greenwich Village. Boo 3/18

CHAPIN, C.C. Fall in, America. REJ 3/30/18

CHAPMAN, JOHN JAY, Autumn. ScM 10/18
  Ode, on the sailing of our troops for France. NoAR 11/17
  Retrospection, YaR 4/18

CHATER, MELVILLE, The Wilful torpedo. YouC 6/28/17

CHEFF, GLADYS BRIGGS. Old. Cen 8/16

CHENEY, JOHN VANCE. The Ditch. LoAG 3/25/16
  The Fallen (in memoriam, May 30). LoAG 5/27/16

John Muir (1838-1914). LoAG 2/2/16
Summer's Ariel. CoV 5/19

CHETWOOD, THOMAS B. The Fountain of youth. PoJ 1/17

CHEYNE, ELIZABETH GIBSON. A Poet to his peoms. Poet 9/15

CHEYNEY, E. RALPH. I, a minor poet. Mas 5/16

CHILD, OSCAR C.A. The Choice. Har 7/16
Reunion. Har 1/17
To a hero. Har 10/16
To a strapless waist. Par 2/18
A Wish. Har 1/16

CHILDS, T.H. The New ars poetica. StJ Autumn#/16

CHILTON, C.A. My answer. CaW 10/19

CHIPP, ELINOR. Before dawn. Ain 11/18
The City. PoJ 8/17
Echoes. PoJ 8/17
I shall not ask. Ain 10/18
Laus veneris. PoJ 8/17
Song. Mid 12/17

CHOCANO, JOSE SANTOS (tr. John Pierrepont Rice).
El Charro. Poet 2/18
The Magnolia. Poet 2/18
Oda salvaje. Poet 2/18
A Song of the road. Poet 2/18

CHOYCE, A NEWBERRY, Memory NYSB 11/3/18

CHRISTIE, CAROLINE. My treasurers. OvM 2/18

CHUBB, THOMAS C. The House of God. NeR 3/22/19

CHURCH, B.B. In this hour. Cri 2/19

CHURCHILL, DAVID. Holocaust. EvM 11/17

CITIZENESS. Contra option. ReM 5/26/16

CLARK, B. PRESTON, JR. Autumn. PoJ 11/17
The Excursion boat. SmS 1/16
Iolanthe. Sms 2/16
Nocture. PoJ 11/15; Cen 11/17
Summer, 1917. Cen 9/17
Venice—November, 1917. BoT 11/7/17

CLARK, BADGER. The Bad lands. Bel 1/22/16
The Drafted man. Cen 3/18
The Fighting swing. ScM 7/18
In the hills. ScM 3/19
Latigo town. Bel 7/14/17
The Long way. Cen 10/15
My enemy. ScM 1/18
My father and I. Cen 3/16
A Night trail. ScM 4/18

Others. Bel 11/16/18
Pioneers. ScM 12/19
Southwestern June. Cen 6/15
The Springtime plains. ScM 4/15

CLARK, CHARLES BADGER, JR. The Medicine man. Bel 1/2/15

CLARK, EVANS. Appeal. Cen 8/15

CLARK, MARTHA HASKELL. Heritage. ScM 4/19
The Little road, YouC 3/9/16
The Old camp chest. YouC 2/22/17
A Song of age. Out 8/15/17
Thanksgiving Day. ScM 11/16
To romance. Out 4/4/17
The Village lights. YouC 5/17/17

CLARK, THOMAS CURTIS. To the singer. CaW 6/19

CLARKE, HELEN ARCHIBALD. Balaustion's Euripides. a dramatic
version of "Balaustion's Adventure" and "Aristophane's Apology." PoL
New Year#/15

CLARKE, JOSEPH I.C. Electric light. CaW 9/18

CLEAVES, CHARLES POOLE. For insight. YouC 11/23/16
The Hero. YouC 2/14/18

CLEGHORN, SARAH N. And Thou too, America. Mas 6/16
But this is also everlasting life. EvM 12/15
Come, captain age. Cen 11/16
A Green Mountain garden, ScM 6/16
The Incentive. Mas 4/15
An Inclosed nun. Cen 1/16
Lamia in Windsor. EvM 10/16
One Love. Son 9-10-/19
Poison. Cen 3/16
Portrait of a lady.. ScM 9/19
The River. EvM 1/17
Spring in Vermont. EvM 4/16

CLEMENTS, COLIN C. A Beggar's complaint, English version. StJ 3/19
Four poems from the Japanese. StJ 10-12/19
The Seasons. StJ 12/18
A Soldier's prayer. Cov. 2/19

CLERFEYT, RENE-MARY. Marronniers. Sms 10/17

CLINE, LEONARD LANSON. Convalescence. DetS 9/8/18
The Leman. Pol New Year#/17
On the banks of the Duero. DetS 11/17/18
On the roof. Lib. 3/18
Street cars. ReM 11/1/18
To MacDowell. Mas 9/17
Washington Avenue. DetS 1/27/18

CLOUD, VIRGINIA WOODWARD. Advent. CoV 1/19

Blue butterflies. Sms 5/15
Dewfall. Lyr. 7/17
Eurydice. Lyr 6/17
Il Maestro. Cen 10/15
In your dream. CoV 10/19
Isle of dreams. Bel 2/2/18
The Little house. Bel 12/18/17
Prelude. Boo 12/16
Through the call of closer days. SmS 10/17

CLOVER, MADGE. Beneath the prairie. LoAG 4/29/16
"Dance nigre." LoAG 5/16/16
The Desert. LoAG 2/5/16
In Carmel Bay. LoAG 4/1/16

CLOVER, SAMUEL. A South Sea ditty. REJ 7/27/18

COATES, ARCHIE AUSTIN. Althea, at her window. Ain 8/19
America's homecoming. BoT 11/23/18
Chanty. EvM 4/19
Gifts. Har 11/19
Lavender. Poet 11/17
Sehnsucht. Lyr 5-6-19
Summer sea. CoV 7/19

COATES. FLORENCE EARLE. America. NYTM 2/25/17
Art and war. Bel 1/9/15
Beatrice before death, on reading Shelley's "Cenci." Min 6/16
Belgium. Bel 9/21/18
The Brave. Har 4/15
Christmas Eve. Bel 12/25/15
The Comrade. PhPL 6/12/18
The Gods remember. Har 10/16
I too have loved. NoAR 1/19
In memory of an American soldier. NoAr 6/19
In the offing. Min 5/17
In war-time, Bel 2/29/15
The Infantry that would not yield. Bel 12/14/18
A Love-song. Bel 12/1/17
The Nest. ScM 1/15
Our land. Har 4/19
Requiem for a young soldier. ScM 11/15
Serbia. PhPL 5/17/18
She will not hear. Out 5/5/15
The Smile of Reims.. Bel 6/2/17
A Soldier. Bel 7/20/18
The Something more. BoT 4/6/18
Time. NoAR 6/15
To one in hospital pent. Har 7/16

COATES, R.M. Musicale to A.H. NeR 6/7/19

COATSWORTH, ELIZABETH J. Arabian dawn. Lyr 5-6/19
  Belated. Poet 12/19
  The Bells. CoV 1/19
  By the canal. Cen 1/19
  Coming events... NeR 12/24/19
  The Coolie ship. Lib 3/18
  The Curse. Poet 12/19
  Daibutsu. NeR 9/24/19
  A Deserted courtyard. Cen 1/19
  The Gate. Poet 12/19
  The Ghouls. Poet 12/19
  In April. Cen 1/19
  Light of love. Poet 12/19
  Loneliness. CoV 6/18; Cen. 1/19
  Love tower. Poet 12/19
  Mandarin garden. Cen 1/19
  The New moon. NeR 5/17/19
  Ora pro nobis. EvM 6/19
  Poster. NeR 1/4/19
  Posters. NeR 3/15/19
  Song from the Swedish. You 6/19
  Spring in China. Poet 12/19
  Spring prayer. Cen 1/19
  To eyes that see. Har 1/19
  To a figurehead. CoV 7/19
  Two rhymes on Spanish proverbs. You 6/19
  The Waves. CoV 7/19
COBB, ANN. Up Carr creek. Out 8/27/19
  War-time in the mountains. Out 5/8/18
COBURN, DOROTHY DAVIS. The Silent violin. BoT 1/2/18
COE, ALICE ROLLIT. The Price o' dreams. ScM 6/19
COE, SAYERS. Newark, the voice of the city. New 9-10/16
COGSWELL, THEODORA BATES. The Little trees of Christmas. ScM 12/17
COHEN, NESSA. My garden at twilight. Lyr 11/17
  A Tone poem of Rimsky-Korsakoff. Lyr 11/17
COHEN, SOLOMON SOLIS. Love called me away. ScM 6/15
COIT, DOROTHY. The Door. PoJ 3/18
COLAHAN, ELLWOOD. The Waterfall. Poet 8/15
COLCORD, LINCOLN. These days. PoRa 7/16
  You who love me. PoJ 4/16
COLE, SAMUEL VALENTINE. William DeWitt Hyde. BoT 10/27/17
COLL, ALOYSIUS. The Birthright. SmS 2/15
  Fame. Out 10/29/19
  Washington, Nat 9/27/19

COLLIER, MIRIAM DE FORD. The Singing month. Mas 2/16 .
  A Spring song. Tri 5/16

COLLINS, CLARISSA WENTWORTH. The Bachelor. SmS 5/17

COLLINS, JOHN H. I am the way. CaW 3/19

COLLYER, ROBERT. Saxon grit. Bel 5/4/18

COLT, FRANCIS. Ballad of Mr. Morgan's collection. CoV 2/16
  Portriat. CoV 2/16
  The Prophet. CoV 5/16
  To one passing. CoV 7/16

COLUM, PADRAIC. The Ballad of Downal Baun. PoR 12/16
  The Beggar-woman sings. SmS 5/15
  The Bison. Poet 7/19
  The County of Mayo. Nat 3/8/19
  The Exile. EvM 6/16
  I can't have grief for everything. NeR 2/15/19
  Polonius and the ballad singers. Poet 7/15
  The Rune master. Nat 11/8/19
  To any poet. Poet 7/19
  The Vultures. Poet 7/19
  The Wanderers. Poet 7/19
  The Wayfarer. Poet 4/15

CONANT , ISABEL. The Oak in holy week. NYTi 4/13/19
  War's alchemy. CoV 7/18

CONDE, MARIA. Autumn. Har 10/18

CONE, HELEN GRAY. Happy country. Son 8/18
  Old burying hill. Son 1/18
  The Way ofthe white souls. ScM 1/19

CONGER, JOSEPHINE, Life. StJ 5/18
  The Man of power. StJ 5/18

CONGER, KATHERINE JANEWAY. A Prayer. GoH 1/18

CONKLING, ELSA. Summertime, Poet 7/16

CONKLING, GRACE HAZARD. About Mexico. Cen 2/17
  After sunset. Cen 2/18
  Amecameca. Poet 12/17
  April in the Huasteca. Cen 5/17
  At the cross roads. GoH 6/18
  The Barberry bush. Cen 9/15
  Bells. EvM 2/17
  The Casualty list. GoH 1/19
  Cedars. You 4/19
  Cretonne tropics. Ain 6/19
  Cuernavaca. Poet 12/17
  The Door-harp. Har 11/16
  Durango. Poet 12/17
  Dusk in the garden. CoV 6/18

Exile. Ain 4/19
Flanders bells. EvM 7/18
The Garden. EvM 2/17
Guadalupe. Poet 12/17
Gulf view. Poet 4/17
Huasteca. Poet 12/17
The Little rose in the dust, my dear. Poet 11/15
Mexico. YaR 7/17
Morning in the Alameda. NoAR 12/18
The Mountain mother. EvM 1/19
The Museum. Poet 4/17
The Nightingales of Flanders. EvM 10/17
Orizaba. Poet 12/17
Pablo. EvM 2/17
Patio scene. Poet 4/17
The Peacock. EvM 2/17
The Pine tree of dusk. SmS 11/17
Popocatapetl. Poet 12/17
Rain. EvM 2/17
Refugees, Belgium, 1914. Poet 11/15
The Ruined cities. EvM 6/16
San Luis Potosi, Poet 12/17
Santa Maria de Rio. Poet 4/17
The Saw-mill on the Connecticut. CoV 10/18
The Song unmade. EvM 7/19
Spring day. Poet 4/17
Sunset. Ain 12/19
Tampico. Poet 12/17
To Francis Ledwidge. YaR 10/18
To the schooner Casco, dear to R.L.S. PoR 8/16
To a soldier in France. Cen 12/17
Velardena sunset. Poet 4/17
Vera Cruz. Poet 12/17
Victory. BoT 11/23/18
Victory bells. EvM 2/19
The Violin remembers. You 12/18
War. GoH 4/18
White birches. GoH 1/18
CONKLING, HILDA. Butterfly. Poet 7/19
By Lake Champlain. Poet 7/17
The Dew-light. Poet 7/19
Easter. Poet 7/19
For you, mother. Poet 7/19
Geography. Poet 7/19
Morning. Poet 7/19
Narcissus. Poet 7/19
Night goes rushing by. Poet 7/19

Poems. Poet 7/19
Polars. Poet 7/19
Rose-petal. Poet 7/19
Seagarde. Poet 7/19
Snow-flake song. Poet 7/19
Snow-storm. Poet 7/19
Songs. Poet 7/16
Spring song. Poet 7/17
Sunset. Poet 7/17
Thoughts. Poet 7/19
To a mouse. Poet 7/17
Water. Poet 7/17
Yellow summer-throat. Poet 7/19

CONNOLLY, SUSAN CORNELIA. To one. SoW 4/15

CONSELMAN, WILLIAM M. Cynara. Par 4/18
In an old fashioned garden. Par 6/18
To a cynic. Par 2/18

CONTARDO, LUIS F. My sister's death (tr. Alice Stone Blackwell). StJ 3/19

CONTRERAS, FRANCISCO. The Charm of the rains (tr. Alice Stone Blackwell). StJ 3/19

CONVERSE, FLORENCE. Millennial episode. LivC 12/22/17

COOK, AMORY HARE. In youth. Har 6/16
Overhead. CoV 2/16
To-day. CoV 1/16
A Wish. CoV 3/16

COOK, CELIA. The Spice-box. YouC 7/5/17

COOK, HAROLD. All. SmS 10/17
Defeat. SmS 8/17
The Last fay. SmS 7/18
The Lost lover. SmS 10/17
The New song. SmS 6/17
Prayer. Sms 5/17
Would that I knew. Har 5/19

COOK, JOHN ORTH. Moriens profectus. CoV 2/17
A Prayer. CoV 9/19

COOKE, EDMUND VANCE. God is a democrat. Foru 8/16
Helen Keller. StJ 9/19
Ireland free. ReM 3/7/19
They who know. ReM 12/7/15
Those two. Har 12/19

COOKE, LE BARON. Apathy. CoV 4/19
Do you remember? Par 9/18
Heights. CoV 4/19
I wonder. CoV 4/19
On Sahara. CoV 4/19

The Wheel of unimportant things. StJ 6/19
COOKE, MARJORIE BENTON. The Cabaret. Sms 1/15
COOKE, ZITELLA. A Restored friendship. YouC 11/2/16
COOLE, RALPH G. Cry of the mothers. LoAG 1/9/15
  Night on the hills. LoAG 6/10/16
  Smoke rings. LoAG 3/20/18
  Two baby shoes. LoAG 1/22/16
  Where the stream runs swift. LoAG 3/17/17
COOLEY, JULIA. The Acolyte. Mid 2/17
  The Effigy. Mid 9-10/18
  Entity. CoV 5/16
  In a corridor of statues (Chicago Art Institute). Poet 5/16
  The Message. Mid 12/16
  Recapitulation in heaven. ChT 10/31/16
  Spring sorrow. Poet 3/16
  To loneliness. CoV 10/19
COOMARASWAMY, ANADA. "Severe consolation." You 12/18
COOPER, BELLE. At church. LoAG 6/10/16
  At four o'clock. LoAG 4/1/18
  Capri. LoAG 3/24/17
  Evensong. LoAG 6/17/16
  Ils ne passeront pas. LoAG 4/28/17
  L'espirit de l'Amerique. LoAG 2/24/17
  Our soldiers dead. LoAG 6/3/16
  Pro patria. LoAG 6/24/16
  Somewhere LoAG 3/3/17
  Sonnet (to Charles Mills Gayley). LoAG 12/16/16
  To a mocking-bird. LoAG 9/23/16
  The Vision. LoAG 7/12/16

COOPER, HOYT. Last road song. Mid 10/16
  The Old Roman road. Mid 1-2/19

COPINGER, L.E. The Letter. EvM 12/18

COPPEE, FRANCOIS. The Cannon (tr. Lillian White Spencer).
    DenP 10/13/18

CORBIN, ALICE. Apparitions. Poet 1/16
  Betsy's boy. SeA 9/17
  Buffalo dance. Poet 2/17
  Candle-light. Poet 1/19
  Change. ChT 10/31/16
  Color notes. Poet 1/16
  Courtship. Poet 2/17
  Cross-eyed Peter's Valentine. SeA 9/17
  Delphy. SeA 9/17
  El Rito de Sante. Poet 1/19
  Fame. Poet 1/19

To a portrait of Lord Byron. ArW 10/17
To a portrait of Whistler in the Brooklyn Art Museum. Poet 10/17
Whistlers's White Girl. Poet 10/17

CRAFTON, ALLEN. From Toul to Metz. EvM 6/19
In time of war I sing. EvM 5/18

CRAIG, ABBIE. August in the melon patch. YouC 8/16/17
Tiger lillies. YouC 7/26/17
Tired of blue. YouC 11/2/16
When doctor brought home his car. YouC 5/25/16
When the piper called. YouC 7/20/16

CRAIG, ANNE THROOP. The Hidden word. PoeL Spring#/17

CRAM, MILDRED HANSON. The Coward. SmS 8/15

CRANSTON, CLAUDIA. A Balloon party. GoH 7/17
Forgotten. SmS 6/15
A song. GoH 8/18

CRAPSEY, ADELAIDE. Amaze. Oth 3/16
Dirge. Cen 2/16
Fate defied. Oth 3/16
The Guarded wound. Oth 3/16
Madness. Cen 2/16
Moon-shadows. Oth 3/16
Night winds. Oth 3/16
November night. Oth 3/16
Release. Oth 3/16
Rose-Marie of the angles. Cen 2/16
Song. Cen 2/16
Susanna and the elders. Oth 3/16
Trapped. Oth 3/16
Triad. Oth 2/16
The Warning. Oth 3/16
Winter. Oth 3/16
Youth. Oth 3/16

CRAWFORD, NELSON ANTRIM. The Apple tree. Mid 9/18, 7-8/19
The Blue spruce. Mid 9/18, 7-8/19
The Catalpa. Mid 9/18, 7-8/19
A Child's grace. YoCh 6/23/18
Disservance. Pag 6/18
A Field of flax. Mid 9/18, 7-8/19
Free. OvM 11/19
The Ginkgo. Mid 9/18, 7-8/19
Hands. Mid 9/18, 7-8/19
Humoresque. SmS 6/18
The Mathematician. NeR 11/10/17
Memory. OvM 2/18
The Oak. Mid 9/18. 7-8/19
Pines. Mid 9/18, 7-8/19

Poplars. Mid 9/18, 7-8/19
Unfulfillment. CoV 9/18
A Voice. Mid 8/19
Willows. Mid 9/18, 7-8/l9

CREW, HELEN COALE. Dead summons. YaR 4/19
"Fortissimi sunt Belgae." Out 1/27/15
A Grace before reading. Out 1/26/16
Koto lies dead. ArW 10/17
My lad. YouC 8/30/17
"O lad! O lad!" Cen 5/15
Sing, ye trenches! Out 5/12/15
These are they sheep, Theocritus. CoV 5/17

CROCKER, M.E. In a walled garden. CoV 8/16
One captive. NeR 11/20/15
Winds. Mid 8/17

CROMWELL, GLADYS. Autumn communion. Poet 3/18
Christmas, Madison Square. PoR 12/16
The Crowning gift. Poet 4/17
Folded power. Poet 3/18
The Fugitive. Poet 4/17
The Mould. Poet 3/18
Star song. Poet 3/18
Winter poetry. NeR 1/4/19
Words. NeR 1/4/19

CROW, MARTHA FOOTE. Ghosts of past time. Poet 12/16
Religion. Poet 12/16
Strangers. CoV 9/18

CROWELL, GRACE NOLL. The Blind child. StJ 10-12/19
The Little house. CoV 11/19
Recompense. ScM 2/18
Wet lilacs. Lyr 5-6/19

CROWELL, MERLE W. Sealed song. SoW 6/15

CROWLEY, STACIA. "Sweet Argos." ScM 5/19

CULNAN, CATHERINE. Song of courage. YouC 6/27/18

CUNNINGHAM, C. The Alien. Poet 2/19

CURRAN, EDWIN. Healing of the world. Har 10/18
The March thaw. Poet 3/18
A Robin in Wall Street. Har 4/19
South winds. NeR 5/3/19

CURRY, ROUTLEDGE. En route. Mas 3/17
I wanted. Mas 5/17
Life's mysteries. Mas 5/17

CURRY, WALTER CLYDE. Death in the trenches. StJ 2/18
Reflections. StJ 6/19
The Street cleaner. StJ 1/18

CURTIS, CHRISTINE TURNER. New England beach. CoV 6/18
   The Old range road. Lyr 12/17
   Separation. You 4/19
   Snowfall in White River valley. Nat 12/14/18
   Under autumn trees. CoV 10/18
CURTIS, GLENN E. The Coquette. Ain 10/18
CUSHMAN, SYLVIA. The Summons. BoT 2/8/19
CUTLER, JULIAN S. The Kid. BoT 12/1/17
   The Old clipper days. BoT 3/6/15
CUTTING, MARY STEWART. April's isle. EvM 5/18
   From a little house. EvM 5/19
   Strange. EvM 6/18
   Triumph. EvM 4/19

D

"D.,H." See Aldington, Mrs. Richard
"D.,M." Two contentments. Mas 10/16
"D.,C.M." The blurred twig. Cen 5/18
DAILEY, CHARLES A. Closing the bar. NYS 3/23/19
DALEY, EDITH. As leaf and fruit. LoAG 2/12/16
   A Blessed isle. LoAG 2/26/16
   Con sordini (with muted strings). LoAG 5/29/15
   A Fear. LoAG 2/12/15
   In an orange grove. LoAG 3/20/15
   Moonpaths. LoAG 5/27/16
   The Red rose. LoAG 2/26/16
   The Secret way. LoAG 4/29/16
   A Valentine. LoAG 2/12/15
   The Valley's crown. LoAG 5/20/16
DALTON, MARY LEE. The Fairy out of the book. YouC 2/17/16
   A Frolic in the orchard. YouC 9/20/17
   The Greatest show on earth. YouC 4/18/18
   The Liberty Bell. YouC 6/29/16
   Lilac and robin. YouC 5/24/17
   The Little flags. YouC 5/25/16
   Lucky Priscilla. YouC 1/10/18
   Moving day. YouC 5/16/18
   The New leaf. YouC 1/6/16
DAMON, S. FOSTER. Apparition. Tou 8/18
   Carnival. You 10/18
   He likens her to a star of heaven. You 10/18
   Idyll. Cen 7/18
   "A Little,-called Pauline." Cen 12/18
   Panel. You 12/18

Triolet. You 10/18

DANFORD, HOMER A. Suburban felicity. ReM 5/23/17
The Visible supply. ReM 3/7/19

DANFORTH, ROY HARRISON. Sister of mine. Mas 10/17

DANIEL, MARY SAMUEL. The Guest. Har 9/15
The Open door. Har 7/15
The Path. Har 2/18

DANNISTON, JOHN. Some who sleep. Son#2/17

D'ANNUNZIO, GABRIEL. On a figure of France crucified (painted
by Romaine Brooks) [tr. Laura Fullerton Gilbert].
PoeL New Year's#/16
To America in arms. Out 8/21/18

DARGAN, E. PRESTON. Erect. Pet 4/15
For a map of Mars. Poet 4/15
Heartily know. Poet 4/15

DARGAN, OLIVE TILFORD. At the gate. ScM 3/17
Ballad of the rich suitor. ScM 11/17
Beyond the war. ScM 1/15
Fatherland. Boo 10/17
The Fourth watch. ScM 12/18
Home. Lib 6/19
On Clingman dome. NYSB 8/11/18
To a Texas primrose. ScM 8/18

DARIO, REUBEN. Daphne (tr. Lister Raymond Alwood). DetS 11/12/19
Nightfall in the tropics (tr. Thomas Walsh). Boo 12/17

DARLOW, GERTRUDE. A Little psalm. LoAG 2/5/16
The Secret. LoAG 4/22/16
Song. LoAG 1/15/16
Words. LoAG 1/9/15

DARRACH, GRACE. If I could write. CoV 7/17
Interim. CoV 7/17
Man's work. CoV 8/17
The Swallows. CoV 8/17

DASHIELL, MARGARET. A Sampler. SoW 4/15

DAUTHENDEY, MAX. The Hours must die (tr. E.B.). Min 6/16

DAVID, ROSS. Apples. Mas 3/17

DAVIDSON, C.H. After a concert. StJ 7/18
All to you. StJ 7/18
Appreciation. StJ 7/18
Battles long ago. StJ 7/18
Becalmed. StJ 7/18
Challenge and answer. CoV 3/17
Compensation. Boo 4/17
Dependence. PoeL Spring#/18

I said when I first saw you. PoeL Autumn#/17
Rencontre. PoeL Spring#/18
Response. PoeL Winter#/16
The Thirst of the antelope. Mas 9/17
To a great man. Boo 5/17
To a librarian. Boo 6/17

DAVIES , GEORGE. The Village street. Lyr 11/17

DAVIES, MARY CAROLYN. After all and after all. Cen 6/17
Ambition. CoV 6/16
The Apple tree said. Poet 9/19
A Ballad of Easter morning. GoH 4/19
The Ballad of a woman. Bel 12/21/18
Blood. PoeL Spring#/16
The Blood-stained cross. Tou 5/18
Borrower. Cen 5/17
A Casualty list. Cen 7/18
The Chinquapin trail. Nat 8/24/18
Cloistered. Poet 12/15
A Club. StJ 10/18
College. Mas 7/16
Communion. Ain 6/19
The Dancer. StJ 10/18
David. Bel 5/17/19
A Day, I-IV. Poet 8/17
The Dead wife. CoV 5/18
The Death watch. Poet 12/15
The Door. CoV 5/18
The Dream bearer. Mas 7/16
Every brook runs blue again. YouC 4/12/17
Fed. ReM 12/13/18
Feet. CoV 10/16
Fifth Avenue and Grand Street. BoT 11/23/18
Firelight. SoW 1/15
"Forever." Par 9/18
'Fraid stars. YouC 3/2/16
Free. Cen 2/18; Mid 9-10/18
A Game. CoV 11/18
A Girl's songs, I-III. Poet 8/17
A Grace. Kis 2/19
A Greenwich Village tea room. Tou 10/18
Grief. PoR 2/17
Guardian. CoV 5/18
Gypsy time. YouC 5/3/17
Gypsying. SoW 7/15
Highlanders, fix bayonets! EvM 7/19
Home fires. Par 7/18
An Hourglass and a sundial. Ain 4/19

To a great man. Ain 9/19
To a poet. Lyr 4/19
To a tree. CoV 5/18
To the women of England. Mas 4/16
Traps. ReM 6/21/18
Trench silhouettes. Tou 12/18
Vintage. Cen 3/18
Volunteer. YouC 1/3/18
A War bride. Par 8/18
What the Christmas tree thinks. YouC 12/21/16
The Wild, wild swans. PoJ 2/16
The Women who laughed. EvM 12/18
The Word. CoV 4/19
Words. Par 7/18
The World is all a wonderland. YouC 10/25/17
Young love. Ain 12/19
Younger than spring is she. CoV 5/16
Youth's a clean sword. Mid 5/17

DAVIS, CHRISTINE KERR. In Kerry. ScM 4/19

DAVIS, FLORENCE BOYCE. The Cow path. Bel 5/26/17

DAVIS, GRACE LOWREY. My garden. GoH 7/19

DAVIS, H.L. A Field by the river. Poet 4/19
Flags. Poet 4/19
The Gypsy girl. Poet 4/19
In the field. Poet 4/19
My step-grandfather. Poet 4/19
Oakland pier: 1918. Poet 4/19
The Old are sleepy. Poet 4/19
Running vines in a field. Poet 4/19
The Spirit. Poet 4/19
The Sweet-tasting. Poet 4/19
The Valley harvest. Poet 4/19

DAVIS, HOMER. Arcana. PoJ 12/16
Memento more! PoJ 12/16
Nomads. PoJ 12/16
Respice finem. PoJ 12/16
The Visitant. PoJ 12/16

DAVIS, MARY WRIGHT. A Songster unknown. YouC 1/24/18

DAVIS, ROBERT H. Hic Jacet! SmS 2/16
Upon seeing Geraldine Farrar through my ear. SmS 7/15

DAW, BEATRICE. Madrigal sans politesse. PoeL New Year's#/18

DAWSON, CONINGSBY. A Hospital in France. GoH 12/17
The Lads away. GoH 3/18
To the girls we left behind. EvM 12/18

DAWSON, ERIC P. Letters from home. GoH 6/18

DAWSON, MITCHELL. Cantina. LiR 5/15
  Girl of jade and ivory. LiR 4/17
  Harpy. LiR 5/15
  In passing. LiR 1-2/16
  Santa Maria del Carmine. LiR 5/15
  Teresa. LiR 1-2/16
  Termaggic. LiR 5/15
  Threat. LiR 1-2/16
  To diverse contemporaries. Oth 7/19
  Under the cypress.

DAY, CLARENCE, JR. Sic semper dissenters. NeR 10/5/18

DAY, DOROTHY. Mulberry Street. Mas 7/17

DAY, SARA. The Atonement. SoW 5/15

DEAN, HARRIET. A Dry-coloured vine. Oth 12/18
  The Pillow. LiR 1-2/16

DEARMER, WILLIAM. My dream garden. EvM 11/16

DE ARMOND, LIZZIE. My servant. YouC 7/26/17

DE BANVILLE, THEODORE. Ballads of fidelity (tr. William
  Van Wyck). LoAG 12/10/17

DE BOSSCHÈRE, JEAN. Chair-maker (tr. Ezra Pound). SeA 9/17
  Electrician (tr. Ezra Pound). SeA 9/17

DE CASSERES, BENJAMIN. The Haunted House. Oth 5-6/16

DE FORD, MIRIAM ALLEN. The Music-maker's child. Poet 1/15

DE GOUROMONT, REMY. Epigrammes: je n'aine plus. Poet 1/15
  La vasque. Poet 5/15

DEHMEL, RICHARD. A Group of poems (tr. Leonora Speyer). StJ 9/19
  Song to my son (tr. E.J. O'Brien). PoeL Autumn#/15
  The Workingman (tr. Leonora Speyer). Nat 7/19/19

DE LA MARE, WALTER. Fare well. YaR 4/17
  Nightfall. YaR 4/17
  Reawakening. Poet 4/17
  Two epitaphs. Poet 4/17

DE LA SELVA, SALOMON. Birches. Ain 9/19
  Candle light. CoV 11/16
  For France. Ain 11/18
  In defense of Helen. Ain 3/19
  In the country. Ain 9/18
  Measure. Har 6/17
  The Merchant. Poet 11/17
  My Nicaragua. Poet 11/17
  One day in Bethlehem. Ain 4/17
  The Pulse of love. Ain 10/18
  The Singer despairs. CoV 11/16
  The Singer exults. CoV 11/6
  So love has taught me. Ain 2/19

Sonnet. NYSB 6/15/19
A Tale from faerieland. Foru 7/15
The Tiny maiden. Poet 11/17
Tropical town. CoV 11/16
Unredeemed. Ain 8/19

DE LISLE, LECONTE (tr. Celia Louise Crittenton). The Heart of
Hialmar. PoeL Vacation#/17
In excelsis. PoeL Vacation#/17
In the soft air, Villanelle. PoeL Winter#/16

DE LISSER, LEICESTER A.N. The Voice. NYSB 6/23/19

DELL, FLOYD. Apologia. Poet 5/15
On reading the poems of Edna St. Vincent Millay. Lib 5/18
Song. Poet 10/19
Summer. Mas 2/17
Two sonnets. Lib 10/18

DELP, CAROLINE MABEL. Dance of death in the sycamores. LoAG 8/5/16
Dusk in the canyon. LoAG 8/26/16
Eucalypti. LoAG 9/2/16

DE MARTHOLD, JULES. France's hymn of Hate (tr. Barbara Henderson).
NYTM 7/4/15

DE MAUPASSANT, GUY. The Bird-catcher (tr. B.A. Botkin). StJ 8/19

D'EMO, LEON. Like a cur on a throne. Cen 11/19

DeMOVILLE, MARY FELIX. The Annunciation. SoW 3/15

DeNERVAL, GERARD. Delfica (tr. Francis Taylor). PoeL New Year's#/15

DeNERY, AMELIE. Ballade des oliviers. Colo 7/15
La chanson des Aiguilles. Colo 7/15
Reims. Colo 7/15

DENISON, ELDREDGE. Love's dwelling place. Par 5/18

DENNEN, GRACE ATHERTON. Conscience. CoV 7/17
A Knitting song. YouC 3/7/18
Revelation. LoAG 2/19/16
The Russian dancers. LoAG 7/8/16
Spring in the westland. LoAG 3/3/17
The Winged victory. LoAG 2/26/16

DENNIS, CHESTER. The Origin of philosophy. Cen 8/17

DENNIS, O.M. Interned. Mad 7/17

DE P.,E. By a window at dusk. For 11/16

DE P.,J. War poem. For 11/16

DE PUE, ELVA. The Foolish virgin lights her lamp. Mas 10/17

DEUTSCH, BABETTE. The Dancers. NeR 1/6/17
The Death of a child. ReM 12/14/17
Gifts. SmS 2/19
Ironic. Mas 6/17
Lures. SmS 6/18

Magic screen. SeA 8/17
Nocturne. ReM 11/23/17
Noumenon. CoV 12/19
Redemption. Son 1-2/19
Ritornello. ReM 6/12/19
Sagesse. ReM 6/12/19
Sea-music. Poet 1/18
Severance. Lib 10/18

Sic semper. Lyr 10/17
Silence. SmS 10/17
The Silver chord. Lib 7/18
The Undelivered. Lyr 2/19

DEWING, E.B. March. Har 4/9

DEXTER, MARION HICKS. The Picture. Ain 6/19

DICKINS, EDITH. The Nativity. ScM 12/19

DICKERMAN, ELIZABETH S. Charles Peguy. PoeL Spring#/17

DIERSSEN, ANNA. Now. ReM 11/16/17

DILLON, KATHLEEN. Two poems for dancing. Oth 10/15

DIMON, DOROTHEA. Little miss April. YouC 3/29/17

DIVINE, CHARLES. The Autobiography of a small town girl. Mas 8/17
A Castle in France. NYSB 1/12/19
Casuals. NYSB 12/22/18
Chateau Thierry. NYSB 1/5/19
The Confessions of a hampered man. SmS 4/17
Dickie Dow, W.S.R. WaGa 12/22/17
Excitement in the barracks. NYSB 6/23/19
A fete day (sketches in Paris). NYSB 2/2/19
Fog. NYSB 10/27/18
He soldiered with Jack in the islands. NYSB 2/2/19
Her confession. SmS 8/17
The Heroes in pajamas. NYSB 11/24/18
The Hob-nail shoes. WaGa 12/29/17
The Impatient soldier. WaGa 1/19/18
In the Cafe de Commerce (the night of November 11, 1918).
    NYSB 1/19/19
In the cathedral at Nevers. NYSB 2/2/19
In celebration of peace. NYSB 1/19
In the city. SmS 6/16
In the danger zone. NYSB 9/8/18
In Montmartre (sketches in Paris). NYSB 11/24/18
In Saint Parize. NYSB 10/27/18
In the street (the night of November 11, 1918). NYSB 1/19/19
Indecision. Mas 7/17
Jerry's prisoner. NSYB 11/24/18
Lines on a load of hay. SmS 6/17

Madelon. NYSB 1/5/19
The Mighty insignificance. NYSB 1/5/19
Moon-song. NYSB 1/19/19
Oh, little moonlit hill. Mas 10/17
The Old Sixty-ninth. NYSB 1/5/19
The Painted fleet. NSYB 9/8/18
A Picture of dejection (sketches in Paris). NYSB 2/2/19
Pork and beans. NYSB 10/27/18
Private Mugrums goes across. NYSB 9/8/18
Private Mugrums on modern conveniences. NYSB 1/12/19
Private Mugrums on "quiet sectors." NYSB 1/12/19
Psychoneuroses. NYSB 12/22/18
A Rainy night (sketches in Paris). NYSB 2/2/19
Revenge: in memory. SmS 5/17
The Road through Moiry. NYSB 1/12/19
The Service stripe. NYSB 1/12/19
Soldier's mail. NYSB 11/24/18
A Song of lovers. Par 10/17
The Spick. NYSB 1/19/19
The Stars in pawn. SmS 6/17
To the papers and the bull. NYSB 1/12/19
The Traffic markers. NYSB 9/7/18
An Unknown mademoiselle. NYSB 11/24/18
Various lines. NYSB 1/5/19
When love will fill your heart. SmS 9/17
When we come back. WaGa 5/4/18
Wind in the spring. SmS 4/18
The World through a porthole. NYSB 1/12/19
DODD, LEE WILSON. Autumnal. Lyr 1-2/18
The Comrade. Poet 1/15
The Hero. Lyr 1/19
A Little grimy-fingered girl. Out 6/12/18
Mirella dances. Poet 10/15
Only not to be too early old. Poet 1/15
Open letter. Lyr 1-2/18
The Parting. YaR 1/18
Plus tard. YaR 1/19
Refusal. Lyr 10/17
The Temple. Poet 1/15
To a neo-pagan. YaR 10/16
Tragi-comic. Lyr 8/17
Variation. Lyr 7/17
DODGE, ANNE ATWOOD. Of gardens. NoAR 3/19
DODGE, ARLITA. The Cabaret dancers. Boo 8/15
Pallas-Athena. Boo 12/16
DODGE, LOUIS. The Cathedrals. ReM 6/25/15

The Flags. ReM 5/7/15
Her garden. ScM 9/17
Impressions. ReM 5/10/18, 5/2/19
The Plea. Har 10/15
The Returning. ScM 9/18
Rhythms. ReM 11/30/17

DODSON, ELLEN MACKENZIE. Invitation. LaAG 5/12/17

DOKU-HO. Love's island (tr. Ian Oliver). Har 12/17

DOLCH, E.W., JR. Behind the "great offensive." Mid 6/17

DOLE, ARTHUR MACDONALD. The Mission bell. LoAG 3/18/16

DOLE, NATHAN HASKELL. The Meteor. NoAR 8/15
Mirage. NoAR 8/15
Plenilune. Lyr 5-6/19
Sea-monsters. NoAR 8/15
Seals. NoAR 8/15
The Summer sea. NoAR 8/15

DOLLARD, JAMES B. To a dead child. CaW 1/17

DOLSON, CORA A. MATSON. Birches. LoAG 1/1/16
The Golden light. SmS 11/16
My mother. SmS 10/15
October days. SmS 10/15

DOLSON, EUGENE. First love. SmS 12/15
A Girl's forgiveness. SmS 2/16
Old houses. Ind 11/13/16

DONEY, MAY. My little ship. CaW 7/19

DONNELLY, FRANCIS P. All things unto God. CaW 3/18
Memories of France. CaW 11/19

DONNER, HERMAN MONTAGU. Song unreleased. Par 9/18

D'ORGE, JEANNE, The Beggar. Poet 8/17
The Convent. Oth 12/17
The Crystal. Oth 5-6/16
Defeat. Oth 4-5/19
Expectancy. PoJ 3/17
The Freshman. Oth 12/17
Goblin. PoJ 3/17
The Incubator. PoJ 3/17
Invitation. Oth 5-6/16
Joy. Oth 12/18
Legend. Oth 5-6/16
The Master. LiR 4/17
The Meat-press. Oth 5-6/16
The Microscope. Oth 5-6/16
Mortality. Oth 5-6/16
The Prayer rug. Oth 4-5/19
The Problem is. Oth 12/17

The Question. Oth 5-6/16
Ruts. Oth 5-6/16
Sea-mood. Oth 12/17
The Statue. Poet 8/17
Stolen. Oth 12/17
To a new friend. PoJ 3/17

DOUGHTY, LEONARD. Looming isles. CoV 9/19

DOUBLEDAY, NANCE. U-ka-lee (to a redwing blackbird). GoH 4/17

DOWNEY, JUNE E. Gold-hunting. PoeL New Year's #/17

DOWNING, ELEANOR. On the Feast of the Assumption. CaW 8/15

DOYLE, FRANCIS X. Adventurers. CaW 5/18
Epitaph. CaW 7/19

DOYLE, HELEN M. My neighbor. GoH 5/17

DRACHMAN, JULIAN M. At sunset. CoV 12/18
Bastille Day. CoV 7/19
Even so. CoV 2/19
Fire-weed in the forest. CoV 11/19

DRAKE, MARIA UPHAM. The Law of life. YouC 10/18/17

DRANE, CECIL ARTHUR. If only I might look. Son 3-4/18

DRANSFIELD, JANE. Friendship's service. LoAG 9/2/16
Trees in winter. Nat 2/8/19

DRAPER, ELIZA ADELAIDE. The Unknown. ScM 1/16

DRAPER, JOHN W. After the 1590's. Mad 8/17
After the Requiem. Colo 2/17
Andante. Colo 10/16
ARIA ITALIANA. Colo 3/15
Ballet Russe. Colo 4/16
Belgia. Colo 11/15
Brussels: Aughst, 1914. Colo 11/15
The Condemned murderer. Colo 12/16
Danse languoreuse. Colo 9/15
De altis. Colo 10/16
Faery repentent. Colo 5/16
From Faery. Colo 1/16
"Les jardins sous la pluie." Colo 8/16
A Story of southern Spain. Colo 1/15
To Ernest Lissauer. Colo 12/15
To a rosinante. Colo 7/16
Whither and why? Colo 9/16
Within cloister gates. Colo 3/16

DREISER, THEODORE. For a moment this wind died. SmS 5/16
They shall fall as stripped garments. SmS 5/16
Wood note. SmS 5/16
Ye tribes. SmS 5/16

DRESBACH, GLENN WARD. At a factory door. PoeL SummerN/17
  Bacchanalia. PoeL SummerN/17
  Battles. PoeL Summer N17
  Chains. CoV 6/19
  Christmas Eve, 1917. Boo 12/17
  Defeat. CoV 6/19
  Dewdrops. Mid 1-2/18
  The Dreamers. Poet 9/17
  The Dreams of one dead. PoJ 8/17
  A Father and his dead son. PoJ 8/17
  Faun song. PoJ 8/17
  The Glory of dreams. PoJ 8/17
  Hymn to Pan. Mid 1-2/18
  I had forgottne. Mid 1-2/18
  The Immortality of dreams. PoJ 8/17
  In New Mexico. Poet 7/19
  Like the wind in the dunes. CoV 9/17
  The Loquacious outlaw. CoV 6/19
  A Mountain nocturne. Mad 8/17
  The Murderer God sentenced. Mid 3-4/18
  A New Mexico hill-song. PoJ 8/17
  Nocturne. Poet 9/17
  O restless spirit. CoV 7/18
  Ocean. PoJ 8/17
  On the road with the wind. PoJ 8/17
  One face in the crowd. Poet 6/17
  The Price of corn. Mid 8/17
  Song. CoV 6/19
  Song for a violin. Poet 11/15
  Song of the new crusade. Boo 10/17
  Song to the dawn wind. Mid 4/17
  Songs while the leaves are falling. Mid 9-10/19
  The Sower who reaped the sea. Boo 9/17
  Summer, 1918. Boo 6/18
  To the night wind. Mid 7/17
  Two songs. Poet 6/17
  When spring comes back. Boo 4/18
  Winds that moved the friendly trees. Mid 1-2/18
DREYFUS, ESTELLE HEARTT. Freesia (to my father). LoAG 2/12/16
  Unfoldment. LoAG 1/10/18
DRINKWATER, JOHN. Anthony Crundle. Cen 11/16
  Dedication to Edmund Gosse. Cen 8/16
  Invocation. Poet 9/16
  Reciprocity. Poet 11/17
  Sunrise on Rydall Water (to E. de S.). Poet 12/15
DRISCOLL, LOUISE. The Blue jay. CoV 7/19
  The Child of God. SeA 11/16

The Doll. You 12/18
Exit—the fool. CoV 5/18
The Fragments. You 12/18
The Garden of the west. Poet 12/18
God's pity. CoV 1/19
Harbury. Poet 2/18
If you have loved a garden. Har 6/19
The Lilacs. Poet 5/15
My garden is a pleasant place. CoV 10/18
The Princess. You 12/18
The Scarf. PoJ 2/17
Treasure. Poet 11/19
A Village church. Poet 5/15
The Word of the wind. BoT 11/23/18

DRISCOLL, MARJORIE CHARLES. The Explorers. YouC 7/6/16
   Her soldier. EvM 2/19

DU FU. Night in a border village (tr. Henry C. Fenn). StJ 6/17

DUANE, MARY MORRIS. Faces. CoV 2/17
   Happiness. CoV 1/17
   I dreamt. CoV 1/17
   In my need. CoV 1/17
   Once. CoV 2/17

DUCLE, ESTELLE. Awakening. CoV 10/18
   True love. Lyr 5-6/19

DUDLEY, CAROLINE. Chaotic peace. Poet 3/16
   Concerning a nobleman. Poet 3/16
   The White wisdom. PoJ 7/15

DUDLEY, DOROTHY. La Rue de la Montayne Sainte-Geneviere. Poet 6/15
   The Moon. Poet 7/17
   November in the park. Poet 11/15
   Paderewski, Chicago: February sixth, 1916. Poet 7/17
   Pine River Bay, Autumn, 1916. Poet 12/17

DUDLEY, HELEN. Dirge. Poet 12/17
   Reed-song. Poet 12/17

DUER, CAROLINE. On a hill near the sea. GoH 8/17
   The Vision. ScM 4/19

DUFFY, ESSIE PHELPS. The Token. YouC 11/30/16

DUNBAR, ALDIS. Enemies. YouC 6/29/16
   Reveille. Mid 10/17
   The Younger brothers. YouC 6/6/18

DUNCAN, WALTER JACK. Cradle song. Del 2/17

DUNN, FLORENCE E. The Soldier. YouC 2/10/16

DUNNING, RALPH CHEEVER. The Home-coming. Poet 1/16

DUNORIER, WILLIAM EDWARD. "'Tis a bleak sea and night sea."
   Colo 7/16

DUNSANY, EDWARD J., LORD. Songs of an evil wood. SmS 6/17
DURBIN, HARRIET WHITNEY. The Milk room. PeHJ 8/17

E

"E." In May. For 11/16
   In a meadow. For 11/16
"E.,A.G." To Tom Daly, after reading a book of his verse.
   LoAG 7/31/15
EARLS, MICHAEL. A Ballad of France. CaW 10/17
   Old Hudson rovers. CaW 10/16
   A Song. CaW 6/19
   A Winter minister. Out 1/17/17
EASTAWAY, EDWARD. Old Man. Poet 2/17
   The Unknown. Poet 2/17
   The Word. Poet 2/17
EASTMAN, MABEL HILLYER. "Yet I am not for pity." Har 11/19
EASTMAN, MAX. Anniversary. Lib 5/18
   Car window. Mas 9/16
   A Chicago portrait. Mas 9/16
   The City. CoV 1/16
   Coming to port. Mas 3/16
   A Dune sonnet. Mas 7/17
   Europe. Mas 12/16
   Eyes. Lib 4/18
   Fire and water. Lib 7/18
   Hours. Mas 4/17
   In my room. Lib 6/18
   Invocation. Mas 4/15
   Isadora Duncan. Lib 3/18
   Kansas. Mas 9/16
   The Lonely bather. Mas 8/17
   A Morning. Lib 11/18
   The Net. NeR 8/7/15
   Painting. Mas 9/16
   A Praiseful complaint. Lib 10/18
   Provincetown. Mas 9/16
   Rainy song. Mas 10/17
   Sea shore. Mas 9/16
   The Sun. Mas 10/16
   Those you dined with. Lib 4/18
   To love. Mas 9/16
   To a mad dog. Mas 6/15
   To Marie Sukloff - an assassin. Lib 8/18
   To Nicolai Lenin. Lib 11/18
   X Rays. Lib 10/18

EASTWOOD, EARL V. The Bleak house. WoW 5/19

EATON, JEANETTE. Rebellion. Mas 8/17

EATON, WALTER PRICHARD. Home-coming. Cen 12/17
  Piegan pines. Cen 4/18

EBERHART, NELLE RICHMOND. The Reaping. Ain 5/19

EDDY, LUCY. Bougainvillea. Poet 2/18
  The Flowering acacia. Poet 2/18
  Iris. Poet 2/18
  The Jacaranda. Poet 2/18
  Lullabies. Poet 2/18
  New-born. Poet 2/18
  The Olive tree. Poet 2/18
  Ophelia roses. Poet 2/18
  Red eucalyptus. Poet 2/18
  Sea-gardens - Avalon. Poet 2/18

EDDY, RUTH BASSETT. In passing. YouC 1/6/16

EDEN, HELEN PARRY. A Mother in England. Ind 12/18/16

EDGETT, EDWIN FRANCIS. All for mother. BoT 5/11/18
  The Blest and the cursed. BoT 5/8/18
  For Belgium. BoT 3/16/18
  In France. BoT 3/25/18
  Old books for new. BoT 4/6/18
  Satan rebukes sin. BoT 6/14/18
  Stand firm at home. BoT 6/5/18
  Thus spake the prophet Isaiah. BoT 3/20/18
  To General Sir Douglas Haig. BoT 11/23/18

EDLUND, GUSTAVE. To Patience Worth. ReM 11/19/15

EDMAN, IRWIN. Braveries. Cen 9/19

EDSON, CHARLES FARRELL. Emil Oberhoffer. LoAG 2/10/17
  Sequoia gigantea. EvM 11/15

EDSON, CHARLES LEROY. Her war garden. Par 9/18
  Summer chores. Puc ?/15

EDWARDS, ELI, pseud. See McKay, Claude

EGAN, MAURICE FRANCIS. The War bride. ScM 9/17

EISENBURGH, JULIA. The Professors. Mas 9/17

ELDER, ADA BARNES. Love's watch. WoW 1/19

ELDRIDGE, PAUL. The Black cat. StJ 10-12/19
  The Daisy speaks. StJ 10/18
  God. StJ 5/19
  Man speaks to man. PoJ 7/16
  The Moon and the ocean. CoV 9/19
  My thoughts. StJ 6/18; CoV 2/19
  Night. StJ 10-12/19
  Time's castanets. StJ 10/18

ELIOT, S.A., JR. The Northeaster. CoV 6/18

ELIOT, T.S. Aunt Helen. Poet 10/15
  Conversation galante. Poet 9/16
  Cousin Nancy. Poet 10/15
  The Hippopotamus. LiR 7/17
  La figlia, che piange. Poet 9/16
  Le directeur. LiR 7/17
  The Love song of J. Alfred Prufrock. Poet 6/15
  Lune de miel. LiR 7/17
  Melange adultere de tout. LiR 7/17
  Mr. Apollinax. Poet 9/16
  Morning at the window. Poet 9/16
  The Portrait of a lady. Oth 9/15

ELLERBE, CECILIA. April's fairest morn. Colo 10/16
  Fulfillment. Colo 11/15
  Madonna's vision. Colo 3/15
  Wistaria. Colo 1/17

ELLERBE, PAUL LEE. The Bells of Sante Fe. NYS 3/9/19

ELLSWORTH, E.D. An Autumn party. YouC 11/16/16

ELLYSON, JOHN REGNAULT. A Colloquy in sleep. Poet 7/16

ELMER, CLARENCE. The Veterans. EvM 5/19

ELMER, HAROLD. To Verlaine and Ernest Dowson. CoV 11/16

EMBRY, JACQUELINE. Cinquains - white and black. StJ 5/19
  Jealousy. GoH 6/19

EMMET, ROSINA H. The Tree. ScM 4/19
  Waiting. ScM 10/19

ENDICOFF, MAX. The Chief librarian. Mas 2/17
  The City. Poet 8/15
  Excavation. NeR 5/15
  The Fixture. Mas 2/17
  The Gold-sprayed voice of the people. Mas 10/16
  The Newcomer. Mas 2/17
  The Public library. Oth 1/16
  The Retired acrobat. Mas 2/17
  The Sea-liner. Oth 1/16
  The Spring storm. Lyr 10/17
  The Subway. Oth 1/16
  The Terminal. Oth 1/16
  The Veteran. Lib 6/18

ENGLISH, VICTORIA. A Woman knitting. CaW 10/18

ENTREKIN, CLARA P. The Day the lads came back. BoT 2/8/19

ERSKINE, JOHN. In the garden. Poet 7/17
  Kings and satrs. Nat 11/15/19
  The Poetic bus-driver. Lyr 10/17
  The Sons of Metaneira. Lyr 6/17

ESKEW, GARNETT LAIDLAW. The Chimes. NYH 6/17/19

EVANS, DONALD. The Exile wall. PoR 2/17
With death and uncouth. PoR 9/16

EVERETT, LEOLYN LOUISE. The Invalid. Cen 3/17

F

"F." To R.A. Mas 8/17

"F.,B.P." A Dare. Nat 1/4/19

FABRE, HENRI. Provencal verse (tr. Elizabeth Shepley Sergeant).
NeR 1/23/15

FAHNESTOCK, ELIZABETH BERTRON. Brotherhood. Out 11/3/15
Home days. Out 11/3/15
I wish --. Out 1/31/17
Service. ScM 2/17

FAIRCHILD, CAMILLE. Airships. PoeL Winter#/16
Song of the stars. PoeL Winter#/16

FANNING, CECIL. Efficiency. ReM 7/21/16

FARMER, ETHEL. The Bonfire. Tri 3/16
In some quiet garden. CoV 7/16

FARQUHAR, JEAN. I have been a god. SmS 11/16
My love. SmS 11/15
Scene D/amour. SmS 6/16

FARRAR, JOHN CHIPMAN. Brest left behind. CoV 7/19

FARRINGTON, HARRY WEBB. Rough and brown. BoT 3/29/19

FAUNCE, FRANCES AVERY. Away. Nat 7/26/19

FAUSET, JESSIE. Again it is September. Cri 9/17
Christmas Eve in France. Ind 12/22/17
The Return. Cri 1/19

FAUST, FREDERICK. The Secret. Cen 2/17

FAWCETT, JAMES WALDO. Return. Min 10/16
Well! well! Mas 1/17

FAY, ALICE M. America speaking. StJ 9/18

FAY, CHARLES EDEY. Autumn. Boo 10/17
The People perish. Boo 12/17

FAY, DOROTHEA. Portrait. CoV 4/19

FECHHEIMER, LEE S. America to her flag. Poet 7/17

FEINSTEIN, MARTIN. "Apres la guerre." Mid 1-2/19
"C'est la guerre." Mid 1-2/19
Dolor. Colo 1/17
A Fool in distress. Mid 5-6/18

FELDMAN, JESSE. After battle. You 12/18
Exile. You 12/18

FELSHIN, S. MANASSEH. A Japanese print. Mas 6/17

FENDELL, SOLOMON J.D. Lobe lasts like a lily. Poet 5/18

FERL, EMILY. Respite. LoAG 5/12/17

FERRIS, WALTER. New love in a street car. Foru 6/15

FICKE, ARTHUR DAVISON. Adventure. CoV 3/17
  The Arbor, a design by Kiyounaga. CoV 4/17
  Arcadian nocturne. Mid 7/16
  Before summer. ScM 5/19
  The Birdcage. Poet 3/16
  Buddha appearing from behind mountains. Poet 11/16
  The Butterfly. Cen 8/15
  The Dancers. Oth 3/16
  For to-day. NoAR 12/15
  The Headland. SeA 12/16
  I am weary of being bitter. Poet 3/15
  Immortals in exile. ScM 3/15
  Like him whose spirit. Poet 3/15
  Meeting. Poet 3/15
  October song. ScM 11/18
  The Pine branch, a painting by Kenzan. Poet 11/16
  Pines on a mountain, a screen by Yeitoku. Poet 11/16
  Portrait of a judge. ScM 7/15
  Portrait of a lady. CoV 3/17
  Portrait of a woman, by Yeisho. CoV 4/17
  Prayer before summer. Boo 11/17
  Rupert Brooke, a memory. LiR 6-7/15
  Snowtime. Poet 3/15
  The Sword of the Samurai. Mid 7/16
  Tables. Mas 12/16
  To the beloved of one dead. ScM 9/17
  To Rupert Brooke, died before the Dardanelles, April, 1915. Poet 6/15
  A Wave of symphony, a screen by Sotatsu. Poet 11/16

FIELD, FLORA. The Flower. Ain 8/18

FIELD, MARY. Justice. Mas 6/16

FIELD, RACHEL LYMAN. Desires. Mas 9/17

FIELD, SARAH BARD. Victory. LiR 4/17

FINCH, LUCINE. Everyman's land. Out 9/19/17
  "Let there be light." Har 1/17
  Two on the battlefield. Out 7/21/15
  When life comes knocking at thy door. Har 7/15

FINERTY, LOUISE FOLEY. The Grave. Bel 3/18/16

FINLEY, JOHN. A la terre Sainte. ScM 12/15
  Ain Karim. ScM 12/18
  Odysseus' bark. ScM 1/19
  A Picture of old age. ScM 10/19

"Telefunken." ScM 3/15
"Via dei." ScM 1/19
Whose day shall this be? Out 9/6/16

FIRKINS, O.W. The Pictures of Jesus in the Louvre. NoAR 5/19
To my country. YaR 1/16

FISHBURN, JOSEPHINE REDMOND. Child poems. You 10/18
So quietly you came. You 12/18

FISHE, ISABELLE HOWE. Epitaph for an unknown soldier. CoV 7/17

FISHER, A. HUGH. The Traitor. Cen 6/16

FISHER, ISOBEL HUME. The Mother. NoAR 1/18

FISHER, MAHLON LEONARD. Ad Finem. Mid 5/16
Always my look is lifted, Son 10/18
Anticipation. Son 9/17
At a child's grave. Bel 1/30/15
The Brothers. Son 11-12/19
Compensation. Son 9/17
Consonance. Bel 3/3/17
Delirium. Foru 1/15
The Hills were wonderfully fair. Son 8/18
I had a dream. Mid 2/17
If one should come. Mid 6/15
In futuro. Son #III/17
Insanity. Son #II/17
Knowledge. Son 11-12/18
The Last pine. Mid 8/17
Legend. Bel 11/27/15
The Lichen. Lyr 5/17
Love of children. Son 1/18
My song be silent. Son 11/17
Obiit. Mid 2/17
The Old house. Son 3-4/19
Oxen. Son 1/18
Per contra. Mid 1-2/18
A Poet to his father. Son 1-2/19
Realization. Foru 3/15
The Road runs fast. Mid 9-10/19
The Roofless brotherhood. Son 8/18
Should beauty sleep. Bel 5/3/19
The Simple thought. Son 11/17
The Sorceress. Bel 12/30/16
Stairways. Son 3-4/18
The Steadfast. Son 11-12/19
Threefold. Son 3-4/19
To nature. Mid 6/16
To us in Eden. Mid 3-4/19
Victory. Mid 4/16

A Village graveyard. Bel 11/27/15
When I am ended. Son 9/17
Where the wings are. Son 10/18
With an antique ring. Son 5-6/19

FISHER, STOKELY S. Under the dead stars. Bel 2/24/17
A Voice from the twilight. Bel 3/8/19

FISKE, ISABELLE HOWE. The House remembers. PoJ 7/16
Made in Germany. PoJ 7/16
Somewhere in France. Poet 11/18
Trade. PoJ 7/16

FITCH. ANITA. The Faeries's fool. Poet 8/16

FITCH, RUTH. Chinese music. Mas 7/17
The Kiss Cen 9/17

FITZGERALD, JAMES B. The Inheritance. PoR 6/16

FITZGERALD, MARTIN. "Carry on, mates!" Out 8/15/17

FITZSIMONS. THEODORE. The Wine-presser. Min 2/16

FLETCHER, JOHN GOULD. At the turn of the year. Poet 12/19
The Beautiful Geisha. PoJ 6/17
Blind people. Poet 12/16
Cliff-dwelling. Poet 3/16
The Clipper ships. NeR 6/15
The Clouds. PoJ 6/17
A Comparison. PoJ 6/17
Dead thoughts. PoJ 6/17
Despair. PoJ 6/17
Distant coasts. PoJ 6/17
Earth. Boo 3/18; YaR 7/19
The Everlasting contradiction. Poet 12/16
The Giants. You 6/19
Give and take. Poet 12/16
The Great silence, to Richard Aldington. PoJ 1/18
Heat. Lyr 8/17
Invocation. Oth 9/15
La Salle Street-evening. Poet 12/17
Lake front at night. Poet 12/17
The Last rally. Cen 12/16
Lincoln. PoR 8/16
London midnight. NeR 9/28/18
The Lonely grave. PoJ 6/17
The March of the dead men. PoJ 12/16
Mexican quarter. Poet 3/16
The Monadnock. Poet 12/17
Mutualability. PoJ 6/17
A New heaven. YaR 4/18
New York, to H.D. Poet 7/15
Night on the beach. Dia 11/22/17

Spindrift. SmS 5/16
Three songs. Lyr 11/17
Voices. SeA 12/16
Voyage. Poet 5/18
Window-candle. SmS 2/17
The Winds of spring. Mas 5/15

FLINT, F.S. Chalfront Saint Giles. PoJ 3/16
Children. Poet 1/18
Evil. Poet 2/16
Gloom. Poet 2/16
In the cathedral. Poet 1/18
Terror. Poet 2/16
War-time. Poet 2/16

FLORANCE, JOHN. The Graduate. Cen 7/17

FLORANCE, RICHARD. Death. SmS 5/15
Envy. SmS 6/15
Twenty-one. SmS 8/15

FLOWER, JEAN. And so it goes. Par 1/18

FOLEY, JAMES W. Some funny little folks. YouC 11/30/16
A Story after school. YouC 5/18/16
The Way of a boy. YouC 6/22/16

FOLGARE, LUCIANA. The Submarine (tr. Anne Simon). LiR 6-7/15

FORD, FORD MADOX. See Hueffer, Ford

FOSTER, ALAN S. The Upset at court. YouC 1/20/16

FOSTER, BERNARD FREEMAN. The Road to Tartary. Har 6/15

FOSTER, JEANNE ROBERT. Petition. Ain 11/19

FOSTER, JOHN B. The Old Oyster Bay. NYS 1/19/19

FOSTER, NANCY K. A California garden. LoAG 10/10/17

FOX, CONSTANCE PRAEGER. Early spring. LoAG 6/24/16
Sea song. LoAG 4/22/16
Unrequited. LoAG 12/18/16

FOX, ELIZABETH. Birth. Mas 4/17

FOX, MOIREEN. Foreboding. Poet 5/17
In absence, I-IV. Poet 5/17
Liadain to Curithir. Poet 3/15
Love. Poet 5/17

FOX, PAUL HERVEY. A Ballad of buccaneers. Bel 1/16/15
A Captain of romance. Colo 6/15
The Golden galleon. ScM 8/17
The Potency of prayer. SmS 7/15
Tobacco ghosts. Colo 10/15

FRALEY, FREDERICK. Testimony. CoV 11/19
To a black-eyed susan. CoV 7/18

FRANCIS, EMMA S. February fourteenth. YouC 2/19/16

Lady moon. YouC 11/2/16
Rolling hoops. YouC 5/11/16
The Seamstress. YouC 3/2/16
Two girls of Binbury town. YouC 5/23/18
When Alice walked in the wood. YouC 6/14/17
The Wrong doctor. YouC 11/9/16

FRANCIS, WILLIAM LAMB. Satyr choir. Colo 1/15

FRANK, FLORENCE KIPER. Afterwards. Poet 12/17
Attack. Poet 12/17
For the young men dead. Dia 4/25/18
He is dead at twenty. You 6/19
The "L" express. Mas 6/15
The Moment. Poet 12/17
"O when will God come as a mighty flood." PoeL Autumn#/15
Three sonnets. PoeL Summer#/15
To L.B. You 2/19
The Two souls. CoV 5/18
Where sympathy pays. Mas 5/15
With child. Poet 12/17
Within my arms. Poet 12/17
A Woman Mid 7/17

FRANK, HENRY. America in the war. StJ 9/18

FRANKAU, GILBERT. How Rifleman Brown came to Valhalla. Cen 4/17

FRASER, DONALD A. Autumn leaves. CoV 10/18

FRAZIER, C. EMILY. Children at Easter. Cri 4/19

FREDERICK, JOHN TOWNER. Eldest curse. Lyr 3/19
November. PoJ 1/18
The Orchard. Poet 10/19
Song. PoJ 1/18
Song of the pantheist. Min 6/17

FRENCH, FRANK ARTHUR. Garlands. PoJ 9/17

FREYTAG, BARONESS VON. The Conqueror. Mas 6.16

FRIEDLANDER, V.H. One fortune of war. Cen 10/15
Transmutation. Har 1/16

FRIEDMAN, EDWARD. Fulfillment. Colo 5/15

FRÖDING, GUSTAV. The Eternal Jew. PoJ 2/16

FROST, ROBERT. Birches. AtM 8/15
The Bonfire. SeA 11/16
The Death of the hired man. NeR 2/6/15
The Gum-gatherer. Ind 10/9/17
The Hill wife. YaR 4/16
In the home stretch. Cen 7/16
Locked out (as told to a child). For 2/17
Not to keep. YaR 1/17
The Road not taken. AtM 8/15

Snow. Poet 11/16
The Telephone. Ind 10/9/16
FRYER, CECILY. Conscience. Poet 5/18
In a gale. Poet 5/18
FUJITA, JUN. Sister. Oth 4-5/19
Tanka. Poet 11/19
FULLER, HENRY B. Postponement. Poet 2/16
Towards childhood. Poet 1/17
FULLERTON, WILLIAM MORTON. Morning in Achaia. ScM 4/17
FURGUSSON. A.R. The City editor. Har 4/15/16
The Copy chopper. Har 4/15/16
The Humorist. Har 4/15/16
Invocation. Har 4/15/16
The Reporter. Har 4/15/16
The War correspondent. Har 4/15/16
FURLONG, MARTHA RICE. Sea-dreams. CoV 10/16

G

"G.,H." Despedida. For 2/17
"G., P.R." Canadian bred. NYS 1/19/19
GAINES. CHARLES KELSEY. The Path of peace. NoAr 6/19
GAINES. RUTH. Paris 1917. Poet 10/18
GAINES, SAMUEL RICHARDS. A Maid ne'er spake. Mad 9/17
GALE, ZONA. The Secret love. Har 10/19
GALSWORTHY, JOHN. At sunset. CoV 6/19
GAMMANS. HAROLD W. Handkerchief. PoJ 1/17
In my winter garden. StJ 1/18
Lady ocean. PoJ 1/17
Pittsburgh murmurs. StJ 4/18
GANETT, LOUISE AYERS. Housetops. Ind 4/21
The Unbroken march. Mas 7/17
GANNON, FRANK S., JR. Influence. CaW 7/18
GARESCHÉ, EDWARD F. Maris Stella. CaW 5/19
Niagara. OW 9/17
Sun-browned with toil. CaW 7/15
The Young priest to his hands. CaW 6/18
GARLAND, ROBERT. A Prayer in khaki. Out 12/26/17 You. SmS 1/16
GARNETT, LOUISE AYRES. Arbor-vitae. Poet 7/19
Comrades. Poet 10/18
Hound at night. Poet 12/19
Keeping cool. Mas 10/17

Know thyself. Poet 10/18
The Lilies of France. Poet 10/18
Little chief. Poet 12/19
Outcast. Poet 12/19
The Prodigal. Poet 12/19
Reflections. Poet 12/19
Song. Poet 12/19
Wither thou goest. Mid 5-6-/18

GARRISON, THEODOSIA. The Broken lute. SmS 7/15
The Conqueror. GoH 8/18
The Declaration of Independence. Out 7/3/18
The Father. EvM 4/17
The Free woman. EvM 8/18
The Healed ones. GoH 12/16
The Heart of woman. GoH 1/19
Her heaven. EvM 1/18
The Hosts of Mary. ScM 12/19
Kindred. GoH 7/17
Love-songs. EvM 7/17
Margot of Alscace. EvM 12/17
The Martyr. Har 6/18
Prayer for the house in trouble. GoH 5/17
A Prayer for mothers of men. GoH 12/17
A Prayer for planting time. GoH 6/18
A Prayer for the road's end. GoH 11/17
A Prayer for those who watch.. GoH 7/18
A Prayer for the world's rebuilders. GoH 9/18
The Puritan. SmS 6/15
The Shepherd who stayed. Cen 12/16
The Soul of Jeanne d'Arc. ScM 1/17
Success. EvM 7/19
These shall prevail. GoH 2/18
The Tinker's song. SoW 3/15
A Voice at the door. Mad 9/17
When himself comes back. Puc 7/17/15
The Windows. Poet 8/18
With the same pride. EvM 6/18

GASKILL, MARIAN N. Crusaders. ScM 11/17

GATES, ELLEN M.H. How strange it seems. Har 8/15
"I shall not cry return." Har 7/15
A Personal desire. Har 6/17

GAY. DOROTHEA. Constrained. Lib 6/18
Estrangement. Mas 2/17
Trees. Mas 10/17
Wind-cry. Mas 4/17, 7/17
Wind harp. CoV 4/19

GEIGER, FRANCES MOORE. A Pagan. CoV 7/17

GEISINGER, W.B. Summer's comin'. LoAG 5/12/17

GEORGE, STEFAN. Oppportunity (tr. E.B.). Min 12/16
Song (tr. E.B.). Min 10/16

GERBAULET, NINA JOY & CLAIRE K. For realms untried. PoR 12/16

GESNER, RICHMOND H. Lexington's heroes. BoT 2/8/19

GESSLER, CLIFFORD FRANKLIN. Free Russia. Nat 8/9/19
To a girl on roller skates. CoV 12/19
Walther von dem Vogelthal. CoV 3/17

GFELLER, C. Yville, Colo 1/15

GIBBON. J. MURRAY. Little grey mother. ReM 6/5/19

GIBBS, DORNEY. Commee il faut. SmS 12/16

GIBRAN, KAHLIL. God. SeA 5/17
My friend. SeA 5/17
On giving and taking. Sea 5/17
Sayings of "the madman." You 4/19
The Three arts. SeA 5/17
The Two hermits. SeA 5/17

GIBSON, CHARLES E. The Other. Boo 6/18

GIBSON, GERALD. To Miriam. SmS 1/17

GIBSON, JUNE. I hate her. SmS 2/17
Jerry heard the crash. SmS 1/17
On my deathbed I am worried. SmS 12/16

GIBSON, LYDIA. Artemis. Mas 3/15
Awakening. Lib 7/19
By a stream. Mas 1/17
City dawn. Mas 6/15
The Coming. Mas 9/16
Dust of dreams. Mas 8/17
Esoeris. Mas 3/15
Green peas. Mas 9/16
A Grove. Mas 8/17
Intimacy. Lib 6/19
Not Years. Mas 8/17
On a hill. Mas 8/17
A Portrait. Mas 10/16
A River in drought. Mas 8/17
Silent. Mas 7/16
Solace. Mas 7/16
The Swimmers's song. Mas 1/17
The Young Girl with the red hair. Mas 3/16

GIBSON, WILFRED WILSON. Back. Poet 8/15
The Blast-furnace. NoAR 3/15
Color. Poet 3/16
The Fear. Poet 8/15

The Going. Poet 8/15
Gold. Poet 3/16
Hill-born. Poet 8/15
Hit. Poet 8/15
The Housewife. Poet 8/15
The Ice-cart. Cen 8/15
In the ambulance. Poet 8/15
In khaki. YaR 10/19
In the orchestra. Poet 4/15
The Kittiwake. YaR 10/19
Medical officer's clerk. YaR 10/19
The News. Poet 1/17
Nightmare. Poet 8/15
Oblivion. Poet 3/16
Sentry go. YaR 10/19
The Shaft. Ind 1/1/17
Tenants. Poet 3/16

GIDDINGS, HELEN. My garden. StJ 4/18

GIDLOW, ELSIE A. At the top of the world. Poet 10/19
Never any fear. Poet 10/19

GIFFORD, FANNIE STEARNS DAVIS. Borrowed wings. GoH 2/17
In an old lodging-house. Poet 3/15
The New house. Har 1/15
To-night. Poet 3/15

GIFFORD, R.B. My fifty dollar bond. NYSB 10/6/18

GILBERT, CHARLES BAKER. It does make a difference, Wordsworth,
    what? Cen 5/17

GILBERT, JULIA. Strategy. SmS 9/17

GILBERT, MORRIS. An Apostrophe. SmS 5/17
Cats. Sms 10/16
A Cigarette in slender fingers. SmS 4/17
Disillusion. Poet 4/19
Epitaph on a madman's grave. Poet 4/19
A Glove. Colo 1/15
He affronts the destinies. SmS 8/18
Irish kisses. Sms 4/17
The Lanthorn or the gleam. YouC 1/18/17
Love came tremendously. SmS 8/17
A Message. SmS 10/18
Miracles. SmS 6/18
Prussians don't believe in dreams. Poet 4/17
The Thing. Poet 4/19
To a French aviator fallen in battle. Poet 4/17
Wars are for youth to wage. Ind. 4/14/17
What I would have. SmS 8/17
What there is. SmS 4/18

Wheels. Lib 6/18
When I die. SmS 5/16
Why he cornered the market. Poet 4/19
GILCHRIST, MARIE EMILIE. A Friend in France. CoV 5/19
Growing older. Nat 6/22/18
Old Eurydamas. Nat 10/26/18
Springtime theft. CoV 5/19
Summer rain. Nat 6/21/19
GILKYSON, PHOEBE HUNTER. The Mother. ScM 12/15
GILLETTE. EUGENIA. Home acre. Cra 2/16
GILLILAN, STRICKLAND. He beat me home. GoH 11/17
Our shifting ambitions. WoW 1/19
Sex obligation. SmS 7/16
GILMORE, EVELYN KING. Sacrifice. YouC 2/28/18
GILMORE, LOUIS. Deity. Poet 6/18
Earth. Poet 6/18
Improvisation. LiR 6/17
Improvisations. LiR 7/17
Pause. Poet 6/18
GILMORE, MARIAN FORSTER. Out of the depths. Boo 11/16
The Triumph of love. Boo 10/16
GILTINAN, CAROLINE, A.N.C., to Joyce Kilmer. BoT 10/5/18
The Breeze. PoR 5/16
The Coward. CaW 11/16
The Disguise. Sta 12/13/19
Epiphany song. CaW 1/17
The First Christmas. CaW 12/19
The Living. BoT 11/19
The Miracle. CoV 5/18
The Revealer. CaW 3/18
To my Victrola. PoJ 12/15
GINGER, BONNIE. April fog. Ain 4/18
It's name. Ain 10/18
GINSBERG, LOUIS. As I came down in the harbor. CoV 1/17
In the hallway. CoV 10/18
Japan nights. CoV 8/16
The Lover thinks of the beloved. CoV 10/18
Nocturne. Foru 7/17
Saturday night. Mas 3/16
Song, summer afternoon. CoV 7/17
GIOVANNITTI, ARTURO. Anniversary. Mas 10/17
The Day of the war, June 20. Mas 8/16
La cisterna. Colo 3/15
Mea culpa. Lyr 10/17
New York and I. Ain 9/18

When the cock crows. Mas 10/17
GIRASCH, PAUL. The Wall. Lib 10/18
GLAENZER, RICHARD BUTLER. The Almoner of night. PoJ 3/17
  The Answer. PoJ 1/16
  Barbados. PoeL Vacation#/17
  Bathtubs. ReM 6/15/17
  Bermuda. Poet 6/17
  Caribbean nights. Poet 2/19
  The Chasm. Poet 12/15
  Christmas in the old world. BoT 12/22/17
  The Coin, Mid 7-8/18
  Conscience. Mid 7-8/18
  The Cure. CoV 9/18
  Dominica. PoeL Vacation#/17
  Dry-point of Mrs. James Luce. CoV 12/19
  The Dual birth. Bot 11/23/18
  First growth. Poet 2/19
  The Golden plover. PoeL New Year's#/16
  Iere. PoeL Vacation#/17
  Indian summer. Boo 11/16
  L'Arc de Triomphe. Oth 5-6/16
  La Pelee. PoeL Vacation#/17
  Lees. PoJ 3/17
  A Letter from Lovelace. PoeL Spring#/17
  The Little donkey. Poet 2/19
  Middle-age. EvM 9/17
  The Minor poet. SmS 7/17
  The Miracle of Montserrat. PoeL Vacation#/17
  Morne fortune. PoeL Vacation#/17
  On the dispersal of the Morgan porcelains. Colo 12/16
  The Passage. Poet 6/17
  A Pittance. CoV 7/17
  Palms (a West Indian rhapsody). Min 11/16
  Pomegranate. Poet 12/15
  Quandary. Poet 6/17
  Roses three. PeoL New Year's#/17
  The Sage. PoJ 1/16
  St. Christopher and Nevis. PoeL Vacation#/17
  St. George's, Grenada. PoeL Vacation#/17
  Sark of the Leewards. Mid 3-4/19
  Scales. Oth 5-6/16
  The Shadow. PoJ 3/17
  The Shoulders of France. CoV 7/17
  Snap-shots of American authors: Howells. Boo 7/17
  Snap-shots of American authors: Morris. Boo 1/18
  Snap-shots of American authors: Tarkington. Boo 7/17

Snap-shots of American authors: Wharton. Boo 7/17
Snap-shots of American novelists: Cable. Boo 9/17
Snap-shots of American novelists: Deland. Boo 10/17
Snap-shots of American novelists: Dreiser. Boo 9/17
Snap-shots of English authors: Bennett. Boo 8/17
Snap-shots of English authors: Conrad. Boo 6/17
Snap-shots of English authors: G.K.C. Boo 10/17
Snap-shots of English authors: George. Boo 8/17
Snap-shots of English authors: Hewlett. Boo 5/17
Snap-shots of English authors: Locke. Boo 6/17
Snap-shots of English authors: Shaw. Boo 5/17
Snap-shots of foreign authors: Artzibashef. Boo 7/18
Snap-shots of foreign authors: Barrie. Boo 7/18
Snap-shots of foreign authors: D'Annunzio. Boo 7/18
Snap-shots of foreign authors: France. Boo 3/18
Snap-shots of foreign authors: Gorky. Boo 7/18
Snap-shots of foreign authors: Loti. Boo 2/18
Snap-shots of foreign authors: Maeterlinck. Boo 7/18
Snap-shots of foreign authors: Rolland. Boo 3/18
Snap-shots of foreign authors: Schnitzler. Boo 7/18
Snap-shots of foreign authors: Sudermann. Boo 7/18
The Snare of the tropics. Cen 8/16
Souvenir of Domenica. Oth 5-6/16
The Star of stars. Mad 8/17
The Stumbling block. Mid 7-8/18
Sure, it's fun! BoT 3/24/15
The Tapestry. Poet 12/15
To an artist. ReM 11/26/15
To Edgar Lee Masters. ReM 6/18/15
To Mea: a realization. PoJ 1/16
To Mea at dawn. PoJ 1/16
To Sarah [Bernhardt]. Boo 5/15
Unanswered. Mad 8/17
Under the Saman. Poet 2/19
Words. CoV 1/19

GLASPELL, SUSAN. Joe (Joseph O'Brien, died Oct. 27, 1915.) Mas 1/16

GLASSIE, HENRY HAYWOOD. Vengeance. Nat 2/15/19

GLEASON, HAROLD WILLARD. The Dream of the naval reservist on his
    first night in service. NYSB 11/17/18
"Fight, Ames! Fight!" NYSB 12/15/18
First aid. NYSB 12/15/18
"Fishers for pick'ril." YouC 8/3/16
A Flurry in stocks. NYSB 12/29/18
Mere Mignolle. NYSB 10/13/18
"Mort pour la patrie." NYSB 12/15/18
Mud. NYSB 6/23/19
The Sunken submarine. NYSB 11/10/18

Union River Bay. NYSB 11/3/18
Vigils. NYSB 9/15/18

GLENDAY, TOM. A Million dead. ReM 1/28/16
Peace. ReM 3/3/16

GLOSSOP, EMMA ELLEN. The Summer cottage. YouC 5/10/17

GLOVER, CHARLES W. Jeannette and Jeannot. ReM 6/4/15

GODOY, JORGE. Beaux. NYSB 11/10/18
The Immortals. NYSB 9/15/18
June. NYSB 6/23/19
Never! NYSB 8/11/18

GOING, CHARLES BUXTON. The Path of glory. EvM 3/16
Repatriated. EvM 8/17
The Resurrection of peace. NYTM 4/4/15
The Sky-scraper. EvM 12/16
They who wail. ScM 11/17

GOLDRING, DOUGLAS. Home. SmS 7/15
Maisonnettes. Oth 1/16
Voyages. Poet 5/15

GOLDSMITH. WALLACE. The Contrast. YouC 2/24/16

GONZALES, JORGE. To the old guitar (tr. Alice Stone Blackwell). StJ 3/19

GOODALE, DORA READ. April-over-the-hill. YouC 4/13/16
The Children of the childless. YouC 2/8/17

GOODELEL. THOMAS D. Two poets. YaR 4/16

GOODLOE. ABBIE CARTER. At parting. ScM 8/16
Overseas, in memory of Alan Seeger, killed in battle, Belloy-en-Santerre,
July 4, 1916. Boo 2/18
The Telephone. Boo 4/18

GOODMAN, HENRY. Memory. Lyr 1-2/18

GOODMAN, WILLIAM MCDONALD. A Doubting brother. SoW 8/15

GOODYEAR, ROSALIE. Beloved madness. Lib 6/18
Consolation. PoR 8/16

GORDON, FLORENCE LEE. Dawn. Mid 5-6/18
Quiet. Mid 5-6/18

GORDON, FRANK S. By Genesseret. Poet 6/18
Dirge for one dying. Poet 6/18
I have but one love. Poet 6/18
I will cling me to a star. PoJ 3/18
Liberty. PoJ 3/18
Lost land. PoJ 3/18
Morning hymn. Poet 6/18
Night. Poet 2/17
On the war-path. Poet 2/17
Sa-a Narai. Poet 2/17
The Smoke prayer. Poet 6/18
Startled waters. Poet 6/18

The Tom-tom. Poet 2/17

GORDON, GEORGE. Dinner at eight. NYSB 12/29/18

GORMAN, HERBERT S. The Burning bush. BoT 1/26/18
Caput mortuum. PoJ 2/16
The Fanatic. NYSB 12/28/19
Gray hills. NYS 3/9/18
The Lost heart. Lib 10/18
The Satrys and the moon. PoJ 2/16
Tread softly, time. PoJ 3/16

GOULD, FELIX, The Kiss of the god. PoJ 1/18

GOULD, WALLACE. Children of the sun. SeA 7/17
My secret. Oth 7/19
Poeme erotique. Oth 7/19
Snows. Oth 4-5/19
To W. Oth 7/19

GOULDING, ERIC ROSS. To the heroic dead. DetS 6/9/18

GRABO, CARL H. Peace. Nat 11/23/18

GRADWELL, W. EWART. La rapatries. NYS 6/25/18

GRAHAM, HOWARD S., JR. Flower love. CoV 2/16
A Toast. CoV 4/16

GRANICH, IRVIN, MacDougall Street. Mas 5/16

GRANVILLE, CHARLES. The Bayonet charge. Poet 1/18
For parents of the slain. Poet 1/18
The Mourner. Poet 1/18
The Question. Poet 1/18
Under orders. Poet 1/18

GRANT, ROBERT. A Hymn. ScM 3/18

GRAVES, HARLEY. Before dawn in camp. Poet 9/17
I came to be alone. Poet 9/17
A Thought when noon is hot. Poet 9/17
White magic. Poet 9/17

GRAVES, ROBERT. The Kiss. Cen 7/19

GRAY, AGNES KENDRICK. A Dying soldier of Venice. BoT 12/8/17
In San Fernando Valley. LoAG 9/2/16
Jeanne d'Arc, the Shepherdess,on a statue by Chapu. BoT 3/30/17
Night on the golden horn. Mid 9-10/18
Our lady of the trenches, statue of the Virgin set up on the
battlefield by soldiers. PoJ 6/17
The Palm tree's song. YouC 3/21/18
Pavane. Mid 9-10/18
Roma aeterna. BoT 6/8/18
To a shamrock growing in California. LoAG 7/1/16

GRAY, DANIEL W. The Death of the lizzie. CoV 11/19
Dust. CoV 11/19

GRAY, MARY. Belleau Hill. Poet 7/19

GREEN, WILLIAM CHASE. To an Italian shepherd boy. CoV 8/16

GREENE, HIRAM MOE. Theodore Roosevelt. WoW 3/19

GREENE, ROY FARRELL. The Little girl who laughed. PeHJ 10/17

GREENHOOD, DAVID. For the gossip of crazy Melendez. You 4/19

GREENWOOD, G. DOUGLAS. Reverie. CoV 7/17

GREENWOOD, JULIA. The Kind heart. Poet 10/18
  The Woodlands. PoeL Summer#/16

GREGG, FRANCES. Pageant to H.D. Poet 1/15

GREGORY, ALLENE. Litany. Poet 10/18

GREGORY, SUSAN MYRA. The Answer. PoJ 7/17
  Death. PoJ 7/17
  Heaven. PoJ 7/17
  Here where we met. PoJ 11/17
  Nocturne. PoJ 7/17
  Now. PoJ 7/17
  Orpheus' song to Eurydice. PoJ 7/17
  September song. PoJ 11/17
  The Secret. PoJ 11/17
  Summer is dead. PoJ 7/17
  To-night. PoJ 11/17

GREIF, MARTIN. Evening. SmS 4/15

GRIDLEY, LOUISE MAY. A Winter evening. GoH 1/18

GRIFFIN, ANNA. Dark Rosaleen's last chaplet. CaW 7/19

GRIFFITH, WILLIAM. Adelina Patti. NYSB 11/2/19
  Apotheosis. Ban 8/20/17
  At the will of the moon. Ban 8/27/17
  Autumn song. Poet 6/15
  Canticle. Poet 6/15
  A Character. Ban 8/27/17
  City pastorals. Int 6/15
  Columbine. Ain 9/18
  The Duel. Ban 8/27/17
  Enigma. Ban 8/27/17
  Evening. Ban 8/20/17
  A forest rendezvous. SmS 9/19
  The Ghostly hound. Ban 8/20/17
  Hadleyburg. Poet 6/15
  The Haunted house. Ban 8/20/17
  He forgets Yvonne. Poet 9/16
  The Home-coming of Pierrot. Bel 8/5/16
  The Hospital. Ban 8/27/17
  The House of the sphinx. Ban 2/12/17
  The Hunt. Ban 8/27/17
  I, who fade with the lilacs. NYSB 8/10/19

I, who laughed my youth away. Ain 8/19
Interlude. Poet 6/15
Love and life. Ban 8/20/17
Magdalen. Ban 8/20/17
Mors omnibus communis. Ban 8/20/17
My dog. Ban 8/20/17
O not the moon. Ban 8/20/17
Oh Chatham beach. Ban 8/20/17
Oubliette. Ban 8/20/17
Pierrette goes. Poet 9/16
At the door. Ban 8/20 17
Pierrot and Pierrette at the window. Bel 8/5/16
Pierrot the conjurer. Ain 2/19
Pierrot gives an accounting. Bel 8/5/16
Pierrot is haunted by the wraith of Pierrette. Ain 7/18
Pierrot mourns the death of Pierrette. Bel 8/5/16
The Protest of Pierrot (1914). Bel 8/5/16
Renunciation. Ban 8/20/17
Requiescat. Poet 6/15
Serenade. Poet 6/15
The Sisters. Ban 8/27/17
Vigil. Ban 8/27/17
War. Ban 8/27/17

GRIGGS, EDWARD HOWARD. Age. StJ 5/19

GRIMES, KATHERINE ATHERTON. Bid them be still. SoW 5/15
The Greatest gift. SoW 3/15

GROFF, ALICE. Herm-Aphrodite-us. Oth 1/16

GRUDIN, LOUIS. All my beautiful moments. Poet 12/17
Background. Lyr 1/19
For the old. Lyr 1/19
Have you no pity? Poet 12/17
I squandered. Poet 12/17
My people. Lyr 1/19
Prayers. Lyr 1/19
Refugee. Lyr 1/19
The River. Poet 2/17
Walls. Lyr 1/19
The Woolworth. Poet 12/17
With my own hands. Poet 12/17

GRUENING, MARTHA. Prepared. Mas 3/16

GRUMAN, HARRY D. The Cynic. Par 5/18

GUEST, EDGAR A. Christmas wishes for 1917. LoAG 12/20/17

GUITERMAN, ARTHUR. A Ballade against critics. Har 8/19
The Conqueror (an Algonquin legend). Har 6/17
The Curse of the antique. Har 9/17
Eiler, a Christmas legend of old Denmark. Bel 12/23/16

Elsewhere, R.F.D. YouC 11/22/17
Gargantua of gotham. Cen 7/18
The Goal. Boo 11/18
Home again. Out 11/26/19
House blessing. BoT 3/31/17
The Idol-maker prays. Har 7/18
Messire Geoffrey Chaucer to hys editor. Boo 10/18
Mexican serenade. Cen 6/18
Mikko the squirrel, a Passamaquoddy legend. YouC 5/16/18
The Quest (a Lithuanian folksong). Bel 9/30/15
Ragnarok. Bel 7/13/18
The Return. Har 11/15
The Scribe's colophon. Boo 4/19
Temperament. Boo 8/18
Training day, a ballad. ScM 10/15
GURLITZ, AMY LANDON. From an office window. EvM 6/19
The Marching men. EvM 4/19
"Vive le roi!" EvM 2/19

HACKETT, FRANCIS. Harry Hawker. NeR 5/24/19
HADLEY, FLORENCE JONES. The Road to Arcady. WrM 6/19
HAGEDORN, HERMANN. Autumn in the Coonecticut hills. CoV 11/18
The Birthday. CoV 1/16
The Boy in armor. Out 1/10/17
The Boy in chapter, Phi Beta Kappa, June 18, 1917. Out 6/20/17
The Bridegroom speaks (lines for the marriage of G.L. and W.D.H.
   CoV 3/16
The Cabaret dancer. Poet 12/15
The Clock. CoV 1/16
Early morning at Bargis. Poet 7/15
Fatherland. Poet 9/15
Fugitive. NoAR 1/16
The Heart of youth. Out 11/24/15
How spring came to New York. Out 4/3/18
I wonder. Out 3/17/15
Judgment. Out 3/14/17
The Just cause. EvM 1/18
Love in marriage. ScM 3/19
An Ode of dedication. Cen 1/17
Philemon to Baucis. CoV 3/16
Resurrection. Cen 1/17
A Rhyme of forsaken ships. Out 12/20/16
Tongues. CoV 6/16
"A Traveler from a distant land." Out 1/3/17

HAGER, ALICE ROGERS. Sea song. LoAG 6/10/18

HAIGHT, ELIZABETH HAZELTON. At Ravello. PoeL 3/15

HAINES, ELWOOD LINDSAY. Twilight song. CoV 7/17
  Walking home. CoV 6/18

HAINES, HELEN. Her names (feast of the nativity of the Blessed
  Virgin, Sept. 8th). CaW 9/16

HAIRIG, MURGURDITCH CHRIMIAN. The Memorial of the lamenting
  soldier (tr. Alice Stone Blackwell). StJ 2/18

HALE, RALPH TRACY. Youth. WoW 8/18

HALCK, VITEZSLAV. Evening songs (tr. Otto Kotouc).
  PoeL Winter#/16

HALIFAX, JEAN. What a good idea! YouC 11/2/16
  Words with wings. YouC 3/22/17

HALL, AMANDA BENJAMIN. Artists. SmS 7/16
  A Child. NoAR 10/18
  Fog. SmS 2/18
  Joy o'living. CoV 6/18
  Panacea. Har 3/19
  Pastoral. CoV 6/19
  Woods' warrior. CoV 1/19

HALL, FREDERICK. The Neutrals. YouC 11/2/16

HALL, HAZEL. Americanism. LoAG 6/20/18
  Captive. Har 10/19
  Company. NeR 5/3/19
  A Falling star. BoT 5/20/18
  The Flowering. Mas 7/17
  Frames. NeR 2/8/19
  From an old portrait. LoAG 6/20/18
  Hands. You 6/19
  Later spring. Mas 7/17
  The Little house. Har 11/19
  My grave. Mid 3-4/19
  Passing. CoV 12/18
  Red Cross knitting. LoAG 6/20/18
  Shut in. NeR 1/25/19
  Smiling. Lib 10/18
  Song. LoAG 5/20/18
  Songs for dreams. CoV 12/19
  The Still return. Lib 7/18
  To a phrase. Poet 7/18
  To a sunbeam. CoV 12/18
  Unanswered. You 6/19

HALL, HERBERT J. The End of the storm. Bel 9/16
  Music of great spaces. Bel 9/29/17
  Slim flutes and viols gay. Bel 6/21/19

The winged victory. Bel 12/9/16

HALL, JAMES NORMAN. A finger and a huge, thick thumb. Cen 1/17
The Three-penny lunch. PoR 9/16

HALL, JEANNIE PENDLETON. The Cloak for the manger. YouC
12/13/17
A Mother cat. YouC 8/23/17
Simeon in the temple. YouC 1/4/17
A Song from the ashes. YouC 7/19/17

HALL, JOHN. Pierrots, scene courts mais typique (after the
"Pierrots" of Jules LaForgue). LiR 5/17

HALL, NEWTON MARSHALL. At a certain place in Flanders. BoT
4/17/18

HALL, RUTH. The Wolf at the door. Poet 8/16

HALLECK, GEORGE. Song: old style. SmS 8/17

HALLET, ETHEL. Regret. PoJ 5/15

HALSEY, ABIGAIL FITHIAN. Life's alchemy. CoV 2/17
The Proof. CoV 1/17
Revelation. CoV 5/19
The Source. CoV 1/17
World builders. CoV 2/17

HAMILL, R.F. I am art. ArW 7/17

HAMILTON, MARION ETHEL. Pink blossoms. Poet 3/19

HAMMOND, ELEANOR. Dew. CoV 9/18
Fog. You 2/19
Goldfish. CoV 9/18
Searching. CoV 9/18
Souls. CoV 9/18

HAMMOND, ELIZABETH. Cradle song of Mary the Mother. NoAR 10/18

HAMMOND, JOHN MARTIN. From the Eighteenth century. SmS 7/15

HAMPTON, EDGAR LLOYD. The Peace call. Cen 3/19

HAMSBY, FLORENCE. Rime and reason. YouC 2/7/18

HANBURY, PATRICK C. The Humorist. Mas 6/16

HANKINS, MAUDE McGEHEE. Daddy Gander rhymes. SoW 8/15
Don't forget. SoW 8/15
The Jitney man. SoW 8/15
The Little mouse in a trap. SoW 8/15
Muckie Matchet. SoW 8/15

HANLEY, Elizabeth. Arrival. CoV 8/16
Little roads. CoV 5/16

HANLINE, MAURICE A. Hate is a sword. CoV 12/18
Ladybird. CoV 12/18
Poetry. CoV 7/18
A Song of Pierrot. CoV 12/18

HANLON, JOHN. The Bridesmaid. Par 8/17
  A French Canadian in hospital. Par 9/18
  The Living God. SmS 1/17
  A Lyric. Par 1/18
  A Song of a southern island. SmS 7/16
  A Spring song of the city. SmS 4/17
  To a reluctant lady. Par 4/18
  Two songs. SmS 7/15
  Two songs of Pan. Par 7l/18

HANLY, ELIZABETH. Aspirations. CoV 7/18
  Back home. BoT 1/26/18
  First to fall (W.C.S., class of '15). Out 3/27/18
  Her garden. YouC 12/27/17
  My wish. Out 12/27/16
  November eleventh. BoT 11/23/18
  Sixteen. CoV 9/17
  The Trees of Picardy. Boo 8/18

HANNIGAN, D.F. The Renaissance of man. Min 1/17

HANSGEN, MATTIE LEE. The Magic key. YouC 12/23/15

HANSON, JOSEPH MILLER. Panama. ScM 3/15

HARDING, D.E.P. The Queen's shrift. CoV 10/17

HARDING, MAUDE BURBANK. Epidemic. StJ 4/19
  A Memory. You 2/19
  Peace. StJ 2/19

HARDING, RUTH GUTHRIE. At the old ladies' home. Bel 10/16/15
  From a car-window. SmS 5/15
  O Mary in thy clear young eyes. Bel 12/18/15
  Song. BoT 9/25/15

HARDY, EVELYN. To a deserted garden. ScM 11/16

HARDY, MARY EARLE. In an April shower. YouC 4/11/18

HARDY, THOMAS. A Hundred years since. NoAR 2/15

HARE, AMORY. April. CoV 8/19
  August moon. CoV 8/19
  Blind. CoV 8/19
  "But there was one who wore a crown." CoV 8/19
  By the hearth. CoV 8/19
  By the window. CoV 8/19
  Chanticleer. CoV 8/19
  The Dead. CoV 8/19
  Gone. CoV 9/17
  Moods. CoV 8/19
  Moon magic. CoV 8/19
  Outside and in. CoV 8/19
  Remembered. CoV 8/19
  "Shine." CoV 8/19

"So slim and swift and glad was she." CoV 8/19
Sonnet I. CoV 8/19
Sonnet II. CoV 8/19
Surgery. CoV 8/19
Unsolved. CoV 8/19
Walking at night. CoV 8/19
HARLAND, MARION. But once. Ind 3/12/17
HARMON, MARK. The Journey. Har 1/22/16
HARPER, ISABEL WESTCOTT. To the gypsy girl. ScM 11/19
HARRISON, JAKE H. April in the south. SoW 4/15
HARRISON, KENDALL. The Heritage. ReM 1/21/16
  His share. ReM 12/15/16
  On a hill-top. ReM 2/18/16
  To a dead soldier. ELM 1/1/16
  "Way for Mr. Atkins." ReM 5/11/16
HART, ELIZABETH. Gloucester nights. ScM 10/17
HART, LOUISE. Inscription on a sun-dial. Poet 7/17
  The Spider's web. Poet 7/17
  Winter. Poet 7/17
HARTE, RICHARD BRETE. To J.L.L., a psychic poem. LoAG 11/20/17
HARTLEY, MARSDEN. After battle. Poet 7/18
  Her daughter. Poet 7/18
  In the frail wood. Poet 7/19
  Scaramouche. Oth 2/19
  Spinsters. Poet 7/18
  Swallows. Oth 3/19
HARTPENCE, ALANSON. Revenge. Oth 8/15
HARTSWICK, F. GREGORY. Elegy written at a country club. Cen 4/17
  The Great big man and the wee little girl. Cen 7/17
  The White gods (with due apologies to Kipling's "Feet of the
    young men"). Cen 4/17
HARVEY, SHIRLEY. Rainy days. Poet 11/18
HASTE, GWENDOLEN. Boot Hill graveyard. Mid 9-10/19
HASTINGS, WELLS. Indentity. Cen 4/16
HATCH, MAY D. Federalized. NYSB 8/11/18
HAUGHAWOUT, MARGARET E. Wyrd. Mas 3/17
HAUPTMANN, GERHARDT. As an Aeolian harp (tr. Bernard Raymund).
    PoeL Summer#/15
  The Poet (tr. L.M. Kneffer). PoeL New Year's#/16
HAUSGEN, MATTIE LEE. The City boy. YouC 10/25/17
HAWKEN, CYRIL C.H. Hope. ScM 4/19
HAWLEY, HUDSON. Just thinking. EvM 7/18
HAWSBY, FLORENCE. The Sand box. YouC 3/30/16

The Tea party. YouC 3/16/16

HAWTHORNE, HAZEL. Fifteen years old. Lib 7/18

HAWTHORNE, HILDEGARDE. Haunted. Har 7/15

HAY, ELIJAH. An Epitaph. ReM 3/16/17
  The King sends three cats to Guenevere. Oth 12/18
  Lolita, a respectable woman. Oth 1/17
  Night. Oth 1/17
  Nightmare after talking with worldly women. Oth 1/17
  Ode in the new mode. ReM 3/16/17
  Philosopher to artist. ReM 3/16/17
  Prism on the present state of poetry. Oth 1/17
  Spectrum of Mrs. X. Oth 1/17
  Spectrum of Mrs. Y. Oth 1/17
  Spectrum of Mrs. Z. Oth 1/17
  Spectrum of Mrs. & so forth. Oth 1/17
  To an actor. ReM 3/16/17

HAY, GREGORY. The Soldier's good-bye. YouC 1/25/17

HAY, JOHN. The Enchanted shirt. ReM 11/22/18

HAYNE, WILLIAM HAMILTON. A Gentleman. ScM 1/18
  Ideals. ScM 8/15
  The Volunteer. ScM 1/16
  When peace comes down. ScM 1/19

HEAD, CLOYD. Epilogue. Poet 10/18
  The German expire-Bismarck, von Moltke. Poet 10/18
  Grotesques, a decoration in black an white. Poet 10/16
  The Marne. Poet 10/18
  Prelude. Poet 10/18
  They march through the streets of Paris. Poet 10/18

HEAD, HENRY. Destroyers YaR 4/17
  Died of is wounds. YaR 1/18
  I cannot stand and wait. YaR 4/16

HEALD, LOUISE. Blue gray eyes. Ain 9/18
  My olden love. Ain 10/18

HEALEY, ROBERT. The Derelicts. Har 2/15

HEAP, JANE. Notes, I-II. Poet 6/17

HEARD, JOHN JR. Victor Chapman, Harvard, 1914. Nat 4/5/17

HEAZLITT, CLARENCE WATT. Winter evening. Lyr 4/19

HECHT, BEN. Romance. SmS 6/15
  Snow monotones. Poet 2/18

HEDRICK, TUBMAN KEENE. Land. ReM 11/22/18
  The Landlord. ReM 11/22/18

HEINE, HEINRICH (tr. Louis Untermeyer). Angelique. SeA 4/17
  Doctrine. SeA 4/17
  Epilogue. SeA 4/17

From the window. SeA 4/17
Losses. SeA 4/17
To George Herwegh. SeA 4/17
A Warning. SeA 4/17

HELBURN, THERESA. The Aviator. Bel 2/12/16
Freesia. CoV 8/16
Resurrection. SmS 12/5
To you. PoJ 3/17

HELLER, SAMUEL. In the train. StJ 5/19

HELLMAN, GEORGE S. Mother's birthday. GoH 5/17
The Princess. Lyr 12/17

HELTON, ROY. In December. NYSB 11/10/18

HENDERSON, ALICE OLIVER. After seeing Kathleen. LiR 8/15
Breaking down beautiful churches. Poet 7/15
How they burned houses down. Poet 7/15
Kathleen. LiR 8/15
Miss Ungeriche's Japanese play. LiR 8/15
A Mountain of fire. LiR 8/15
Ribbons in the sun. Poet 7/15
The Snow flakes. LiR 8/15
War. Poet 7/15

HENDERSON, ANNA M. A Prayer. Cri 4/18

HENDERSON DANIEL M. Adventure street. EvM 9/18
Alan Seeger: soldier-poet. CoV 7/18
The Brushwood fire. McCl 10/18
Dawn. EvM 3/18
The Flag of man. EvM 4/19
The Gray battalion. NYSB 2/9/19
The Living. McCl 11/17
Love and lyre. CoV 10/19
Marshall bluebird. EvM 4/19
A Nature-lover passes. Har 8/19
The New York Public Library. Boo 11/17
The Poet's path. CoV 12/19
A Soldier in Manhattan. NYSB 2/9/19
Soldier's all. Out 9/12/17
Youth and death. Lyr 5-6/19

HENDERSON, PETE. The Blacksmith. For 11/16

HENDERSON, ROSE. Earth and stars. Mas 9/17
Faces. Lib 10/18
Hands. PoJ 3/17
Neighbors. PoJ 3/17
Night. CoV 12/19
On the mountain. CoV 9/17
The Pagan. NeR 3/15/19

A Plains wife. CoV 9/17
Red-blooded. CoV 10/18
The Shack. PoJ 3/17
Spring-New Mexico. Poet 4/10
To one in the trenches. Dia 12/20/17
When war came. Lib 4/18
The wind. CoV 10/18

HENDERSON, RUTH E. The Dark. Nat 12/13/19

HENDERSON, W.J. The Afternoon. ScM 7/18

HENDRIX, MRS. WILLIAM SAMUEL. Do I love thee? Mad 9/17
October's child. TeR 10/19
Rose dreams. Mas 8/17

HENRY—HIRSCH. Under the evening star (tr. McPherson). NYTr 12/1/18

HENSLEY, ALMON. Somewhere in France, 1918. EvM 8/18

HEPBURN, ELIZABETH NEWPORT. "I am too proud." Ain 8/18

HERALD, LEON. Youlia. DetS 1/19/19

HERDER, SUZETTE. To a flower. Poet 5/16

HERENDEEN, ANNE. The Day. EvM 6/19
I am always trying to find out about things. Mas 7/17
R.T.P. Lib 11/18

HERFORD, OLIVER. Britannia salvatrix. Har 12/18/16
Epilogue, spoken by Miss Rose Coghlan at the closing of Wallack's
    Theatre, in New York, on May 1, 1915. BoT 5/1/15
The Illustrator's apology. Boo 11/16
To a cow. Cen 2/17
To the crocodile. Cen 3/16
To a flea. Cen 6/16
To a gold fish. Cen 11/15
To a hen crossing a road. Cen 6/18
To a lion. Cen 12/15
To a sheep. Cen7/18
The Whip-poor-will. Cen 3/15

HERFORD, WILL. That God made. Mas 2/16

HERRON, VENNETTE. Reminiscence. Ain 5/19

HERSEY, HAROLD. The After dawn. Par 8/18
Art. Ain 5/19
A Ballad of memories. Min 5/16
Benedicte. Min 11/16
The Buddha. Ain 4/19
Disillusion. SmS 7/16
Fragment. Par 6/18
An Hour of grace. Par 4/18
Irony. Par 9/17
The Last word. Par 11/17

The Lutanist. SmS 12/16
The Meeting place. Par 5/18
The Painted lady. Ain 9/18
Silhouettes of the city. Min 1/16, 3/16
To one older. SmS 1/16
Victory. Min 1/17

HERSEY, MARIE LOUISE. My soldier boy. BoT 5/2/17
Unidentified. BoT 1/2/18

HERVEY, JOHN L. Ballade of the libido. ReM 6/8/17
A Chinese ideograph. Colo 8/15
Ex-voto, to John Myers O'Hara, with homage for "Sappho" and "Pagan
  Sonnets." ReM 8/13/15
From dawn to dawn-epanastrophe. ReM 3/30/17
Gli Condottieri. Colo 10/15
The Nameless one, Gettysburg cemetery, U.S.A. ReM 5/26/16
Pallisy. ReM 7/5/18
The Parthenon. ReM 11/26/15
Running water. ReM 3/10/16
Socrates. ReM 2/4/16
Walt Whitman. ReM 12/7/15

HETZEL, MARGARET HUNT. Aprille's love song. Mas 7/17
The Fool. Mas 9/17
When I have tea. Mas 5/17

HEWETSON, GEORGE BENSON. Father Lacombe, O.M. II. CaW 2/17
The Homeless God. CaW 10/17
The Process. CaW 10/18

HEWITT, ETHEL M. Bois etoile. Har 10/17
Ivolry. Har 11/19
Lover with wings. Har 1/19

HEWITT, STEPHEN H. Glastonbury, vobis parta quies. Foru 2/16

HEYSER, PAUL. On the death of a child (tr. Bernard Raymund). PoeL
  Spring#/15

HEYWARD, DuBESE. An Invocation. CoV 12/18

HICKENLOOPER, JEAN. Content. Mid 10/16

HICKEY, EMILY. Arraigners and poets. CaW 6/17
At Lustleigh. CaW 10/16
A Cry in the springtime. CaW 4/19
Devon. CaW 10/16
Killed (aged 19, 20, 21). CaW 9/17
September. CaW 10/16
The Spirit indeed is willing, but the flesh is weak. CaW 4/15
To my guardian angel. CaW 10/16
The War's story. CaW 5/19
"Whose, then, shall those those things be?" CaW 10/19

HICKEY, JAMES C. Doubts. Nat 4/26/19

HILL, ELIZABETH. To little April. YouC 4/13/16

HILL, FRANK ERNEST. AT the foot of the market. Foru 5/15
By grace of battle. Foru 4/15

HILLMAN, CAROLYN. The Blue strand. BoT 5/1/18
June fancies. BoT 6/8/18
The Sign. BoT 4/19/19
Sugar mice. Poet 12/19
Wreaths. Poet 12/19

HILLMAN, GORDON M. 'Is missus. BoT 7/6/18

HILLS, ELIJAH CLARENCE. Spanish graves. PoJ 3/16

HILLYER, ROBERT SILLIMAN. Interval. NeR 2/15/19
An Invitation. NeR 9/23/18
The Mirrors. Son 11-12/19
Premonition. NeR 12/28/18
Return. NeR 2/15/19
The Sea-gull. SeA 6/17
Summer night. StJ 1/18
Thermopylae and Golgotha. Nat ?/19
To Congress concerning the bill for universal military service. Mas 4/17
To a scarlatti passepied. NeR 2/26/16
Two sonnets. Lyr 1/19; NeR 2/15/19
Vigil. Son 11-12/19

HINCHMAN, WALTER S. Autumn by the sea. CoV 1/16

HINDMAN, JULIA MAXEY. Flowers. SoW 6/15

HIRES, HARRISON S. The Benefactor. Mas 8/17

HITCH, ALFRED. Beauty. Poet 8/17

HOBART, ETHEL. A Legal holiday. NeR 9/7/18
Song for worship. NeR 5/10/19
To F.F. NeR 11/2/18

HOFFMAN, C. GOUVERNEUR. To the anglo-saxon aviators. ScM 5/18

HOFFMAN, PHOEBE. The Civil engineers. CoV 10/19
The Down-trail. CoV 6/18
The Freight yards. CoV 7/16
Lilies that sleep. Mid 11-12/18
The Locket. CoV 1/16
The Runner. CoV 1/19
The Salvation Army's song. 1/17
The Song of the aviator. CoV 2/17
To an oats field on a hill-side. CoV 10/18
The Up-trail. CoV 6/18

HOFMANNSTHALL, HUGO VON. Death (tr. C.W. Stork). PoeL Spring#/18

HOKE, TRAVIS. Supreme laughter. Poet 1/17
The Ultimate. Poet 1/17

HOLBROOK, H.W. Adieu. Min 5/17

Art. Mid 5-6/18
Conquest. Mas 7/17
Triolet. Mid 4/17, 11-12/18
HOLBROOK, NELLIE. The Robin in the rain. CoV 4/17
HOLBROOK, WEARE. The Birch. StJ 5/18
Pioneers. CoV 12/18
Souvenir. StJ 2/19
Vale. NYSB 6/15/19
HOLDEN, EMERY MAY. America. Out 7/26/16
HOLDEN, RAYMOND PECKHAM. After the storm. CoV 1/19
February twenty-second. CoV 8/17
Funeral. CoV 9/17
Passers-by I-VI. Poet 6/18
HOLLAND, NORAH M. Remonstrance. Mad 7/17
HOLLEY, HORACE. Creative. Poet 5/15
Cross patch. Poet 4/16
Divinations. Oth 5-6/16
During music. PoJ 4/16
Foreword. PoJ 4/17
Hertha. Oth 7/15
The Idiot. Oth 7/15
Invocation. Foru 6/16
Life. Foru 6/16
Lovers. Poet 5/15
Orchard. Foru 6/16
Recession. PoJ 4/16
Renaissance. SmS 2/15
She. SmS 11/16
The Soldiers. LiR 4/17
The Soldiers: an impression of battle. Foru 1/15
Twilight at Versailles. Poet 5/15
You. Oth 7/15
HOLLIDAY, TERRELL LOVE. An Ode to ankles. Par 11/17
Sidestepping Circe. Par 12/17
The Years. Par 2/18
HOLMES, RALPH F. Paradise. DetS 11/21/18
HOLT, ISABELLA. Lament. Tri 3/16
HOLZ, ARNO. The Song (tr. L.M. Kneffer). PoeL Spring#/16
HOOKE, HILDA M. The Vagabond. CoV 11/19
HOOKER, BRIAN. Acquaintance. Cen 12/18
The Bridge. HarW 3/18/16
Braodway. HarW 1/29/16
The Church. HarW 3/11/16
The City. HarW 4/1/16
Horizons. HarW 2/26/16

Madison Square: Christmas. HarW 2/19/16
The Maker of images. YaR 4/15
The Old tree. HarW 2/12/16
Riverside. HarW 3/25/16
To any woman. Tou 7/18
The Wanderer. Har 11/17
Washington Square: the Arch. HarW 3/4/16

HOOLEY, LOUIS RICHMOND. The Reward. SmS 4/18

HOOPER, ELEANOR TILESTON. Dick and his sister. YouC 8/23/17

HOPKINS, ERNEST J. Redemption. Lib 11/18
To a cubist maid. LoAG 3/17/17

HOPKINS, GERTRUDE. The Fear. Cen 5/16
The Ferry. CoV 2/17
The Flame and the smoke. CoV 2/17
Land of the free. CoV 2/17
The Shop. CoV 3/17
Webs of dawn. CoV 5/17
The White-bloomed boughs. SmS 5/15

HOUSE, NATHAN CALEB. The Moth. PoJ 7/15

HOUSE, ROY TEMPLE. To a dead mouse in a trap. Poet 4/19

HOUSEMAN, LAURENCE. The Old moon. Har 7/18
The Quick and the dead. Cen 3/19
Song. Boo 4/18
Summer night. Har 6/19
The Wood maze. Boo 7/18

HOW, LOUIS. Rachel comforted. Har 2/15

HOWARD, KATHARINE. Belgium. Poet 12/16
Grapes and cigarettes. PoJ 1/16
The Host of dreams. Poet 7/17
Lost angels. LoAG 8/26/16
Sacrifice. PoJ 1/16

HOWE, HERBERT CROMBIE. As from a belfry. Bel 8/7/15
The Cherry tree. Mas 9/16
Ravens. Mas 7/17

HOWE, M.A. DE WOLFE. Crucifixions. Nat 3/29/17
The Day. YouC 8/3/16
The Ship builders. BosH 7/22/17

HOWE, MARTYN. Ophaly. PoJ 11/17

HOWE, R. HEBER, JR. A Mountain madrigal. BoT 4/6/18

HOWELLS, MILDRED. If this be all. NoAR 8/15
"Oh, tell me how my garden grows." Har 8/15

HOWLAND, CHARLES P. The Mountains of destiny. NeR 4/3/15

HOYT, FLORENCE. The Adventures of the jets. YouC 6/8/16
More adventures of the jets. YouC 7/6/16

HOYT, HELEN. Action poem. Poet 8/15
  Annunciation. Poet 8/15
  Anticipation. PoJ 11/17
  Arches. Poet 3/17
  Ascension. Poet 12/18
  At the museum. Poet 12/18
  Before the storm. PoJ 11/17
  The Book. CoV 5/17
  Candle shadows. Mid 9/17
  Certitude. CoV 3/16
  Come to me out of the dark. Tri 1/16
  Comparison. Mas 9/15
  Continuance. Poet 3/17
  Converse. Lyr 6/17
  Countervalence. CoV 3/16
  Creation. PoJ 1/16
  The Dancer. Poet 3/17
  Desire. Oth 4/16
  Difference. Poet 12/18
  Escape. Oth 4/16
  The Field and the coulter. PoJ 10/15
  Finis. Mas 8/16
  The Fishers. Cen 6/15
  Flirtation. Mas 8/16
  For you a transient joy. Oth 4-5/19
  The Garden. SeA 6/17
  Gods. Cen 12/17
  Golden bough. Mas 8/16
  Gratitude. Mas 8/16
  Happiness betrays me. Poet 12/18
  The Harp. Poet 12/18
  Hey Nonino. Poet 3/17
  I have found my beloved. Poet 12/18
  In the Art Institute. Mas 8/16
  In the next yard. SeA 8/17
  Interlude. Poet 12/18
  Kin. Poet 3/17
  Landscape. Mid 5-6/19
  The Letter. Poet 3/17
  The Little house. PoJ 1/17
  Living. LiR 8/15
  A Look. Cen 1/16
  Make believe. CoV 3/16
  The Measure. PoJ 1/16
  Memory. Poet 12/18
  Men-folks. Poet 3/17
  Menaia. Mas 9/15

Miss Smith. Lib 4/17
Name. Poet 12/18
The Newborn. Poet 8/15
October. CoV 10/18
Oh, we shall meet. Poet 12/18
Patience. Lib 4/18
A Place on a hill. You 12/18
Poem to be danced. Poet 3/17
Ravelling. Mas 8/16
Remonstrance with sleep. PoJ 11/17
Return. Mas 9/15
Revelation. Cen 8/17
Riddle. Oth 4/16
Rock and sea. StJ 9/19
"Rooming." LiR 8/15
The Root. Poet 12/18
Royalty. Lyr 11/17
The Sense of death. Poet 8/15
Sky-humor. Poet 3/17
Sparrows. Lib 4/17
Stature. Poet 12/18
Thought with a child. Cen 10/16
Time to love on feeling its approach. Mas 9/15
To a vine and workmen cut down. Poet 3/17
To Dorothy. Mid 7/8-18
Trees of memorial. PoJ 11/17
Triumph. Poet 12/18
The Unchanging. Mas 7/16
Under the tree. Poet 3/17
Unity. Lib 10/18; Poet 12/18
Vegetable store. Oth 3/19
Vita nuova. Oth 4/16
Weather. Mas 9/15
Weeds. ReM 6/19/19
With words. ReM 4/6/17
Words out of waking. LiR 5/15
HUCKFIELD, LEYLAND. An April night. CoV 4/18
Avon memories. You 4/19
The Bogging of death. Mid 1-2/18
Break-up in the South Saskatchewan. CoV 5/17
Death song of the mad god who made the Grand Canyon. Tri 3/16
Haunted reaping. Poet 7/15
The Laborer in the mists. Mid 1-2/18
A Midnight song. CoV 5/17
The Muse in church. Poet 7/15
Off Catalina. CoV 10/17
Oh! For a dark-green hill-top. CoV 4/18

The Old gods march. CoV 4/18
The Singing skull. CoV 12/19
HUEFFER, FORD MADOX [FORD MADOX FORD]. The Sanctuary.
    Poet 4/18
The Silver music. Poet 4/18
To Mrs. Percy Jackson. Poet 3/17
What the orderly dog saw. Poet 3/17
A Winter landscape. Poet 3/17
HEUFFER, VIOLET HUNT. See Hunt, Violet
HUEY, MAUD MORRISON. In search of happiness. YouC 5/11/16
The Mediums. YouC 8/9/17
O little bird, teach me to sing. YouC 2/1/17
The Perfect seed. YouC 6/14/17
HUGER, R.D. The Rust of unused powers. Poel Spring#/15
HUGGINS, DOROTHY. Que la vie est belle. Boo 3/17
HÜHNER, LEON. Night. Boo 4/17
HUIGINN, E.J.V. America. BoT 4/28/17
The boys of Uncle Sam. Bot 1/12/18
In no man's iand. BoT 4/27/18
Viva Italia! BoT 6/4/18
HUMPHREYS, MARY. Awakening. CoV 3/17
"Dawlin!" CoV 3/17
A New-world ruin. ReM 8/31/17
Nothing serious. ReM 9/21/17
Spring. CoV 5/17
HUNN, CLARKE FOX. The Laughter. PoR 2/17
Manhattan. PoJ 5/16
Scherzando. PoJ 5/16
HUNNICUT, NAT C. The Last hour. CoV 8/17
A Lover's revenge. CoV 9/16
HUNT, ELIZABETH R. — And no birds sing. ReM 4/5/18
Labor and capital. ReM 7/3/19
Main floor G2 center. ReM 2/8/18
Music. ReM 7/3/19
HUNT, FERN-DELL. The Difference. LoAG 11/20/17
HUNT, RICHARD. Gas-lamp ghost. Poet 4/18
June. PoJ 7/17
The Scarlet tanager. Poet 9/17
Song in early April. Poet 4/18
Song of the killing liars. LiR 6-7/16
To a golden crowned thrush. Poet 5/16
HUNT, VIOLET [VIOLET HUNT HEUFFER]. A Call in hell.
    Poet 2/15
Is it worth while? Poet 4/18

Kensington High Street. Poet 3/17
What the civilian saw. Poet 3/17
HUNTER, MINERVA. The Fairies' masquerade. Lyr 10/17
Who would believe? Lyr 1/19
HUNTINGTON, C.S. Snow. CoV 2/19
HUNTINGTON, FRANCIS V. Desert invocation. Cen 2/15
The Tennis players. Cen 5/15
HUTCHINSON, ELEANOR. Hearts a-singing. Har 11/18

I

"I.,A.P." Wanted. Mas 5/16
IDE, EDWARD. Laughing in and out. Cri 8/17
INGERSOLL, EDWARD P. Manhattan. Mas 5/16
INGLIS, ANTIONETTE. An Elfland story. YouC 8/9/17
INGRAM, JUNE. The Mothers who lose. Son 8/18
INMAN, ARHUR CREW. Fate. StJ 12/16
Hunger song. StJ 12/16
In the crow's nest. StJ 12/16
Song of the south-sea god. StJ 12/16
INNES, LAURENCE EDWARD. I go to kill. BoT 8/17
INSKEEP, ANNIE DOLMAN. Birth, not death. LoAG 6/10/16
Life's tapestry. LoAG 6/10/16
IRELAND, BARON. The Romance of Veronica de Peyster. SmS 2/16
IRIS, SCHARMEL. Lake Michigan at night. Poet 9/17
The Old man. Poet 9/17
War-time cradle song. Poet 9/17
Your neighbor and mine. Poet 9/17
IRVING, MINNA. First aid. NYS 1/19/19
Lady bug. NYS 3/9/19
Larks in Flanders. NYS 3/2/19
The Log of the seven seas. NYS 2/16/19
IRWIN, INEZ HAYNES. Singing in Paris - 1917. Lib 7/18
IRWIN, WALLACE. An Ancient Scottish ballad. Cen 5/18
ISH-KISHOR, JUDITH. Dawn. Lyr 5/17
Introspection. Lyr 8/17
ISH-KISHOR, SULAMITH. The First day. Lyr 11/17
Morning song. Lyr 1/19
On the east side. Lyr 5/17
IVERSON, SADE. Who wants the blue silk roses? LiR 5/15
IVINS, PERRY. Camping. Lyr 6/17
IWANA, HOMEI. The Cup of darkness (tr. Eunice Tietjens). StJ 3/17

J

JACKSON, CATHARINE EMMA. Piping. Har 7/18

JACKSON, LEROY F. Charley. Mid 7-8/19
The Coyote. Mid 7-8/19
The Northwester. Mid 10/17
The Strange adventures of a little boy. YouC 12/30/15
Sunday. Mid 7-8/19

JACKSON, LUCY. Driving in the park. CoV 5/16

JACKSON, ROBERT MACAULEY. The Funeral. SmS 11/15

JACKSON, VIRGINIA P. Africa. Cri 2/19

JAMES, EDWARD M. A Picture. You 12/18

JAMISON, ROSCOE C. Negro soldiers. Cri 9/17

JANVIER, GEORGE W. I walk through darkening aisles. CoV 4/17

JENKINS, GEORGE B., JR. Arcady. Par 9/18
Corinne. SmS 6/16
I offer you my slightly battered heart. Par 8/18
I shall say "hello" indifferently. Par 9/18
Lines to a co-respondent. Par 9/18

JENKINS, OLIVER. The Old cathedral. BoT 12/13/19
On and on. BoT 11/12/19
Sparks. BoT 12/24/19
Tinsel. BoT 11/15/19

JENKS, TUDOR. A Portrait by Velasquez. Bel 2/26/16
A Timely petition. Out 7/11/17

JENNEY, FLORENCE G. April birdsong. CoV 4/19

JENNINGS, G.B. Bernice. SmS 3/18

JENNINGS, LESLIE NELSON. Arabesque. Lyr 3/18
Arrestment. Dia 11/16/18
Awakening. Sun 11/17
Ballade of aesthetes. Boo 2/17
Bars. Ain 10/19
Black magic. Mas 4/17
Castlebar. Lib 6/18
The City. CoV 3/17
Curtain. Mid 7-8/18
Dēnouement. SmS 2/18
Design for old desire. PoJ 3/18
The Dusk of empire. Foru 12/17
Earth has no tears. Son 10/18
Ephemerae. NeR 10/19/18
Epilogue. NeR 8/17/18
Evincement. Min 4/17

Candles. Oth 5-6/16
The Dance. CoV 10/16
Dilemma. Poet 3/17
The Door. Poet 3/17
Eclipse. Oth 3/19
Glass. ,h 5-6/16
The Haunt. Poet 2/15
The Horns of peace. Poet 3/17
The Interpreter. CoV 10/16
The Last poet. SmS 4/15
The Mad woman. CoV 10/16
The moon's betrayal. SmS 2/15
The Old home. PoR 12/16
Old youth. Poet 3/17
Olives. Oth 7/15
The Plum tree. CoV 5/16
Salome. PoJ 1/17
Shadow. Oth 2/19
Sisters of the rose. Poet 2/15
Song for a spring night. SmS 2/16
Stars. SmS 9/17
Translation. SmS 10/17
The Tree toad. Poet 3/17
Vale, H.D.J. ReM 4/27/17

JOHNS, PEGGY BAIRD. Trilium. Mas 9/17

JOHNSON, ANNE PORTER. The Heart's way. PeHJ 8/17
October. PeHJ 10/17
On the way. PeHJ 11/17
The Wanderer. PeHJ 9/17
The Winter fire. PeHJ 2/18

JOHNSON, BURGES. A Difference. EvM 12/18
His temples. Har 11/16
The Nursery. EvM 2/17
Play. Har 5/18
The Service. Har 2/15
Toul. NoAR 2/19
When daddy sings. EvM 4/17

JOHNSON, CONSTANCE. In a hospital. EvM 1/19

JOHNSON, FENTON. The Artist. Oth 4-5/19
Aunt Hannah Jackson. Oth 2/19
Aunt Jane Allen. Oth 2/19
The Barber. Oth 2/19
The Cotton picker. Lib 8/18
Dreams. Oth 4-5/19
The Drunkard. Oth 2/19
The Gambler. Oth 2/19

How long, O Lord! Poet 6/18
The Lost love. Poet 6/18
Rulers. Lib 8/18
The Sunset. Lib 8/18
Tired. Oth 1/19
Who is that a-walking in the corn? Poet 6/18

JOHNSON, GEORGIA DOUGLAS. Again it is the vibrant May. Cri 5/18
Desert-bound. Cri 4/18
Guardianship. Cri 10/17
Heritage. Cri 10/17
Hope. Cri 10/17
Let me not lose the dream. Cri 10/17
The Mother. Cri 10/17
My boy. Cri 10/17
Prejudice. Cri 5/19
Tears and kisses. Cri 8/17
To the mantled. Cri 5/17

JOHNSON, IDA JUDITH. The Bishop. CoV 11/16
Changed. CoV 12/19
Flood. Poet 5/18
The Minstrel. Poet 5/18

JOHNSON, JAMES WELDON. A Modern poet to his baby son. NYS 1/20/19
To America. Cri 11/17
The White witch. Cri ?/15

JOHNSON, ROBERT UNDERWOOD. "And then?" YouC 3/1/17
Constance. Har 4/8/16
The Corridors of Congress. NoAR 5/15
Goethals of Panama. NYTr 5/2/15
The Little room of dreams. ScM 8/17
Oriole and poet. Har 2/16
Reading Horace. HarW 3/4/16
Two flags upon Westminster towers, April 20, 1917. Ind 6/2/17

JOHNSON, ROSSITER. A Book re-opened. Mad 8/17
The Dark Ages. Colo 4/16
A Valentine. Colo 2/17
A Veteran by the wayside. Colo 5/15

JOHNSON, WILLIAM SAMUEL. Buttadeus (a battle episode of July, 1915). Foru 6/16

JOHNSTON, FLORENCE POYAS. New Mexico. Cen 12/15

JOHNSTON, MARIE. Where the trinity flows. LoAG 5/16/16

JOHNSTONE, JULIAN. Tantramar. CaW 7/18
Winooski Falls. CaW 5/17

JONAS, ROSALIE M. Ballade des belles milatraisses. ArW 7/17

JONES, CHARLES C. Good advice. NYTM 12/31/16

JONES, HOWARD MUMFORD. The Afternoons. Foru 8/16
  Aphrodite. Poet 4/16
  At sunset. ReM 12/27/18
  Dawn. Foru 8/16
  De profundis. CoV 9/16
  Driftwood. ReM 12/27/18
  First impressions. Foru 8/16
  Fog. ReM 12/27/18
  The Garden in September. Mid 2/16
  Gargoyles: a Eunise. CoV 12/16
  In Hood's canal. ReM 12/27/18
  Influences. ReM 12/27/18
  The Last conquistador. TeR 1/19
  Librarians. Mid 6/17
  Night. Foru 8/16
  Night vision. ReM 12/27/18
  November on the dunes. Poet 12/16
  Phonology. Mid 6/17
  The Professor muses, physic lecture room before class. Poet 4/16
  Seabeck. ReM 12/27/18
  Six academic sonnets. CoV 9/18
  A Song of Butte. CoV 11/18
  Tides. ReM 12/27/18
JONES, MARY. Cadwalader. ScM 2/19
JONES, RALPH M. Bed-time. CoV 5/19
  I saw the spring come riding. YouC 5/2/18
  Mary. CoV 9/18
  The Two towns. YouC 5/24/17
  Verbiage. YouC 2/15/17
JONES, RUTH LAMBERT. The Call of the unknown. Lif 9/5/18
  The Coming. Lif 5/22/19
  Comparison. Boo 9/19
  Dream. Lif 1/23/19
  Echoes. CoV 12/19
  Harmon B. Craig (Verdun - July 16, 1917). Bot 8/?/17
  "Lest we forget." BosH 5/31/19
  Puzzle. Lif 5/15/19
  To her. CoV 12/19
  To an Indian in vaudeville. Lif 8/29/18
  War pictures. CoV 7/18
  Wounded. CoV 7/18
JONES, THOMAS S., JR. At sundown. PoJ 4/16
  The Garden. BoT 12/21/18
  The Gifts of peace. BoT 12/21/18
  The Great poets. Har 4/17
  The Hills. PoJ 4/16

The Last spring. PoJ 4/16; BoT 12/21/18
The Miracle of song. PoJ 4/16
Sanctuary. BoT 12/21/18
To Maude Adams. NYTi 3/25/17

JORDAN, CHARLOTTE BREWSTER. Susanna Sempler's sample.
    YouC 3/9/16
A Visit to Ireland. YouC 4/19/17

JOSEPHSON, MATTHEW. See Rilke, Rainer Maria

JOYCE, JAMES. Alone. Poet 11/17
Flood. Poet 5/17
A Flower given to my daughter. Poet 5/17
Nightpiece. Poet 5/17
On the beach at Fontana. Poet 11/17
She weeps over Bahoon. Poet 11/17
Simples. Poet 5/17
Tutto e sciolto. Poet 5/17

JOYCE, W.H. The War spirit. LoAG 1/16/15

JUDSON, JEANNE. Christmas Eve, 1918. CoV 12/18
Faith. CoV 12/18
Song of little things. CoV 12/18

JUDSON, MARGARET. In the night. Poet 2/19

JURGELIONIS, KLEOFAS. Lament, Lithuanian folk-song. Poet 6/16

K

"K.,H." The Disembodied. SmS 4/15

KAUFFMAN, REGINALD WRIGHT. In after years. SmS 12/15
Prometheus. Mas 2/15
Recognition. Cen 11/19

KAUFFMAN, RUTH WRIGHT. To the gardeners. Har 11/15

KEARNEY, CLYTIE HAZEL. Lost moon. CoV 9/19

KEELER, CHARLES. Ganga devi. Colo 8/15

KEGEL, WILHELM. The Ends justify. Oth 1/16

KEIKINTVELD, JEANETTE. The Happy lover. DetS 10/6/18
Through empty years. DetS 8/25/18

KEITH, HENRIETTA JEWETT. May comes laughing. Nat 5/17/19

KELKNAP, P.H. Inseparable. Ain 4/19

KELLEY, ETHEL M. The Other child. Har 1/16
The Rainy day. YouC 3/1/17
Roses. Har 6/18
Waiting for Santa Claus. YouC 12/13/17

KELLY, BLANCHE. The Mirror. CaW 9/17

KEMP, HARRY. And is it true? Par 4/18

The Angel's anthem. Ind 12/11/16
Cleopatra dead. SmS 10/16
The Dead lover. Ain 2/19
Defeat. SmS 4/18
The Dream. SmS 1/18
Even when I pray. Ain 3/19
The Guestless room. Par 8/18
He did not know. Cen 10/19
Her handkerchief   Par 7/18
How many women tall and fair. SmS 10/17
Idealism. SmS 12/17
If you had been unkind. Ain 9/18
Jim. Par 6/18
A Lad and a lass together. Par 10/17
The Leafless bough. SmS 9/17
March night. HoG 3/16
The Moth's complaint. SmS 10/16
Old-fashioned song. Cen 7/19
A Phantasy of heaven. SmS 1/18
Rain. Ain 10/18
The Rainbow. Ain 8/18
Rebellion. Mas 7/16
Resurrection. Mas 3/16
Solomon's song. SnaS 12/18/17
The Storm. Ain 5/19
The Stormy star. Mas 6/16
To Fiametta. Ain 8/19
Towards dawn. Foru 7/17
Travel. Mas 4/15
The Traveler. Ain 12/19
The Tryst. Par 2/18
Unforgotten. Par 10/17
The Warden's son. SmS 9/17
What else to do? Par 1/18
The Wheel of life. SmS 12/17
Why should we strive? Par 11/17
The Wind died yesterday. SmS 8/18
The Wisdom of the wise. Ain 4/19
Zenobia. Mas 2/16

KENNEALY, J.J. The Sleepers. Har 5/19

KENNEDY, CHARLES W. A Christmas prayer. ScM 12/17
Memory. ScM 6/17
"You who once walked beside me." SmS 4/19

KENNEDY, SARA BEAUMONT. Fragments. SoW 3/15

KENNON, HARRY B. Black gum. ReM 12/15/16
A Book review. ReM 2/16/17

Camouflage. ReM 9/7/17
Mary. ReM 12/17/15
Music visible. ReM 4/21/16
Problem. ReM 12/24/16
Psychology. ReM 3/23/17
To Amy. ReM 4/25/19
What rabbit? ReM 6/5/19

KENT, ARTHUR V. The Leader. Poet 4/16
The Wild honey of wisdom, to E.L.L. Poet 4/16

KENYON, BERNICE LESBIA. Distraction. Son 9-10/19

KENYON, JAMES B. The Airman. Har 2/18
The Changeless round. Ain 8/18
Related. Bel 4/1/16
Renascence. Har 6/17

KENYON, THEDA. In an old fashioned garden. CoV 5/19
November. Lyr 11/17
Sanctuary. CoV 5/19
To a tear bottle. Cov 7/17

KERN, JOHN. The Proud lady. SmS 4/18

KERVAN, ALTE STILWELL. The Organ man. YouC 3/16/16

KESSLER, KARL W. But she isn't. Par 7/18
I admit something. Par 2/18
The Lesson. Par 11/17

KETCHUM, ARTHUR. Before the swallow dares. YouC 3/28/18
Holiday. SmS 1/15
Holy week. YouC 4/20/16
A Place of stars. LivC 12/22/17
A Waite-songe for Chrystmasse. YouC 12/21/16

KEYES, FRANKLIN C. A Ballad of dying. CaW 11/19

KILLACKY, U.H. "Noli me tangere." CaW 4/17

KILMER, ALINE. Age invading. Out 3/14/17
An Autumn walk with Deborah. PiR 10/18
A Didactic poem to Deborah. ScM 3/17
Dorothy's garden. ScM 1/17
The Garden child. Out 5/24/16
High heart. GoH 3/18
I shall not be afraid. GoH 2/19
In spring. GoH 4/18
My mirror. Boo 3/19
Things. Boo 7/19
Violin song. NYSB 6/8/19

KILMER, JOYCE. The Annunciation. QW 7/17
The Ashman. CoV 4/16
August Fourth, Nineteen Sixteen. Boo 12/18
Beauty's hair. PoJ 4/16

A Blue Valentine, for Aline. Poet 3/17
In memory of Lieutenant Rupert Brooke. Boo 9/15
The New school. Out 11/24/15
Prayer of a soldier in France. GoH 4/18
The Proud poet. Bel 5/27/16
The Robe of Christ. CoV 1/16
Roses. CaW 6/17
Rouge bouquet. ScM 9/18
The Singing girl. CaW 10/16
The Singing soldier. NYTi 1/19/19
The Thorn. Poet 3/17
To an adventurous infant on her birthday, August, 1915. Boo 12/18
To the memory of three poets. PoR 6/16
To my mother, October, 1915. Boo 12/18
Valentine written for his mother, 1913. Boo 12/18
The Visitation. QW 7/17
Wealth. Bel 9/18/15
The White ships and the red. NYTM 5/16/15

KIMBALL, FLORENCE T. Betrayal. Lyr 6/17
Might I be prince. Mad 8/17
Pier 6. CoV 6/19

KIMMEL, STANLEY PRESTON. Vespers. LoAG 5/5/17

KING, ALICE. Creation. SmS 12/16

KING, GEORGIANA GODDARD. Compline. ScM 2/19
In the key of blue. Foru 4/15
To a Chinese air. Foru 5/15

KING, SARA. Apathy. PoJ 6/16
Cry. PoJ 6/16
If it be true. ScM 11/15
Interlude. PoJ 6/16

KING, TERENCE. Cur deus homo. CaW 3/19

KINNEY, MURIEL. My friend the catbird. Poel Summer#/17
The Type. PoeL Summer#/17

KIRCHWAY, FREDA. To a soap-box orator. Mas 2/15

KIRK, WILLIAM F. Come again, Uncle Sam! Par 5/18

KIRKLAND, JEANNE. Good bye. Mas 3/17

KIRKWOOD, KATHLEEN. The Block party. EvM 2/19

KITTREDGE, HERMAN E. The Dream-flower. Lyr 10/17

KIZER, HELEN BULLIS. The Brides. SmS 12/15

KLYCE, LAURA KENT. Interlunacy. Boo 3/19

KNAPP, ETHEL MARJORIE. A Miniature. YouC 10/10/16

KNAPP, G. PRATHER. Cost. ReM 2/28/19

KNEVELS, GERTRUDE. Main street. YouC 6/1/16
Mourning. Out 11/7/17

KNEVELS, MARY EASTWOOD. The Hills. Poet 5/17
  Wood paths by the sea. Poet 5/17

KNIBBS, HENRY HERBERT. Apunyi ayis. LoAG 1/9/15
  Sunshine over Yuma. SmS 3/15

KNIGHT, LULA W. The Wind in the trees. Poet 7/16

KNISH, ANNE. Opus 181. Foru 6/16
  Opus 344. Oth 1/17
  Opus 360. Oth 1/17
  Opus 371. Oth 1/17
  Opus 380. Oth 1/17
  Opus 389. Oth 1/17
  Prism on the present state of poetry. Oth 1/17

KNOTT, HENRY. The Three geraniums. WoW 4/19

KOLARS, MARY B. Spring faithfulness. Boo 5/17

KOOPMAN, HARRY LYMAN. The Centennial of Keats' poems, London,
    1817. BoT 8/1/17

KRAMER, BERT. When silence reigned. Par 9/17

KREYMBORG, ALFRED. Again. Poet 4/17
  Animals. Boo 12/17
  Arabs. Oth 3/19
  Bell. PoJ 2/17
  Carbon-dioxide. Oth 1/19
  Convention. Oth 2/16
  Courtship. Poet 4/17
  Dirge. Poet 4/17
  Earth wisdom. Oth 2/16
  Idealists. NeR 2/26/16
  Improvisation. Oth 2/16
  In a dream. PoJ 1/16
  In the next room. Oth 2/16
  June. PoJ 2/17
  Lanes. Poet 4/17
  Lightning. PoR 7/16
  Little folks. Oth 2/16
  Love was dead. Poet 4/17
  Lure. PoJ 2/17
  Man tells. Oth 2/16
  Midnight caprice. Oth 12/18
  The Nobility. SeA 8/17
  Nun show. Oth 7/19
  Old manuscript. Poet 2/16
  Others. PoJ 2/17
  Overhead in an asylum. Oth 7/15
  Pennies. NeR 1/1/16
  Preludes. Boo 11/17
  Primer. PoJ 2/17

Progress. NeR 2/26/16
Red chant. Cri 11/18
Self esteem. PoJ 2/17
Sir Hobbledehoy. Poet 4/17
A Sword. Oth 2/16
To H.S. Oth 2/16
To W.C.W., M.D. Oth 2/16
Toward love. Oth 2/16
The Tree. NeR 1/1/16
Trees. PoJ 2/17
Variations. Oth 7/15
Vision. Oth 4-5/19
Vistas. Oth 2/16
When the willow nods. Poet 3/18
The Whip of the unborn. Oth 2/16
Woman tells. Oth 2/16
Worm. NeR 5/18/18
1914. Poet 4/17

KUDER, BLANCHE BANE. The Fairy town. Lyr 8/17

KUEFFNER, LOUISE MALLINCKRODT. The Land of desire. Min 3/17
Mother of joy. CoV 4/18
The Prairie. Oth 1/16
The Sea. Oth 1/16
The Wind of the world. Min 12/16

L

"L.,A.L." To Henry Leverett Chase. ReM 7/30/15
The Water wind. ReM 7/30/15
"L.,L." Spider song. For 11/16
"L.,M." I, too will write vers libre. For 2/17
LACKEY, ALEXANDER McK. Sonnet. Mas 5/17
LACOSTE, LUCIE. Waiting. SmS 12/16
LAFFITTE, KATE C. America. LoAG 3/20/18
LAIRD, ALAN. Tertium quid. SmS 4/18
LAIRD, WILLIAM. And I also. Mid 3-4/18
The Anchor. CoV 4/17
An Apple eater to a coquette. CoV 7/18
Buds. Poet 2/16
Foresight. Mid 3-4/18
Interlude. Lyr 7/17
A Prayer. CoV 1/19
Schumann-Heink in Pittsburgh. CoV 11/16
A Song of heavens: from France. CoV 1/19
A Stable-yard. Mid 3-4/18

Thoughts on a long road. CoV 7/17
To a mountain peak. CoV 11/16
To a new passion. CoV 2/17
To a young man. CoV 11/16
The Two thiefis. CoV 10/17
Ulysses returned. CoV 8/17

LAMB, LOUIS ALBERT. Matters grow worse. ReM 6/22/17

LANG, DAVID. I made my sorrow into a song. CoV 2/19
Old song. Har 3/19

LANGHORNE, MARGARET. Morning song. SmS 10/17

LAMPTON, W.J. Art and artist. ArW 6/17

LANE, J.M. After a summer shower. SmS 7/16

LANSING, JOHN G. In extremis. ScM 8/15

LAPRADE, M. The marmot and the marmoset. Har 12/19
Peace with honor. Har 10/19

LARNED, WILLIAM TROWBRIDGE. Ballade of the last straw.
ReM 7/27/17

LASKER, RAYMOND. Justice. Colo 7/16

LATHAM, PETER. Advice. CoV 4/18
Contradiction. CoV 2/18

LAVALLE, JOHN, JR. Over Ypres. Cen 6/19

LAWRENCE, D.H. Bread upon the waters. Poet 2/19
Casualty. Poet 7/19
The Child and the soldier. Poet 7/19
Daughter of the great man. Poet 7/19
Gloire de Dijon. Lyr 1-2/18
The Grey nurse. Poet 7/19
I am like a rose. Lyr 3/19
The Jewess and the V.C. Poet 7/19
Message to a perfidious soldier. Poet 7/19
Moonrise. Poet 7/18
Mother's son in Salonika. Poet 7/19
Mourning. Poet 7/19
Neither moth nor rust. Poet 7/19
Nostalgia. Poet 2/19
Obsequial chant. Poet 2/19
On the balcony. Lyr 8/17
Pentecostal. Poet 2/19
People. Poet 7/18
Prisoner at work in a Turkish garden. Poet 7/19
Resurrection. Poet 6/17
River roses. Lyr 10/17
"Rose of all the world." Lyr 1/19
Sighs. Poet 7/19
Tommies in the train. Poet 2/19

War baby. Poet 2/19
Zeppelin nights. Poet 7/19
LAWRENCE, JOSEPHINE. Memory. Bel 2/17/17
LAWRENCE, REBECCA PARK. Ecce mysterium. Poet 7/15
LAWRENCE, SEABURY. The Lost lightship. NYSB 11/10/18
Paths of glory. NYSB 8/11/18
Poetry. NYSB 9/15/18
The Stoker. NYSB 9/1/18
Tale of a regimental (and monumental) cook. NYSB 8/11/18
LAWSON, W.P. A Voice. Mas 9/16
LEA, FANNIE HEASLIP. His girl. GoH 6/18
LEAMY, EDMUND. The Road to Larchmont. NYSB 11/3/18
Sea-hunger. CoV 7/19
LEAR, MARIE B. A Melody. Lyr 3/19
LEAVENWORTH, ANNIE CRIM. Crowning gift. Lyr 4-6/19
LEBLANC, MAURICE. Presentment (tr. Mrs. William Flewellyn Saunders).
ReM 8/6/15
LE BRAZ, ANATOLE. The Song of the blowing wind (tr. Elizabeth S.
Dickerman). PoeL Summer#/16
LECLERC, MARC. The Passion of our brother, the poilu. Boo 12/18
LEDOUX, LOUIS V. Mater Dolorosa. Har 5/16
Persephone in hades. PoR 6/16
Song of the daughters of Celeus. Har 6/16
Whip-poor-will. YaR 7/19
LEDWIDGE, FRANCIS. Had I a golden pound. Cen 5/18
The Lanawan shee. Cen 1/18
The Sylph. Mad 9/17
To one who comes now and then. Cen 3/18
To a sparrow. Cen 4/19
LEES, AGNES. The Answer. Poet 5/17
At dawn. Poet 9/15
Bach at the organ. YouC 3/22/17
Bark-bound. Poet 1/19
A Blinded poilu to his nurse. Boo 5/18
The Broken tie. Poet 1/19
Claude Debussy. Poet 5/18
The Doll. Poet 5/17
The Dream child. PoR 2/17
Eastland waters. Poet 2/16
Evening. Poet 5/17
Footsteps. YouC 12/23/15
In the morgue. Poet 1/19
The Keeper of the lock. PoR 7/16
Long distance line. Poet 9/15
Moving pictures. Boo 6/15

The Nesting linnet. YouC ?/?/15
An Old woman with flowers. Poet 1/19
Peace. Poet 12/18
The Quest. PoR 2/17
Radium. PoJ 6/15
Red pearls. Int 10/16
Shakespeare. Poet 4/16
The Slacker. Poet 1/19
The Sweeper. Poet 1/19
Three quests. Poet 9/15

LEE, HELEN A. Robin singing rain. YouC 6/15/16

LEE, MARY EFFIE. Morning light. Cri 11/18

LEE, MUNA. Addendum. SmS 1/18
  Behind the house is the Millet plot. Poet 1/16
  Bereavement. SmS 2/16
  But still. SmS 2/17
  The Cabbage field. SmS 3/18
  Compensation. Poet 8/17
  Concerning all the poets of the world. SmS 9/17
  The Dreamer. SmS 12/16
  The Fall of the year. SmS 10/18
  From a book of phrases. SmS 12/17
  Genesis. SmS 6/17
  Go out across the hills. SmS 2/17
  Harvest. Poet 1/16
  I shall not sing again of love. Poet 1/16
  I thought love would come gloriously, with a clash. Oth 5-6/16
  I took my sorrow into the woods. Poet 1/16
  I who had sought God blindly in the skies. Poet 1/16
  It is only then. SmS 4/17
  Lips you were not ahungered for. Poet 1/16
  Love song. SmS 4/18
  Magdalen. Poet 1/16
  Mahhavis. Poet 8/17
  Now have I conquered that which made me sad. Poet 1/16
  An Old grief. SmS 7/17
  The Perfect song. SmS 10/16
  Regret. Ain 10/19
  Shadows, I-II. Poet 8/17
  A Song at parting. SmS 5/16
  Song for a harp. SmS 1/17
  A Song of happiness. Poet 8/17
  Song of an old love. SmS 2/18
  The Stars are colored blossoms. SmS 11/16
  Though you should whisper. Poet 1/16
  The Tryst. SmS 5/17
  Twilight song. SmS 12/16

Two love songs. SmS 10/17
The Unforgotten. SmS 1/16
A Villanelle of forgetfullness. CoV 7/16
Wi' thoughts of my love. SmS 7/17
Windblown, I-III. Poet 8/17
You. SmS 6/17

LE GALLIENNE, HESPER. The Garland of memories. Har 4/19
The Patient gods. Har 8/19
To the southern sea. Har 8/16
A Villanelle of life and death. Har 12/19

LE GALLIENNE, RICHARD. Ballade of Amaryllis in the shade.
    Puc 6/5/15
Ballade of the junk man. Puc 5/15/15
Ballade of his lady's immortality. Ain 8/18
Ballade of the modern bard. Har 10/19
A Ballade of pot-pourri. Har 6/19
A Bookman's ballade. Har 11/19
Carpe diem. Ain 11/19
The Chalice. Har 10/18
Desiderium. Har 11/17, 7/19
The Face eternal. Ain 4/19
Homeward bound. Har 10/16
In the woods at midsummer. Ain 8/19
Joyous gard. Har 4/19
The Lost paradise. Har 4/17
Sacred idleness. Har 5/18
Sailing companions. Har 2/17
Sea sorcery. HarW 4/29/16
Violin music. Har 3/16
When I am very old. Har 11/16
When I go walking in the woods. Har 6/15
Wood flower. Har 8/16
The Wood nymph. Har 8/17
Woman - a prayer. Ain 6/19

LEINSTER, MURRAY. To - (whom I loved last year). Par 12/17
You kissed me. Par 4/18

LELAND, ROBERT DeCAMP. Memorabilia. PoJ 7/17

LEMONT, JESSIE. Mnemosyne. Har 6/19

LEONARD, DOROTHY. At Horseshoe beach. Cen 8/17
A Day of rain. Cen 10/18
The Minuet. Cen 1/18
My daughter's hair. Cen 4/17

LEONARD, PRISCILLA. Desolation. Out 5/22/18

LEONARD, WILLIAM ELLERY. Above the battle (1616-1916 and
    thereafter). Mid 6/16
As I listened by the lilacs. StJ 6/19

LeROY, HARRIET CROCKER. A Mother in England. YouC 10 11 17
LESEMANN, MAURICE. Woodwinds. You 4 19
LESLIE, SHANE. Oblivio dei. ScM 3/17
LETTS, W.M. The Connaught rangers. YaR 4 18
  The Road that goes west. YaR 10/18
LEWIN, ALBERT. Evening. Colo 2/15
  Feet of the wind. PoJ 2/17
  "I am never merry when I hear sweet music." Colo 12/16
  "I loved thee not." Colo 8/16
  Keats. Colo 6/16
  The Lake's cool covert. Colo 3/16
  The Lanquid day. Colo 12/15
  L'armour et la vie. Colo 6/15
  The Maudlin moon. Colo 8/15
  My cloud. Colo 1/16
  The Old moon. Colo 3/15
  The Passer. Colo 12/16
  Twilight. PoJ 2/17
  A Valentine. Colo 2/16
LEWIS, ADDISON. 1915. ReM 12/3/15
LEWIS, CHARLTON. Pro patria. YaR 7/17
LEWIS, EMILY SARGENT. The Abbess. CoV 10/17
LEWIS, JAY. Moon-wandering. Boo 4/17
LEWIS, KATHARINE PARK. Apprehension. CoV 5/19
  Gold. EvM 9/17
  The World is full of bonny lads. CoV 5/17
LEWIS, MARGARET. Yellow leaves. SmS 2/17
LEWIS, NANCY. Rhymed ragout. LoAG 12/16/16, 12/30/16, 1/6/17,
  1/20/17, 2/3/17, 2/17/17, 3/3/17
  The Wonderful year (William J. Locke). LoAG 12/9/16
LEWISOHN, LUDWIG. Love in autumn. SmS 10/15
  The Two loves. Foru 5/15
LIEBERMAN, ELIAS. Bolshevik inn. NYTi 2/7/19
  Brothers. Out 8/9/16
  Builders of Babel. BoT 11/23/18
  From a bridge car. HarW 3/18/16
  Gargoyles. StJ 10-12/19
  The Ghost. SnaS 12/18/17
  A Humorous sage. AQ 12/6/18
  The Nation to its foreign born. EvM 3/16
  Nocturne. Out 5/10/16
  The Parade of the drafted. NYTi 2/24/18
  The Quest of Pierrot. Puc ?/17
  The Singer. CoV 4/19
  Soldini, vaudeville violinist. EvM 2/17

Theodore Roosevelt, American. AQ 2/19
Tired eyes. StJ 12/18
Violets and the woman. Ain 6/19
Wilson at the Coliseum. NYTi 2/18/19

LILLIE, MARIE ELMENDORF. The Recluse. Poet 3/16

LINCOLN, ELLIOT C. Montana night. CoV 12/19
Mrs. Senator Jones. CoV 12/19

LINDERMAN, FRANK B. My friend Pete Lebeaux. ScM ?/19

LINDSAY, VACHEL. The Apple-blossom snow. Foru 8/16
Booker Washington trilogy. Poet 6/16
The Broncho that would not be broken of dancing. SeA 8/17
The Chinese nightingale. Poet 2/15
The Daniel jazz. Oth 1/19
The Empire of China is crumbling down. Poet 9/18
The Eyes of Queen Esther and how they conquered King Ahasuerus. CoV
  4/18
The Flower of mending. Foru 8/16
Hail to the sons of Roosevelt. NYSB 2/9/19
How I walked alone in the jungles of heaven. NeR ?/?/18
How Samson bore away the gates of Gaza. Poet 10/17
In memory of Joyce Kilmer. NYSB 2/16/19
Mark Twain, an inscription for your volume of Hunkleberry Finn.
  ReM 12/3/15
Mark Twain and Joan of Arc. Poet 7/17
Niagara. Poet 7/17
Our mother Pocahontas. Poet 7/17
The Praise of battlement. Foru 8/16
The Sea serpent chantey. Oth 3/19
Sew the flags together. BoT 11/23/18
The Soap-box. Poet 10/17
What the burro said. ChHE 5/7/15
What the sexton said. Foru 7/16

LING CHEN-PING (tr. Henry C. Fenn). Home thoughts from the hills.
  StJ 6/17
The Mandarin philosophizes. StJ 6/19
Sunset. StJ 6/19

LINN, EDITH WILLIS. A Marching song for America. Lif 7/12/17
The Ruin. Pea 12/16
To a whistle blow by a boy. CnR 12/7/16

LINN, MABEL. Madrigal. Poet 5/17
Spring. Poet 5/17

LINTON, RALPH. Returned. EvM 5/19
Shells. EvM 12/18
When. EvM 10/18

LI PO (tr. Sasaki and Maxwell Bodenheim). Drunk. LiR 6/17
Gently-drunk woman. LiR 6/17

Mountain-top temple. LiR 6/17
Perfume-remembrance. LiR 6/17

LIPPMAN, ALICE D. Fifth Avenue sky-scrapers. Poet 4/19
Vagabonds. Poet 4/19

LIPPMANN, JULIE M. A Prayer in time of peace. GoH 1/19

LIPPMANN, L. BLACKLEDGE. At parting. CoV 10/16
A Child's garden. CoV 6/16

LITTELL, PHILIP. Not a sparrow falleth. Mas 1/15

LITTLE, DOROTHY I. Vigil. CaW 6/19

LIVESAY, FLORENCE RANDAL. The Battlefield. Poet 4/19
Gold ladies. CoV 12/19
The Kalina. Poet 11/16
Marusenka's wedding. Poet 4/19
My field. Poet 11/16
Old Ruthenian folk-song. Poet 10/15
Parting. Poet 4/19
The Return of Dresbenucha (April). Poet 4/19
Ruthenian lovers. Poet 11/16
Song of the Cossack. Poet 10/15
Song of departure. Poet 11/16
Song of the drowning Cossack. Poet 4/19
The Ukrainian national anthem. PoeL Summer#/15
An Ukrainian war-song. PoeL Summer#/15
The Young recruits. PoeL Summer#/15

LIVINGSTON, STEPHEN TRACY. A Song of victory. BoT 3/16/18

LONG, HANIEL. Ascutney in shadows. PoJ 6/16
At parting. Har 8/18
A Book on economics. Poet 5/18
The Cause of this I know not. Poet 5/18
The Cross. Oth 1/19
The Cuban in the states. Poet 5/18
A Dawn figure. Oth 1/19
The Day that love came down to me. CoV 4/16
Dead men tell no tales. Poet 5/18
The Death of Alexander the Great. CoV 6/19
The Diver. Oth 1/19
Girl swimmers. Oth 1/19
Grotesques. Oth 1/19
The Herd boy. Poet 5/18
His deaths. PoJ 11/17
The Ides of March. Poet 12/15
In the pines. Oth 1/19
The Infant to his father. PoJ 6/16
Madness. Poet 5/18
Near his bed. Poet 12/15
Renegades from Boston. PoJ 6/16

Seeger. Poet 5/18
Shoes. Poet 5/18
Song. Poet 5/18
Song of young Burbage. Poet 5/18
Star-dust. Poet 5/18
Summer afternoon. Oth 1/19
The Terror. Poet 5/18
Through the window. Poet 12/15
The Newark. New 9-10/16
To sculptors. Oth 1/19
The Urchin. Oth 1/19
Vacation protest. Mas 6/16
With compliments. PoJ 6/16

LONG, JOHN LUTHER. The Moon in the moat. CoV 4/17

LONG, LILY A. He buildeth his house. Poet 7/16
The Poet's part. Poet 7/16

LOUYS, PIERRE. For the monument of Le Conte de Lisle (tr. Celia Louise
    Chittenton). PoeL Vacation#/17

LOVEMAN, ROBERT. Song. SmS 8/15, 10/15

LOVING, PIERRE. Dawn in the city. CaW 9/17
A Japanese teacup. Colo 8/15
The Newspaper. Colo 5/16
The Rose in hell. Colo 5/16
Sea vision. Colo 2/17
Song of opiates. Colo 7/15
To a child on her second birthday. Colo 12/15
To Madame Sarah Bernhardt. Colo 10/16
To Maurice Hewlett. Colo 6/16
The Trust of Florence. Colo 10/15

LOW, BENJAMIN R.C. For the dedication of a toy theatre. ScM 4/15
Jack o'dreams. PoR 5/16
A Measure of the immeasurable. BoT 11/23/18
These United States. BoT 2/7/17
Underground. PoR 11/16

LOW, PAGE. The Housewife. SmS 1/16

LOWELL, AMY. After a storm. NeR 8/7/15
Aliens. NeR 8/7/15
Appuldurcombe Park. Poet ?/18
The Artist. Poet 9/19
An Aquarium. ReM 7/7/16
Autumn. Poet 3/17, 9/19
Autumnal equinox. ScM 9/17
Balls. Poet 9/19
The Bather. Har 8/17
Battledore and shuttlecock. ScM 8/16
Before war is declared. BoT 2/28/17

The Bookshop. Poet 9/19
The Breaking out of the flags. Ind 6/2/17
Business as usual. BoT 2/16/18
The Camellia tree of Matsue. Poet 3/17
Camouflaged troop-ship. Dia 11/16/18
A Comparison. Oth 8/15
The Cornucopia of red and green comfits. Ind 11/3/17
The Cross-roads. PoR 9/16
Desolation. Poet 3/17
The Diamond shoal lightship. NoAR 12/18
Disillusion. Poet 3/17
Document. Poet 3/17
Dreams in wartime. LiR 6/18
The Dusty hour glass. Ind 3/5/17
The Emperor's garden. Poet 3/17
Ephemera. Poet 3/17
Eucharis Amazonica. GoH 4/17
Fenway Park. Poet 9/15
Flotsam. SeA 11/16
The Flute. Cen 12/18
Free fantasia on Japanese themes. Cen 2/18
Frimaire. ScM 8/19
From China. Poet 3/17
The Fruit shop. YaR 7/15
The Garden by moonlight. Boo 9/18
Gargoyles. ReM 4/18/19
Good gracious. Poet 9/19
The Grocery. Mas 6/16
Guns as keys: and the great gate swings. SeA 8/17
Illusion. Poet 3/17
Impressionist picture of a garden. Tri 4/16
In a time of dearth. Cen 9/16
In time of war. You 10/18
Interlude. Boo 12/18
July midnight. Lyr 7/17
A Lady to her lover. Poet 10/18
The Landlady of Whinton Inn tells a story. Poet 1/18
Lead soldiers. Poet 9/15
Little ivory figures pulled with strings. NoAR 10/19
A Lover. Poet 3/17
Madonna of the evening flowers. NoAR 2/18
Malmaison. LiR 6-7/16
May evening in Central Park. Poet 9/15
Meditation. Poet 3/17
Memorandum confided by a yucca to a passion vine. Boo 11-12/19
Number 3 on the docket. PoR 5/16
Ombre Chinoise. YaR 1/17
On a certain critic. LiR 3/17

On the mantlepiece. Boo 5/19
One of the "Hundred views of Fuji" by Hokusai. Poet 3/17
One winter night. Tou 12/18
Orange of midsummer. SeA 4/17
The Painter on silk. Poet 9/16
Paper fishes. Poet 3/17
The Paper garden. HoG 2/16
The Paper windmill. Cen 12/15
Patterns. LiR 8/15
Peach-color to a soap-bubble. Poet 9/19
The Peddler of flowers. Oth 8/15
The Poem. Mas 4/16
Poetry. You 10/18
Pyrotechnics. Poet 5/16
Quincunx. Har 7/19
Red slippers. Poet 4/15
Sea coal. NeR 8/7/15
Sea-blue and blood-red. NoAR 4/17
Solitaire. Poet 4/15
A Sprig of Rosemary. ScM 7/18
Strain. Poet 9/15
Streets (adapted from the Poet Yakura Sanjin, 1769). Poet 3/17
Sugar. Ind 12/29/17
Sunshine. Poet 3/17
To a husband. Poet 3/17
To two unknown ladies. NoAR 6/19
Trades. YaR 1/17
Trees. Oth 8/15
Trees in winter. NoAR 10/19
Twelve loyal fishermen. Ind 11/24/17
The Two rains. Dia 1/28/18
Vernal equinox. Poet 9/15
Vicarious. You 10/18
William Blake. YaR 1/17
A Year passes. Poet 3/17
1777. Poet 8/16
See Ayscough, Florence for poems written with Amy Lowell

LOWENGRUND, ALICE C. A Prayer, America, 1918. CoV 7/18

LOWREY, PERRIN HOLMES. Afternoon. CoV 4/19
April in Killarney. CoV 4/16
Dawn. Cov 4/19
Night. CoV 4/19
An Old violin. Colo 2/17
Periwinkles. CoV 4/18
Silence and I. Ain 8/18
Twilight prayer. CoV 4/19

LOY, MINA. The Black virginity. Oth 12/18

Love songs. Oth 7/15
LUCE, MORTON. The Sea and the moon. Son 3-4/19
LYMAN, DEAN B., JR. Pomegranates. Poet 5/18
LYNE, CASSIE MONCURE. A Boyish memory. SoW 2/15
LYON, ANNE BOZEMAN. Kumquat trees. StJ 2/19
LYSTER, MARGARET. Dawn. Poet 10/19
   The Painted saint in the wood. Poet 10/19
   Song for parting. SmS 7/18

M

"M. and M." Parents. For 2/17
"M, O.T." The Child. For 2/17
   The Father. For 2/17
"M., M.S." Bondage. CaW 7/17
"M., P.S." A Valentine. For 2/17
"M.S.M." Knights-errant. CaW 10/17
   A Song for a man. Boo 4/19
   To my favorite author. CaW 4/18
"M.,V." Lullaby. For 2/17
"M., W M." The Prune. ReM 1/3/19
McALMON, ROBERT M. Aero-laughter. Poet 3/19
   Aero-metre. Poet 3/19
   Consecration. Poet 3/19
   Consummation. Poet 3/19
   Perspicuity. Poet 3/19
   Volplanteer Poet 3/19
McCALES, W.F. Chloe. Boo 8/15
McCALLUM, MELLA RUSSELL. The Frog. Mid 3-4/18
McCARTHY, DENIS A. Daddies and laddies. youC 1/13/16
   Fanny and fuss and feathers. YouC 5/4/16
McCARTHY, JOHN RUSSELL. Adventuring. Poet 8/16
   Ballad. Bel 2/15/19
   Come down, Walt! Poet 5/19
   Daisies. SmS 5/17
   The Dance in the wood. Colo 6/16
   Dandelion. SmS 4/17
   Dreams. Bel 4/12/19
   God's blue. Colo 9/15
   Goldenrod. Poet 8/16
   June. Bel 6/17/16
   The Maple in spring. CoV 5/19
   The Perfect ghost. Par 7/18
   Pine. CoV 1/17

Satisfaction. Oth 1/16
The Still trees. Bel 3/23/18
Sunday morning. Oth 1/16
The Thief. Oth 1/16
Violet CoV 3/17
The Way of a maid. Bel 3/2/18
When comes that hour. Mid 3-4/19
Wild aster. Poet 12/19
Wild rose. SmS 5/17

McCLELLAN, WALTER. In the night. Mid 5-6/16
To V.C.G. Mid-11-12/19

McCLURE, JOHN. All they that pass by. SmS 5/15
Ballad of broken tomes. Bel 4/19/19
Ballad of his own fireside. SmS 2/17
Carol. SmS 12/16, 1/18
The Celts. Sms 10/16
Chanson naive. SmS 9/17
The Dreams. SmS 1/18
Ego. SmS 6/15
Elf's song. SmS 8/17
The Everlasting yea. SmS 5/16
Finis. Sms 7/17
Heart's-ease. Oth 1/16
Homage. SmS 4/17
Home. SmS 7/17
I could forgive. SmS 5/17
Lady of delight. SmS 6/18
The Lass of Galilee. SmS 10/15
Les revenants. Par 6/18
The Merry men. SmS 8/15
The Needy poet invoketh the gods. SmS 5/15
Philosophy. Poet 3/16
Retort courteous. SmS 7/18
Somnambulist. Oth 1/16
Song. SmS 3/18
Songs of his lady. SmS 6/16
These be the gifts. SmS 2/18
To a lady. SmS 12/15
To his lady. Poet 3/16
Visitants. Oth 1/16
Wanderer. SmS 4/18
Wanderers. Oth 1/16

McCLUSKEY, KATHERINE WISNER. Confessional. CoV 10/19

McCOLL, JOHN. An Anti-climax. Par 9/18
A Wayfaring song. Par 6/18

McCONNELL, ANNA B. Accuracy. CoV 11/19

McCORMICK, ANNE. Pompeii. Boo 1/18
  Song. SmS 12/15

MCCOURT, EDNA WAHLERT. The City market place. PoeL
    Summer#/16
  The Cloud woman. PoeL Vacation#/17
  The Desert. PoeL Vacation#/17
  The Lost lover. PoeL Vacation#/17
  The Lovers. PoeL Vacation#/17
  Scarlet wings. PoeL Vacation#/17
  The Water lily. PoeL Vacation#/17
  Wenewelir. PoeL Vacation#/17

McCOY, SAMUEL. The Future - voyageurs' song. ScM 5/15
  The Guardian angels. CoV 6/16
  The Hobby horse. CoV. 6/16
  Independence Hall. Mas 6/16
  Old lady. ScM 4/19
  Sarran. Boo 4/19
  To a flower girl. CoV 6/16

McCRACKEN, W.D. Broadway. EvM 5/19
  The Glad hand. EvM 4/19

McCRAE, JOHN. The Anxious dead. EvM 10/18

McCULLOUGH, ANNIE WILLIS. Father's day.. YouC 7/5/17
  The Road to story-book land. YouC 8/2/17

MacDONAGH, THOMAS. Wishes for my son. Out 5/17/16

MacDONALD, ARTHUR ROYCE. Private Nucome. EvM 1/19

McDONALD, CARL. The Ould Irish landlord. Boo 3/18
  A Poet's epitaph. Boo 5/18

MacDONALD, FRANCIS C. Optima memoriae. ScM 11/16

MacDONALD, LILIAN. The Absent. LoAG 3/11/16
  The City-bound. LoAG 2/26/16
  A Toast. LoAG 2/26/16

McDONOUGH, PATRICK. Via longa. CaW 6/16

McDOUGAL, MAY CARMACK. The Glittering drudge. StJ 4/19

MacDOUGALL, ALLAN ROSS. Retrospect. Tou 10/18
  A Snapshot. SmS 6/15
  Song. Tou 10/18
  Spring Nineteen Eighteen. Tou 10/18
  When Alms Glick sang. ChDN 4/22/18

McCAFFEY, ERNEST. Aeroplanes. LoAG 1/20/18
  After many days. LoAG 2/26/16
  America (marching song.) LoAG 11/1/17
  Ballade of Berenice. LoAG 3/10/18
  Ballade of Herostratus. LoAG 12/18/16
  Ballade of the Jewess. LoAG 1/10/16
  Ballade of Knossos of the wide-wayed streets. LoAG 3/18/16

McGUCKIN, MILDRED CRISS. Dawn. Colo 12/16

McGUINNESS, MARY C. Song. Lyr 3/19

MACHADO, ANTONIO. To Juan R. Jimenez (tr. Leonard L. Cline).
    Dets 4/7/18

MACHAR, J.S. On Golgotha (tr. Otto Katouc). PoeL Vacation#/17

MacINTYRE, CARLYLE F. Ad matrem. LoAG 5/12/17
    The Dreamer in the sun. Ain 11/19
    The Magic inn. Ain 10/19
    Spring in Europe. Ain 6/19

McKAY, CLAUDE. [Eli Edwards, pseud.]. After the winters. Lib 7/19
    The Barrier. Lib 7/19
    A Capitalist at dinner. Lib 7/19
    The Harlem dancer. SeA 10/17
    If we must die. Lib 7/19
    Invocation. SeA 10/17
    The Little peoples. Lib 7/19
    The Negro dancers. Lib 7/19
    A Roman holiday. Lib 7/19

MACKAY, ISABEL ECCLESTONE. Killed in action. Foru 7/17

MacKAYE, ARVIA. By the summer sea. PoR 8/16
    Fire castles. LiR 8/15
    The Purple gray. Poet 7.16
    The Unknown race. LiR 8/15
    Zephyr. LiR 8.15

MacKAYE, PERCY. American consecration hymn (music by Francis
    MacMillen). Out of 5/8/18
    The Battle call of alliance. NYTM 5/6/17
    Choral song. HarW 3/18/16
    Christmas, 1915. Foru 1/16
    Consummation. BoT 12/7/18
    Eliot to Wilson. Ind 11/6/16
    Les soeurs (to Madame Sarah Berhnardt). BoT 5/19/17
    Liebknecht or Hohenzollern. Ind 4/28/17
    Marching with Pappa Joffre. BoT 5/12/17
    On first hearing an English skylark. PoJ 7/15
    The Return of August. Ind 8/9/15
    The Returning. BoT 12/7/18
    Russia, 1917. CoV 4/17
    To Marshal Foch. BoT 11/23/18

MacKAYE, ROBIN. The Swimming pool. LiR 8/15
    To a turtle. LiR 8/15

McKEEHAN, IRENE P. Invictus. Foru 5/15

MACKELLER, DOROTHEA. Encounter. Har 3/15

McKENNA, EDMOND. After the strike. Mas 4/15
    In the outer sanctum. Mas 7/15

To the suicides. Mas 2/15
War changes. Mas 1/15

McKENZIE, JAMES PROCTOR. Hey, ca' thro'. SmS 4/18

McKINNEY, E.L. Next to pure reading matter. Cen 5/17
One who benefits. Cen 3/17
The Pitiable penguin and his awkward appetite. Cen 10/16
Vers libre liberated. Cen 4/17

McKINNEY, ISABEL. Cavalier tunes. YouC 2/10/16
The Life of quilts. YouC 5/4/16
When singing April came. Poet 4/18

McKINSEY, FOLGER. A Love song. SmS 1/15
I sing of love. SmS 1/15

MacLEAN, CHARLES AGNEW. To Grace. Ain 2/19

McLEANE, JAMES, JR. A Broken friendship. NeR 11/9/18
Lilies: a memory. NeR 10/19/18

MacLEISH, ARCHIBALD. Grief. YaR 4/15
On a memorial stone. Lyr 4/19

McLEOD, IRENE. The Absent lover. YaR 7/18
At parting. YaR 10/17
Discharged. YaR 10/17
Mary. YaR 7/17
Missing. YaR 7/18

McMaster, BRYCE. Brimstone butterfly. ChHE 5/4/18

MacMILLAN, MARY. Carpe diem. You 10/18
The Family pew. Lib 3/18
Inspiration. SmS 10/17
The Little golden fountain. SmS 6/15
Nausica sings before the coming of Ulysses. SmS 6/18
Truth. Mas 6/16

McMULLEN, DYSART. The Challenge. Out 5/30/17
To a young soldier. EvM 7/18

McNAUGHT, ELMOND FRANKLIN. Gray morning. Poet 7/17
Spring morning. Poet 7/17

MACOMB, CATHERINE SISK. The Homecoming. SmS 1/15

McRAYE, BETTY. Sweethearts. SmS 7.15

MACREADY, M.A.K. The Piper. Har. 8/18

MacTAVISH, SANDY. Golf. LoAG 1/20/18

MADONE, A. A Mood. SmS 1/15

MAHDESIAN. ARSHAG D. The Snow (tr. Alice Stone Blackwell). StJ 2/18

MALA, YENOMDRAH. The Body and the soul. NeR 12/21/19

MALLARMÉ. STEPHANE. Les fleurs (tr. Francis Taylor). PoeL
Spring#/15

MALLEY, AUGUSTUS DAVID. An Archangel's query. CaW 4/17

MANN, DOROTHEA LAWRENCE. Can it be peace? BoT 11/23/18
  Candle'glow. BoT 7/22/17
  L'envoi. Cen 12/18
MANN, KARL. Loot. Lyr 11/17
  My ultimate lady. Lyr 8/17
MANNING, FREDERIC. Anacreontic. Poet 1/17
  Sacrifice 19022. Poet 7/17
MARGETSON, GEORGE REGINALD. The light of victory. BoT 4/24/18
MARIAN, GEORGE. The Home-coming. Poet 7/19
MARKHAM, EDWIN. Our believing Thomas. Ind 10/23/16
  Peace over earth again. PeHJ 12/17
MARKHAM, KIRAH. Love. SmS 10/18
  Mood. SmS 2/18
MARKS, JEANNETTE. Beside the way. Out 2/7/17
  His name? Bel 6/23/17
  The Marriage barge. PoJ 7/15
  The Tide. CoV 1/17
  Two candles. NoAR 8/19
  When they come. SmS 5/16
MARLATT, EARL. Love untold. Poet 12/17
  People. Poet 12/17
MARLOWE, DIANTHA HORNE. The Milkweed bird. YouC 9/13/17
MARQUIS, DON. Pen for the dedication of a home. HoG 1/16
  The Towers of Manhattan. ScM 6/15
MARQUIS, NEETA. Rain at night. SmS 1/16
  A Sibelius symphony. CoV 12/18
MARSH, GEORGE T. Exit. ScM 3/18
MARSHALL, MARGUERITE M. The Calling. Ain 9/18
  Desires. Ain 10/18
  In City Hall Park. Ain 6/19
  Longacre Square. Ain 4/19
  Moma moderna. Ain 8/18
  Resurgam. Ain 10/19
  A Song of loves mortal. Ain 11/19
  "Who hath desired the sea." Ain ?/17
MARTIN, EDWARD SANFORD. The Battleship remarks. ScM 2/15
MARTIN, JULIA. The Golden touch. PoJ 11/15
MARTIN, LANNIE HAYNES. Reunion. LoAG 6/16/17
  Widowhood. LoAG 6/16/17
MARTINEZ, ENRIQUE GONZALES. The Owl and the swan (tr. Muna
  Lee).
  Boo 6/19
MASEFIELD, JOHN. The Central. ScM 8/15
  The Choice. CoV 1/17

The End. ScM 10/15
Revelation. Har 9/15
Unconquered. ScM 8/15
The Unexplored. ScM 8/15
Which. ScM 10/15
The Will to perfection. YaR 4/17
The Wind-barren. YaR 10/16
The World's beginning. ScM 10/15

MASON, EDWARD WILBUR. The Oriole. Cra 4/16

MASON, LOWELL. Playing the war game. Out 1/9/18

MASON, ROSALIND. A Child's grace. Poet 6/16
Fair weather and I happy. Poet 6/16
Happiness. Poet 6/16
Vision. Poet 6/16

MASSECK, CLINTON J. At thirty he sings of a day in spring. Poet 8/16
A Day and its journey. Oth 5-6/16
Down the wind. Poet 8/16

MASTERS, EDGAR LEE. All life in a life. Poet 3/16
Arabel. Poet 11/15
At Decapolis (Mark, Chap. V). ReM 4/26/18
At Fairbanks. Poet 6/19
Autochthon. ReM 7/14/16
Battin' flies. ReM 6/5/19
Botticelli to Simonetta. NYSB 3/9/19
Boyhood friends. YaR 1/17
Christmas at Indian Point. ReM 12/15/16
Clay Bailey at the side show. ReM 3/22/18
The Cocked hat. ReM 12/3/15
Come, William et al. ReM 4/14/16
The Conversation. Poet 11/15
Dear old Dick (in memory of Richard E. Burke). ReM 8/10/17
The Death of Sir Launcelot. SmS 9/15
Epitaph for us. YaR 1/19
Father and daughter. LiR 8/15
George Joslin on "La Mencken." Poet 6/19
Henry Murray. Poet 6/19
Hokku. LiR 6-7/16
In memory of Bryan Lathrop. Poet 6/17
John Cowper Powys. ReM 5/5/16
A Lady. ReM 2/14/19
The Lake boats. ReM 2/9/17
The Letter. ReM 3/30/17
The Loom. ReM 8/3/17
The Loop. NeR 1/1/16
Mt. Calm. ReM 1/21/17
My light with yours. ReM 4/20/17
Neanderthal. ReM 10/5/17

Oh you Sabbatarians! ReM 3/7/19
The Old court house. ReM 5/29/19
Pulling the tooth. ReM 5/4/17
Recessional in time of war, medical unit - . ReM 12/28/17
A Republic. Nat 9/27/19
Silence. Poet 2/15
Simon surnamed Peter. ReM 12/7/15
Song of the human spirit. Poet 10/17
Song of men. Poet 10/17
Song of women. Poet 10/17
Spoon River anthology. ReM 1/1/15, 1/15/15
Spoon River revisited. NeR 11/23/18
The Star. ReM 2/25/16
The Subway. Oth 5-6/16
Theodore Dreiser. ReM 11/12/15
To-morrow is my birthday. ReM 9/14/17
Toward the gulf. ReM 12/14/17
The Wedding feast. ReM 1/25/18
Widow La Rue. ReM 1/19/17
Wilbur Rankin. ReM 5/28/15
Wild birds. ReM 2/14/19
Winged victory. ReM 2/22/18
The World's desire. Poet 4/19
The World's peace. BoT 11/23/18
MASTIN, FLORENCE RIPLEY. Americus. Poet 1/18
April night. Mas 6/17
David. Poet 1/18
The Dream. Mas 6/16
Dream free. PoJ 9/17
Dryad. Mas 7/17
I walked among the gray trees. PoJ 4/16
In the subway. Mas 8/16
Isidor. Poet 1/18
Lucretia. Poet 1/18
A Manhattan yard. Mas 3/17
Moth moon. PoJ 9/17
Off the Maine coast. PoJ 9/17
The Old-fashioned garden. Mas 7/17
Roderick. Poet 1/18
Shadows on Bedford Hill. Lib 5/18
The Teacher speaks. Mas 5/17
To one loved. Mas 8/17; Lib 4/18
MATHISON, MINNA. The Happy heart. Mid 11-12/18
MATSON, NORMAN H. Propaganditti. Mas 3/17
MATSON-DOLSON, CORA A. The Old mother. SmS 7/15
MATTICK, IRVIN. In the spring. Tri 2/16

MAVITY, NANCY BARR. The Living Pan. Boo 7/18
A Pilgrimage. Boo 2/18
To my daughter - three days old. Boo 5/19
The Unforgiven. CoV 1/19
Violets. Boo 6/18

MAYER, EDWIN JUSTUS. Epitaph. Lyr 3/19
Sonnet. Mas 9/17, 10/17

MAYNARD, LAURENS. Ave post saecula. PoeL Winter#/17

MAYNARD, THEODORE. Annunciation. CaW 3/19
Dirge. NoAR 7/19
Gratitude. CaW 4/17
If ever you come to die. Lyr 5-6/19
Laus deo. CaW 11/18
Mater desolata (to Margaret Pearse). CaW 2/17

MAYSI, KADRA [Katherine Drayton Mayrant Simons]. The Franc-Tireur.
    NYTM 5/6/17
Gypsy song. Mas 6/17
Lines on a Chinese landscape drawn in a book of Chinese verse. Lyr 12/17
The Taking of Bagdad. CoV 8/17

MEAD, EDNA. To an old letter. Har 1/16

MEADOWCRAFT, CLARA PLATT. The Open path. Har 1/18

MEARSON, LYON. Rondeau of any soldier. Har 1/19

MEDHURST, FRANCIS. The Children's isle. Har 11/16

MEDUSENHAUPT. Jealousy. Mas 3/17

MEEKER, MAJORIE. At sea. Poet 5/19
Daisies. Poet 5/19
Madeleine. Har 11/18

MEIERS, CHARLES P. Master of the sea. LoAG 1/9/15

MERCANTINI, LUIGI. The Gleaner of Sapri. PoeL Winter#/16

MERINGTON, MARGUERITE. Peace and victory. NYSB 3/23/19
Perdita. ScM 8/15

MERKLE, ROBERT. Murderer. Par 4/18

MERRICK, HYDE BUSTON. The Drab little lady. PoeL Summer#/16

MERRILL, MARGARET BELL. In the midst of them. ScM 5/18

MERTEN, JACK. He looks at God with opera-glasses. You 12/18
Japan, about 1877. You 12/18
Romance. You 12/18

MESQUIDA, ANNA BLAKE. The City of heritage. New 9-10/16
Tribute. New 9-10/16

METCALF, THOMAS NEWELL. Turkish Dick. Cen 3/17
Unfortunate Fanny. Cen 6/17

MEYER, JOSEPHINE A. Epitaph. Ain 12/19
Finale. Ain 5/19

MEYER, LUCY RIDER. Dey's a li'l six feet of groun', somewhere
    (a spiritual). Out 12/17/19

MEYER, MYRTLE COLLMAN. The Lost spell. CoV 9/17

MEYNELL, ALICE. Length of days: to the early dead in battle, 1915.
    NoAR 3/15

MEZQUIDA, ANNA BLAKE. Great heart. GoH 6/19

MICHAEL, WILLIAM. Ambrosia. CoV 4/16

MICHELSON, MAX. The Adversary. Poet 3/17
  The Bird. Poet 7/15
  Death. Poet 11/18
  A Dilettante. Poet 11/18
  Fire. Poet 3/17
  Girls. Poet 11/18
  The Golden apple. Poet 11/18
  Gone. Poet 3/17
  A Helen. Poet 11/18
  A Hymn to night. Poet 5/16
  In the park. Poet 5/16
  Knowledge. Poet 3/17
  La mort de Paul Verlaine. Poet 11/18
  A Lady talking to a poet. Poet 11/18
  Love lyric. Poet 5/16
  Masks. Poet 11/18
  Midnight. Poet 5/16
  Myrrh. Poet 11/18
  The Newcomers. Poet 5/16
  "Newly seeded." Poet 3/17
  Night moods. Poet 3/17
  O brother tree. Poet 7/15
  Off. Poet 3/17
  On a windy afternoon. Poet 3/17
  Pain. Poet 11/18
  A Petit bourgeois. Poet 11/18
  Playing horse. Poet 3/17
  A Polish girl. Poet 3/17
  Portrait, to H.M. Poet 3/17
  The Red light. Poet 5/16
  A Rich gentleman. Poet 11/18
  Storm. Poet 5/16
  The Tired woman. Poet 2/18
  To a woman asleep in a street-car. Poet 11/19
  The Traitor. Poet 11/18
  Traveler. Poet 3/17
  The Willow tree. Poet 5/16

MIDDLETON, SCUDDER. The Beloved. PoR 1/17
  The Bird. CoV 4/19

Children. Bel 5/6/16
The Clerk. CoV 6/16
Dream-rover. YaR 4/19
The Empty room. YaR 4/19
The Girl. CoV 9/18
In Union Square. CoV 4/16
Interlude. PoJ 1/17; CoV 4/19
The Lost comrade. PoR 2/17
The Lost singer. Dia 11/2/18
Love's pilgrimage. SmS 4/15
Overheard. Har 10/19
The Poets. CoV 1/17
The Prisoners. Bel 3/16/18
The Return. CoV 2/17; Nat 12/21/18
Romance. YaR 4/19
The Servant. Mas 7/17
Song in the key of autumn. Cen 11/19
Spring. Boo 4/18
The Stranger. Poet 4/17
The Sun. YaR 4/19
To an old couple. Poet 4/17
The White magician. Foru 6/16
The Worker. Har 12/19
1918. BoT 11/23/18; ReM 12/6/18

MIFFLIN, LLOYD. Balboa in Panama - 1513. ScM 4/15
Sonnet. ScM 4/15

MIKI, ROFU. On the grass (tr. Eunice Tietjens). StJ 3/17

MILLAY, EDNA ST. VINCENT. Afternoon on a hill. Poet 8/17
Alms. Ain 6/19
Ashes of life. Foru 8/15
Blue-beard. Foru 5/16
Daphne. Ain 11/18
The Death of autumn. Nat 10/25/19
The Dream. Foru 7/15
Elaine. Nat 11/16/18
Figs from thistles. Poet 6/18
If you were dead. Foru 5/16
Indifference. Foru 3/15
Inland. Ain 11/19
Kin to sorrow. Poet 8/17
The Little tavern. Poet 8/17
Love resurgent. Ain 4/19
The Penitent. Poet 6/18
Possession. Son 10/18
Recuerdo. Poet 5/19
Rondel. Ain 3/19
Rosemary. Ain 10/19

The Spires of St. Patrick's. CaW 1/19
To arms. IlS 6/9/18
To a lark at morn. BoT 1/19/18
The Trysting. BoT 5/29/18
Wayside song. BoT 10/30/18
MILLER, JOHN, JR. Niagara. Tri 2/16
  Ravage. Poet 9/16
MILLER, KARL H. A Memorial Day revery. SoW 5/15
MILLER, MARY WILLIS. Cards. Lyr 10/17
MILNE, A.A. From a full heart. EvM 5/19
MINAS, LOOTFI. The Infinite desire (tr. B.A. Botkin). StJ 10-12/19
MINER, JESSICA S. And yet. ScM 3/17
MINOT, ELIZABETH. Chicken and corn pone. BoT 2/6/18
  Viva Italia! BoT 11/17/17
  With Frankincense and Myrrh. BoT 2/1/19
MINOT, JOHN CLAIR. Abijah and Abner. YouC 8/10/16
  Abijah and his fiddle. YouC 4/27/16
  The Baby Pan. YouC 4/12/17
  Barbara Bell. YouC 3/30/16
  Bid the land o' dreams good-bye. YouC 1/18/17
  The Boy and the flag. YouC 6/14/17
  The Brook that runs to France. YouC 5/23/18
  Bubbles. YouC 3/23/16
  Buster's visit to dreamland. YouC 1/18/17
  Chums. YouC 2/24/16
  E pluribus unum. YouC 6/28/17
  The Frog choir. YouC 3/16/16
  Good old major. YouC 11/15/17
  The Happiest highway. YouC 6/15/16
  Jack-in-the-pulpit. YouC 4/5/17
  The King's new year's test. YouC 1/3/18
  Poppy and her goat. YouC 4/6/16
  The Surf sprites. YouC 7/6/16
  The Sword of Arthur. YouC 5/24/17
  Virginia Dare. YouC 2/17/16
  When April is on the way. YouC 3/29/17
MIRON, SALVADOR DIAZ. Snow-flake (tr. Alice Stone Blackwell).
  StJ 8/18
MISTRAL, FREDERIC. The Communion of saints (tr. Edward J. O'Brien).
  PoeL Summer#/15
MITCHELL, AGNES LEWIS. King Bluster. YouC 2/3/16
MITCHELL, LALIA. Memories. Par 12/17
MITCHELL, LANGDON. In a smoking car. NeR 2/12/16
MITCHELL, R.S. A Fig tree. Dia 11/22/17

MITCHELL, RUTH COMFORT. A Ballad of Doris Ritter. Cen 7/18
   Barbara. Cen 2/16
   The Choosing. CoV 10/19
   Compensation. Har 4/19
   El poniente. Cen 2/16
   The Foreign nun is sitting in the sun. CoV 9/18
   "From her late residence." ReM 1/10/19
   In the court of abundance. PoR 10/16
   Jane Addams. AtM ?/19
   A Letter. Cen 10/17
   A Mountain mummer. BoT 4/22/16
   My grief that I married a gypsy man. Cen 5/18
   The New motherhood. Cen 3/16
   The Night court. Cen 9/15
   The Old maid. Cen 7/15
   Papyrus. SmS 12/15
   Quien sabe? SmS 5/15
   Revelation. SmS 11/15
   St. John of Nepomuc. Poet 1/16
   Symphonie pathetique. Cen 7/16
   Venetian boats. Cen 10/16
   The Vinegar man. SmS 6/15
   The Wishing bridge. Cen 6/16

MIXTER, FLORENCE KILPATRICK. The Candle. Mid 5-6/19
   The Dead. Mid 3-4/18
   December augury. CoV 9/17
   Elegy. Mas 7/17
   Estranged. Mid 5-6/19
   A Greek coffee house. Mas 8/17
   In memory of. Mid 5-6/19
   Prologue. Mid 5-6/19
   St. Patrick's Cathedral. Mid 3-4/18
   The Summons. Mid 5-6/18
   To a child. Poet 12/17
   The Wild cat. Lyr 1/19

MOMBERT, ALFRED. The Heavenly drinker (tr. John William Scholl).
   PoeL Summer #/15

MONAHAN, MICHAEL. Revanche. SmS 12/17

MONNETTE, ORRA EUGENE. End of the road. LoAG 12/2/16
   Hope. LoAG 12/16/16
   The Marsh. LoAG 2/3/17
   A Revery. LoAG 3/17/17

MONRO, HAROLD. Elegy in 1915 (B.H.W.). Foru 5/16
   Strange meetings. Poet 9/16

MONROE, HARRIET. America. Poet 12/18
   April - North Carolina. Poet 4/18

Azaleas. Poet 4/18
The Blue ridge. Poet 4/18
The Fringe-bush. Poet 4/18
A Lady of the snows. Poet 8/15
The Laurel. Poet 4/18
A Letter of farewell. Poet 1/17
The Meeting. Poet 4/18
The Mocking-bird. Poet 4/18
Mountain song. Poet 8/15
The Mountaineer's wife. Poet 4/18
My porch. Poet 4/18
The Oak. Poet 4/18
On the porch. Poet 8/15
The Pine. Poet 8/15
The Question. Poet 4/18
The Rose-bush. Poet 4/18
To W.J.C. Poet 11/16
Vernon Castle, killed in the aviation service, Feb. 15, 1918. Poet 3/18
The Water ouzel. Poet 8/15
White. Poet 4/18
MONTALVO, RICARDO FERNANDEZ. Her floating tresses (tr. Alice
    Stone Blackwell). StJ 3/19
MONTANYE, C.S. Orientale. Par 9/18
MONTGOMERY, L.M. Two foes. CoV 5/19
MOORE, JOHN TROTWOOD. By the eternal. SoW 2/15
MOORE, MARIANNE. Appellate jurisdiction. Poet 5/15
    Counsel to a bachelor. Poet 5/15
    Diogenes. CoV 1/16
    Masks. CoV 1/16
    Poetry. Oth 7/19
    Radical. Oth 3/19
    Sun. CoV 1/16
    That harp you play so well. Poet 5/15
    The Wizard in words. Poet 5/15
MOORE, REBECCA D. Her dream. YouC 4/6/16
MOORE, T. STURGE. Isaac and Rebekah. Poet 8/16
MOORE, WILLIAM DYER. King Arthur's return. TeR 10/19
MORELAND, ANNA. My poor verses. DetN 1/26/19
MORELAND, JOHN R. Bereavement. Min 6/16
    Gifts. Min 6/17
    The Kiss. Min 6/16; ReM 9/1/16
    The Living lie. Mas 9/17
    Loss. Min 5/16
    Tears. Min 12/16
    Waiting. Min 6/16

What would you give? Min 4/17
When I am dead. Min 11/16
Worthless. Mad 9/17

MORGAN, ANGELA. The Doer. Out 12/31/19
It is my glory. CoV 10/18
Open the gates. EvM 9/18

MORGAN, EMANUEL. Bare. Oth 12/18
Dead. Oth 12/18
In memory of a night. DetS 6/23/18
New. Oth 12/18
Old. Oth 12/18
Opus 45. Foru 6/16
Opus 81. Oth 1/17
Opus 88. Oth 1/17
Opus 96. LiR 7/17
Opus 97. Oth 1/17
Opus 103. Oth 1/17
Opus 106. Oth 1/17
Opus 115. Oth 1/17
Prism on the present state of poetry. Oth 1/17
Tame. Oth 12/18
Wild. Oth 12/18

MORGAN, EDWIN J. Sea-song. Colo 12/16

MORGAN, HARRIET. Lines for music. SmS 4/15

MÖRIKE, EDUARD [tr. P.H. Thomson]. Fiar Rohtraut. PoeL Spring#/16
Foresaken. PoeL Spring#/16
'Tis she. PoeL New Year's#/16

MORLEY, CHRISTOPHER. Do you ever feel like God? SmS 12/17
Elegy written in a country coal-bin. Cen 2/17
Lines for an eccentric's book plate. Boo 5/18
O. Henry - apothecary. EvM 2/17
On first looking into a subway excavation. Cen 3/17
Pedometer. Cen 12/16
To a Broadway hotel. SmS 3/18
To a very young gentleman. Cen 1/18

MORRIS, JEAN. In heaven. Mas 6/16
Psyche. Foru 6/16
The Temple. Foru 3/16

MORRIS, O.M. Mary. ReM 2/4/16

MORRIS, OLIVETTE. An Afternoon stroll. YouC 5/17/17
The Buttercup test. YouC 4/18/18
Dottie and the downies. YouC 7/6/16
The Little birds. YouC 5/30/18
A May morning. YouC 5/18/16
Sewing in the garden. YouC 9/6/17
The Spick-span dress. YouC 10/11/17

Waiting for Santa. YouC 12/14/16

MORRISON, JOHN. The Day of Washington. YouC 2/15/17
   The Empty nest. YouC 11/16/16
   The Farm where the farmer was a boy. YouC 8/23/17
   A Flag-day pledge. YouC 6/8/16
   Fooling the teacher. YouC 5/2/18
   The Frogville picnic. YouC 5/10/17
   If only wants come true! YouC 1/25/17
   The Magic coin. YouC 3/28/18
   The Mousermobile. YouC 9/13/17
   A Party in the marshes. YouC 5/2/18
   A Rainy day ramble. YouC 3/2/16
   The Ride on the roller. YouC 1/20/16
   The Shipbuilders at home. YouC 7/23/16
   The Thanksgiving of the bunnies. YouC 11/22/17
   The Three propoises. YouC 7/12/17
   Towser and the moon man. YouC 5/18/16
   The Trouble with school. YouC 10/11/17
   The Vacation trip of the school house. YouC 8/10/16
   Why the Eskimo boys are afraid of Santa Claus. YouC 12/21/16

MORSELL, MARY. At heaven's gate - one soul to another. CoV 12/18
   Four walls. CoV 12/18
   I find no words to sing of love. StJ 4/18
   The Masque. Lyr 4/19
   The Scissors grinder. CoV 5/19
   Vain hope. Par 7/18

MORTLAND, M.A. A Prayer in war-time. Bel 8/31/18

MORTON, CARREL. Reverie over a demi-tasse. Mas 6/17

MORTON, DAVID. The Adventurer. Mid 3-4/19
   After three years. Son 11-12/18
   Beauty like yours. CoV 10/18
   Confession. SmS 10/18
   Conspiracy. PoJ 7/16
   The Dead. Foru 10/15
   A Dinner. SmS 6/17
   The Doors of Dover. EvM 9/19
   England and the sea. NoAR 1/19
   Firelight. SmS 12/17
   Five o'clock. Bel 2/23/18
   For Bob, a dog. SmS 6/16
   A Garden wall. Boo 9/19
   A Gentleman from Stratford sees the play. Bel 2/22/19
   Home. SmS 12/16
   "I shall not ask too much." Foru 3/16
   Immortalis. Bel 8/4/17
   Joyce Kilmer, 1886-1918. NYSB 12/8/19

The Kings are passing deathward. Bel 1/4/19
Lamplight. SmS 3/18
Love song. SmS 3/18
Maple Avenue. Bel 10/12/18
Mariners. Har 8/19
Napoleon in hades. Cen 10/17, 10/18
November dusk. Son 11-12/18
An Old lover. Har 11/18
An Old woman: in war-time. Bel 11/25/16
Phantoms. PoJ 2/17
Poems. Boo 6/19
Resurgam. PoJ 2/17
Returned. NYSB 2/16/19
Revelation. PoJ 2/17
Reverie. SmS 2/17
Shackles. SmS 6/18
"Shipping news." CoV 7/19
Ships in harbor. NYSB 3/23/19
Snow dusk. Lyr 3/19
Sonnet. SmS 2/18
The Spring that comes to Flanders. GoH 5/19
Stranger. SmS 4/18
Swallows. SmS 1/18
That day you come. SmS 12/16
To one dead. Cen 2/17
To the unknown. SmS 6/16
To William Griffith, he that is Pierrot. NYSB 7/27/19
Transfiguration. Ain 9/19
A Tryst. SmS 10/17
When I am dead. PoJ 2/17
William Winter. Cen 9/17
Winter. SmS 2/16
Wooden ships. Boo 4/19
Writs. Boo 11-12/19
You. SmS 7/17
A Young girl dead. CoV 7/19

MORTON, FRANCIS McKINNON. The Little cloud sheep. PeHJ 12/17

MORTON, JOHNSON. A Fine solution. YouC 5/17/17
Half past eight. YouC 5/24/17

MOSHER, ADA A. A Journey's end. Son 9/17

MOSHER, MARTHA B. Haunted. Lyr 1-2/18
The Sea speaks. Lyr 10/17

MOUNT, RICHARD. Her fan, her veil. DetS 10/14/18
Villanelle. DetS 4/24/18
Why. DetS 11/10/18

MOUNTAIN, HARCOURT. Poems after the Chinese. SmS 3/15

MOWRER, PAUL SCOTT. Mist on the moor. PoeL Vacation#/17
    Order. Cen 1/17
    The Phantom washerwoman. PoeL Vacation#/17
    The Voice of the dead. PoeL Vacation#/17
MUCKLEY, HELEN. Changes. Poet 5/19
    The Deceiver. Poet 5/19
MUIR, HENRY D. The Murderess. CoV 10/16
MUIR, MARJORIE. Song. SmS 4/17
MULLER, JAMES ARTHUR. Sempach, a ballad of patriotism. ScM 11/15
MULLER, JULIUS W. Prisoner of Belshazzar. CoV 10/19
MUNGER, ROBERT. The Sleepers. YaR 7/18
MUNKITTRICK, R.K. Tommy's stamp book. YouC 5/31/17
MUNROE, FREDERICK MITCHELL. My soul. SmS 8/15
MUNSTERBERG, MARGARETE. Two sonnets on paintings by Jean
    Francois Millet. StJ 9/19
    The Unseen. StJ 4/19
MURPHY, CHARLES R. Assurance. Nat 9/28/18
    The Deserted garden. Mid 4/17
    Martyrs of misfaith. Nat 3/22/17
    Sonnet. CoV 7/18
    To France. CoV 11/19
MURPHY, ETHEL ALLEN. The Lost Love. SmS 7/17
MURPHY, WILLIAM DENNISTOUN. Theodore Roosevelt. NYS 2/9/19
MURRAY, ADA FOSTER. The Flags. Boo 10/18
MURRAY, ROY IRVING. Day's end. ScM 1/19
MURRAY, THOMAS J. The Longshoreman. CoV 12/18
    Satiety. Par 11/17
    The Tea ships. Nat 4/5/19
    The Trees of Haddonfield. NYTi 3/23/19
MUSE, WILL D. The Sentry. SoW 8/17
MUSGROVE, CHARLES HAMILTON. The Scarlet thread. Poet 10/15
MUTH, EDNA TUCKER. The Freshman. Mid 11-12/19
MYRRH, HUGH. Best sellers, a libretto for writing chaps. For 2/17

N

"N.,C.A." Flowers. Min 6/17
    Vision. Min 12/16
NAJERA, MANUEL GUTIERREZ. A Wish (tr. Alice Stone Blackwell).
    StJ 8/18
NEALLEY, ROSE D. The Rain elves. CoV 6/16
NEFT, BERTHA. Mood. PoR 11/16
NEGRI, ADA. The Little soldier unknown (tr. Rudolph Altrocchi). PoeL

Vacation#/17

NEIHARDT, JOHN. And the little wind. Cen 6/15

NAKRASSOV, NIKOLAI ALEKSEYEVICH. Mothers (tr. Eugene M. Kayden). PoeL Spring#/15

NESBIT, E. Spring in war-time. Har 6/15

NESBITT, MARIAN. To a friend. CaW 3/17

NEWSMITH, JOSEPH A. Oku, Nogi and Nodzu. YouC 1/10/18

NEVIN, HARDWICKE. Girl o' wisp. CoV 5/17
A Home. CoV 7/17
Trenches. Cov 7/18

NEWBOLD, RICHARD. After storm. Colo 5/16
Hope. SmS 2/16
Tramp royal. Colo 3/16

NEWBOLT, HENRY. Sir Pertab Singh. ReM 11/1/18

NICHOLL, LOUISE TOWNSEND. The Black house. CoV 5/18
Blossoms. Ain 10/18
The Child's mother. Ain 5/18
The Common stick. CoV 10/18; ScM 4/19
Cowardice. Mid 9-10/18
For a child named Katharine. Mid 12/17
A Prayer. GoH 12/16
Revelation. CoV 9/19
Sands MacCree. Foru 4/15
September. Nat 9/14/18
Song for April. ScM 4/19
Spring. Nat 9/14/18
Weaver. Mid 9-10/19

NICHOLS, ROBERT. Dawn on the Somme. CoV 4/19
The Exile (Chinese lyrics). NYSB 2/23/19
The Flower of flame. Poet 11/19
Invocation. Cen 11/19
Li-Po, his catch upon being more drunken than ever. NYSB 2/23/19
Modern love song. Poet 7/19
On the hillside (lyrics from the Chinese T'ang period). NYSB 2/23/19
Plaint of an humble servant. Cen 5/19
Poem made by Po-Chui to the honor of an old fashioned harp of his. NYSB 2/23/19
The Secret. Cen 3/19
The Secret garden. Cen 12/18
Separation. NYSB 2/23/19
Threat. Lyr 4/19
A Wandering thing. Poet 7/19

NIES, KONRAD. Heimatsaat. Colo 2/16

NIETZSCHE, FRIEDRICH. The Seventh solitude (from Dionysos-Dithyrambs) [tr. L.M. Kneffner]. PoeL Spring #/16

NOBLE, ROSE CARY. Fulfillment. ScM 1/17

NOGUCHI, YONE. Hokku. Poet 11/18

NORDEN, PETER. Good morning. Poet 7/16

NORMAN, H.L. Crooning creeds. StJ 8/19

NORMILE, F. Conquest. Lib 7/19
  Depths. Lib 7/19
  Morgot. Lib 6/19

NORRIS, MARY RACHEL. Pax Beata. Har 4/15

NORRIS, WILLIAM A. Ballad of stars. PoJ 1/18
  Morn and eve. NeR 5/18/18
  Sonnet. NeR 2/26/16
  The Whispering leaves. CoV 5/19

NORTH, JESSICA NELSON. A Warning. Cen 4/17

NORTHCROSS, ELEANOR HAMMACK. The Dead daughter. YouC
    4/19/17

NORTON, GRACE FALLOW. Fly on! Poet 12/15
  "Good-by, proud world, I'm going home!" Har 8/19
  Hark to the wind of the world. Poet 12/15
  I give thanks. Poet 12/15
  Make no vows. Poet 12/15
  A Song of love. SmS 2/15

NOSREME, H.O. Puss and her tail. Ind 12/4/16

NOVAK, RUTHELE. A Day in May. Cov 7/19
  Heroism. CoV 7/19
  The Man at the plow. CoV 7/19

NOYES, ALFRED. Christmas, 1919. Out 12/17/19
  Ghosts of the new world. Boo 7/17
  Kilmeny. Boo 6/17
  The Lord of misrule. NoAR 5/15
  Old Cap'n Storm-along. Boo 6/17
  The Old meeting-house. YaR 4/19
  (On a certain goddess, acclaimed as "new" but known in Babylon), "five
    criticisms." NYSB 3/2/19
  (on certain of the Bolsheviki), "idealists," "five criticisms." NYSB 3/2/19
  (On cretain realists), "five criticisms." NYSB 3/2/19
  (On fashions in art), "five criticisms." NYSB 3/2/19
  (On many recent novels by the conventional unconventionalists), "five
    criticisms." NYSB 3/2/19
  Princeton in war time. Out 6/13/17
  The River of stars. Cen 7/15
  A Spell for a fairy. Har 3/15
  The Union. YaR 10/18
  "A Victory celebration." NYSB 12/8/18
  Wireless. Boo 6/17

NYE, MRS. JOHN PALMER. My bonny lad. OSB 5/26/18

O

"O.,B.J." The Hills of California. LoAG 2/19/16

O'BOLGER, T.D. Counsels of O'Riordan, the rainmaker. Poet 12/16

O'BRIEN, EDWARD J. April twilight. StJ 6/18
  Aran cradle song. CoV 1/16
  The Call. Har 4/19
  Coelum chorale, in honorem assumpationis B.V. Mariae,
    Reginae Coeli. PoJ 5/15
  A Dream of flame. CoV 5/16
  The Drifting man (John Millington Synge, 1871-1909). Bel 6/24/16
  Elegy. Boo 10/18
  Eucharist. CoV 4/18
  Flower. LiR 4/17
  Foam. LiR 4/17
  For one who went west (Joseph Mary Plunkett). StJ 3/17
  Hellenica. Oth 1/16; Lib 11/18; Mid 11-12/18
  The Hole. CoV 7/16
  The Hosting of the Sidhe. PoeL Summer#/15
  Hymn to light. Boo 4/18
  The Lament at the wedding. Mid 6/16
  The Last piper. BoT 2/4/15
  Light concealed. StJ 6/18
  Magic. Tri 5/61
  The Meeting. CoV 4/18
  Mirrored light. CoV 4/18
  A New England idlyl. CoV 5/16
  Ode in time of remembrance. BoT 2/13/18
  On the day of achievement. BoT 11/23/18
  The Path. Har 4/18
  Sea flame. CoV 4/18
  The Shepherd boy. ScM 11/16
  The Shroud. CoV 2/16
  Song. BoT 2/4/15
  Stilled music. StJ 4/19
  To an April skylark. Mid 4/16
  To Brigid MacDonagh of Inishmaan. CoV 2/16
  To a skylark. CoV 4/18
  Under the stars. BoT 12/26/15
  Wild air. SmS 7/18
  Woodways. CoV 5/19

O'BRIEN, JEAN. Praise of love. Poet 8/16
  Prayer. Poet 8/16

O'CONNELL, MARTIN. Empty hands. CaW 12/18
  Why. CaW 4/18

O'CONNOR, ARMEL. Apportionment. CaW 10/16
  The Wise virgins. CaW 8/17
O'CONNOR, VIOLET. A Great mystery. CaW 2/18
O'CONOR, NORREYS JEPHSON. All Saints' Day. LivC 11/3/17
  Evensong. Boo 10/17
  Goodbye. Bel 3/24/17
  The Hills of dreams. Bel 2/26/18
  In memoriam: Francis Ledwidge (killed in action, July 31, 1917).
    NYTr 8/16/17
  Jerusalem retaken. Boo 2/18
  The Listeners (with a copy of Walter de la Mare's book). Son #2/17
  Moira's keening. CoV 10/19
  Moon fancy. CoV 6/18
  Prayer for St. Patrick's Day. BoT 3/6/18
  The Response of the shee. Colo 1/16
  Summer's end. ArW 10/17
  Times and customs. BoT 3/15/19
  To a fireside companion. CoV 4/19
  To Lord Dunsany. Bel 5/10/19
  To one in Kerry. Colo 1/16
O'DONNELL, CHARLES L. Drought. CaW 6!5
  Forgiveness. Poet 5/16
  Magi. Boo 12/17
  Martin of Tours. Poet 12/16
  A Road of France. Poet 7/19
  A Road to Ireland. CaW 3/17
  Transformation. Boo 11-12/19
  Trelawney lies by Shelley. Boo 5/19
  Village churches. CaW 1/19
OGILIVIE, WILL H. The Plow. Out 7/28/15
O'HARA, JOHN MYERS. Dawn at Lesbos. ScM 12/18
  Evocation. SmS 10/16
  Lethe. Sms 7/16
  New songs of Sappho. PoR 9/16
  Parentalia. ScM 12/17
  Vale. PoJ 12/15
O'HARA, STEPHEN J. The Parting. Par 9/17
OLIVER, JENNIE HARRIS. Lone trail. CoV 11/18
  Noon trail. CoV 11/18
OLIVER, WADE W. Night piece. You 2/19
  Winter night. You 12/18
OLIVIER, SYDNEY. Transparency. Ain 11/19
OLSON, TED. Clouds. CoV 11/19
O'NEIL, DAVID. The Ancient burden. ReM 9/17/15
  Apathy. ReM 9/17/15

The Ascent. Poet 11/17
An Astronomer. ReM 9/17/15
The Beach. Poet 11/17
Child's eyes. PoJ 9/17
Complaint. ReM 9/17/15
Enslaved. Poet 11/17
First love. ReM 9/17/15
Freedom. Poet 11/17
Greatness. ReM 9/17/15
The Heights. ReM 9/17/15
Human chords. Poet 11/17
Inheritance. Oth 12/17
Lime light. Oth 12/17
Love. PoR 9/16
Love song from the trenches. PoJ 9/17
March. PoJ 9/17
Messages. ReM 9/17/15
Moods and moments. ReM 9/17/15
A Navajo poet. Oth 12/17
One way out. ReM 9/17/15
Our son Jack. ReM 9/17/15
The Peasants. Poet 11/17
Peasants at war. PoJ 9/17
Poverty. ReM 9/17/15
The Prodigal son. Oth 12/17
Regeneration. Oth 12/17
Solitude. LiR 1-2/16
A Troop ship. PoJ 9/17
The Unquiet. Oth 12/17
A Vase of Chinese ivory. ReM 9/17/15
Vernal showers. ReM 9/17/15
Victory. ReM 9/17/15
Walt Whitman. PoJ 9/17
War's aftermath. PoJ 9/17
O'NEIL, GEORGE. The Cobbler in Willow Street. Cen 5/19
The Fisherman. SmS 6/18
For the woods destroyed. ReM 3/22/18
Le cynge. SmS 6/18
Margot. Poet 5/19
The Marvel. Poet 5/18
On the light reeds. ReM 3/22/18
Sparrow. Poet 5/19
Spring's crocus-fingers. ReM 3/22/18
They pass. ReM 3/22/18
O'NEIL, IDA. To a Persian manuscript. Nat 8/2/19
O'NEILL, ROSE. Your despair and my despair. Har 5/19
OPDYKE, OLIVER. The Day of days. BoT 4/26/18

OPPENHEIM, JAMES. America. SeA 3/17
  The Ancient of days. Lyr 8/17
  Golden death. Cen 10/16
  Good morning. Cen 8/16
  A Handful of dust. Ene 5/15
  In the pause of ominous foreboding days. SeA 8/17
  Laughter. Cen 11/15
  Memories of Whitman and Lincoln. SeA 5/17
  Morning and I. Cen 9/17
  Out. EvM 12/16
  Prelude (to "Creation"—a drama). SeA 1/17
  The Red month. Cen 9/16
  The Song of the uprising. SeA 9/17
  Under the bell. EvM 11/16
  The Young world. Dia 2/28/18
OPPER, EMMA A. Lais to her dog. ScML 5/15
O'REILLY, AMADEUS. To a bluebird. BoT 11/1/17
  Two. BoT 3/20/18
O'REILLY, MILES. April 20, 1864. NYSB 8/11/18
ORR, BETTY. The Forfeit. Poet 7/17
ORR, HUGH ROBERT. They softly walk. You 4/19
ORR, PATRICK. Annie Shore and Johnnie Doon. Poet 1/15
ORTIZ, LUIS G. My fountain (tr. Alice Stone Blackwell). StJ 8/18
O'SEASNAIN, BRIAN PADRAIC. End of the trail. NeR 12/7/19
  The Lost world. CaW 4/19
  The Silences. CaW 8/19
O SHEEL, SHAEMAS. Isolation. Min 6/16
  William Butler Yeats. Min 6/16
O'SULLIVAN, SEUMAS. Have thou no fear. SmS 10/15
  The Roses. SmS 1/15
  Resurgam. SmS 6/15
OTHON, MANUEL JOSE. The Stars (tr. Alice Stone Blackwell). StJ 8/18
O'TOOLE, PHELIM. A Futurist fantasy. ReM 12/14/17
  L'aveugle. ReM 1/18/18
  The Rider. ReM 12/21/17
  Specters and expecters. ReM 12/14/17
  Washington pie: or the public buildings of Medicine Hat. ReM 3/9/17
OVINGTON, MARY WHITE. Mary Phagan speaks. NeR 8/28/15
OXENHAM, JOHN. M-U-D. Boo 7/18

P

"P,E.W." Red Cross. Mas 9/17
PACKARD-DU BOIS, G. Easter thoughts. Pas 3-4/18

Who goes there? Pas 1-2/18

PAGET, BLANCHE. Impotence. Lyr 11/17

PAGET, REGINALD. Cruisers on the Hudson. Lyr (Supplement) 6/17
  Evening. Lyr (Supplement) 6/17
  Fog. Lyr (Supplement) 6/17
  June. Lyr (Supplement) 6/17
  Noon. Lyr (Supplement) 6/17
  Translation from Goethe's "Iphigenie auf Tauris." Lyr (Supplement)
    6/17
  Translation of the Song of the Parcae. Lyr (Supplement) 6/17

PAINE, ALBERT BIGELOW. The Deserted house. SmS 8/16
  The Frozen brook. Cen 3/16
  Insomnia. Cen 9/16
  The Star dreamer. Har 11/16
  Summer night. Cen 6/16
  The Superman. Har 6/16

PALEN, LEWIS STANTON. The Postern gate to the land of dreams.
    HarW 3/25/16

PANGBORN, GEORGIA WOOD. The Dead maids and the daffodils.
    ScM 4/19
  Morning on the beach. Poet 6/15
  The Mother speaks. Har 5/16
  The Walk on the moor. Poet 6/15

PARADISE, VIOLA T. Clothes. Poet 8/17
  Death. Poet 5/18
  Early spring night. Poet 5/18
  Midnight rain. Poet 5/18
  Thoughts. Poet 5/18
  Wind and moonlight. Poet 5/18

PARKER, E.W. Nora. Tou 7/18

PARKS, M.M. March. YouC 3/8/17

PARMENTIER, FLORIAN. Espoir. Par 8/18
  Les langues de la nuit. SmS 9/17

PARRISH, EMMA KENYON. Des' a-nappin. CoV 11/18
  The feet of the anathoth. Colo 1/17
  White and gold. CoV 12/19
  Yssaen. CoV 8/16

PARSONS, MABEL HOMES. The Fantasy of life. PoeL Summer#/17
  Mist. PoeL Summer#/17

PARSONS, MARY CATHERINE. My Valentine. YouC 2/8/17

PARTRIDGE, PAULINE. Sacrament. Poet 7/18

PASCAL, RENE. Entreaty. SoW 4/15

PATKANIAN, RAPHAEL. The New generation (tr. Alice Stone Blackwell).
    StJ 2/18

PATRICK, ASA ANDERSON. The Ancient Miracles. Colo 6/16

Lotus and cherry. Colo 4/15
PATTEE, FLORENCE M. Merry May. YouC 5/3/17
PATTERSON, ANTOINETTE DE COURSEY. The Birches. Poet 9/18
  Carnage. Poet 5/16
  A Day in the open. Ain 7/18
  Enchanted land. Mad 9/17
  The Firs in autumn. CoV 10/18
  Glamour. CoV 6/18
  Guerre a mort. Ain 5/19
  Honors. Poet 10/18
  In late autumn. Ain 11/18
  The Moon. CoV 2/16
  Restlessness. CoV 5/16
  The Sea to-day. Ain 11/19
  Sheila Eileen. Poet 5/16
  The Shower. Ain 3/19
  Spinning Song. CoV 3/16
PATTERSON, JEAN RUSHMORE. King Albert comes! Out 10/1/19
PATTERSON, MARJORIE. Fulfillment. Lyr 12/17
  Harlequin's Valentine. CoV 2/19
PATTERSON, WINNETA. Going home at night. LoAG 5/8/15
PATTON, BESS HAFER. The Boudoir clock. PoJ 3/17
PATTON, GEORGE S., JR. Might-right. LoAG 6/23/17
PATTON, MARGARET FRENCH. Comfort. CoV 9/18
  Needle travel. Mas 7/15
  The Sound of the needles. Mas 6/16
PATTON, MIRIAM KEEP. The Clock. Mas 5/17
  On your birthday. Har 3/15
  Song. Har 2/15
PAUL, DOROTHY. Hagar. Cen 4/16
  The Threshing-floor. Cen 4/18
PAYSON, MAHDAH. To any mountain. Poet 9/16
PEABODY, JOSEPHINE PRESTON. All Soul's eve. PoR 11/16
  Men have wings at last. BoT 2/13/15
  Portrait of a daughter. CoV 11/19
  To King Albert. BoT 11/23/18
PEACH, ARTHUR WALLACE. Question. Colo 6/16
  The Reason. SmS 4/15
PEARCE, LEILA MILLER. The Habitue. CoV 8/16
  Machine made. Oth 3/16
PEARSALL, ADAM. Romance. Pag ?/19
PEARSON, RUTH R. To Woodrow Wilson. Lib 4/18
PECK, GLENNA HUGHES. Weariness. Mid 9-10/18
PECK, KATHRYN. Blockade. Nat 5/31/19
  In the day nursery. Lib 4/18

PECK, SAMUEL MINTURN. The American marines. BoT 3/15/19
  Communion. Har 1/18
  The Reprimand. BoT 3/15/19
  The Winter rain. BoT 2/8/19

PEEPLES, LUCIA. Mine. Poet 1/18

PEGUY, CHARLES. Saint Genevieve (tr. Elizabeth S. Dickerman).
  PoeL Spring#/17

PEMBERTON, MURDOCK. Cross section. ReM 5/18/17
  Stock. Cen 6/16
  What befell old Attica? BoT 5/31/19

PENNINGTON, ALICE DAMROSCH. In church. NeR 11/20/15

PENNYPACKER, GRACE F. What baby wants. YouC 6/21/17

PERCY, WILLIAM ALEXANDER. A Ballad of St. Sebastian. Bel 3/25/16
  Before dawn. Colo 6/16
  Fulfillment, after a battle: 1916. NoAR 1/17
  In our yard. Bel 8/25/17
  In the night. CoV 7/18
  A Little page's song (13th century). CoV 6/16
  Lullaby. CoV 7/18
  The Man in white. Bel 4/21/17
  Overtones. Bel 3/17/17
  Poppy fields. Bel 4/27/18
  Sanctuary. Bel 1/20/17
  The Song you love. CoV 5/17
  The Swallows. Bel 1/18/19
  This soldier generation. CoV 7/19
  To an old tune. CoV 1/18
  A Volunteer's grave. NoAR 6/19
  A Wond song. Bel 1/5/18
  The Young squire. Bel 7/27/18

PERKINS, HELEN STANDISH. A Careful maid. YouC 2/28/18

PERRY, EUGENE. West to east. Bel 4/13/18

PERRY, HAROLD E. Liberty gold. BoT 4/24/18

PERRY, Lilla Cabot. A Friend. Har 8/16

PETERSON, FREDERICKA. Aetna. Nat 4/12/19
  Deported. Nat 2/22/19
  "Great possessions." Nat 12/28/18
  Northern summer. NeR 8/7/15
  To a friend. Nat 5/10/19
  Urashimataro. NeR 11/20/15

PETRUNKEVITCH, WANDA. Death and the aviator. Poet 8/15
  Inconsistency. Poet 8/15

PETTEE, Florence M. The Incense jar. PoJ 2/17
  The Who-bird. YouC 9/6/17

PETTUS, MARTHA ELVIRA. Sister Teresa (in memoriam). CaW 8/19

PEYER, ETHEL R. When I grow old. Har 6/15
PEYTON, JOHN R. The Censor. Poet 7/19
PFEIFFER, EDWARD H. The Mystery. SmS 1/15
PHELPS, ARTHUR L. An Old man's weariness. Poet 7/18
    There was a rose. Poet 7/18
    You died for dreams. Poet 7/19
PHILLIPS, CHARLES F. Birth. CaW 6/18
    The Crimson snow (Bethlehem, 1916). CaW 12/16
    The Fool of God. CaW 12/18
    Music. CaW 7/17
    November vigil. CaW 11/18
    An Old masterpiece. CaW 9/17
    The Soldier's mother (from a letter from the trenches). CaW 5/17
    The Star born. CaW 8/18
    Uncas Island revery. Lyr 7/17
PHILLIPS, STEPHEN. The Hatching of war: a dramatic fragment.
    NoAR 1/15
    A Woman to Shakespeare. Cen 1/15
PHILLPOTS, EDEN. On Eylesbarrow. ScM 11/19
PICKENS, WILLIAM. The Riveters. BaA 5/29/18
PICKERING, RUTH. To Arthur B. Davis. Lib 4/18
PICKTHALL, MARJORIE L.C. April song. SmS 4/15
    Mary shepherdess. ScM ?/15
    "Not here, not here the rose." SmS 3/15
    Quiet. Dia 10/25/17
    Singing children. YouC 12/14/16
PIER, ARTHUR STANWOOD. Shipbuilders. BoT 7/22/17
PIERCE, FREDERICK E. Silos. YaR 10/18
PINCKNEY, CLARA. A Coasting song. YouC 1/10/18
    The Open fire. YouC 1/29/16
    The Story of Billy. YouC 7/27/16
    The Summer boarders. YouC 8/9/17
    The Visit. YouC 12/30/15
PINCKNEY, JOSEPHINE L.S. Nuptial. CoV 9/19
PINDER, FRANCES DICKENSON. Inland. CoV 9/19
    Peace. CoV 1/19
    Vagabond. CoV 11/18
PINIFER, ALICE. The Gypsy. Mid 5-6/19
    The Lily. CoV 4/17
    Pine trees and snow. CoV 2/19
    Plowman. CoV 4/17
    Spring trumpets. CoV 4/17
PIPER, EDWIN FORD. Annie. Mid 3/17
    At her dugout. Mid 12/17

At the postoffice. Mid 12/17
The Banded. Mid 12/17
Barbed wire. Mid 1/17
The Boy on the prairie. Mid 3/17
Breaking sod. Mid 2/17
By the road. Mid 1/17
The Church. Mid 4/17
The Cowboy. Mid 1/17
The Drought. Mid 2/17
Dry bones. Mid 1/17
The Ford at the river. Mid 2/17
The Games. Mid 12/17
The Gathering. Mid 12/17
Gee-up thar, mules. CoV 4/19
The Grasshoppers. Mid 3/17
Have you an eye? Mid 10/17
The Horse thief. Mid 1/17
I'll go a piece with you. StJ 4/19
In a public place. Mid 12/17
Jarvis waited. Mid 12/17
Joe Taylor. Mid 12/17
The Jumper. Mid 12/17
The Key. Mid 12/17
The Last antelope. Mid 1/17
The Man with the key once more. Mid 12/17
Meanwhile. Mid 4/17
Mister Dwiggins. Mid 12/17
Moon-worship. Mid 12/17
The Movers. Mid 1/17
Nathan Briggs. Mid 12/17
The Neighborhood. Mid 12/17
Once on a time. Mid 1/17
The Prairie fire. Mid 2/17
The River once more. Mid 3/17
Road and path. Mid 12/17
The Schoolmistress. Mid 3/17
The Settler. Mid 1/17
The Sod house. Mid 2/17
Ten cents a bushel. Mid 4/17
Three per cent a month. Mid 4/17
Water barrels. Mid 2/17
The Well. Mid 2/17
The Well digger. Mid 2/17
The Windmill. Mid 2/17
PITT, CHART. The Chosen sons. HarW 1/1/16
The Eyes of war. EvM 11/17
In rainbow land. NYTM 4/22/17

The Mail team. HarW 12/18/15

PITTS, MABEL PORTER. The Individualist. LoAG 4/15/16

PLUNKETT, GEORGE NOBLE. Urania. CaW 11/16

POHL, H.J.O. An Up-to-date wail. LoAG 6/23/17

POHLAND, LAURA. The Flute. DetN 1/26/19

POLLOCK, CHANNING. Afterward. Cen 5/18

POLLOCK, LEWETTE BRAUCHAMP. Then and now. EvM 9/18

POOLE, LOUELLA C. Charles Dickens. BoT 4/19/19

POORE, DUDLEY. Ode in time of battle. NeR 5/15/15

PORCHER, FRANCES. Spring in Virginia. ReM 3/12/15

PORTER, CHARLOTTE. Quoth the duck. PoeL Winter#/16
   Shop-flowers and shrine-flowers. StJ 9/19

PORTER, ETHEL HALLET. Wood magic. LoAG 12/9/16

PORTER, GENE STRATTON. "Whitman." NYSB 5/25/19

PORTERFIELD, G.A. A Carol for Christmas: 1917. Bel 12/22/17
   In hospital. Bel 7/28/17

PORTOR, LAURA SPENCER. The Shepherds. Har 12/19

POSTGATE, MARGARET I. The Veteran. Poet 8/18

POTTER, MIRIAM CLARK. Dreams for three. YouC 2/8/17
   A Feast at happy highlands. YouC 7/26/17
   The Gigglequicks. YouC 1/27/16
   The Gigglequicks and Bobby. YouC 12/27/17
   The Gigglequicks and mother. YouC 3/30/16
   The Gigglequicks at bedtime. YouC 2/24/16
   The Gigglequicks at home. YouC 7/13/16
   Little sister of the moon. YouC 6/15/16
   The March wind. YouC 3/7/18
   The Sandman's wife. YouC 1/11/17

POTTLE, EMERY. The Day's journey. GoH 71/17
   In Italy. Har 6/17
   To an Italian statue. Har 4/18

POUND, EZRA. Albatre. SmS 8/15
   Atthis. Poet 9/16
   Dans un omnibus de Londres. Poet 9/16
   Dogmatic statement concerning the game of chess: theme for a
      series of pictures. Poet 3/15
   Exile's letter, from a Chinese of Rihaku (Li Po). Poet 3/15
   The Fish and the shadow. Poet 9/16
   Her little black slippers. SmS 10/15
   Homage to Q.S.F. Christianus. Poet 9/16
   Image from Orleans. Poet 3/15
   Impressions of F.M. Arouet (de Voltaire). Poet 9/16
   Love-song to Eunoe. SmS 7/15
   Near Perigord. Poet 12/15

Pagani's. Poet 9/16
Poems from the Propertius series. Poet 3/19
Provincia deserts. Poet 3/15
Three cantos, I. Poet 6/17
Three cantos, II. Poet 7/17
Three cantos, III. Poet 8/17
The Three poets. Poet 9/16
Villanelle: the psychological hour. Poet 12/15

POWEL, HARFORD, JR. A letter to W. Peirce in Paris. CoV 12/16

POWELL, ARTHUR. The Fighter. CoV 7/18
Illumination. Boo 3/17
A Song of Villon's. CoV 4/16

POWELL, H.A. A Conscientious objector. NYSB 10/13/18

POWERS, CHARLES J. At Jesus' bruised knees. CaW 4/19

POWERS, MABEL. An Iroquois thanksgiving. Out 11/22/16

POWYS, JOHN COWPER. The Hope. Poet 10/18

PRADO, PEDRO. The Three Marys (tr. Alice Stone Blackwell). StJ 3/19

PRATT, ANNA M. An April fool. YouC 4/4/18
A May frolic. YouC 5/10/17
A Winter blanket. YouC 2/1/17

PRENTICE, MADELINE. To the unnamed. Ain 3/19

PRESTON, ANNIE A. The Belcroft chimney. GoH 3/19

PRESTON, KEITH. The New Noah. ReM 2/21/19

PRICE, C.A. A Native of Peru. ScM 4/19
Ubique. ScM 2/17
When school begins again. YouC 9/13/17

PRICE, EDITH BALLINGER. Revelation. CoV 12/18
To a child. CoV 12/18
White thorn cottage. CoV 12/18

PRICE, N.O. A July jingle. YouC 6/28/17

PRICE, RUTH CLAY. And yet—. Pag ?/19

PROUDFEET, ANDREA HOFER. The Ship's prow. Poet 5/19

PROUTY, ADELAIDE. An April battle-ground. Out 4/3/18

PRUDHOMME, SULLY. France (tr. Marie Louise Hersey). BoT 6/13/17

PULSIFER, HAROLD TROWBRIDGE. America to France and Great
Britain. Out 4/24/18
Clarion. Out 3/16
The Lusitania. Out 5/26/15
Phantoms. Out 1/3/17
The Shadow of silence. Out 5/15/18
The Strong young eagles. Out 7/3/18
To a school-mate—killed in action. Out 3/20/18
To an unborn child. PoJ 10/15
Wild bird. Out 2/6/18

PUTNAM, NINA WILCOX. Souvenir de ta tendresse. Ain 6/19
PUTNAM, SHIRLEY. Marsh mists. Colo 4/16
PYNE, JOHN. Aurore et Crépuscule. NeR 2/26/16
PYNE, MARY. The River bank. Har 6/19

Q

QUILL, JOHN. When pedagogues do their turn. LoAG 3/18/16
QUINTER, GEORGE E. From the beach. CoV 10/19
QUIRK, CHARLES J. A Song. CaW 11/17

R

"R.,H.C." A Song of young things. Out 7/5/16
"R.,M." Intellectual inhibition. Mas 7/17
   Quiet. Mas 7/17
"R.,P.T." Plums. Poet 7/18
"R.,S." LInes written in a barber shop. For 11/16
RABELL, DU BERNET. "I planted once in a garden." Ain 2/19
RAGSDALE, LULAH. The Illiterate. PoJ 4/17
RAINSFORD, W. KERR. Faugh-a-ballagh. Out 4/24/18
   To a Phoenician tomb on the coast of Africa. Out 8/7/18
RAMOS, EDWARD. Chanson triste. Oth 3/16
   In the green wood. PoJ 7/15
   L'arbre mystique. Oth 3/16
   Rapiers a deux points (to G.K.). Oth 3/16
   Touch me not. PoJ 10/15
   Unclean. PoJ 10/15
RAND, KENNETH. Credo. YaR 1/15
   "Limited service only." Bel 11/30/18
RAND, ROBERT. Graves of dreams. Poet 5/19
RANDALL, HERBERT. Gutter song. BoT 3/25/17
   The Sunshine path. YouC 7/5/17
   When Jamie the Piper comes back. BoT 8/17
RANSOM, JOHN CROW. Roses. CoV 12/18
RAPHAEL, ALICE. Phantoms. SeA 6/17
RASKIN, P.M. The Game. StJ 9/19
REVANEL, BEATRICE W. Amen. Boo 1/18
   Broomgrass. CoV 9/18
   Certainty. CoV 9/18
   The Day you went. CoV 1/19
   The Humorists. CoV 11/19
   Sonnets from an unknown (found on the body of an Irish officer).

CoV 5/18
To you. CoV 1/19
RAYMOND, RUTH ILSE. Youth. LoAG 10/30/16
RAYMUND, BERNARD. At sunset. Mid 6/17
   Caprice. Mid 11-12/19
   December woods. Mid 11-12/19
   Dedication. You 4/18
   If I go down. Mid 11-12/19
   Lachrymae rerum. PoJ 3/17
   The Lovers. PoJ 3/17
   Romance. Mid 11-12/18
   Shepherd's pipe. Colo 9/16
   White magic. Mid 11-12/19
   REDFIELD, ROBERT, JR. Ambition. CoV 4/18
   In Moulins Wood. Poet 8/18
   Return to the front. Poet 8/18
REDPATH, BEATRICE. The Cat. SmS 11/16
   Five o'clock. SmS 8/15
   The Release of the soul. Foru 7/15
REED, EDWARD BLISS. The Dawn. YaR 10/16
   Three friends. YaR 10/16
REED, JOHN. Fog. ScM 8/19
   Hospital notes, I-III. Poet 8/17
   Love at sea. Mas 5/16
   Proud New York. Poet 4/19
REEDY, WILLIAM MARION. The Conquerors. ReM 4/20/17
REES, ARTHUR D. Cares that infest the day. Poet 12/18
   Longings for home. Poet 12/18
   The Melancholy plaint of the Russian song. Poet 12/18
   Tears, idle tears! Poet 12/18
   Unseeing the seen. Poet 12/18
REESE, LIZETTE WOODWORTH. All Hallows. SmS 11/16
   Arraignment. Son ?/17
   Burning the leaves. SmS 3/15
   Chloe to Amaryllis. Boo 12/17
   Cupboards. Mid 5-6/18
   Ellen hanging clothes. CoV 5/18
   Haworth parsonage. Foru 1/15
   Her son. CoV 11/19
   His mother. CoV 2/19
   Lilac dusk. Mid 9/17
   The Little shoe. ScM 4/19
   Monday. SmS 2/15
   Not I. CoV 5/19
   Odors. Son 5-6/18
   The Rector. SmS 6/16

The Secret. SmS 2/16
A Song. Lyr 6/17; SmS 3/18
Tankle-tinkle-tank. Foru 2/15
To myself. Boo 2/18
Triumph. Son 11-12/18
The Wood thrush. Mid 5-6/19

REEVES, MARY. My lesson. CaW 1/18

REICH, HARRY, JR. Prelude. Mas 4/17

REID, BRUIN. Ho, hum. SmS 1/16

REID, PEGGY. Old glory. DetN 1/26/19

REPS, PAUL. Once in a blue, blue moon. Mas 10/17

RETHY, JOSEPH BERNARD. Amor sin morte. PoJ 7/17
To an old man. Mas 2/15

RHYS, ERNEST. A Breton night. Poet 4/16
Death and the jester. Poet 4/16
Nesta's morning song. Poet 4/16
Romance. Poet 4/16
Sonnetina: Punch and Judy. Poet 4/16
The Woman of sorrows. Poet 4/16

RICE, CALE YOUNG. After parting (a woman speaks). Bel 6/15/18
Atavism. Bel 8/11/17
The Faring of Fa-Hien. Bel 1/19/18
In the deep midnight. Cen 11/15
King Amenophis (a screed for deported Belgians). Bel 11/17/17
Last lines of the poet of Suma. Cen 12/15
New dreams for old. Cen 7/16
The Plainsman. Bel 2/3/17
Questions. Cen 5/17
Revolution. Cen 6/17
A Sidmouth lad. Foru 2/15
Solitary sea-gull. Bel 2/9/18
Young April. Cen 4/18

RICE, FREDERICK GARNETT. You. Mas 10/16

RICE, GRANTLAND. The Vanished country. NYTr 3/10/15

RICH, H. THOMPSON. Afterwards. Poet 11/17
Desire. Poet 6/16
The Drinker. Poet 6/16
I come singing. Poet 11/17
In a bungalow. Mad 9/17
In the manner of Edgar Lee Masters. ReM 9/8/16
Longing. Mad 7/17
Lyric. Par 8/17
Nocturne-remeeting. Ain 12/19
Note. PoJ 1/17
Pierrette sings. Par 4/18
Poetry. PoJ 1/17

Pyrotechnics. PoJ 1/17
Quandry. PoJ 1/17
The Scarlet tanager. Foru 9/16
The Scissor-man. Foru 7/17
She sings. Mad 8/17
Transposition. SmS 4/15
"World without end, amen!" PoJ 1/17
You came and went. Poet 6/16

RICH, LILA. Frozen heart. Poet 7/17
Praise. Poet 7/17
The Snowstorm. Poet 7/17
War. Poet 7/17

RICHARDS, JOHN. Easter, 1918. Out 7/17/18

RICHARDSON, JAMES E. Algol in Perseus. CoV 3/16
At the sculptor's. CoV 5/16
The Borderland. CoV 8/16
The Bunty shoe (New Jersey pine barrens). CoV 10/16
By summer hill. CoV 1/16
The Dragon-fly. CoV 9/16
Eclipse. CoV 5/16
In a library. CoV 1/16
The Plough. CoV 1/16
Sonnet. CoV 9/16
The Vase. CoV 9/16
A Word on the stars. CoV 3/16

RICHARDSON, JOSEPH HAMILTON. The Lode star. SoW 4/15

RICHARDSON, MABEL KINGSLEY. Pastel for March. Mid 3-4/19
A Short story. CoV 19/19
Strangers. Mid 7-8/18
Ubiquity. CoV 7/18

RICHMOND, CHARLES ALEXANDER. Between the lines. Out 7/26/16
Brother Jonathan. Out 2/16/16
Brother Jonathan speaks his mind. Out 3/15/16
Brother Jonathan's trials. Out 5/13/16
For the sailors at sea. Out 2/20/28
The Lord's prayer. Out 12/22/16
A Song. ScM 6/16

RICKARD, OSWALD M. The Aviation meet. YouC 9/27/17
The Fourth in the Arctic. YouC 7/?/17
King-ger-ump and the flixie-flies. YouC 8/17/16
Kitbird land. YouC 6/21/17

RICKETT, EDMOND. A Ballade of the liris. ScM 4/15

RIDGE, LOLA. Blossoms. Oth 12/18
Dawn-wind. Poet 10/18
Dorothy. Oth 1/19
Dreams. NeR 11/9/18

Easter dawn. Oth 7/19
The Edge. Poet 10/18
The Everlasting return. NeR 11/16/18
The Fiddler. Poet 10/18
Friends. Ain 12/19
Iron wine. Poet 10/18
Jaguar. Oth 3/19
The Song. Poet 10/18
The Spoiler. Ain 8/19
Unveiling. Ain 10/19
The Woman with jewels. Oth 12/18

RIDGELY, TORRENCE. To children. NeR 1/4/19

RIHANI, AMEEN. Renunciation. Har 8/15

RILEY, JAMES. Assurance. CoV 5/16

RILKE, RAINER MARIA. The Angels (tr. Sarah T. Barrows).
   PoeL Winter#/16
Autumn (tr. Matthew Josephson). Lyr 11/17
Autumn day (tr. Sarah T. Barrows). Boo 10/16
The Book of hours (tr. Sasha Best). PoeL Winter#/15
Glimpse of childhood (tr. Marharete Munsterberg). PoeL New Year's#/16
A Grave hour (tr. Sarah T. Barrows). PoeL Winter#/16
My battle-cry (tr. Sasha Best). PoeL Spring#/15
Presentment (tr. Sarah T. Barrows). PoeL Winter #/16

RITTENHOUSE, JESSIE B. Defeat. Har 3/18
Freedom. SmS 11/17
Frost in spring. Har 3/16
The Ghost. ScM 11/17
The Ghostly galley. PoJ 1/17
My wage. GoH 8/17
Patrins. CoV 7/17
Presence. Har 5/19
Silence. PoJ 1/17
The Waterfowl. Har 9/18
Words. Lyr 7/17

RIVENBURGH, ELEANOR. The Gift. Par 8/17

RIVOLA, FLORA SHUFELT. Fledglings. Mid 3-4/18
Heart-cry. Mid 7-8/19
Kinship. Poet 5/18
Lincoln. Mid3-4/18
The Mother's meeting. Mas 7/17
Promise. Mid 7-8/19
The School-house revival: a fragment. Mid 3-4/18

RIZAL, DON JOSE. The Last farewell (tr. E.M. Patten). PoeL Summer#/15

ROBBINS, JACOB. Judas. Lyr 12/17

ROBBINS, LEO. White sisters. StJ 7/18

ROBERTS, DOROTHY GWYNNE. An Unknown Princess (lines on the painting by Leonardo Da Vinci). Boo 8/17

ROBERTS, ELIZABETH MADEX. Twilight. You 12/18

ROBERTS, JOHN. Those burglars. SmS 7/15

ROBERTS, MARY ELEANOR. The Coquette to the apple-eater. CoV 9/19
English portraits in the Morgan Gallery. CoV 8/16
Hilda's garden. CoV 7/17
Love, the enemy. CoV 9/16
Moon in the morning. CoV 6/16
The New curriculum. BoT 2/28/17
A Poet in the city. CoV 9/19

ROBERTS, THEODORE GOODRICH. As you turn the year. Boo 3/15

ROBERTS, WALTER ADOLPH. Ballade of the fourth year of the war. Mas 10/17
The Celt. Cen 12/19
For poets slain in the war. Ain 2/19
Place de la Concorde. Par 10/17
Tiger lily. Ain 11/19
Villanelle of the living Pan. Ain 5/19
Villanelle of Montparnasse. Ain 9/18
"The Woman rebel" (to Margaret Sanger). Mas 5/16

ROBINS, NELSON. The Best. YouC 1/27/18
On growing old. ArW 7/17

ROBINSON, CHARLES MULFORD. The Fields of Flanders. Out 4/10/18

ROBINSON, CORRINE ROOSEVELT. From a motor in May. Out 5/5/15
"If I could hold my grief." PoR 8/16
The last leaf in spring. ScM 12/17
The Path that leads nowhere. ScM 4/16
To Italy. ScM 11/18
To peace, with victory. BoT 11/23/18
Tradition. ScM 8/15
Uriel. ScM 3/17
We who have loved. SmS 9/15

ROBINSON, EDWIN ARLINGTON. Alcaics. CoV 2/19
Bokardo. Poet 9/15
Demos. NoAR 1/19
Discovery. Lyr 4/19
Firelight. You 10/18
Flammonde. Out 1/16/15
The Flying Dutchman. Nat 11/9/18
John Brown. Lyr 1/19
London Bridge. Lyr 1/19
The Mill. NeR 7/2/18
Neighbors. YaR 1/19
The New jester. BoT 11/23/18
Nimmo's eyes. ScM 4/16

Old King Cole. ScM 5/15
Pauvrette. Out 6/30/15
A Song at Shannon's. Lyr 3/19
The Three taverns. Lyr 5-6/19
The Unforgiven. ScM 11/15
The Valley of the shadow. AtM 12/18
The Wandering Jew. Out 12/24/19
ROBINSON, ELOISE. April. CoV 4/19
August. CoV 4/19
Blue roses. Dia 6/20/18
The Bridge. CoV 5/18
Clytie swims at dawn. PoRA 2/17
Fatherland. Poet 10/18
June. CoV 4/19
October. CoV 4/19
Quiet. ScM 3/18
Remembering. Out 1/9/18
Resurrection. Out 3/17/15
Rose mongers. ScM 6/16
Sweat-shop flowers. Mas 9/17
The Trees. Poet 7/18
War. Poet 5/17
ROBINSON, GERTRUDE. Riding the storm. PeHJ 11/17
Tide o' the year. PeHJ 2/18
ROBINSON, PRISCILLA Q. Christmas Day. StJ 12/18
ROBY, HENRY W. Charge of the surgeon's corps. ReM 8/13/15
ROCHE, JOHN PIERRE. La guerre est finie. CoV 2/19
Life as a gage you flung. CoV 7/18
Pierrot sings. Poet 3/16
ROCKWELL, LEO L. Invitation. Colo 8/16
The Old man of the sea. Colo 4/15
RODKER, JOHN. Backtalk. Oth 10/15
Because some lover. Poet 6/17
The Betrayal. Oth 10/15
Celtic. Oth 10/15
Columbia becomes "advanced." Oth 10/15
The Compassionate pilgrim. Oth 10/15
Day-dreaming. Oth 10/15
Dead queens. Poet 6/17
The Emperor's nightingale. Oth 10/15
Excuses himself for being concerned at her going. Oth 10/15
Going home. Oth 10/15
Her first love. Oth 10/15
In defence. Oth 10/15
In a garden. Poet 6/17
Interlude-nostalgie de l'infini. Oth 10/15

The Lunatic. Oth 10/15
Pierrot. Oth 10/15
The Plot thickens. Oth 10/15
The Searchlight. Poet 10/19
Twilight I, II. Oth 10/15
Under the trees. Poet 1/16
ROE, ROBERT J. The Eternal battle. CoV 11/19
The Link. CoV 11/19
Mountains. NeR 12/31/19
Worship. CoV 11/19
ROFFEY, HALL. Qualche cosa veduta. Poet 1/15
ROGERS, ROBERT. The Pendulum. Mas 2/16
ROLLINS, LEIGHTON. Song at dusk. StJ 10-12/19
ROOF, KATHARINE METCALF. Mirage. Ain 12/19
ROONEY, JOHN JEROME. Saint Michael. CaW 9/18
ROOSEVELT, KERMIT. "To Camoens in Mesopotamia." ScM 12/18
ROOT, E. MERRILL. Rain. CoV 12/19
A Tragedy of errors. CoV 11/18
RORTY, JAMES. The Conquerors. Poet 9/19
ROSE, A.C. Moon magic. SmS 7/15
ROSENBERG, ISAAC. Break of day in the trenches. Poet 12/16
Marching Poet 12/16
ROSENTHAL, DAVID. Paliacco. Mas 4/17
The Paint box. Oth 12/17
Sylvanettes. Oth 12/17
ROSENZWEIG, M.E. Hope. StJ 1/18
ROSSER, FLAVIA. Widowed. You 6/19
ROSSNER, OSCAR H. To a dancing child. Mas 8/15
ROSTAND, EDMOND. The Tomb of Achilles-sonnets (tr. Edith Hopekirk).
     NYTM 7/25/15
The Windows beautiful. EvM 10/18
ROTH, CLARE BEACH. A Florida sunset. SoW 8/15
ROTH, SAMUEL. After. BoT 6/7/17
After the feast. BoT 5/9/17
Declaration. BoT 5/9/17
Earth longs not. BoT 6/7/17
Ghosts. CoV 2/17
Human speech. Poet 6/18
If I should speak. CoV 1/17
In memory of Auguste Rodin. BoT 11/21/17
In memory of Reginald Paget. Lyr (Supplement) 6/17
Kol Nidre. Poet 6/18
Let me be calm. Min 3/17
A Lost spring. CoV 4/17

Mourning. Mid 7-8/19
Shelley. CoV 2/17
Should you turn from me. BoT 5/9/17
Sonnets on Sinai. Men 12/17
Sundown. Mid 7-8/19
Trifles. CoV 1/17
The Wanderer. BoT 6/7/17
ROWLANDE, RUTH. Love's lure. WoW 6/19
ROYER, JESSICA. Then. EvM 6/18
RUDLEDGE, ARCHIBALD. The Friend. YouC 2/24/26
RUE, LARS. The Ideal death-bed. SmS 4/17
RUFFIN, WILLIAM E. HENRY. Columbia. CaW 7/16
RUMMONS, CONSTANCE. Souvenir. Mid 11-12/18
RUNNER, OLIVE. Freedom. Poet 9/18
RUSSELL, A.J. Song of the rough-barked tree. Bel 5/31/19
RUTHERFORD, JANET MELDRUM. A Ballad. CoV 7/19
RYDBERG, VICTOR. Heaven's blue [Himlem bla] (tr. Ernest W. Nelson).
    PoeL Summer #/16
RYDER, B.B. Coasting. YouC 2/17/16
RYDER, CHARLES T. Dedication. Bel 7/31/15
    Not without hope. Bel 10/?/15
    Whip-poor-will. Bel 3/27/15

S

"S.,A.E.H." In desolation. CaW 7/16
    To any mystic. CaW 7/16
"S.,G.H.S." On being asked for a poem. CoV 2/17
"S.,E.R." Tribute. YouC 7/27/16
"S.,E.S." To a schoolmistress. Mas 9/17
"S.,M.E." Oh, grave, where is thy victory? Par 10/17
"S.,S.S." And death came. Oth 6/16
"S.,T.J." An Answer. CaW 8/19
    Holy communion. CaW 9/18
SABEL, MARX G. Appearances. Poet 10/19
    Before the gates. CoV 1/19
    A Burlesque queen. CoV 4/17
    The Conqueror. CoV 4/17
    En passant. CoV 1/17
    Moonshine. CoV 10/17
    The Musician. CoV 7/17
    The Politician. CoV 4/17
SAINSBURG, HELEN. Epithalamion. Oth 10/15

Spring. Oth 10/15
ST. JOHN, EDNA. Communion. LoAG 4/1/16
SALESKI, R.E. What is eternal. PoeL Autumn#/15
SALMON, ARTHUR. The Pilgrims. Coll 2/2/18
SAMAIN, ALBERT. Visions (tr. Sasha Best). PoeL Spring#/15
SAMPSON, HENRY A. After hearing an anthology of fugitive verse.
    REJ 7/27/18
  All hail, romance. REJ 3/23/18
  By the sea: a memory. REJ 4/6/18
  Dawn. REJ 2/16/18
  Death of Ase (Peer Gynt suite). REJ 3/2/18
  Death of Samson. REJ 3/23/18
  Golgotha. REJ 4/20/18
  In memoriam. REJ 2/23/18
  On an old hymn book (published in 1780). REJ 5/11/18
  On the death of a young boy. REJ 4/20/18
  Poe. REJ 3/2/18
  Prologue to a book of verse. REJ 2/23/18
  Song of the liberated. REJ 10/12/18
  Sonnet to a sonnet. REJ 2/9/18
  Stephen Phillips, bankrupt. REJ 3/9/18
  To F.L.W. REJ 3/30/18
  To H.M.: in memoriam. REJ 3/9/18
  To a genial old man. REJ 5/11/18
  To R.P.A. REJ 2/9/18
  Ventosus. REJ 4/6/18
  "Victory" of Samothrace. REJ 3/30/18
  The Wave. REJ 2/16/18
SAMUEL, MAURICE. Remembering now. Lyr 8/17
SANBORN, JOHN. "Certainly, it can be done!" SmS 4/15
SANBORN, MARY FARLEY. The Barrel stave. PoJ 8/17
  He stands behind the counter. PoJ 2/18
  The Kursaal at Reims. BoT 5/9/17
  The Passing of the five senses. PoJ 4/16
  The Verses. ReM 5/18/17
SANBORN, PITTS. Grandees of Spain. Oth 4/16
  Rue des trois conils (To E.L.) Oth 4/16
  Sauce supreme (to E.L.). Oth 4/16
  Vie de Bordeaux. Oth 4/16
SANBORN, ROBERT ALDEN. Charles Chaplin. PoJ 3/17
  The Crowd. PoH 5/15
  Democaust. POJ 11/15
  The Deserted balloon. Oth 3/16
  Dust to dust. PoJ 11/15
  The Island. Poet 7.17

Little caribou makes big talk. Poet 11/19
Rain song, an Algonquin medicine song.. StJ 8/19
SARGENT, DANIEL. Peace. ScM 2/15
SARGENT, IRENE. Tom's a-cold. Colo 3/15
To the Adriatic. Colo 6/15
SASSOON, SIEGFRIED. The Dugout. CoV 7/19
Night on the convoy. Lib 6/19
SATTERLEE, MARY. Nona Goble. Par 5/18
SAVAGE, CLARA. Flight. GoH 3/18
SAWYER, RUTH. Bondage. GoH 6/17
SAXON, HELEN A. Departure. YouC 1/10/18
The Recruit. YouC 8/17/16
SCHAFF, HARRISON H. To England. PoR 12/16
SCHAUFFLER, GOODRICH C. Chalandry. Poet 7/19
SCHAUFFLER, ROBERT HAVEN. Earth's Easter: MCMXVI. Out 4/26/16
The Harmonies of heaven. Lyr 7/17
Love song. Min 4/17
The White comrade. Out 1/24/17
SCHAUKAL, RICHARD. Wind of June. Min 12/16
SCHEFFAUER, ETHEL TALBOT. The Lost kingdom. Poet 1/15
The Valiant dust. Bel 6/3/16
SCHELLING, FELIX E. From under the knife. CoV 4/18
Life. CoV 2/18
A Thought obvious. CoV 4/18
SCHMUCKER, SARA. Blow, breezes of the western sea. LoAG 11/6/16
Louise and I. LoAG 10/16/15
My lady dauntless. LoAG 7/22/16
SCHNACK, FRITZ. Echo (tr. William Saphier). LiR 3/15
SCHNEIDER, PAULINE. An Old woman in spring. Lib 7/18
SCHNITTKIND, HENRY T. A Jewish prayer. StJ 3/19
Night on the seashore. StJ 2/19
SCHOONMAKER, FRANK M. The Brook. Poet 7/17
The Bubble. Poet 7/17
O poet. Poet 7/17
To a sparkling piece of crystal. Poet 7/17
SCHUELER, ELSIE LASKER. To the Prince of Morocco. (tr. Louise M.
Knueffner.). PoeL Winter#/16
SCHUYLER, MARGARETTA. In the corner by the wall. Mas 2/17
The Little ugly duckling. Mas 6/17
Sea myths. Lib 3/18
SCHWARTZ, ISABELLA. Renunciation [Eusagung] (tr. E.W. Triess).
PoeL New Year's#16
SCOLLARD, CLINTON. An Alien. ScM 8/17

Allah, il allah. CoV 3/16
Apple-trees. Har 5/18
April song. Bel 4/20/18
An Arcadian. SmS 7/17
Autumn wanderers. Bel 11/9/18
Beckonings. Out 4/17/18
Bereavement. Par 8/18
Blow, ye blithe airs. SmS 6/18
Dawn. Par 6/18
Deep harbor. Min 6/16
Dreams. Bel 7/8/16
Dusk at the pyramids. Bel 2/6/15
An Egyptian dawn. CoV 3/17
Embers. Bel 1/11/19
The Eternal presence. Bel 1/29/16
An Exile. Har 3/17
Fairy gold. NYS 1/19/19
The Flutes of faery. Bel 1/6/17
The Frogs of Windham. Bel 2/19/17
Glamour. Lyr 6/17
Guerdons. Min 6/16
High noon at Salo il Carroccio, an Italian monthly. BoT 11/23/18
A Hill in Picardy. Ind 10.2/16
In time of victory. BoT 11/23/18
The Inn of the five chimneys. PoJ 5/16
Jericho. Out 4/10/18
Keats. Boo 1/17
The Khan. Lyr 1/19
Kinship. Bel 8/3/18
The Last red leaf. Bel 12/2/16
Love's need. SmS 4/15
The Morning walk. Bel 6/16/17
My library. Boo 1/18
My songs. SmS 9/17
The Phylactory. Par 5/18
The Piper. Bel 3/22/19
The Playhouse of dreams. Bel 3/13/15
A Prayer. Har 5/19
The Promise of March. NYS 3/2/19
Rainbows. YouC 4/12/17
Recompense. Ain 10/18
The Reed-player. CoV 4/17
The Ride of Tench Tilghman. ScM 12/15
Roses in the rain. Har 5/17
A Shop in Portland Town (to Thomas Bird Mosher). Bot 10/10/17
Snow. Ain 5/19
Song. Par 4/18

Song in autumn. Bel 10/13/17
A Southern garden. Bel 12/20/17
The Spirit. Har 8/17
A Summer song. Har 6/19
To Madison Cawein. Bel 8.12/16
The Torch. Ain 8/18
Vagabondage. Bel 5/20/16
The Voice. Out 8/25/15
The Watcher. ScM 4/19
The Whisper of the sands. Bel 12/11/15
Winter music. Har 2/18

SCOTT, CYRIL KAY. The Desert, PoJ 8/17
Lights at evening (All Saints' Day).   PoJ 8/17
Off shore. PoJ 8/17
On the San Francisco. PoJ 8/17
Spring in the high desert. PoJ 8/17

SCOTT, DUNCAN CAMPBELL. Ode on the hundredth anniversary of the
    birth of James Russell Lowell. BoT 2/19/19
To a Canadian aviator who died for his country in France. ScM 8/17

SCOTT, EVELYN. Argo. PoJ 2/19
The City at midnight. Poet 11/19
Conservatism. Poet 11/19
Destiny. PoJ 2/18
Fear. Poet 11/19
Japanese moon. PoJ 2/18
Little pigs. Poet 11/19
Lullaby. PoJ 2/18
Mail on the ranch. Poet 11/19
The Naiad. PoJ 2/18
Night. PoJ 2/18
Penelope. Oth 4-5/19
Rainy season. Poet 11/19
Ship masts. Poet 11/19
The Silly ewe. Poet 11/19
The Storm. Poet 11/19
Tropical flowers. Poet 11/19
Twenty-four hours. Poet 11/19
The Vampire bat. Poet 11/19
Women. Oth 2/19
The Year. Poet 11/19
Young girls. Oth 2/19
Young men. Oth4-5/19

SCOTT, MARGRETTA. The Black silence. PoJ 5/16
The Chimney pots of London. PoJ 5/16
David. Poet 7/19
Dolly Parker. Poet 7/19

Jeune. Poet 6/16
Pastel. Poet 6/16
Provincial. Poet 5/15
Release. Mas 10/16
Scherzo. Poet 6/16
A Vivid girl. Poet 5/15

SHANNON, JAMES. Hands. Mas 9/17

SHARMAN, LYON. The City. Poet 7/17
Cloud-loved. Poet 7/17
Fish. Poet 7/17
Magicians and the gods. Poet 7/17
Porcelains. Poet 7/17
A Swallow. Poet 7/17

SHARP, ELIZABETH. Sundown. SmS 8/18

SHAW, ADELE. The Time of the golden rod. SoW 9/15

SHAW, FRANCES. The Beckoning moon. Poet 7/15
The Birds of God. Poet 5/17
Broadway at night. Mas 9/17
The City lights from a skyscraper. Poet 7/15
The Dream gift. Poet 5/17
Grandmother. Poet 3/19
The Harp of the wind. Poet 7/15
The Last guest. Cen 4/16
Little lonesome soul. Poet 5/17
The Organ angels. Poet 7/15
The Ragpicker. Poet 7/15
Tree voices. Poet 7/15
World lullaby. Poet 3/19

SHAW, M.A. The Turning year. Mid 11/17

SHEPARD, MORGAN. Birthdays. YouC 1/13/16

SHEPARD, ODELL. The Adventurer. Bel 7/10/15
Certain American poets. SmS 1/16
Comrades. YouC 1/13/16
Earth-born. SmS 11/15
The Elm. CoV 6/18
Evening. SmS 6/16
The Flock at evening. Boo 2/18
The Goldfinch. YouC 6/7/17
God's picture. Mas 8/17
Housemates. YouC 2/3/16
In the dawn. BoT 11/23/18
Lightning. BoT 12/7/19
Love among the clover. SmS 2/15
Metempsychosis. CoV 11/19
Morning. SmS 6/16
A Nun. Poet 3/17

An Old inn by the sea. Boo 1/18
Vanitas. SmS 5/16
Vistas. SmS 4/15
Waste. BoT 11/2/17

SHERMAN, ELLEN BURNS. A Drift-wood fire. ScM 1/16
  The Earth's threnody. Nat 1/25/17
  The Second genesis. Lyr 4/19

SHERMAN, ISAAC R. Pursery Rhyme. Mas 5/16

SHERMAN, STUART. Redemption. Nat 8/3/19

SHERWIN, LOUIS. another hymn of hate. SmS 1/18

SHERWOOD, CHALRES L. My ten buckeyes. Poet 11/18

SHERWOOD, MARGARET. My soul. ScM 4/17
  The Old technique. ScM 3/15

SHIELDS, PIERRE. June. NYSB 6/23/19

SHILLABER, B.P. A Few rhymes for Mrs. Otis Merriam's seventieth
    birthday anniversary, from an autograph album. PoeL Spring#/19

SHILLITO, EDWARD. For the youthful dead. ScM 9/18
  Missing. ScM 6/15

SHIRLEY, FRANK A. In the Alameda. PoJ 2/17

SHORE, VIOLA BROTHERS. Brown arms. Ain 8/19
  In summer. Par 9/18

SHUEY, MARY WILLIS. Blue and white. Mid 9-10/18
  Patchwork. CoV 1/19
  Portrait of an old woman. CoV 1/19
  Quilts. Poet 9/18
  Re-deal. Mid 9-10/18
  The Second wife. CoV 1/19
  Welcome. Mid 9-10/18

SHUMAKER, HARRIET HALL. Perpetuated. CoV 9/16

SHUMWAY, HARRY IRVING. Seeing is believing. Par 6/18
  She had presents of mine. Par 12/17

SIAMANTO. Thirst (tr. Alice Stone Blackwell). StJ 2/18

SIEBACH, MARGARET R. Home from school.. YouC 6/8/16

SIEGRIST, MARY. The League of Nations. NYTi 3/9/19

SIFTON, PAUL F. Wolverine winter. Poet 1/18

SILL, LOUISE MORGAN. The Old woman. ScM 11/15
  Remembering. PoeL Summer#/16

SILVA, VICTOR DOMINGO. Cain (tr. Alice Stone Blackwell). StJ. 3/19

SIMMONS, LAURA. After Omar—100 yards. Par 8/17
  The Ally. ArW 6/17

SIMONS, KATHERINE D.M. See Mausi, Kadra

SIMPSON, WILLIAM H. Maytime. Poet 5/19

SJOLANDER, JOHN P. Aftermath. TeR 1/19

Blinding light. TeR 1/19
A Butterfly. TeR 1/19
The New creation. TeR 1/19
SKINNER, CONSTANCE LINDSAY. Chief Capilano greets his namesake
    at dawn. Poet 2/17
Hasheesh. SmS 3/15
I hear song waking. LoAG 12/18/15
I sing of the desired. CoV 6/19
Indian spring. CoV 6/19
Interlude. CoV 6/19
Kan-il-lak the singer to Nak-ku: Nak-ku answers. Poet 1/16
Sea song. CoV 6/19
Spring dawn. CoV 6/19
Spring to the earth witch. Poet 2/17
Summer dawn (Tem-eyes-kivi). Poet 1/16
The Wild Woman's lullaby. ScM 12/16
SLADE, WILLIAM ADAMS. Hymn for America. NYTM 3/17/18
SLATER, MARY WHITE. Barefoot sandals. Poet 11/17
Europe—a retrospect. Fra 1/17
When spring comes up the April hill. Mas 7/17
SLATON, VIVIAN VAUGHAN. War blight. NYTM 7/11/15
SLEDD, BENJAMIN. To England afterthought. NYTi 2/23/19
SLOAN, J. BLANDING. Kiss. Oth 12/17
Lee crystal. Mas 10/17
Pam. Oth 12/17
SLOAN, VANDERVOORT. Chicago winter along the Illinois Central
    tracks. CoV 2/19
SLOSSON, MAY PRESTON. The Nation's burden. Ind 1/15/17
SLYKE, B.K. In winter. Poet 2/19
Orpheus in the street. Poet 2/19
SMERKA, OTTO. From the bridge. EvM 5/16
SMERTENKO, J.J. Hunter's monotone. Nat 8/16/19
SMITH, AMY LEBREE. Branded to that typical plainsman, L.S. Poet 8/16
SMITH, C. FOX. Mother Carey. Boo 8/18
Sailor town and shipmates. Boo 9/18
Songs in sail. Boo 9/18
SMITH, CLARK ASHTON. The Desert garden. Ain 2/19
Fires of snow. Poet 7/15
Forgetfulness. Son 5-6/19
In November. Ain 12/19
In Saturn. Son 1-2/19
In the wind. Poet 7/15
The Mummy. Son 5-6/19
Sepulture. SmS 10/18
SMITH, EFFIE. Autumn winds. Har 9/17

SMITH, ELIZABETH PARKER. Songs. StJ 12/18

SMITH, ESTHER MORTON. Eastward in the "commonwealth."
    CoV 1/17
  The Fog drifts in. CoV 3/17
  The Tawny trail. CoV 11/18

SMITH, G.H. Christmas at the zoo. YouC 12/23/15

SMITH, HARRY. Monopoly. Mas 3/17
  Time-clock. Mas 3/17

SMITH, HARRY DUGDALE. A provider. Mas 7/17
  Smouldering volcanoes. Mas 6/17

SMITH, HELEN EMERY. Her gift. Ind 2/26/17

SMITH, IDA K. To Baboushka. GosD 2/28/18
  What is the news today? GosD 2/18/18

SMITH, J. THORNE, JR. Autumn in the subway. SmS 9/17
  Curse and be merry. Mas 1/17
  What do I know of the war? Mas 7/17

SMITH, JOHN. The Prussian alaphabet. LoAG 4/10/18

SMITH, LEWIS WORTHINGTON. Aglavaine. Poet 9/15
  Driftwood. Poet 9/15
  Image-imaginings. ArW 7/17
  The Road to June. CoV 5/16
  Salome. CoV 9/19

SMITH, MRS. LEWIS WORTHINGTON. The Camel driver. StJ 4/19
  The Spoils. StJ 8/19

SMITH, MARION COUTHOUY. By order of the people. Out 11/24/15
  The Final star. Har 10/16
  The Flight and the passing. PoeL New Year's#/16
  In no-man's land. Out 7/18/17
  The Legion of death (the women soldiers of Russia). Out 10/31/17
  An Old French "seventy-five." YouC 4/18/18
  Salutation. StJ 6/17
  The Supreme flight. EvM 10/18
  A Toast. YouC ?/?/15
  Vale. NYTi 2/2/19
  Verdun. Nat 4/5/17
  The Waterfall. CoV 9/17

SMITH, MAY RILEY. The Child in me. Foru 7/16

SMITH, NINNA MAY. The ugly woman. SmS 5/17

SMITH, NORA ARCHIBALD. The Compassion of the swallows
    (a Galician legend). YouC 3/29/17
  The Feet of the children. Out 4/3/18
  Morning in the market (Williamsburgh Bridge). PoR 11/16
  Moving pictures. StJ 10-12/19
  War work. GoH 4/18

SMITH, PAUL G. "Unknown." EvM 5/19

SMITH, RUTH MAURINE. City pigeons. Mid 11-12/18
  Motoring at night. Mid 11-12/18

SMITH, SAMUEL F. Symbol of innocence. PoeL Spring#/15

SMYTH, FLORIDA WATTS. The Hosts of Kamehameha. CoV 8/16

SNELLING, FLORENCE D. March in Tryon. Poet ?/19

SNOW, JANE. A Childless wife. Mas 8/17
  A Mother. Mas 8/17
  A Society woman. Mas 8/17
  A Suffragist. Mas 8/17

SNOW, ROYALL. Beacon. StJ 10-12/19
  Mystery. You 4/19
  Night-train. StJ 10-12/19
  A Tragic nocturne. StJ 10-12/19

SOLOMON, M. WALTER. Autumn. StJ 4/19
  Early spring. StJ 4/19
  Myth of snowfall. You 4/19

SOTHERN, E.H. God. ScM 1/18

SOULE, GEORGE. Solitude. LiR 5/15

SOUTH, IRA. Caribbean lullaby. ScM 11/19
  The Joke. ScM 11/19
  Regret. ScM 11/19
  Uncertainty. ScM 11/19
  Vale. ScM 11/19
  Victory. ScM 11/19
  Wisdom. ScM 11/19

SPAULDING, EDITH B. Mo leannean shee. Colo 1/16

SPEAKMAN, HAROLD. Her son. Del 10/18
  Sacrament. EvM 7/18
  The Toilers. EvM 9/17

SPENCER, LILIAN WHITE. The Closed churches. DenP 5/30/19
  Columbia remembers. DenP 5/30/19
  Columbia speaks. DenP 1/26/19
  Columbia waits. DenP 1/26/19
  Hail and farewell. DenP 2/9/19
  Matres Dolorosae Americae. DenP 2/9/19
  Villanelle. DenP 2/9/19

SPERANZA, GINO C. Endangered. Out 8/14/18

SPEYRE, LEONORA. All souls. CoV 11/18
  April on the battlefields. CoV 7/18
  The Chinese tapestry. Lyr 1-2/18
  A Crabbed song of spring. CoV 4/18
  Decoration Day. Bel ?/?/19
  Enigma. CoV 2/19

The Exposed mummy. Nat ?/?/19
The Feather. StJ 4/18
First snow on the hills. Dia ?/?/19
Fog at sea. StJ 2/18
Gossips. CoV 6/19
Judgment day. Lyr 1/19
Lover's parting. StJ 3/19
The Naturalist on a June sunday. CoV 6/19
A Note from the pipes. Nat 3/29/19
The Queen bee flies. Lyr 3/19
Rendezvous. CoV 6/19
Sea-gulls. Boo 7/19
The Summer of peace. Nat 6/28/19
Summer sorror. Cen ?/19
To Saint-Gauden's statue in Rock Creek Cemetery, Washington.
   ScM 1/17
To the victors and the vanquished. Nat 12/7/18
When Baba dives. StJ 4/18
The Workman. Nat 7/19/19

SPICER, ANNE HIGGINSON. Alan Seeger. BoT 2/21/17
Easter, 1918. ChT 3/31/18
Flanders flowers, 1918. ChT 2/2/18

SPINGARN, JOEL ELIAS. The Three dreams. Mas 6/15

SPOFFORD, HARRIET PRESCOTT. At dawn. ScM 12/17
The Empty room. ScM 2/15
The End of the road. Har 4/18
Out of the east. ScM 8/17
The Vanishing. Har 3/15

STACKHOUSE, ELSIE. Bells. Lib 7/18
Brick pathway. Lib 7/18
My garden. Lib 7/18
Pipes. Lib 7/18
Playtime. Lib 7/18
Wishes. Lib 7/18
Words. Lib 11/18

STAFFORD, WENDELL PHILLIPS. Invocation. AtM 5/15

STAHEL, LUISA REMONDINO. The Shepherdess. PoJ 8/17

STAIT, VIRGINIA. Hunger. CoV 11/19

STANLEY, HAL. Metamorphosis. SmS 10/15

STANTON, STEPHEN BERRIEN. Dauntless. ScM 6/16
The Riddle. CoV 10/18

STARBUCK, MARY S. A North Sea watch. PoJ 3/16

STARBUCK, VICTOR. Ballad of adventures. YouC 11/29/17
Home-coming. Har 12/19
The Idler. Poet 2/15

The Little houses. Cen 1/19
Night for adventures. Poet 8/16
The Poet. Poet 2/15

STARCK, MARY. A Song of winter. YouC 2/15/17

STARRETT, VINCENT. The Man who talked with Lafayette. Foru 7/17

STEARNS, HAROLD CRAWFORD. At dusk of day. CoV 10/18
Brothers. Mid 9-10/18
Caoine. SmS 4/17
Echoes. Bel 10/26/18
Enfant de Paris. Par 8/18
God is singing. StJ 6/18
I have made two songs for you. SmS 7/18
In a hospital. Mas 3/17
The Jester. SmS 8/17
A Little song. CoV 10/18
Nocturne. Lyr 3/19
A Prayer. BoT 6/1/18
Reuben Roy. Poet 11/18
The Schoolmaster. Bel 2/16/18
Sounds. StJ 6/18
There are two ladies in our little town. SmS 10/17
To you whom I dared not see. Par 12/17
The Tread of Pan. SmS 10/18
Vale, Kenneth Rand. Bel 12/17/18

STEELL, WILLIS. The Ace. NYSB 8/11/18
Books for soldiers. NYSB 9/15/18
Bring me my dead (Columbia). NYSB 9/15/18
Notify Ed. NYSB 6/23/19
A Pipe. NYSB 9/18/18
Poets after July first. NYS 2/16/19

STEPHANSON, STEPHAN G. At close of day (tr. Mrs Asak Johnson).
    StJ 6/17

STEPHENS, JAMES. Check! Har 3/15

STEPHENSON, BASIL. Dreamer of dreams. CoV 7/18
To the unknown dead. CoV 7/18

STEPHENSON, DAISY D. In December. YouC 12/21/16
Little dream ponies. YouC 4/13/16
The Sumberland sea. PeHJ 12/17
Warning Easter bunny. YouC 4/20/16

STERLING, GEORGE. Altars of war. Bel 3/29/19
Autumnal love. Ain 9/19
The Common cult. Bel 11/3/17
The Deserted nest. ScM 10/16
The Dust dethroned. DetS 3/23/19
Farmer Haynes' niece. ReM 12/15/16
The Glass of time. Bel 5/19/17

Life is motion. Oth 7/19
Meditation. Oth 12/17
Of the surface of things. Poet 10/19
The Paltry nude starts on a spring voyage. Poet 10/19
Peter Parasol. Poet 10/19
Peter Quince at the clavier. Oth 8/15
The Place of the solitaires. Poet 10/19
Ploughing on a sunday. Poet 10/19
The Silver plough-boy. Oth 8/15
Six significant landscapes. Oth 3/16
Song. Oth 3/16
Sunday morning. Poet 11/15
Tattoo. Oth 3/16
Thirteen ways of looking at a blackbird. Oth 12/17
Three travellers watch a sunrise. Poet 7/16
Valley candle. Oth 12/17
The Weeping burgher. Poet 10/19
The Wind shifts. Oth 12/17

STEWART, LUELLA. Desire. Poet 10/19
The Last hour. CoV 12/18

STEWART, MARY. The Young men lie dead. Ind 11/13/16

STIELER, K. (tr. Margarete Munsterberg). Anathema. StJ 6/17
Child voices. StJ 6/17
Dreams of wandering. StJ 6/17
Frauenworth. StJ 6/17
Moonlight night. StJ 6/17
On the shore. StJ 6/17
Resignation. StJ 6/17
Roses. StJ 6/17
Secret greetings. StJ 6/17
Silent woe. StJ 6/17

STIX, HELEN. Hendon Flying Field at morning. Tri 3/16

STOCKETT, M. LETITIA. Pomengranates. CoV 9/19

STOCKTON, JAMES LEROY. The Admonition of the hills. Bel 3/6/15

STODDARD, ANNA GLENN. The Friend. Cen 1/16

STOKES, WILLIAM H. Refuge. LoAG 6/10/16
Spenser's "Hymnes." LoAG 6/3/16

STONER, ELIZABETH R? The Crutches tune. EvM 4/19

STORK, CHARLES WHARTON. Appearances. Min 3/17
The Artist's rondeau. For 11/2/17
Autumn ballet. LiR 4/17
The Ballad of Morgan Le Fay. Lyr 7/17
The Demon steed. Lyr 6/17
A Dream of England. Nat ?/?/19
Dream song. Mad 9/17

"Just go back." Kis 2/19
"Kismet." Kis 2/19
Love—of olden days. Kis 2/19
The Marne, 1918. Kis 2/19
Mother. Kis 2/19
Mother o' mine. Kis 2/19
My dearest. Kis 2/19
"My Valentine—and thine." Kis 2/19
"No man's land." Kis 2/19
"Over the top." Kis 2/19
"Realization." Kis 2/19
"Sacrifice!" Kis 2/19
A Thought. Kis 2/19
The Trees of winter. Kis 2/19
Today we rejoice and tomorrow we mourn. Kis 2/19
Twilight. Kis 2/19
When baby came. Kis 2/19
"Where the mountain scrapes the sky." Kis 2/19
Winter. Kis 2/19
Winter days. Kis 2/19
Winter's here. Kis 2/19
"With a ting-a-ling-a-ling." Kis 2/19
"Vale!-Theodore Roosevelt." Kis 2/19
"Ye who have no sons—give your gold!" Kis 2/19
Youth learns. Kis 2/19
Youth's rosy vision. Kis 2/19
Youth's way. Kis 2/19
SUCKOW, RUTH. Guest importunate. Lyr 2/19
An Old woman in a garden. Tou 8/18
Song in October. Mid 9-10/18
SUDDUTHN, H.T. THE World League for Peace. NYTi 1/26/19
SULLIVAN, ALAN. Not for thine eyes. Har 9/18
Time hath no lance to wound her. Har 7/19
To my children asleep. Har 7/16
To one killed in action. Cen 10/17, 10/18
SUMMERS, EVE BRODLIQUE. Of ruined cities. Poet 7/19
SUTHERLAND, HARRIET. A Brave boy. YouC 6/1/16
The Dropped stitch. YouC 6/6/18
An Easter race. YouC 4/5/17
The Falling moon. YouC 5/9/18
One day at a time. YouC 1/4/17
The Puzzle of legs. YouC 7/12/17
Ten little autumn leaves. YouC 11/29/17
When Bobbie runs the car. YouC 2/3/16
When the guests are gone. YouC 8/17/16
SUTHERLAND,MARJORIE. Lilies of the valley (D.W.) Mid 8/16

The Night nurse. Mid 6/17

SUTTON, E. In prayse of ye pipe. ScM 12/15
The Trailing Arbutus. Cen 5/15
The Wind in the corn. ScM 9/15

SWAIN, CORINNE ROCKWELL. A Ballade of ambition. Cen 7/18
Ode. Cen 8/17
Rondel. Cen 8/17

SWAN, CAROLINE D. A Blaze of silver. CaW 12/18
The New wine. CaW 7/17
The Sea winds. CaW 615
The Sleeping Christ. CaW 1216

SWASEY, ROBERT. The city in summer. Oth 1/16

SWIFT, ELIZA MORGAN. Can it be true? ScM 7/16
On the prairie. ScM 5/18
The Village central. ScM 12/16
What shall I bring you? ScM 9/18

SWIFT, IVAN. The Poet's shift. SmS 5/15

SWINBURNE, ALGERNON CHARLES. Dies irae. ReM 12/13/18
Recollections. Cen 8/17

SYMONDS, HARRIET WHITNEY. In March, winds riot. YouC 3/2/16

SYMONS, ARTHUR. At the three fountains. Poet 5/17
Cleopatra in Judaea. Foru 6/16
Dreams. Poet 8/18
An Epilogue to love. SmS 2/18
In the Campagna. Har 12/16
Iseult of Brittany. PoJ 3/16
To a grey dress. Poet 8/18

SYRIAN, AJAN. Armenian marching song. Poet 8/18
"I sing of my wife while I live." Poet 6/15
The Immigrant at Columbia. Poet 6/15
The Prayer rug of Islam. Poet 8/18
The Syrian lover in exile remembers thee. Poet 6/15
Syrian mother's lullaby. Poet 8/18

SYRKIN, MARIE. The Wonder. You 12/18

T

"T.,E.D." Exaltation. LoAG 8/10/17

"T.,J." The Temple steps. PoeL New Year's#/16

TAFEL, ANNA. One blind. CoV 12/18
Rain at evening CoV 12/18

TAGGARD, GENEVIEVE. An Hour on a hill. Har 12/19

TAGORE, RABINDRANATH. The Child. GoH 5/17

East and west. Ind 10/2/16
Epigrams. Poet 9/16
Love lyrics (tr. Basanta Koomar Roy). StJ 10-12/19
My prayer. GoH 10/16
TANNER, ELEANOR. The Rose window. CaW 6/15
TATNALL, FRANCIS DORR SWIFT. The Stars before the dawn. Har 6/15
TAYLOR, C.J. The Lure of the blue Carib. NYS 2/9/19
TAYLOR, DEEMS. An Eating-song. Cen 8/17
TAYLOR, KATHARINE. Clinging earth. Nat 11/23/18
Tristram in the wood. ScM 11/18
TAYLOR, MALCOLM. Drinking song. NeR 5/8/15
Even-song. NeR 4/8/16
TEALL, EDWARD N. Allies. NYSB 11/3/18
Road and the book. NYSB 11/10/18
Senex confronts a mirror. NYSB 8/11/18
Three. NYSB 11/17/18
TEALL, GARDNER. The Threshold, new year's. StJ 1/19
TEASDALE, SARA. After death. Bel 3/4/16
Alone. YaR 10/18
April song. ReM 9/3/15
August moonrise. ScM 9/18
The Ballad of St. Kevin. ReM 12/15/16
Barter. Poet 6/17
Because. ReM 6/15/17
Bitterness. SmS 5/15
Blue squills. Poet 4/18
The Broken field. YaR 17/16
By a brook. CoV 6/18
Change. SmS 10/18
Child, child. ScM 7/16
The Cloud. Har 7/15
The Coin. NYSB 2/9/19
Come. SmS 6/15
The Cup. Har 3/18
Day and night. ScM 12/19
Debtor. YaR 10/18
Desert pools. ReM 9/3/15
Dew. Cen 5/16
Did you never know? NYSB 1/26/19
Doctors. Bel 8/28/15
Doubt. Lyr 6/17
Driftwood. Cen 12/18
Dusk in June. ReM 9/3/15
Ebb tide. ReM 6/15/17
Flames. Har 2/16
Florence. ReM 8/27/15

The Fountain. ReM 8/27/15
The Ghost. Har 10/17
Gray eyes. CoV 4/19
Houses of dreams. Mas 7/17
"I am not yours." ReM 8/27/15
I have loved hours at sea." Har 3/19
"I know the stars." Har 8/19
Immortal. ReM 9/3/15
In a burying ground. Bel 10/27/17
In the carpenter's shop. ReM 9/3/15
In a hospital. Har 3/16
In memoriam: F.O.S. ReM 8/27/15
In memory of J.L.W. Bel 1/25/19
It is not a word. Poet 9/19
Jewels. Cen 6/16
The Lamp. ReM 6/15/17
Leaves. Poet 10/15
Lessons. Poet 6/17
The lighted window. Cen 6/15
Lights. PoJ 9/17
Meadowlarks. CoV 4/19
Morning. Poet 10/15
Mothers. GoH 3/18
My heart is heavy. Poet 9/19
Nahant, 1918. Nat 9/21/18
Naples. ReM 8/27/15
The Net. CoV 4/19
The New Moon (from a hospital window). SmS 6/16
New year's dawn. ReM 9/3/15
Nightfall. SmS 5/18
A November night. ScM 11/16
Old days. SmS 5/16
Old tunes. ScM 1/19
Open windows. YaR 7/16
Other men. SmS 1/17
Pain. YaR 7/16
Peace. Cen 5/15
The Philosopher. GoH 12/16
Places. NYTr 6/1/19; ScM 6/19
A Prayer. YaR 6/16
Red maples. Bel 3/30/18
Refuge. Poet 6/17
Rest. SmS 4/18
Rome. ReM 8/27/15
Schooners. EvM 8/17
The Sea wind. SmS 2/15
Servitors. Boo 12/18

The Silent battle. ReM 3/30/17
The Singer. PoR 5/16
Song. ReM 8/27/17; Poet 9/19
Song-making. YaR 10/18
Sons. EvM 1/18
Spirit's house. Poet 6/17
Spray. Tou 7/18
Spring in wartime.
Spring rain. Cen 5/17
Spring torrents. Poet 9/19
Spring, 1918. Cen 5/18
Stars. NYSB 1/26/19
The Strawberry man. Bel 4/14/17
Stresa. ReM 8/27/15
Summer night, Riverside Drive. Cen 9/15
Summer storm. SmS 6/18
Sunset, St. Louis. ReM 12/14/17
Swans. SmS 6/15
There will come soft rains. Har 7/15
Thoughts. ReM 8/27/15; Cen 11/19
To the mother of a poet. NoAR 10/15
Tonight. McCl 8/17
The Treasure. SmS 8/18
Villa Serbelloni, Bellaggio. ReM 8/27/15
The Voice. Poet 9/19
What do I care? Poet 9/19
When we are happiest. EvM 3/18
While I may. ReM 8/27/15
Winter dusk. YaR 10/18
Winter stars. Coll 2/9/18
Wisdom. Har 2/17
Wood song. Poet 6/17

TENCH, IMMANUEL. The End of ends. Son #3/17

THAYER, STEPHEN HENRY. At the grave of Emerson. Colo 12/16
  Masqued. Colo 4/15

THOMAS, AGNES HAAS. White magic. SmS 1/17

THOMAS, BLANCHE. The City. NoAR 1/16

THOMAS, EARL BALDWIN. Behemia. Par 10/17

THOMAS, EDITH M. All souls. Har 11/18
  At the close of day. CaW 9/16
  Audience. Cen 1/15
  The Brother's keeper. NYS 2/16/19
  Demos. StJ 6/17
  The Drinking-fountain. EvM 7/18
  Fairyland fencing. NYS 3/9/19
  The Ground swell. ScM 11/15

Her tears-and mine. ScM 3/19
House beside the way. NYTi 2/2/19
The Knot in the skein. EvM 4/17
Mirror-dance. Cen 6/15
O restless leaf. Har 11/15
Other self. Mad 7/17
The Red-Cross nurse. Har 3/15
The Soul and its Lethe. NYS 3/23/19
Stars in a well. StJ 6/17
Their garments. ScM 5/16
Thistledown. Har 1/15

THOMAS, ELIZABETH H. A Lively game. YouC 3/29/17
Lullaby. Mas 3/17
Monochrome. Mas 3/17
Old woman. Mas 3/17
A song for the sea. YouC 7/19/17
Spring rain. YouC 3/23/16

THOMAS, HENRY C. A Girl dancing on the shore. Poet 8/18
Hay. Poet 8/18

THOMAS, MARTHA B. Blizzard in the country. NYS 1/19/19

THOMPSON, DAPHNE KIEFFER. Indiana. Poet 5/16

THOMPSON, RALPH M. The Daughters. SoW 6/15
The Florist. WoW 4/19
The Married man. Par 12/17
Prophets. Par 1/18
Veterans. SoW 6/15

THOMPSON, WILL. Before you came. Par 2/18
Camels. Cen 12/17
A Little town in Senegal. EvM 8/18
The Marines. EvM 12/18
My ships. EvM 4/17
North of Celebes. EvM 2/17
A spring night. Par 8/18
That Roman spring. Par 5/18
Two friends. EvM 7/18
Two sparkling eyes. Par 1/18

THOMSON, O.R. HOWARD. Betrayal and absolution. CoV 11/18
The Crisis. NYTi 4/20/18
The Modern comedy. CoV 7/16
The Procession. CoV 10/19
The Return of the victor. WiG 5/22/19

THORN, ALIX. The Stepping-stones. YouC 10/25/17

THORNE, J.H. Lyrics of love. SmS ?/15
Two little lyrics. SmS 12/5

THORNTON, KORNILLY. St. Jean de Luz. Mid 3/16

THORNTON, MARION MALLETTE. The Attic. Har 7/17
THORTON, L.M. The Reason. Par 5/18
THURSTON, CHARLOTTE W. Before the dawning. ScM 1/18
THURSTON, HELEN. Fields of France. BoT 5/1/18
TIETJENS, EUNICE. The Bacchante to her babe. Poet 3/15
  Chinese new year. Poet 12/16
  Crepuscle. LiR 1/17
  The Dream. LiR 1/17
  Festival of dragon boats. LiR 1/17
  The Great man. Cen 6/15
  The Hand. SeA 7/17
  Kang Yi. LiR 1/17
  The Most sacred mountain. Poet 12/16
  Narrative, psalm to my beloved. TeR 6/15
  New China: the iron works. SeA 7/17
  Night-watch in the life saving station. PoR 1/17
  Our Chinese acquaintance. Poet 12/16
  Poetics. LiR 1/17
  A Scholar. Poet 12/16
  The Son of heaven. LiR 1/17
  Song. SmS 12/17
  A Song of loneliness. SmS 1117
  The Story-teller. Poet 12/16
  Three spring poems, in imitation of the Japanese. TeR 6/15
  Transcontinental. ReM 7/9/15
  To a West Indian alligator. LiR 6-7/15
TINCKOM-FERNANDEZ, W.G. Blue Hill Bay. Nat 2/1/17
  War silhouettes. Boo 9/15
TIROWEN, KENNETH. Quandry. SmS 7/18
  Then and now. SmS 10/18
TOBEY, BERKELEY. The Cripple. Mas 3/17
  The Monkey. Mas 3/17
TOD. The Progress of prohibition. For 2/17
TOMLINSON, MAY. Consolation. TeR 1/19
TONKIN, KATHARINE. By some strange way. NeO 8/18
  The Way the trees break the skyline. NeO 10/17
TOOKER, HELEN VIOLETTE. Realization. Cen 6/16
TORBERT, ALICE K.C. In defense of bad housekeeping. CoV 3/17
TORRENCE, RIDGELY. Eye witness. ScM 12/16
  I will send the comforter. NeR 2/26/16
  Invitation. NeR 12/28/18
  Jean singing. NeR 12/28/18
  The Map (a fragment). PoR 10/16
  Peace. BoT 11/23/18
  Sea dream. NeR 11/10/17

The Son. NeR 2/26/16
Survivors. Poet 1/17
TOUMANIAN, HOVHANNES. When some day (tr. Alice Stone Blackwell).
  StJ 2/18
TOURKAN, BEDROS. She (tr. Alice Stone Blackwell). StJ 2/18
TOWNE, CHARLES HANSON. After reading "A Harvest of German
  Verse." Boo 10/16
Art. Boo 9/15
Beauty. Cen 7/15
The Blind. Har 7/16
Carouse. Cen 10/19
The Debutante. Har 4/19
The Hosts of April. EvM 4/17
How will it seem. Har 4/18
In an Italian garden. Cen 8/18
Life's loveliness. Har 7/19
The Little book shop. Cen 8/16
The Loiterer. Har 3/16
Mysteries. Har 6/15
New Year's Eve. PeHJ 1/18
A Northern coast. Cen 11/15
The Old loveliness. GoH 12/16
On finishing a wonderful book. Boo 11/16
On first looking into the manuscript of Endymion. Poet 4/15
On seeing a nun in a taxicab. SmS 12/17
A Prayer for the old courage. Har 3/18
The Quarrel. SmS 2/16
Ruins. Out 6/19/18
The Shell. Har 10/17
Silence. Har 4/15
The Slave. SmS 11/16
Sunday evening. EvM 6/18
Telephones. SmS 2/18
To my country. EvM ?/?/15
To one in heaven. GoH 6/17
The Victors. NoAR 4/15
TRAPNELL, EDNA VALENTINE. Echoes. CoV 9/17
Heritage. CoV 2/19
Song. CoV 6/19
Unhistoried. CoV 9/17
TRASK, KATRINA. The New banner. NYTi 4/15/17; WoW 7/19
TRAUBEL, GERTRUDE. Finality. PoJ 12/16
The Fool. PoJ 12/16
TREE, IRIS. Afterwards. Poet 11/18
Sonnet. Lib 6/19
TRENCH, HERBERT. Night on Monte Rosa, ode from Italy in

Moonshine. Par 8/17
TUCKER, ALLEN. Candles. ScM 9/18
TUCKER, IRWIN ST. JOHN. In an art museum. Lib 7/19
TUCKERMAN, FLEMING. Bella Venezia. NYH 12/8/17
  Lincoln's birthday. NYH 2/12/18
TURBYFILL, MARK. The Adventurer. Poet 8/18
  After thought. LiR 11/16
  Benediction. Poet 8/18
  Burden of blue and gold. You 6/19
  Chicago. Poet 10/19
  Counsel. You 6/19
  End of summer. Poet 10/19
  The Forest of dead trees. Poet 8/18
  Journey. Poet 10/19
  Lines written on moutainside at night. You 10/18
  Mellow. Poet 8/18
  The Moments halt a little while before the day. You 10/18
  My heart, like hyacinth. Poet 8/18
  Oh that love has come at all. Poet 5/17
  Prayer for sophistication. Poet 5/17
  Pulse of spring. Poet 5/17
  Rain night. You 2/19
  The Rose jar. LiR 6-7/16
  A Song for souls under fire. Poet 8/18
  A Song of givers and takers. Poet 10/19
  Strangers. Poet 5/17
  Thin day. LiR 6-7/16
  To a cool breeze. Poet 5/17
  Without chaperon. Poet 8/18
TURCHEN, PETER. I am a woman. SmS 2/16
TURNBULL, GRACE H. Tubal-Cain. ArW 7/17
TURNER, ALVA N. Dora Northern. Oth 7/19
  Hazel Dean. Oth 7/19
  Lillian. Oth 7/19
TURNER, GRACE. Epitaph. CoV 4/19
  Sonnet. CoV 6/18
TURNER, LIZINKA CAMPBELL. Distinguo. Lib 5/18
TURNER, NANCY BYRD. Alleluia! YouC 4/5/17
  The Best time o' year. YouC 11/9/16
  Bobby to grandma. YouC 2/10/16
  A Butterfly. YouC 5/9/18
  The Culprit. YouC 3/30/16
  A Curious gardener. YouC 4/11/18
  A Curious thing. YouC 2/17/16
  Early on the fourth. YouC 6/27/18
  Easter, 1918. YouC 3/21/18

U

UNDERWOOD, WILBUR. Bethlehem. ReM 12/13/18
UNGER, HOWARD. We who have lost. Poet 5/18
UNNA, SARAH. The Victors. Poet 12/19
UNTERMEYER, JEAN STARR. Autumn. Cen 10/17
  A Ballad. Mas 1/16
  Birth. Mas 6/16
  Caged. SeA 11/16
  Church sociable. Lib 3/18
  Clay hills. Poet 9/18
  Clothes. PoR 8/16
  Discover me again. Poet 9/18
  High tide. Mas 1/16
  A Man. Poet 1/17
  Mirage. SmS 12/15
  Moonrise. Mas 9/17
  The One wish. Mas 1/16
  The Potteries. Mas 9/16
  Rain. Poet 1/17
  Resignation. SmS 10/16
  Songs. Mas 3/16
  Spring. Lib 10/18
  The Summons. Mas 10/16
  A Teacher. Mas 1/16
  Tolerance and truth. Mas 3/16
  Zanesville. Mas 10/16
UNTERMEYER, LOUIS. Advice. Lib 6/18
  Almost. Mas 5/15
  The American. CoV 4/19
  Armistice. NeR 5/3/19
  Arts and the man. Cen 2/18
  Asleep. Bel 4/26/19
  Battle hymn of the Russian Republic. Mas 9/17
  Beauty. Poet 6/16
  The Beloved. Poet 5/19
  Confidence. SmS 5/18
  Conquest. Poet 5/19
  Creation. GoH 1/17
  Daybreak. Cen 8/18
  The Dead horse. Mas 8/15
  A Derelict. Lib 5/18
  Distances. SmS 7/18
  Driven. Cen 11/16
  Dust. Cen 4/19
  The Eighth day. CoV 4/17
  End of the comedy. Poet 5/19
  Enough. Lyr 10/17

Eve speaks. YaR 1/16
Fantasy. Bel 6/1/18
Forest lake. Cen 3/18
Habit. Lib 5/18
Hands. YaR 4/18
Havens. SmS 7/15
Highmount. YaR 1/17
Home. Poet 9/16
The Hostile hills. NeR 10/12/18
In a minor key. Mas 7/17
Insurrection in April. Lib 6/19
Ishmael. Mas 8/17
Jerusalem delivered. YaR 7/18
Joe-pye-weed. CoV 2/16
The Last day. SmS 2/18
Last wishes. Cen 1/19
The Laughers. Mas 6/15
Lovers. CoV 3/17
Magic. Poet 6/16
A Man. Cen 6/16
Nocturne. SmS 4/18
"On the field of honor." Lib 8/18
On the Palisades. Cen 10/15
On your way. Bro 7/5/18
Out of the storm. SeA 7/17
The Park revisited. EvM 11/17
Picnic on the grass. Lib 5/18
The Pilgrimage. Lib 3/18
Portrait of an American. Mas 8/15
Portrait of a child. PoR 5/17
Portrait of a Chopin-player and his audience. SmS 2/15
Portrait of a dilettante. NeR 2/26/16
Portrait of a jewelry drummer. Mas 8/15
Portrait of a patriot. Mas 1/17
Portrait of a poet. Cen 11/15
Portrait of a Supreme Court justice. Mas 8/15
Prayer for courage. Cen 6/18
Prayer for a new house. GoH 2/18
The Red seas. ReM 1/17/19
Retrospect. Cen 12/19
Return of the soldier. BoT 11/23/18
Rhetoric. NeR 3/8/19
The Road. Bel 11/18/16
The Robber. SmS 3/15
The Score board. Lib 6/18
A Side street. SeA 12/16
The Sleepers. Mas 10/16

A Street walker. Lyr 5/17
Supplication. YaR 7/19
Swimmers. YaR 7/15
Ten years old. Bel 8/10/18
These times. Foru 5/15
To a child of a revolutionist. Cen 12/15
To England (upon the execution of the three Irish poets—Pearse,
    MacDonagh and Plunkett—after the Uprising). Mas 8/16
To a gentleman reformer. Mas 8/15
To my mother. EvM 2/17
To a war poet. Mas 1/15
To a weeping willow. Mas 4/16
Toward liberty: a prayer. GoH 7/17
Truce. Mas 5/16
Victories. PoJ 1/16
The Victory of the beat-fields. Cen 5/15
The Wave. SeA 2/17
Wind and flame. Mas 4/17
Windy days. Lib 3/18
The Wise woman. Bel 5/11/18
Wonder. SmS 1/18
Words. SmS 1/18
Worship. SmS 11/17

UNTERMEYER, RICHARD. As to God, as to heaven. Poet 7/15
As to truths. Poet 7/15
A Story. CoV 6/16

UNDERWOOD, JOHN CURTIS. The Accountant. Foru 6/15
Camp followers. Foru 6/15
The Construction gang. Foru 6/15
Covent Garden, Biskra. Foru 6/15
Fleet manoeuvers. Foru 2/15
Helen, les forts. Foru 6/15
La Gitana. Foru 6/16
Mill children. Foru 6/15
The Old. Foru 6/15
The Open question. Foru 2/15

UPPER, JOSEPH. Questionnaire. CoV 12/19

UPTON, MINNIE LEONA. Hoptoad's new goat. YouC 3/29/17
The Little old melodeon. You 7/13/16
A Shower in grandmother's garden. YouC 6/20/17

UPWARD, ALLEN. Baldur. Poet 5/16
Finis. Poet 5/16
Goldenhair and curlyhead. ReM 12/14/17
Holidays. Poet 5/16

URBINA, LUIS G. (tr. Alice Stone Blackwell). Birds. StJ Autumn#/16
From "The March Toward the Ideal." StJ Autumn#/16

The Last sunset. StJ Autumn#/$6
The Mass at dawn. StJ Autumn#/16
The Moonbeam. StJ Autumn#/16
On the lake. StJ Autumn#/16
The School-teachers. StJ Autumn#/16
Spare the nests. StJ 8/18
A Sunny morning. StJ Autumn#/16
Sunset. StJ Autumn#/16
The Triumph of the blue. StJ Autumn#/16
Witchcraft. StJ Autumn#/16
UTTER, R.P. Frost without wind. NeR 9/21/18

V

"V.,D." "By their works—." For 2/17
VALE, CHARLES. "K" ("Schola novi Castelli: Nunquam non nova").
   Foru 9/15
 Requiem. Foru 10/15
 To Rupert Brooke. Foru 9/15
 Turnhurst. Foru 8/15
 The Unnamed dead. Foru 10/15
VALENTE, JOHN. In a city of iron. Foru 4/16
VALENZUELA, JESUS E. A Song of hands (tr. Alice Stone Blackwell).
   StJ 8/18
VANAMEE, GRACE D. Roosevelt. NYTi 1/8/19
VAN BUREN, D.B. The Eternal question. NYTi 2/16/19
 A Prayer. NYTi 3/2/19
VAN BUREN, FREDERICK, JR. The Convert. ScM 8/16
VAN CLEVE, FLORENCE. Tears. LoAG 9/23/16
VAN DOREN, MARK. The Librarian. SmS 10/15
VANDRAKE, R.F. The Graduate. SmS 12/15
VAN DYKE, HENRY. America for me. WoW 7/19
 The Bells of Malines. Har 12/16
 Flood-tide of flowers in Holland. ScM 12/17
 The Glory of ships. ScM 2/17
 The Heavenly hills of Holland. Har 8/17
 Homeward bound. BoT 5/23/17
 Jeanne d'Arc returns. ScM 4/17
 The Name of France. Out 9/19/17
 The Peaceful warrior. ScM 7/18
 The Proud lady. Har 12/17
 Righteous wrath. Out 1/9/18
 Storm-music. ScM 1/17
 War-music. ScM 12/16

VANNAH, KATE. His prophecy. CoV 9/19
VAN RENSSELAER, MARIANA GRISWOLD [Mrs. Schuyler]. The
    Bell-bouys speak. NoAR 7/17
  In the night. Har 5/18
  Of Shakespeare's sonnets to "Mr. W.H." Son 9-10/19
  A Song for winter. Har 12/17
  With malice toward none. NoAR 5/15
VAN SYYKE, BERENICE K. Furlough. CoV 5/19
  Home. CoV 5/19
  I stood at twilight. CoV 8/17
  If earth receives my soul again. Lib 7/19
  Unfulfillment. CoV 5/19
VAN WYCK, WILLIAM. Acrostic. LoAG 3/11/16, 6/17/16
  Ballad of dead women. LoAG 6/10/16
  Ballad of lost ideals. LoAG 9/30/16
  Ballade to Francois Villon. Ain 3/19
  A Cannibal yarn. LoAG 9/10/17
  Contrasts. LoAG 6/3/16
  Diana. LoAG 6/23/17
  The Doves. LoAG 11/25/16
  Envy. LoAG 9/1/17
  Fifth Avenue. LoAG 1/1/18
  In woodland ways. LoAG 1/1/18
  Interrogation. LoAG 7/21/17
  Jefferson Court. LoAG 1/1/18
  Jester to his bubble. LoAG 5/29/15
  Junipero Serra. LoAG 5/29/15
  Love and sorrow. LoAG 11/6/15
  Lullaby. LoAG 7/17/16
  The Mandarin. LoAG 1/1/18
  Ode. LoAG 7/7/17
  Pan makes lament. REJ 5/?/19
  Pierrot. LoAG 8/10/17
  Pierrot inconstant. LoAG 8/20/17
  Pioneers. LoAG 3/18/16
  A Rondel of parting. LoAG 2/17/17
  Sniggle Fritz. LoAG 5/29/15
  Song. LoAG 10/21/16, 12/2/16
  Song of the war spirit in man's soul. LoAG 5/8/15
  Sonnet. LoAG 7/22/16, 7/21/17, Ain 10/19
  A Sonnet for Helen. LoAG 5/12/17, 7/14/17
  South Ferry and Bowling Green. LoAG 1/1/18
  Spoon River Anthology reflections. LoAG 8/15/16
  To a blind poilu. REJ 3/2/18
  To a French governess. LoAG 6/1/18
  To myself. LoAG 2/10/17

Une chanson pour Pierrot. LoAG 7/14/17
Villanelle. LoAG 6/17/16
Washington Square. LoAG 1/1/18

VAN ZILE, EDWARD S. The battle hymn of democracy. NYTM 3/25/17

VAROUJAN, DANIEL. Alms (tr. Alice Stone Blackwell). StJ 2/18

VEDDER, MIRIAM. Choice. CoV 12/18
The Eternal comforter. Lyr 4/19
Sequence. CoV 12/18
The Watchman. CoV 12/18

VERDER, D.H. A Place to dream. CoV 10/18

VERNON, LUE F. After the storm. LoAG 2/27/15

VERSTEEG, CHESTER. To a child at play. LoAG 12/2/16

VITTORELLI, JACOPO. Anacreontics (tr. E.K. Herron). PoeL Winter#/16

VON DROSTE, ANNETTE. The Pool (tr. P.H. Thomson). PoeL
Spring#/16

VON HEIDENSTAN, VERNER. For love of country (tr. Charles Wharton
Stork). Ind 4/2/17

VON HOFHANNSTHAL, HUGO. Change. Min 12/16

VON LILIENCRON, DETLEY. From childhood (tr. Bernard Raymund).
PoeL Autumn#/15
On the lonely hallig. PoeL Spring#/16

VON LILIENCRON, LETLEV [tr. Sasha Best]. In a large city.
PoeL New Year's#/15
The Mill. PoeL Spring#/15

W

"W.,A.A." Reply to the editor. For 2/17

"W., C.D." To my father. CoV 8/17

"W.,E." Love unconfessed. Mid 5-6/18

"W.,E.R." The Ship adventure. For 2/17

"W., F.L." Shop talk. For 2/17
The Song unsung. For 2/17

"W.,M.C." Some wife to some husband. BoT 12/15/17

"W.,S.C." The Artist's rondeau. For 2/17

WADDELL, ELIZABETH. The Dear little bullet. Mas 4/15
The First gun. Mas 9/15
For lyric labor. Mas 9/17
Incarcerated. Mas 6/16
The Job. Mas 2/16
Making a safe. Mas 8/17
The Tenant farmer. Mas 8/16
Top' o' the pot. Mas 2/15

What of the night. Mas 3/17
WADE, BLANCHE ELIZABETH. Topys-turvy. YouC 2/22/17
WAGENHALS, MARGARET HAMILTON. The Music box. CoV 12/19
WAGGAMAN, MARY T. The Writings of St. John of the Cross. CaW 11/17
WAGNER, CHARLES L.H. The Path that brings me home. BoT 2/9/18
WAGSTAFF, BLANCHE SHOEMAKER. April idyls. PoJ 4/17
  Beauty like a bird. SmS 6/16
  The Dancers. SmS 7/15
  A Daughter to her mother. Min 1/17
  The Dream. Mad 8/17
  The Home-seeker. Min 4/17
  I know that you whom I love to-day. SmS 7/15
  If I could take this love from out my heart. CoV 2/17
  Imprisoned. SmS 6/17
  Joy like a wild bird. PoJ 7/16
  Mourn not for me. PoJ 4/17
  Narcissus. PoJ 11/15
  No more. Har 7/19
  Nocturne. PoJ 4/17
  O vita! O mors! Min 5/16
  The Theft. SmS 11/15
  Three marriage songs. PoJ 3/16
  When life is done. Mas 7/17
WALDO, FULLERTON L. Down and out. CoV 2/17
  On the shore. CoV 10/16
WALDRON, MARION PATTON. Holiday. Coll 2/2/18
  Victory. Cen 7/17
WALDRON, WINIFRED. Hoofs. Poet 6/18
  Swallows. Poet 6/18
WALEY, ARTHUR, tr. Chinese poems. Poet 1/18, 2/18
WALDER, ANNE KENDRICK. Waiting. Mas 9/17
  When in the quiet stretches of the night. Mas 7/17
WALKER, DOROTHY LILLIS. Song. LoAG 5/12/17
WALKER, LAURA MARQUARD. Suggested by a bas-relief of Victory.
    PoeL Spring#/15
WALLACE, JOHN H. Beyond the last trench. Mid 7/17
WALLESER, JOSEPH. Beside the master. Poet 6/17
WALLIS, J.H. Fraternity. Cen 6/17
WALSH, THOMAS. All the beasts of the forest. Lyr 10/17
  The Embers speak. Boo 10/17
  Friar Laurence O'Farrell, -Longford, 1651. PoR 12/16
  In a garden of Granada. HoG 4/16
  The Maids of honor. Bel 7/24/15
  Quis desiderio. CaW 1/17

Saint Francis to the birds. ScM 7/16
Sister Gregoria. CaW 8/15
The Stigmata. ScM 12/17
To a bird at sunset, Seville, 1886. CaW 8/15
To Francisco Goya in the Gallery of Madrid. Cen 5/15
To Joyce Kilmer. CaW 10/18
To a lady painted by Utamare. Lyr 7/17
The Village barber (tr.). NYSB 2/16/19
The Village mayor (tr.). MYSB 2/16/19
Villancice. Lyr 3/19
War. ScM 5/16

WALTER, ELIZABETH. Una ex hisce morieris. Colo 4/15

WARD, LYDIA AVERY COOLEY. In an April tomb. LoAG 4/22/16
Shakespeare. SoAG 4/22/16

WARD, ROBERT EMMET. After the journey. ScM 12/16
Eliza. Cen 10/16
From exile. ScM 5/17

WARE, A. Reflections. PoJ 6/16

WARE, GORDON. The Lullaby. SoW 7/15

WARE, RICHARD D. The Constitution of the League of Nations.
NYS 3/9/19
My dog. NYSB 12/8/19
The Pacifist. BoT 5/8/18
Where Lincoln stood. BoT 2/16/18

WARING, JOHN M. The Ghost. CoV 10/17
The Soul's goodbye. CoV 11/18
Ye highway men. CoV 10/17

WARNER, HARRY. Ferdinand and Florebelle. Par 7/18
Reductio ad absurdum. Par 4/18

WARREN, G.O. Remembering. ScM 3/19
Secrecy. Poet 3/19

WARREN, GRETCHEN. The pilgrim's way. PoeL Summmer#/15
Sacrifice. PoeL New Year's#/16
Spring and winter. PoeL New Year's#/16
The Storm. PoeL Summer#/15
The Wild bird. Poet 7/16

WARREN, KATHARINE. Frost-song. Har 10/15

WARSHAW, J. High lights in the story of Susanna. PoeL Spring#/17

WASHBURN, BEATRICE. The Road to Asola. Bel 1/27/17

WASHBURN, CLAUDE C. Flowers in France. Bel 2/5/16

WASHBURN, MABEL THACHER ROSEMARY. To Jesus, from a tired
heart. CaW 6/17

WASHINGTON, JOSEPHINE T. Cedar Hill saved. Cri 2/19

WASHINGTON, MARY J. Peace on earth. Cri 1/19

WATERS, MIRIAM VAN. Art is born. LiR 4/17

WATKINS, LUCIAN B. Ballade to Paul Laurence Dunbar. Cri 12/18
  Frederick Douglass - orator. Cri 8/17
  Paul Laurence Dunbar - poet. Cri 8/17
  Peace. Cri 3/19
  Samuel Coleridge - Taylor - musician. Cri 8/17
  Star of Ethiopia. Cri 8/18
  These, 7:17 a.m., December 11, 1917. Cri 1/18
  War. Cri 3/19

WATSON, ANNAH ROBINSON. The Queen - a mother. LivC ?/18

WATSON, EDWARD WILLARD. Gaea. CoV 5/17

WATSON, EVELYN. First confession. CoV 6/16
  Fulfillment. Son 11/17

WATSON, LUCIA NORWOOD. At mass for the soul of Sister Helena.
    Boo 10/17

WATSON, ROSAMUND MARRIOTT. The Garner. EvM 4/16

WATSON, VIRGINIA. America's burdens. Har 4/19
  Cana. Har 1/19
  Uncharted. Har 11/15

WATTLES, WILLARD. Acceptance. CoV 9/17, 10/17
  "Against my second coming." Out 10/10/17
  A Beautiful woman told me once. Mid 3-4/18
  The Bench. AQ 6/17
  Bon voyage. Mid 3/17
  The Builder. Poet 10/17
  But it is the dead love. CoV 9/17, 10/17
  Courage, mon ami! CoV 9/17, 10/17
  Dawn. Out ?/17
  Difference. Poet 10/17
  Ding dong bell. Poet 10/17
  Evoe. Mid 9-10/18
  Fragments. CoV 9/17, 10/17
  Gray old mother. Mas 8/17
  Ha! ha! CoV 9/17, 10/17
  Heaven. Poet 10/17
  How little knows the caliph. SmS 6/18
  Hrolf's thrall - his song. Poet 10/17
  I am that I am. Mid 6/16
  I do not love my love because. Mid 9-10/18
  I have had great pity. CoV 11/17
  I know a trail on Toby. HoG 11/16
  I now, Walt Whitman. Mid 12/17
  In memory, Robert Clayton Westman of Massachusetts died in France,
    August 10, 1918. Poet 11/19
  An Indian love song. CoV 5/19
  Laugh with me. CoV 9/17, 10/17

Clairaudient. CoV 11/19
Dawn. CoV 11/19
WEDGE, WILLIAM G. Indecision. CoV 10/18
WEFT, BERTHA. "Before love came." Colo 5/16
WEITBREE, BLANCHE. The Little people. LoAG 12/20/17
WELLES, WINIFRED. After sorrow. CoV 9/16
  A Child to her mother. CoV 10/19
  Communion. NoAR 2/18
  Gesture. NoAR 9/19
  Hail and farewell. NoAR 9/17
  In love. NoAR 9/18
  In an old home. CoV 9/16
  Lifetime. NoAR 2/18
  Loud youth. PoJ 4/17
  Meadow balm. Ind 2/19/17
  Moonflower. NoAR 9/17
  One voice. Cen 2/17
  Plaint. Mad 7/17
  Portrait of a lady at the piano. PoJ 4/17
  Resemblance. CoV 10/19
  School. NoAR 9/18
  Setting for a fairy tale. NoAR 9/19
  Threnody. NoAR 9/17
  To Narcissus. CoV 5/18
  Humiliation. Lib 11/18
WELLS, AMOS R. New glory. YouC 5/30/18
WELLS, CAROLYN. The Boaster. YouC 3/15/17
  The Disappointed centipede. Har 10/19
  A Merry petition. YouC 5/3/17
  On first reading the "new" poetry. Boo 6/19
  The Ultimate bliss. EvM 1/19
WELLS, CATHERINE. War. Poet 11/15
WELLS, JOHN D. Findin' fault. WoW 2/19
WELLS, STUART. The Silent army. Bel 5/22/15
WELSH, ROBERT GILBERT. At odds. Cen 3/16
  The Burial of the dead. CoV 10/18
  Conquerors. Cen 9/17
  The Djinn. Poet 9/18
  The Floor-walker. Cen 12/16
  His father's business. Cen 3/17
  Mother. Cen 9/16
  Readers. Poet 9/18
  Ripples on the Nile. CoV 10/18
  Russian sable. ReM 6/30/16
WENCLAW, RUZA. Children playing. Mas 4/17

Hills. Mas 7/17

Mountains. Mas 4/17

"The New freedom" for women. Mas 3/17

The Orator. Mas 4/17

Regret. Mas 6/17

WENDELL, DOUGLAS CARY. The Song of the sea. CoV 7/18

When the fleet comes in. CoV 7/18

WENTWORTH, C. Ante amorem. CoV 9/19

Youth. Lib 7/19

WEST, ALVIN. I wonder. CoV 6/16

Not of the wood. CoV 5/16

Yesterday. CoV 6/16

WEST, ANDREW F. Last Christmas in the holy land. ScM 1/19

WEST, H.S. Song. StJ 5/19

WETHERALD, ETHELWYN. The Adventures of figure one. YouC
8/2/17

WETHERILL, J.K. Chinoiserie. Poet 12/15

The Heart of the highroad. Poet 12/15

WHARTON, EDITH. Battle sleep. Cen 9/15

"On active service." ScM 11/18

With the tide. SatE 1/19

You and you. ScM 11/18

WHARTON, JAMES. Invocation. SmS 3/15

WHARTON, WILLIAM BAKEWILL. To England. ScM 9/18

WHEELER, D.E. The Baking of a man. Ain 2/19

Midwinter mist. Ain 3/19

The Plaint of the city trees. Ain 8/18

Triolet triste. Ain 9/18

WHEELOCK, GERTRUDE MERCIA. The Private. YouC 2/7/18

WHEELOCK, JOHN HALL. Alone. Poet 11/15

The Artist. CoV 7/19

Beethoven. Poet 11/15

Challenge. PoJ 12/15

Country churchyard. CoV 4/16

Dawn on mid-ocean. YaR 1/19

The Dead dream. SmS 8/15

Dear earth. CoV 6/18

The Dear one. PoR 2/17

Departure. PoR 6/16; PoJ 12/16

Eagles of democracy. Cen 9/19

Earth. YaR 7/17

Evening. Lyr 7/17

Exile from God. ReM 4/5/18

Holy light. Poet 6/17

Human. ScM 8/19

Hymn of man, 1917. ScM 6/17
Life. SmS 7/18
The Lonely poet. YaR 1/19
Long ago. Har 8/16
Love dethroned. You 10/18
The Man to his dead poet. CoV 2/17
Mockery. Bel 9/8/17
Moonlight night. ScM 10/18
The Moonlight sonata. Poet 9/17
Pilgrim. Boo 9/18
The Presence. SmS 11/15; CoV 6/18
Return after death. CoV 2/16
Sleep. Cen 4/17
Song at night. Poet 11/15
Storm and sun. ReM 5/31/18, 8/?/19
The Thought. PoJ 12/15; AmA 4/17
To Blanche. CoV 1/17
The Unknown beloved. Lyr 5/17
Vanished. ScM 4/17
Whip-poo-will. PoJ 12/15
Wisdom and beauty. PoJ 12/15
The World-sorrow. Har 6/18
Zenith. PoJ 6/17

WHICHER, GEORGE MEASON. At the grave of Keats. Har 5/16
  For the eighth of December (the birthday of Horace). Nat 12/6/19
  The Home of Horace. ScM 2/15
  "I heard the nightingale in temple sing." Cen 5/15
  A Spring. Har 2/17

WHITAKER, ROBERT. Twenty thousand days under the sun. Nat
  10/19/18

WHITE, ELIOT. The Blueberries of the church acre. NYS 2/9/19
  Passing Cape Maisi. NYS 3/2/19

WHITE, FLORENCE C. Doing her bit. Par 2/18
  Her text. Par 8/17

WHITE, GRACE HOFFMAN. The Beauty of Abraham Lincoln. Min 1/17
  Freedom. Min 12/16

WHITE, JAMES TERRY. Poetry. ArW 6/17
  The Thought of you. Ain 3/17
  We shall remember them. BoT 4/3/18

WHITE, LOUIS A. Music and apple blossoms. LoAG 6/24/16

WHITE, VIOLA CHITTENDEN. Dutch slumber song. PoR 8/16
  Liberated. StJ 8/19
  The Litany of the comfortable. NeW 5/18
  To a star fish. PoR 8/16

WHITELOCK, WILLIAM WALLACE. The God of battle. YouC 1/20/16

WHITESIDE, GEORGE M. Looking forward. Colo 12/16
WHITESIDE, MARY BRENT. Change. NoAR 6/18
  The Children. Har 5/17
  On the terrace. CoV 7/19
  To a princess of Egypt, in a museum. ReM 9/1/16
WHITFORD, ROBERT CALVIN. Bathsheba. Poet 5/17
  Hostilities. Mas 6/17
  The Seeker. TeR 10/19
  The Ukelele. Mas 6/17
  The Victory. SmS 4/15
  The Young wife. CoV 4/16
WHITNEY, HELEN HAY. Fireworks. Har 2/16
WHITNEY, MYRA. The Spelling lesson. YouC 11/8/17
WHITON, JULIET. For England. ScM 8/18
  A Pagan's prayer. ScM 6/16
WHITS, JAMES TERRY. Somewhere in France. Lyr 5-6/19
WHITSETT, GEORGE F. Freedom. Mas 9/17
WHITTIER, MARY IRA. At the breakfast table. PoJ 12/15
WICKHAM, ANNA. After annunciation. Poet 1/17
  Completion. Poet 1/17
  My lady surrenders. Poet 1/17
  Sentiments. Poet 1/17
  The Silence. Poet 1/17
WICKHAM, HARVEY. O sister nations! America to the Allies - 1917.
    NYSB 10/13/18
  O you who may come after. NYTi 2/2/19
WIDDEMER, MARGARET. After the war. Nat 2/1/19
  And if you came. Bel 4/22/16
  And if your heart is wearying. CoV 7/19
  Bird-flight. CoV 5/17
  Changeling. PoR 7/16
  The Child-heart. SmS 4/17
  The Cloak makers. Nat 4/19/19
  A Cyprian woman: Greek folk song. Poet 2/15
  The Dancers. Har 7/18
  Dream country. Lyr 5/17
  The Faun's sweetheart. Tri 2/16
  Forgetfulness. NYSB 2/9/18
  Garden dream. Dia 11/8/17
  Gifts. Tou 12/18
  A Girl to her mirror. YouC 1/31/18
  God's places. ReM 12/15/16
  Good-bye, my lover. EvM 12/17
  The Gray magician. Boo 4/18
  The Great ships come. GoH 2/18

When youth went. GoH 11/16
Whistle fantasy. Cen 10/17, 10/18
Wind litany. Cra 9/16
The Woman speaks. GoH 1/17
The Young singing soldiers. Tou 12/18
Youth. Bel 4/3/15
Youth-song. Poet 10/17
WIER, CLYDE. Musical mood. Colo 2/15
WILBUR, HARRIETTE. A-m-e-r-i-c-a. YouC 8/16/17
F-l-a-g. YouC 11/8/17
WILBUR, RUSSEL J. Theodore Roosevelt: Anthesis I-II; The Cross
    moving blade I-IV; Envoy; The Golden thread; The Highbrow press;
    The Liberal; Moralistic Roosevelt; The Pair of shears; The Philistine;
    Proem; Sun spots I-II; Temperment; Truth astringent; 1912; 1920. NeR
    8/10/18
WILCHINSKY, MARTHA L. Rain in the city. Mas 12/16
WILCOX, CHARLES. The Cynic. Par 6/18
Remorse. Par 8/18
WILCOX, ELLA WHEELER. Are you loving enough? EvM 8/17
Let us give thanks. GoH 11/17
Poll parrot's reply. YouC 7/27/16
Prayer at Eastertide. GoH 4/17
WILDE, GEORGIA. The Ore train. CoV 11/19
With the British at Messines Ridge. Lyr 10/17
WILKINS, BENJAMIN OGDEN. My lost love. Ain 4/19
WILKINSON, ANDREWS. Visions of the twilight. StJ 4/19
WILKINSON, FLORENCE. Blanche of the quarter. Poet 1/16
The Child in Tuscany. YouC 11/16/16
The Little cafe-Montparnasse. Poet 1/16
The Motor-man. ScM 10/18
WILKINSON, MARGUERITE. Birth. Poet 11/15
A Change song. CoV 2/17
The Charwoman. Poet 11/15
A Curse. CoV 11/18
The End. CoV 11/18
Fiat lux. Mas 9/17
Flowers. Ind 3/19/17
Food and clothing. CoV 11/18
The Food riots. Mas 5/17
For the child that never was. CoV 11/18
For great thoughts of great men. Lyr 3/19
Garments. NoAR 7/19
A Grave. PoJ 2/17
Grey rains. Mid 11/16
In passing. SmS 11/16

The Little boat. SmS 6/16
Love song. SmS 2/18
Makers of little lyrics. Lyr 3/19
My life. CoV 5/16
The Old hunter, a rune of forever and ever. Bel 4/17/15
The Old maid and the violet vendor. Mas 8/15
Once your love pleased me. SmS 1/18
Quia fuisti. CoV 5/16
Shadows. CoV 5/16
Song for my mate. SmS 7/16
Springtime - by an outsider. Bel 5/29/15
Springtime in a San Diego canyon. LoAG 6/26/15
Summer in Coronado. Poet 8/16
The Sun. CoV 4/16
Sunset. SmS 6/17
Varial to her restless lover. CoV 3/17
Vista. CoV 11/18
A Walk in springtime. SmS 5/18
Whence? CoV 4/16

WILLIAMS, ELLA ROYAL. Life contentment. Min 1/16

WILLIAMS, FRANCIS HOWARD. Lacrina victor. CoV 4/19

WILLIAMS, MARK WYNE. Clemenceau. BoT 5/8/18
Park Street and the archbishop. BoT 3/13/18

WILLIAMS, MARTHA McCULLOCH. Fairings. Ain 3/18
An Old wind. Cra 3/16

WILLIAMS, OSCAR C. At a cabaret. StJ 10-12/19
Bubbles. CoV 7/19
Dreams. CoV 10/19
I built my house upon the sand. CoV 7/19
In grief. StJ 5/19
Love's eyes. EvM 12/18
Memory. EvM 9/18
O little waif. CoV 10/19
O send me singing on the way. EvM 3/19
The Purpose. EvM 6/18
Rain and night. Bel 3/15/19
Self. EvM 5/19
Sonnet. StJ 12/18
Winter dusk. Lyr 3/19

WILLIAMS, WARWICK F. The Open path. NYH 12/26/17

WILLIAMS, WILLIAM CARLOS. Apology. Poet 11/16
Appeal. Oth 8/15
Berket and the stars. Poet 3/19
Chinese nightingale. Mas 1/17
The Comic life of Elia Brobitza. Oth 4—5/19
Complete destruction. Poet 3/19

A Confidence. Poet 5/15
The Dark day. Poet 3/19
Epigramme. Oth 2/16
Epitaph. Poet 3/19
A Friend of mine. Poet 3/19
The Gentle man. Poet 3/19
History. Poet 7/17
Le medecin malgre lui. Poet 7/18
Lines. Poet 3/19
Love song. Poet 11/16
M.B. Poet 12/16
Man in a room. Poet 3/19
Marriage. Poet 11/16
Memory of April. Poet 3/19
Metric figure. Oth 2/16
Metric figures. Poet 5/15
Naked. Poet 11/16
Night. PoJ 12/16
The Ogre. Oth 8/15
The Old worshipper. Poet 11/16
Pastoral. Oth 8/15
Play. Poet 3/19
The Poor. Poet 3/19
Romance moderne. Oth 2/19
The Shadow. Poet 5/15
Sick African. Mas 1/17
Slow movement. Poet 5/15
Smell! Poet 7/17
The Soughing wind. Poet 3/19
Spring. Poet 3/19
Stroller. Poet 3/19
Sub terra. Poet 5/15
Summer song. Poet 11/16
Thursday. Poet 3/19
Time the hangman. Poet 3/19
To a solitary disciple. Oth 2/16
Touche. Oth 2/16
Tract. Oth 2/16
Trees. PoJ 12/16
The Young laundryman. Poet 3/19
WILLIAMSON, ESTELLE M. To the Hoya, a plea for universal peace.
LoAG 12/25/15
WILLIE, WOODBINE. Prayer before an attack. Out 7/31/18
WILSON, CALVIN DILL. The Old gods. Poet 6/18
WILSON, CAROLYN C. The Funeral. NeR 4/5/19
WILSON, CHARLOTTE. Veiled moonlight. ScM 12/19

WILSON, ELEANOR ROBBINS. April. YouC 4/11/18
  Motherhood. GoH 1/19
WILSON, GLENN. Le jardin du petit trianon. LYR 10/17
WILSON, HARLOW. The Rime of the merry heart. YouC 3/8/17
WILSON, HELEN L. From a statistical clerk. Mas 8/16
WILSON, JOHN FRENCH. Week end sonnets. CoV 7/19
WILSON, McLANDBURGH. As mothers see it. NYTM 1/7/17
  The Courier. NYS 2/16/19
  Study in natural history. NYS 3/23/19
  There is no peace. NYTi 2/2/19
  There will be no place like home. NYS 1/19/19
  Three mothers. YouC 5/10/17
  We are alone. NYS 3/2/19
WILSON, MARGARET ADELAIDE. Ants in the grass. CoV 10/16
  Dan Myers. Cen 4/15
  Gervais. YaR 4/16
  Insects of a day. YaR 7/19
  Morning. PoJ 12/16
  To a record of her voice. CoV 2/16
  To the spoilers. CoV 3/16
WILSON, STANLEY KIDDER. Impromptu. CoV 5/19
  The Irrelative. Boo 9/15
WINKE, CHARLES H. The Forest fires. AmP 9/19
WINSLOW, ROSE [Jane Burr, pseud]. Fire-bird. Mas 10/16
  Geraniums. Mas 7/16
WINTER, LOUISE. Thy hands. Har 11/16
WINTERS, ARTHUR Y. Carl Sandburg. You 2/19
  Concerning Blake. Poet 9/19
  Little rabbit. Poet 9/19
  Montezuma. Poet 9/19
  The Old weep gently. Poet 9/19
  On the mesa. Poet 9/19
  Round eyes. Oth 4-5/19
  Slag. You 2/19
  White song. Poet 2/19
  Wild horses. Poet 9/19
WIRTH, GRACE MAY. Gardening. YouC 6/22/16
WISTER, MARY CHANNING. After the concert. CoV 10/19
WITHINGTON, ROBERT. Les champs de dieu. BoT 11/24/17
WOLFF, ADOLF. Fireflies. Oth 5-6/16; Poet 9/16
  Lovescape. LiR 4/17
WOLJESKA, HELEN. The Strange assembly. SmS 10/17
  The Worship of satan. SmS 8/15
WOOD, ALICE BOISE. O feet that once were wee. BoT 12/27/17

WOOD, CHARLES ERSKINE SCOTT. The Buddha. Poet 5/19
  Fuchsias and geraniums. Poet 5/19
  Kitty. Poet 5/19
  A Song of beauty. Mas 6/16
  Songs from "The Adventurer." Poet 5/19
  Venus and Mars. Mas 2/15
WOOD, CLEMENT. Alien. Lib 11/18
  Ballade of tame oats. Par 1/18
  The Battle line. CoV 8/18
  Berkshires in April. Poet 4/18
  Black night. CoV 8/18
  Coin of the year. Poet 12/17
  The Coming. Lyr 2/19
  Day of love. CoV 8/18
  De glory road. Ind 2/12/17
  The Earth turns south. Lyr 2/19
  Faces. Lyr 2/19
  Flower of the dust. Lyr 2/19
  Forest of men. Lyr 2/19
  The Golden miracle. Mas 4/15
  Harvest. CoV 8/18
  I pass a lighted window. CoV 8/18
  I would not die in April. Cov 8/18
  If the seas dry. CoV 8/18
  Into green pastures. Lib 5/18
  The Learners. GoH 3/19
  The Link. Poet 4/16
  Love the devourer. Lib 5/18
  Love-givers. CoV 8/18
  Narcissus. Mid 5-6/18
  The Night cometh. Cen 10/17, 10/18
  November. Ain 11/18
  O dear brown lands. Poet 12/17
  October. CoV 8/19
  The Painted year. Ain 10/18
  The Passing. Lyr 2/19
  The Perfect vision. Lyr 2/19
  The Poem. CoV 8/18
  Prayer. Lyr 2/19
  A Prayer. Mas 4/15
  Prelude. SeA 12/16
  The Primal goads. Lyr 2/19
  Rebirth. CoV 8/18
  Red song. CoV 8/18
  The Red tide. Ain 9/18
  Restless birth. Lyr 2/19
  The Return. CoV 8/18

Revolution. Lyr 11/17
Rose song at dusk, to S.T. CoV 5/17
Seed-time. Poet 1/17
Shadows of the peach trees. PoR 2/17
Silence. Mas 1/17
The Smithy of God, a chant. New 9-10/16
Snowfall. CoV 8/18
Soul-drift. Mid 3-4/18
Source. Tou 1/19
Spring. Mas 5/15
Spring piece. Poet 4/16
The Star-bees. Mas 9/15
To yesterdays. Par 8/17
Tomorrow. Lyr 2/19
Victory—without peace. BoT 11/23/18
Wealth of love. Ain 4/19
When I love you. CoV 8/18
A Young god. Lyr 2/19
Young moon. Lyr 8/17

WOOD, MILDRED CUMMER. Country showers. Lyr 3/19
Easy parting. Poet 8/18
The Marsh. Lyr 4/19
World without end. SmS 11/16

WOODBERRY, GEORGE EDWARD. Albert of Belgium. NYSB 12/8/18
Allies. ScM 5/18
The Cheat. ScM 9/17
The Ebb. ScM 9/17
Edith Cavell. ScM 2/16
Faneuil Hall. BoT 4/10/18
Ho! The springtime! ScM 4/19
"Immortal love." ScM 12/16
Italy. BoT 5/20/18
The Old house. Har 2/17
On the Italian front, MCMXVI. NYTM 4/1/17
The Onyx. ScM 9/17
Peace. NoAR 4/15
Piquart. ScM 2/16
The Rock. Lyr 6/17
Roumania. NoAR 5/18
Sonnets written in the fall of 1914. NYTM 9/19/15
The Statue. ScM 9/17
"Thou creative silence strange!" ScM 9/17
Three sonnets. ScM 12/16
To General Armando Diaz. BoT 11/23/18
Vale! ScM 9/17

WOODBRIDGE, HOMER. E. In a mountain park. NeR 2/1/19

WOODRUFF, HELEN SMITH. Cotton's gwiner sell. SoW 1/15

WOODS, WILLIAM HERVEY. At the door. ScM 2/19
  An Attic window. YouC 4/4/18
  Dumb witness. ScM 12/15
  The Explorer. Cen 9/15

WOODS, BERTHA GERNEAUX. The Giver. YouC 5/23/18
  Her son. YouC 4/25/18
  The Three. YouC 5/9/18
  The Waif. YouC 3/23/16

WOODWARD, NAJAH E. Absence. CoV 3/17

WOODWORTH, EDITH IVES. Aspiration. Bel 6/29/18
  Madrigal. ScM 6/15

WOOLDRIDGE, POWHATTAN JOHNSON. Evening. Boo 4/17
  Fairy shores. Boo 6/17
  Success. Boo 1/17

"WORTH, PATIENCE" [i.e. Pearl L. Pollard Curran]. Ah, garden's
    way a-bloomin'. PatW 1/18
  And the skies hung lowerin'. PatW 12/17
  At the early dawn I'd claim. PatW 3/18
  Aw! Ye seekin' babbies! PatW 5/18
  Ayle! ayle! ayle! PatW 12/17
  The Blade. PatW 4/18
  The Break of cloud. PatW 8/17
  Brother o' the path. PatW 5/18
  A Call to arms. PatW 12/17
  Christ-tide. ReM 12/7/15
  The Cleansing. PatW 3/18
  Comrade vagabond. PatW 1/18
  Day hat a merry. PatW 9/17
  Dear deaded bud, awithered. PatW 11/17
  Dear sorrow. PatW 4/18
  The Deceiver. PatW 1/18
  Dust, gray dusts, blow! PatW 1/18
  The Endless voice. PatW 1/18
  Eternal spring. PatW 8/17
  Fade thee, lights o'day. PatW 9/17
  Far hill, sunk amid the blue. PatW 10/17
  Fearing, fearing heart. PatW 11/17
  The Feet of youth. PatW 3/18
  The Fellow-player. PatW 5/18
  The Field awaved, aswayed and golded o'er. PatW 5/18
  The Flag. PatW 1/18
  Food o' moon beams. ReM 10/8/15
  Gentleness and might. PatW 1/18
  Go, rains, thou hast washed the earth. PatW 11/17
  God's twilight. PatW 9/17
  A God's wish unto thee. PatW 9/17

Golgotha. PatW 4/18
Hope and faith. PatW 4/18
Is it finished? ReM 12/13/18
Jesus by the sea. ReM 4/14/15
Larks a-singing high. PatW 5/18
Lullaby. ReM 10/8/15
The Marching hosts. PatW 3/18
Mary. PatW 12/17
The Mill. PatW 4/18
The Miracle. PatW 4/18
Mother. PatW 8/17, 1/18
My ship. PatW 8/17
My song. PatW 1/18
Oh, he is gentleness. PatW 11/17
Oh, like unto a pit am I - deep! deep! PatW 1/18
Oh, my brothers. PatW 5/18
Oh, my wee, bonny craftie. PatW 11/17
Oh thou my all. PatW 8/17
Oh, ye anguished hearts. PatW 1/18
The Old, old song. PatW 4/18
The One thing. PatW 5/18
Out from naughts do I to cunger me. PatW 4/18
Perchance. PatW 4/18
The Player. PatW 4/18
'Pon a spring's burst, a babe was fleshed. PatW 5/18
A Prayer. PatW 8/17
Resurrection. ReM 4/14/15; PatW 2/18
Satisfaction. PatW 5/18
The Scarlet sign. PatW 12/7
Sea dreams. PatW 1/18
The Seekers. PatW 8/17
Seeking, seeking, seekin', see, I be. PatW 3/18
The Shadow land. PatW 1/18
A-Singin' o'er the sea's wave. PatW 3/18
The Singer. PatW 4/18
Slumber, slumber, slumber. PatW 4/18
The Soldier. PatW 3/18
Song of my heart. PatW 8/17
Stop, oh day! Speed ye not on. PatW 1/18
Sweet hath hung the eve. PatW 4/18
Sweet spillin'. PatW 1/18
Swing thee, cradled moon. PatW 9/17
A Thank tide tale. ReM 11/19/15
Thanklessness. PatW 4/18
There's a spot afar within a sea - my isle. PatW 1/18
Tinklin' bells o' eventide. PatW 3/18
To the warsmen. PatW 5/18

A Token. PatW 3/18
Tutored not, unlearned am I. PatW 3/18
The Two sisters. PatW 3/18
The Unheard sounds. PatW 3/18
Victors ever. PatW 3/18
We two together. PatW 4/18
A Weary song. PatW 8.17
The Weeping earth. PatW 3/18
When love came. PatW 5/18
Where the cool morn bathes. PatW 4/18
Where morn's liss, lieth o'er the young spring's field. PatW 11/17
Where my love was born. PatW 1/18
Wry day. PatW 8/17
Ye dank, dank, teared, gray day. PatW 5/18
Yea, I be a-thempt o' song. PatW 12/17
WRIGHT, CUTHBERT. The New Platonist, circa 1640. NeR 8/7/15
WRIGHT, ISA L. From the lowest. ScM 9/18
   Mother's smile. PeHJ 1/18
WRIGHT, THEODORE LYMAN. An Enemy hungers. Nat 11/30/18
WYATT, EDITH. April weather. Poet 1/15
   City whistles. Poet 12/16
   Clover. Poet 1/15
   On the great plateau. Poet 1/15
   Sleep. Poet 12/16
   Summer hail, To F.W. Poet 1/15
WYATT, MARY L. Three little maids. YouC 11/22/17
WYETH, JOHN ALLAN. The Tryst. Har 5/19
WYNE, MADELINE YALE. Cotton fields. Poet 7/15
WYNNE, ANNETTE. The Analyst. Liv 9/18
   April is a baby. YouC 3/28/18
   Arbon Day. YouC 4/4/18
   Because God lavished. Sur 6/8.18
   Before it's time to go to bed. Tea 11/18
   The Blessed madman. CoV 1/19
   Crucified. Lib 4/18
   Days. Tea 11/18
   Detachment. CoV 1/19
   Each dawn. Tea 11/18
   Each new day slips out of my hand. Tea 11/18
   Every day's a little year. Tea 11/18
   A Fiddle is a strange thing. Lib 4/18
   Gardens. Dia 6/6/18
   Her veins are lit with strange desire. Mas 9/17
   I had a thought that love would come. EvM 3/18
   If ever power. Sur 5/11/18
   I'm a pirate. Bea 6/2/18

In a factory. Mas 10/17
Indian children. YouC 3/7/18
A Little song. Lib. 8/18
Love came and laughed. SnaS 4/18
Love need not have nothing else to do. Lib 3/18
May. YouC 5/9/18
My friends. YouC 5/2/18
O it's joy to sing with the hair flung free. Mas 8/17
Palos, Spain, 1492. Tea 11/18
Play. Lib 5/18
Song of a spend-thrift. Liv 10/18
Song of the elegant lady. CoV 1/19
Spectators. SnaS 8/18
To my enemy. Lib 7/19
The Torturers. SmS ?/19
Twelve months in a row. Tea 11/18
Was it the grass was green? Lyr 2/19
What grew in Joan's garden? BoT 11/23/18
When the song is done. Mas 10/17
Who would sing a gay song? Liv 8/18

X

"X107." April weather. Har 10/16
   Forgive. Har 10/16
   If such love came. Har 10/16
   My song. Har 10/16
   Spring in the city. Har 10/16
   Why? Har 10/16

Y

"Y., S." The Madman. NewR 5/3/19
YBARRA, THOMAS T. Ode to work in springtime. NYTi 5/27/17
YEATS, WILLIAM BUTLER. Broken dreams. LiR 6/17
   The Collar-bone of a hare. LiR 6/17
   The Dawn. Poet 2/26
   A Deep sworn vow. LiR 6/17
   Ego dominus tuus. Poet 10/17
   The Fisherman. Poet 2/16
   The Hawk. Poet 2/16
   In memory. LiR 6/17
   Memory. Poet 2/26
   Men improve with the years. LiR 6/17
   One woman. Poet 2/16
   The Only jealousy of Emer. Poet 1/19

The Phoenix. Poet 2/16
A Prayer for my daughter. Poet 11/19
Presences. LiR 6/17
The Scholars. Poet 2/16
There is a queen in China. Poet 2/16
The Thorn tree. Poet 2/16
The Wild swans at Coole. LiR 6/17

YEHOASH. The Art of walking (tr. T.H. Childs). StJ Autumn#/16

YOFFIE, LEAH RACHEL. A Synagogue in Poland. Nat 6/7/19

YORICK. The Song of the Civic League. ReM 12/22/16

YORKE, THEA. Self-love. Kis 2/19

YOSANO. MRS. AKIKO. The Heart of a woman of thirty (tr. Eunice
    Tietjens). StJ 3/17

YOSHII, ISAMO. Songs (tr. Eunice Tietjens). StJ 3/17

YOUNG, ANNE W. The Name. Mas 4/16

YOUNG, ELIZABETH CARRINGTON. My Snowdrop. YouC 2/1/17

YOUNG, ELLA. Fiametta. Poet 6/17
    Greeting. Poet 6/17

YOUNG, SARSFIELD. Poem of nature. SmS 12/16

YOUNG, STARK. To C. NoAr 2/17

YOUNG, WILLIAM. Before the deluge. YaR 10/15
    The Hunging. YaR ?/15
    Journeys to go. YaR 10/17

YOUNGS, MARY. The Boreen a Mharu. ScM 5/17

Z

"Z., R.A." Drifting. For 11/16

ZAMACOIS, MIGUEL. Ballad of the boy who was seven. (tr. William Van
    Wyck). LoAG 6/26/15

ZAMORA. LUIS A. A Secret (tr. Alice Stone Blackwell). StJ 3/19

ZANGWILL, ISRAEL, A Passover sermon. Lyr 11/17
    Spring, 1917. Lyr 11/17

ZARD, CLAIRE BU. Comfortable. Mas 9/17
    Hands. Par 8/18
    A Question. Mas 6/17

ZATURENSKY, MARYA. The Four horsemen. CoV 9/19
    Invocation. CoV 9/19
    A Song of parting. Ain 11/19

ZIEL, E. Abendeier (tr. E.M. Patten). PoeL Winter#/16

ZOBEL, MYRON. I am a pessimist. Cen 9/16
    My love. SmS 2/16

ZORACH, MARGUERITE. Hong Kong. Oth 1/16

Lalla ram. Oth 1/16
The Moon rose. Poet 9/18
ZORACH, WILLIAM. The Abandoned farm. Poet 5/17
Look, the sea! Poet 9.18
ZUMSTEIN, IDA McINTOSH. Magic. GoH 2/18

H
1
A4
v.500

37246

	DATE DUE		

North Hennepin
Community College Library
7411 85th Avenue North
Brooklyn Park, MN 55445

H ✓
1
A4
v. 500

THE ANNALS

© 1988 *by* The American Academy *of* Political *and* Social Science

ERICA GINSBURG, *Assistant Editor*

All rights reserved. No part of this volume may be reproduced or utilized in any form or by any means, electronic or mechanical, including photocopying, recording or by any information storage and retrieval system, without permission in writing from the publisher.

Editorial Office: 3937 Chestnut Street, Philadelphia, Pennsylvania 19104.

For information about membership* (individuals only) and subscriptions (institutions), address:

SAGE PUBLICATIONS, INC.

2111 West Hillcrest Drive   275 South Beverly Drive
Newbury Park, CA 91320   Beverly Hills, CA 90212

From India and South Asia,   *From the UK, Europe, the Middle*
write to: *East and Africa, write to:*

SAGE PUBLICATIONS INDIA Pvt. Ltd.   SAGE PUBLICATIONS LTD
P.O. Box 4215   28 Banner Street
New Delhi 110 048   London EC1Y 8QE
INDIA   ENGLAND

SAGE Production Editors: JANET BROWN and ASTRID VIRDING
*Please note that members of The Academy receive THE ANNALS with their membership.

Library of Congress Catalog Card Number 88-061071
International Standard Serial Number ISSN 0002-7162
International Standard Book Number ISBN 0-8039-3172-7 (Vol. 500, 1988 paper)
International Standard Book Number ISBN 0-8039-3171-9 (Vol. 500, 1988 cloth)
Manufactured in the United States of America. First printing, November 1988.

The articles appearing in THE ANNALS are indexed in *Book Review Index; Public Affairs Information Service Bulletin; Social Sciences Index; Monthly Periodical Index; Current Contents; Behavioral, Social, Management Sciences;* and *Combined Retrospective Index Sets.* They are also abstracted and indexed in *ABC Pol Sci, Historical Abstracts, Human Resources Abstracts, Social Sciences Citation Index, United States Political Science Documents, Social Work Research & Abstracts, Peace Research Reviews, Sage Urban Studies Abstracts, International Political Science Abstracts, America: History and Life,* and/or *Family Resources Database.*

Information about membership rates, institutional subscriptions, and back issue prices may be found on the facing page.

Advertising. Current rates and specifications may be obtained by writing to THE ANNALS Advertising and Promotion Manager at the Newbury Park office (address above).

Claims. Claims for undelivered copies must be made no later than three months following month of publication. The publisher will supply missing copies when losses have been sustained in transit and when the reserve stock will permit.

Change of Address. Six weeks' advance notice must be given when notifying of change of address to insure proper identification. Please specify name of journal. Send change of address to: THE ANNALS, c/o Sage Publications, Inc., 2111 West Hillcrest Drive, Newbury Park, CA 91320.

37246

The American Academy of Political and Social Science

3937 Chestnut Street   Philadelphia, Pennsylvania 19104

Board of Directors

ELMER B. STAATS	RANDALL M. WHALEY
MARVIN E. WOLFGANG	HENRY W. SAWYER, III
LEE BENSON	WILLIAM T. COLEMAN, Jr.
RICHARD D. LAMBERT	ANTHONY J. SCIRICA
THOMAS L. HUGHES	FREDERICK HELDRING
LLOYD N. CUTLER	

Officers

President
MARVIN E. WOLFGANG

Vice-Presidents
RICHARD D. LAMBERT, *First Vice-President*
STEPHEN B. SWEENEY, *First Vice-President Emeritus*

Secretary	*Treasurer*	*Counsel*
RANDALL M. WHALEY	ELMER B. STAATS	HENRY W. SAWYER, III

Editors, THE ANNALS

RICHARD D. LAMBERT, *Editor*   ALAN W. HESTON, *Associate Editor*

THORSTEN SELLIN, *Editor Emeritus*

Assistant to the President
MARY E. HARRIS

Origin and Purpose. The Academy was organized December 14, 1889, to promote the progress of political and social science, especially through publications and meetings. The Academy does not take sides in controverted questions, but seeks to gather and present reliable information to assist the public in forming an intelligent and accurate judgment.

Meetings. The Academy holds an annual meeting in the spring extending over two days.

Publications. THE ANNALS is the bimonthly publication of The Academy. Each issue contains articles on some prominent social or political problem, written at the invitation of the editors. Also, monographs are published from time to time, numbers of which are distributed to pertinent professional organizations. These volumes constitute important reference works on the topics with which they deal, and they are extensively cited by authorities throughout the United States and abroad. The papers presented at the meetings of The Academy are included in THE ANNALS.

Membership. Each member of The Academy receives THE ANNALS and may attend the meetings of The Academy. Membership is open only to individuals. Annual dues: $30.00 for the regular paperbound edition (clothbound, $45.00). Add $9.00 per year for membership outside the U.S.A. Members may also purchase single issues of THE ANNALS for $7.95 each (clothbound, $12.00).

Subscriptions. THE ANNALS (ISSN 0002-7162) is published six times annually—in January, March, May, July, September, and November. Institutions may subscribe to THE ANNALS at the annual rate: $66.00 (clothbound, $84.00). Add $9.00 per year for subscriptions outside the U.S.A. Institutional rates for single issues: $12.00 each (clothbound, $17.00).

Second class postage paid at Philadelphia, Pennsylvania, and at additional mailing offices.

Single issues of THE ANNALS may be obtained by individuals who are not members of The Academy for $8.95 each (clothbound, $17.00). Single issues of THE ANNALS have proven to be excellent supplementary texts for classroom use. Direct inquiries regarding adoptions to THE ANNALS c/o Sage Publications (address below).

All correspondence concerning membership in The Academy, dues renewals, inquiries about membership status, and/or purchase of single issues of THE ANNALS should be sent to THE ANNALS c/o Sage Publications, Inc., 2111 West Hillcrest Drive, Newbury Park, CA 91320. *Please note that orders under $25 must be prepaid.* Sage affiliates in London and India will assist institutional subscribers abroad with regard to orders, claims, and inquiries for both subscriptions and single issues.

THE ANNALS

of The American Academy *of* Political *and* Social Science

RICHARD D. LAMBERT, *Editor*

ALAN W. HESTON, *Associate Editor*

————————— FORTHCOMING —————————

See page 3 for information on Academy membership and
purchase of single volumes of **The Annals.**

CONTENTS

BOOK DEPARTMENT CONTENTS

SOCIOLOGY

ECONOMICS

ANNALS, *AAPSS*, **500**, November 1988

Eliminating the Federal Budget Deficit Without Recession

By F. GERARD ADAMS

ABSTRACT: The federal government's budget deficit of more than $150 billion, some 3 to 4 percent of gross national product, is widely perceived as a serious problem. This article considers policy for wiping out the deficit without recession. Simulations of the Wharton econometric model show that a tax increase would have some slowing effect on the economy but would not cause a recession. Recognition of the possibilities for monetary stimulus, once the deficit is in hand, suggests that the domestic budget deficit can be eliminated without causing an economic slowdown. On the other hand, fixing the domestic budget deficit does not automatically deal with international trade imbalance, which will require other policies and/or international policy coordination in order to be corrected.

F. Gerard Adams is professor of economics and finance at the University of Pennsylvania, where he is also director of the Economics Research Unit and codirector of the Center for Analysis of Developing Economies. He has worked extensively on econometric models of nations, commodity markets, energy, and industries. He has been a consultant to the United Nations, the U.S. Department of the Treasury, the U.S. Department of Commerce, the Federal Reserve, and the World Bank. His most recent book is The Business Forecasting Revolution *(1986).*

IN the mid-1980s, the federal government deficit burgeoned to the range of $150 to $200 billion, some 3 to 4 percent of gross national product (GNP), causing the government debt to more than double in an eight-year period. Congress has not, so far, been able to establish a credible deficit-reduction program. Only a few old-fashioned Keynesians and supply-siders,[1] a strange alliance, argue that the deficits are not serious. The economics profession and the public at large widely perceive the deficits to be excessive and dangerous. The next president will have to take the bull by the horns and undertake a serious deficit-reduction program.

The political difficulties of deficit reduction are well known; even when Congress has, so to speak, locked the cupboard and thrown away the key, it has been able to make only little headway toward a deficit-reduction target. Today, prospects of slow economic growth, a recession sooner or later, and the fact that deficit improvements in 1988 have been achieved by some one-time quick fixes threaten to worsen the budgetary outlook for 1989 and 1990. But many people fear that significant actions to increase taxes now or, if it is still possible, to reduce expenditures further could have adverse macroeconomic consequences for the economy. Some social scientists have spoken of a political business cycle triggered by the change in the presidency, curiously enough a cycle that would occur regardless of which party wins the election in November 1988. The argument is that the next president's efforts to

reduce the deficit early in the new term will result in recession.

The questions we pose in this article are, Is the deficit damaging to U.S. economic performance? And is it possible to devise a policy mix—fiscal policies and corresponding monetary policies—that would avoid or minimize the recessionary impact of deficit reduction?

THE BURDEN OF THE DEFICIT

The U.S. deficit is largely, but not exclusively, a result of the policies of the last ten years. From annual deficits running at the level of $50 billion in the late 1970s, the deficit began to shoot up as a result of the dual pressures of the Kemp-Roth supply-side tax reductions and the expansion of defense expenditure. It is clear that Congress did not have the will to make major cutbacks in entitlement programs. In the face of these forces, there was simply no hope of further squeezing domestic nonentitlement programs sufficiently to wipe out the deficit. As summarized in Table 1, the deficit reached $220.7 billion in fiscal 1986 and was reduced, but only to $150.5 billion, in fiscal 1987, largely as a quirk of the tax-reform law.

Projections of the deficit by the Office of Management and Budget call for a reduction of the deficit in fiscal 1989 and beyond. But the Congressional Budget Office, which is normally more objective on these matters, places the deficit at $158 billion in 1988 and $176 billion in 1989—assuming constant programs, the current-services projection—and other observers have projected even larger figures ranging as high as $200 billion.

Some comments on the evolution of the deficit are appropriate here. In nominal terms, the deficit today is approximately three times the figure in 1980, but

1. The Keynesians can be represented by Robert Eisner, "Presidential Address," *American Economic Review* (in press); the supply-siders by Paul Craig Roberts, *The Supply Side Revolution* (Cambridge, MA: Harvard University Press, 1984).

TABLE 1
FEDERAL GOVERNMENT REVENUES AND EXPENDITURES (Billions of dollars)

Fiscal Years	Revenues					Outlays				Surplus (deficit)
	Individual income taxes	Corporate profits taxes	Social insurance taxes	Other	Total revenues	National defense	Civilian	Net interest	Total	
1975	122.4	40.6	84.5	31.6	279.1	86.5	222.6	23.2	332.3	−53.2
1980	244.1	64.6	157.8	50.6	517.1	134.0	404.4	52.5	590.9	−73.8
1985	334.5	61.3	265.2	73.1	734.1	252.7	564.2	129.4	946.3	−212.2
1986	349.0	63.1	283.9	73.1	769.1	273.4	580.4	136.0	989.8	−220.7
1987	392.6	83.9	303.3	74.3	854.1	282.0	584.0	138.6	1004.6	−150.5
Congressional Budget Office current-services estimates										
1988	390.0	99.0	330.0	78.0	897.0	287.0	617.0	151.0	1055.0	−158.0
1989	415.0	107.0	352.0	79.0	953.0	295.0	683.0	151.0	1129.0	−176.0
1990	454.0	119.0	380.0	83.0	1036.0	306.0	731.0	166.0	1203.0	−167.0
1991	494.0	126.0	407.0	95.0	1122.0	320.0	765.0	184.0	1269.0	−147.0

SOURCE: Congressional Budget Office, Washington, DC.

as a percentage of GNP, the deficit is not correspondingly bigger—it represented 3.4 percent of GNP in 1987 as compared to 2.2 percent in 1980 (Table 2). There has been a significant improvement since the mid-1980s as spending has been checked while nominal GNP has continued to rise. But it is also worth noting that the deficit roughly equals the increase in defense spending since 1980; that net interest payments, which are rising rapidly, about equal the deficit; and that today's deficit approximately matches the cuts in income taxes of the Reagan supply-side program.

The federal deficit should not be looked at in isolation. On the positive side is that state and local governments have been running substantial surpluses, some $50 billion per year going into their employee retirement funds. On the negative side is the fact that the public sector is dissaving, that is, spending more than it is taking in, at a time when the private sector is saving very little. The public deficit offsets domestic private saving. As a percentage of GNP in 1987, personal savings amounted to 2.7 percent, whereas the government deficit amounted to 2.4 percent, 3.4 percent federal less 1.0 percent state and local surplus.[2] This picture is in stark contrast to that in some other countries. In most countries, deficits are as high, relative to GNP, as in the United States, but they are offset by a high private-savings rate. Japan and Italy are good examples. In these countries, excessive private saving is absorbed by the public sector, whereas in the United States, private and public sectors alike draw a limited savings flow.

2. The corporate sector also plays an important role in providing gross savings flows, representing 12.3 percent of GNP in 1987. The vast bulk of this represents allowances for depreciation. Foreign capital inflows amounted to 3.1 percent of GNP.

The impact of the deficit in theory

A frequent analytical approach to the deficit is to look at it in terms of the fundamental national-account identities.[3] For example, from the product side:

(1) $Y = C + I + G + X - M$

and from the resource side:

(2) $Y = C + S + T$

where Y = gross national product; C = consumption; I = investment; G = government expenditures; X = exports; M = imports; S = savings; T = taxes. Subtracting equation 2 from 1 and rearranging the terms yield

(3) $I = S + SD + CF$

where the government surplus or deficit is

$SD = T - G$

and the foreign capital inflow, or the negative of the foreign deficit, is

$CF = M - X.$

Equation 3 is an identity. It must hold at all times.

The natural, but not always correct, inference from this equation is that given S and CF, a higher deficit—that is, a more negative SD—will result in a smaller investment, or I. In effect, it is said that the government deficit crowds out investment, in this illustration, dollar for dollar. Using the same scheme, it can be said that given the low level of S and the high negative value of SD, investment in the United States is being supported almost entirely by foreign capital inflows. The inference is often drawn that to reduce its

3. For a detailed discussion of the theoretical impact of the deficit, see any macroeconomics textbook, for example, R. E. Hall and J. B. Taylor, *Macroeconomics*, 2d ed. (New York: Norton, 1988).

TABLE 2
SALIENT ECONOMIC STATISTICS

Calendar Year	Real GNP (% change)	Consumer Price Index (% change)	Unemployment (% of labor force)	Output per Manhour (% change)	Personal-Savings Rate (% of personal income)	Fiscal Deficit Billions of dollars	Fiscal Deficit % of GNP	Current-Account Balance Billions of dollars	Current-Account Balance % of GNP
1980	-0.2	13.5	7.2	-0.8	7.1	-61.3	-2.2%	1.9	0.1%
1982	-2.5	6.5	9.7	-0.5	6.8	-145.9	-4.6%	-8.7	-0.3%
1984	6.8	3.8	7.5	2.0	6.1	-169.6	-4.5%	-107.0	-2.8%
1985	3.0	3.2	7.2	1.2	4.5	-196.0	-4.9%	-116.4	-2.9%
1986	2.9	2.6	7.0	1.7	4.3	-204.7	-4.8%	-154.1	-3.6%
1987	2.9	3.0	6.2	0.8	3.7	-152.0	-3.4%	-164.8	-3.7%
Forecast (WEFA Group)									
1988	2.5	4.0	6.0	1.2	4.1	-164.4	-3.5%	-147.9	-3.1%
1989	2.4	4.8	6.1	1.7	3.8	-164.6	-3.3%	-147.8	-2.9%
1990	1.8	4.1	6.5	1.6	3.1	-155.2	-2.9%	-148.0	-2.8%

SOURCE: WEFA Group, Bala Cynwyd, PA.

12

foreign deficit the United States should put its house in order by reducing the fiscal deficit or by increasing its savings rate. Similarly, it is argued that a higher savings rate or a lower fiscal deficit will permit a higher rate of investment. This analysis contains a grain of truth, but, as is typical of simplified presentations, it misses some fundamental considerations.

There is no question about the identity. It is binding. The critical issue is whether the causation is from right to left or from left to right and whether the elements that make it up are determined independently. If *CF, SD,* and *S* are externally and independently determined, they limit *I.* A country that has little or no saving, high public deficits, and few capital inflows lacks real resources for investment. That is the situation in many developing countries, and it is applicable to some extent, as we explain further later in this article, to the U.S. economy. If, on the other hand, we see *S* or *CF* as endogenous variables responding to the economy's needs for investment capital, or if the shortage of domestic saving is offset by foreign capital, the identity does not constrain investment.

So long as the economy is operating below full employment, savings can adjust. Suppose, for example, that *S* depends on *Y* and that production depends on demand. An increase in investment spending, *I*, will stimulate demand, production, and income, *Y*, until enough savings are available to meet the desired level of investment, so long as there are sufficient real resources available, that is, so long as the economy is not bumping against a capacity ceiling. The typical textbook discussion of the multiplier describes this situation. But such a discussion also points out the implications in the opposite direction. A cutback in government spending or an increase in taxes to balance the budget tends to reduce demand. There is no automatic offset through higher investment. Unless other stimuli operate, perhaps through the monetary system, an improvement in the fiscal deficit may well be bought at the expense of a lower GNP. That is the basis for fears of a political business cycle, noted previously.

A focus on the economy's operating below capacity should not cause one to lose sight of the considerations that apply under the assumption of full employment. Samuelson's neoclassical synthesis meets this objective by arguing that monetary and fiscal tools can be used to maintain the economy near full employment. Once that target has been achieved, the available flows of domestic saving and/or foreign capital limit investment. In that case, the causation in equation 3 is from right to left. A high government deficit, given private saving, will generate capital inflows or crowd out investment.

From a long-term perspective, too, and from a cross-country perspective, if underutilization associated with recessions is considered temporary, high levels of investment are associated with high savings rates.[4] And, in turn, high rates of investment are associated with high rates of growth. Such a view is supported by economic theory and by empirical studies.

So-called growth accounting studies point clearly to capital as a major determinant of growth and productivity.[5] Consequently, there is little doubt about the long-run role of investment, and

4. "The finding that countries' investment rates are highly connected with their national saving rates has been confirmed by many studies." Michael Dooley, Jeffrey Frankel, and Donald J. Mathieson, "What Do Saving-Investment Correlations Tell Us?" *IMF Staff Papers*, 34(3):503 (1987).

5. Edward F. Denison, *Trends in American Economic Growth, 1929-1982* (Washington, DC: Brookings Institution, 1985).

presumably of saving and foreign capital inflows, as determinants of economic performance. It is feared that dissaving by the public sector—that is, deficits—will ultimately eat into the nation's growth potential.

Monetary effects. Recognition of the financial sector represents a refinement of the model that provides a mechanism through which the deficit can be seen as affecting the growth process. The argument runs through the demand and supply of money. Deficits must be financed. If deficits are financed by borrowing from the private sector, there are increased demands for available funds and the interest rate is likely to be pushed upward. If the deficit is financed, directly or indirectly, through foreign capital inflows, interest rates must be high enough to make investment in U.S. assets attractive to foreigners. Servicing a growing foreign debt may make that situation increasingly more difficult. In other words, fiscal deficits are likely to cause higher interest rates, which in turn reduce investment. Alternatively, if the deficits are financed by money creation, while there is no immediate interest-rate impact, there is inflationary potential through excessive growth of money supply.

The open economy. The increasing internationalization of the United States in the world economy represents another important element in the evaluation of the impact of the deficit. Not only is the U.S. economy wide open to trade in goods and services, but massive international capital flows have affected the process. Capital flows, the reverse of the current-account deficit, are an element in the investment identity. The resources available to the U.S. economy have been enlarged as imports exceed exports. This process began in earnest in the mid-1980s

as the tax cut stimulated U.S. economic expansion and as domestic needs were satisfied increasingly by foreign producers. As shown on Table 2, the U.S. current account, near balance in 1981, progressed to deficits of $107 billion in 1984, $154 billion in 1986, and $165 billion in 1987. The links between the fiscal deficit and the foreign deficit are complex, but the linkage during the 1980s is unmistakable (Figure 1). Unfortunately, it does not follow that fixing the domestic fiscal deficit will automatically repair the foreign balance.

Despite the drastic depreciation of the U.S. dollar, the current-account deficit has not been significantly reduced. International adjustment processes are typically slow. Once supply channels for suitable manufactured goods have been established in the low-wage countries, it will be difficult to turn purchasing patterns back to domestic sources.

Another perspective on these questions is to note that the decline in the value of the U.S. dollar would have been far greater were it not for the inflow of foreign capital. That also means that, were foreigners to lose confidence and cut back on their allocations of capital to the United States, a further decline in the dollar could be averted only with an increase in interest rates. Fears of such an occurrence motivated the stock market crash of 19 October 1987 and are still a factor in the volatility of the stock market.[6]

The U.S. economy is between a rock and a hard place. One alternative is that foreign capital inflows continue. In that case, there will be a continued buildup of

6. Nicholas Brady, chairman of the Brady Commission, has suggested that "the real trigger was that the Japanese . . . sold an enormous amount of U.S. government bonds." *Wall Street Journal,* 22 Apr. 1988.

FIGURE 1
THE TWO DEFICITS OF THE UNITED STATES

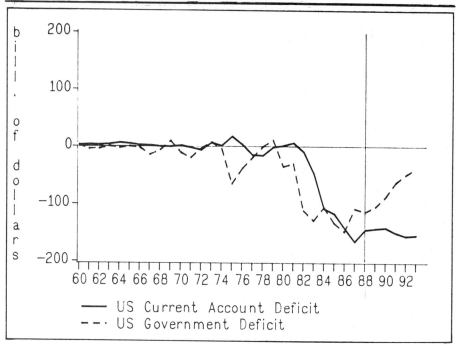

SOURCE: WEFA Group, Bala Cynwyd, PA.

foreign debt and debt-service payments. The growing interest burden should translate into ever larger required capital inflows and increasing indebtedness. Some have termed this the black-hole hypothesis. The other possibility is that foreigners become disenchanted with the United States as a place to put their capital. Insufficient capital flows would translate into U.S. dollar depreciation, which would cause inflation or higher interest rates or, more likely, both.

With these considerations in mind, most economists do not look on the deficit with equanimity.

The impact of the
deficit in practice

Is it possible to discern the adverse impact of the deficit in the U.S. economic experience of the past decade? This is a challenging and perhaps disillusioning question. We will try to answer by looking at the evidence, but we must recognize at the outset that a clear-cut answer is not available.

The promises of the supply-siders never materialized. From a fiscal perspective (Table 1), there was no upward surge of tax revenues that might have offset the reduction in tax rates. There was no broad cutback in government spending, though, of course, there was a restructuring from spending on civilian programs toward spending on defense.

If we look at economic performance (Table 2), we see significant stimulus to the economy particularly during the period from 1982 to 1985. The stimulus was a traditional Keynesian one, from demand

rather than from supply. Since 1985, economic expansion has continued but at a much slower pace, as the continued impact of tax reduction was offset by huge growth of the trade deficit. The demand stimulus was dissipated by drawing on imports.

Nevertheless, economic performance in the United States has been moderately favorable, particularly as compared to some of our European trade partners. There has not been a recession since the early 1980s. There are still no significant signs of recession in spite of the October 1987 stock market crash. Unemployment has gradually declined to 5.4 percent. While there are still pockets of structural unemployment, in many parts of the country, labor markets are already quite tight. Yet, so far inflation has not resurged. In other words, the worst forecasts of the critics of the deficit have not materialized.

Does this mean that we do not need to fear the impact of the deficit? The repercussions of the mixture of loose fiscal and tight monetary policy have been severe. Contrary to some predictions, the personal-savings rate is exceedingly low; it has declined from 7 percent in 1980 to less than 3 percent in 1987. High interest rates have held down investment expenditures. The high value of the U.S. dollar combined with stimulus to demand opened the floodgates to imports, and the precipitous drop in the dollar since 1985 is only recently beginning to have a favorable impact on U.S. exports and imports.

It is difficult, however, to pin down the effect of deficits on growth. On the one hand, as we have noted, the deficits contributed a macroeconomic stimulus during the early 1980s. On the other, they may account for the persistence of high real interest rates during much of the 1980s. There is little doubt that invest-

ment has accounted for a comparatively low share of the nation's product and, more disturbing, that the growth rate of total output and output per capita, productivity, has been very slow. Can this be called simply a sign of economic maturity, or is it the mark of a country that has squandered its resources on current consumption and military expenditures? It is not clear whether this conundrum will be disentangled. Most economists will attribute the weak growth performance of the U.S. economy to a variety of factors of which the high level of the federal deficit is only one.

SIMULATING ALTERNATIVE POLICY SCENARIOS

The challenge to the policymaker is to adjust the policy levers available so as to drive the economy at the speed and direction that satisfy, as much as possible, our multiple economic goals. This is a difficult task in view of the complex interactions and trade-offs of the modern economy. For example, achievement of a balanced budget must be weighed against its potential cost in lost output and unemployment. The difficulty is also one of timing because policies affect the economy with various time lags, an issue that is important in responding to our question of whether we can wipe out the deficit without incurring a recession.

In the past two decades, simulation with large-scale econometric models has become the standard analysis tool for policy evaluation by government officials in the Council of Economic Advisers and by business economists alike. The procedure is as follows:[7]

7. For discussion of model applications for forecasting and simulation, see F. Gerard Adams, *The Business Forecasting Revolution* (New York: Oxford University Press, 1986).

1. The model is used to establish a base projection scenario usually assuming no policy change. This simulation should be realistic, adjusted to recent values of the principal economic variables, and including the best possible appraisal of the external environment and of all the forces over which the policymaker has no control. This simulation or forecast serves as the base against which the impact of alternative policies is compared.

2. A variety of multiplier tests are carried out to evaluate how the economy responds to different possible policy measures. Specified policy changes are made, one at a time, and the results of model simulation are compared to the base simulation: for example, an increase of 1 percent of GNP in government spending will have an X percent impact on GNP, unemployment, and the price level. The timing of the result—how quickly the policy impact will be apparent, how long it will last, whether it will eventually fade away, and so forth—is also very important.[8]

3. Using the information about policy responses gained from the multiplier studies, the policymaker puts together policy scenarios aimed at achieving the economy's targets. Advanced optimal-control techniques allow the computer to select the mix of policies that come closest to the economy's various targets.[9] But the old-fashioned cut-and-try approach still seems to be the most practical procedure. Successive simulation experiments are carried out.

We begin with a realistic program of tax increases and expenditure reductions aimed at achieving budgetary balance. The initial tax increase policy assumed may not be sufficient to approximate the goal of budget balance, so an adjustment in the tax-increase assumption may be necessary. In turn, once an appropriate tax-increase policy has been reached, the simulation may leave the economy with too low a GNP and too high a level of unemployment. The policymaker must then introduce other policies—in this case, probably monetary policies—designed to stimulate economic activity to offset the recessionary impact of the tax increase. This sometimes represents a challenging task.

A variety of alternative deficit-reduction measures could be imposed. It is difficult, at this time, to visualize further deficit reduction through expenditure cuts. There is little room with regard to domestic programs, and even further steps in the direction of disarmament would probably not greatly reduce total spending in the short run. Consequently, we concentrate on tax increases as a method of deficit reduction. There are numerous possibilities with respect to taxes: taxes on income, profits, energy, value added, tobacco and alcohol, and so forth have all been considered. But the simplest and most straightforward approach is an increase across the board in personal and corporate income taxes.

In order not to damage the economy, a reasonable approach would be to reduce the deficit gradually. At the same time, a realistic target might be to maintain the other parameters of economic performance near their base projection levels. A

8. For comparison of model simulation performance, see Lawrence R. Klein and E. Burmeister, *Econometric Model Performances* (Philadelphia: University of Pennsylvania Press, 1976); F. Gerard Adams and Lawrence R. Klein, "Performance of Quarterly Econometric Models of the United States: A New Round of Model Comparisons" (Paper prepared for the Model Comparison Seminar, Washington, DC, 1988).

9. For a discussion, see D. A. Kendrick, *Feedback: A New Framework for Macroeconomic Policy* (Boston: Kluwer Academic, 1988).

6 percent rate of unemployment, a 4 to 5 percent inflation rate, and an average 2 percent growth rate may not be quite the target values that an economic decision maker might choose, but they appear to be consistent and are probably as close to optimum levels as we will be able to achieve. The foreign-balance situation is also important.

In economic theory, the policy target can be achieved so long as the number of policies available is equal to or greater than the number of targets. Thus if we seek budget balance and full employment—and other considerations do not matter!—only two policies—for example, fiscal and monetary policy—are needed. But in practice, the targets that are being sought are multiple, and the achievement of one target frequently means a trade-off with another. The policy instruments themselves entail costs, so that certain values may not be economically or politically acceptable; for example, very high marginal income tax rates may entail serious adverse incentive effects. Finally, the U.S. economy is increasingly open to the rest of the world, and domestic policies must be consistent with the international economic stability of an open economy.

THE POLICY SIMULATIONS

The objective of our policy simulations[10] was to determine whether it is possible to achieve budget balance without a recession. Our base forecast (Table 3) shows an economy with federal budget deficits declining from $156 billion in 1987 to $100 billion in 1992. This base

forecast already visualizes some upward adjustment of taxes, reflecting the assumption that the next president, regardless of his party, will have to confront the deficit situation and at least make a partial adjustment. Our concern here is whether a more complete adjustment to wipe out the deficit will lead to recession. At the same time, the economic environment remains reasonably stable with unemployment at 6 to 7 percent and inflation around 5 percent. Unfortunately, this is also a sluggish economy, with annual growth only around 1.5 percent per year from 1988 to 1990 and rising to 3 percent thereafter.

In an effort to achieve fiscal balance, we impose in alternative simulations an income tax increase. In our first alternative simulation, personal income taxes are increased by $20 billion, $40 billion, and $60 billion in 1989, 1990, and 1991, respectively. Increases in corporate income taxes are $5 billion, $10 billion, and $15 billion, respectively. While these are substantial increases as seen from the point of view of the taxpayer—tax surcharges of 15 percent on individuals and 10 percent on corporations—they are quite small from the perspective of the entire national economy. The tax increases amount to approximately 1 percent of GNP. They are, however, approximately sufficient to wipe out the deficit in the 1990s.[11] The initial simulation makes only the tax change. The response of the monetary and foreign sectors is left up to endogenous determination by the forces operating in the model. With respect to monetary policy, this means that monetary reserves are left unaltered.

The results of the simulations are summarized in Table 3. The impact of the

10. The base forecast and the policy simulations were done using the WEFA Group's Wharton model. The work was done at the University of Pennsylvania, and the author is solely responsible for the results.

11. The remaining federal deficit is offset by the surplus of state and local governments.

TABLE 3
BASE FORECAST

	1989	1990	1991	1992
GNP (billions of 1982 dollars)	3961.4	4025.1	4162.4	4288.6
GNP (billions of dollars)	5086.4	5406.1	5867.4	6347.3
GNP deflator (1982 = 100)	128.4	134.3	141.0	148.0
Federal surplus-deficit (fiscal year)	−153.5	−146.1	−121.9	−100.0
Current account (billions)	−126.4	−111.9	−106.5	−114.0
Private consumption	2582.9	2616.7	2694.0	2772.6
Public consumption	782.3	791.5	805.9	822.1
Nonresidential investment	464.3	466.2	481.7	496.0
Residential investment	186.3	189.6	199.3	208.7
Federal funds rate	8.5	7.7	7.5	8.0

NOTE: Forecast prepared at the University of Pennsylvania, April 1988.

tax increases (Table 4) is to reduce the deficit sharply to the $50 billion level in 1990 and to some $30 billion in 1992. What is the cost of this improvement in terms of economic activity and employment? Deficit reduction does not create sufficient demand elsewhere to offset the negative impact on the demand side. In this case, the impact is not sufficient to drive the economy into recession, but it is negative nevertheless. The already slow growth from 1988 to 1992 is reduced by 0.3 percent annually, so that by 1992, the level of GNP is 1 percent lower than it otherwise would have been. The unemployment rate is 0.3 percent higher. There is a favorable impact on the trade balance, amounting to some $15 to $20 billion in 1991 and 1992, but we note that the short-run impact on the trade deficit is considerably smaller than the improvement in the fiscal deficit.

Opponents of fiscal adjustment have sometimes failed to keep in mind that an improvement in the federal deficit offers possibilities for monetary improvements as well. The lessened need for Treasury financing on the one hand and the greater possibility for Federal Reserve stimulus on the other suggest that, if the fiscal situation can be improved, there will also be room for some improvement of the monetary situation. Thus we have combined in a second alternative simulation (Table 5) the fiscal adjustment examined previously with a loosening of the monetary situation, providing somewhat more money and a somewhat lower federal funds rate. The federal funds rate has been cut by 1 percent and reserves have been increased progressively by $2 billion annually, reaching an increase of $8 billion, almost 10 percent, by 1992. The results of Simulation 2 are interesting in that, even though monetary policy acts slowly, monetary easing wipes out the negative economic impact of deficit reduction. By 1992, real GNP and employment are pretty much the same in this simulation as in the base forecast. Inflation is not greatly affected. The deficit is in check; the economy has easier money.

We might have hoped that this readjustment would result in a higher level of business investment at the expense of consumption, a factor that might have produced faster growth. Unfortunately, our expectations were not fulfilled. There

TABLE 4
SIMULATION 1: TAX-INCREASE ALTERNATIVE (Deviations from the base forecast)

	Deviations from the Base Forecast				Effect as a Percentage of Base			
	1989	1990	1991	1992	1989	1990	1991	1992
GNP (billions of 1982 dollars)	-8.1	-21.5	-36.9	-42.2	-0.2%	-0.5%	-0.9%	-1.0%
GNP (billions of dollars)	-10.2	-28.7	-53.3	-68.4	-0.2%	-0.5%	-0.9%	-1.1%
GNP deflator (1982 = 100)	0.0	0.0	-0.0	-0.1	0.0%	0.0%	-0.0%	-0.1%
Federal surplus-deficit (fiscal year)	23.7	46.1	67.6	67.6	-15.4%	-31.6%	-55.5%	-67.6%
Current account (billions)	2.1	7.6	15.8	23.1	-1.7%	-6.8%	-14.8%	-20.3%
Private consumption	-6.8	-17.8	-30.5	-36.3	-0.3%	-0.7%	-1.1%	-1.3%
Public consumption					0.0%	0.0%	0.0%	0.0%
Nonresidential investment	-2.4	-7.5	-15.2	-21.8	-0.5%	-1.6%	-3.2%	-4.4%
Residential investment	0.0	0.3	0.9	2.2	0.0%	0.2%	0.5%	1.1%
Federal funds rate	-0.1	-0.2	-0.3	-0.5	-0.6%	-2.4%	-4.5%	-5.6%

NOTE: Simulation prepared at the University of Pennsylvania, April 1988.

TABLE 5
SIMULATION 2: TAX-INCREASE AND MONETARY STIMULUS ALTERNATIVE (Deviations from the base forecast)

	Deviations from the Base Forecast				Effect as a Percentage of Base			
	1989	1990	1991	1992	1989	1990	1991	1992
GNP (billions of 1982 dollars)	−5.5	−1.1	0.3	3.1	−0.1%	−0.0%	0.0%	0.1%
GNP (billions of dollars)	−6.4	1.4	6.0	12.8	−0.1%	0.0%	0.1%	0.2%
GNP deflator (1982 = 100)	0.0	0.1	0.1	0.2	0.0%	0.1%	0.1%	0.1%
Federal surplus-deficit (fiscal year)	26.1	57.5	91.1	100.6	−17.0%	−39.4%	−74.7%	−100.6%
Current account (billions)	1.9	4.0	6.5	9.3	−1.5%	−3.6%	−6.1%	−8.2%
Private consumption	−6.3	−13.2	−22.4	−25.5	−0.2%	−0.5%	−0.8%	−0.9%
Public consumption								
Nonresidential investment	−1.8	−1.9	−1.3	0.7	−0.4%	−0.4%	−0.3%	0.1%
Residential investment	1.9	11.2	19.6	24.8	1.0%	5.9%	9.8%	11.9%
Federal funds rate	0.6	−1.0	−1.0	−1.0	7.3%	−13.1%	−13.3%	−12.5%

NOTE: Simulation prepared at the University of Pennsylvania, April 1988.

is a little less consumption, but this translates into higher residential construction, which is most sensitive to the financial situation, rather than business investment, which is largely motivated by demand and requirements for production facilities.

CONCLUSION

What can we conclude from this exercise? Can we wipe out the deficit without recession? Wiping out the deficit with a program of deficit reduction, in the absence of other adjustments, does have a negative effect on economic activity, but quantitatively the economy is large and the deficit, though substantial, is not as important relative to the economy as it once was. Given the assumption of a reasonably healthy economy, wiping out the deficit does not produce an outright recession, only a somewhat slower economy. Once we recognize that a monetary stimulus will be possible—indeed likely, once the deficit is in hand—we see that even the modest recessionary impact of deficit reduction can be offset.

Will wiping out the fiscal deficit take care of the international deficit? The results of the simulations would suggest that there may be a modest improvement, but, not surprising, that improvement largely disappears when the monetary stimulus is used to offset the negative impact of deficit adjustment. This would suggest that other tools are necessary to take care of the external deficit. It should be noted that substantial depreciation of the dollar has already taken place and that further effects on the balance of payments are still to come. Nevertheless, the simulations do not lend encouragement to the notion that once the fiscal deficit is in order, the external deficit—current account—will automatically be fixed as well.

Finally, it is important to note that the time for unilateral policy is past. Policy action in the United States on the deficit needs to be coordinated with policy actions by other countries seeking to maximize jointly the objectives of the United States and its trade partners.

ANNALS, *AAPSS*, **500**, November 1988

Can the U.S. Dollar Survive as a World Reserve Currency?

By FREDERICK HELDRING

ABSTRACT: Following World War II, the United States emerged as the world's single, dominant economic power. That role is diminishing, however, as European nations, Japan, and newly industrialized countries of the Pacific basin begin to exert more economic influence in the world marketplace. As we move to an age of more shared economic power, it seems unlikely the U.S. dollar will survive as the only world reserve currency. A natural extension of this pluralism would be the development of a single, international currency that would be freely accepted by all nations for the purposes of international transactions. An international institution would issue the currency and maintain the support and cooperation of member nations.

Frederick Heldring is chairman of Philadelphia National Bank (PNB) and vice chairman of CoreStates Financial Corp. He began his career with PNB in 1950. Mr. Heldring is chairman of the Greater Philadelphia International Network and president of the Global Interdependence Center. He is a member of the Council on Foreign Relations in New York and of the Executive Committee of the Philadelphia Committee on Foreign Relations. He received a B.S. degree from the University of Pennsylvania's Wharton School in 1951, having previously attended the Free University of Amsterdam.

THE evolution or elevation of the dollar to the role of world reserve currency mirrored the rise of the United States as a world economic and political power in the post-World War II period. The status of a currency as a reserve currency is achieved by a gradual process that leads to general acceptance of the currency, based on the markets' confidence in a currency and the sovereign government that stands behind it. Like the dollar's rise to the status of reserve currency, its relative demise in that role is—and will continue to be—a gradual one that mirrors our nation's shrinking role as the dominant economic power in the free world. As the United States shares its economic and political power with other countries, the role of the dollar as the world reserve currency will inevitably recede. For reasons I will discuss, I view this evolution as both natural and desirable.

THE ROLE OF WORLD RESERVE CURRENCY

The role of reserve currency carries with it certain responsibilities that have the potential for becoming burdens. A reserve currency acts as the anchor to the world monetary system, and the country managing it has a responsibility to keep its economic house in order. The most pivotal part of that responsibility is for the central bank to preserve the purchasing power of the reserve currency, that is, to avoid inflation as well as to maintain world confidence in the government's commitment to do so. Otherwise, the anchor for the world monetary system is either lurching about, as in the case of the large swings in the inflation rate that occurred in the 1970s and early 1980s, or it is drifting, as in the late 1960s, when the inflation rate gradually climbed upward,

so-called creeping inflation. Neither situation represents a very effective anchor, for boats or for monetary systems. The domestic economic problems caused by inflation and the associated movements in interest rates and exchange rates mean that it is always and everywhere advisable for a nation to avoid policy-induced swings in the purchasing power of its currency. In the case of a reserve currency, however, these disruptions become international in scope as the movements in prices, interest rates, and exchange rates have important and immediate worldwide implications.

In addition, reserve-currency status creates the desirability of a nation's keeping an orderly economic house in other areas as well. With respect to fiscal policy, not only is prudent management of fiscal deficits called for, but responsible government spending and tax policies are also desirable. For example, a balanced fiscal budget in which excessive, wasteful government spending was paid for by high or distorting tax rates would not be desirable. To function effectively as a reserve currency, financial markets are needed that are well organized, efficient, and relatively free of capital controls and restrictions so that capital can flow freely in and out of assets denominated in its currency. Similarly, the markets for tradable goods need to be relatively free of protectionist restraints so that goods as well as capital can flow in and out of the country without artificial barriers. Finally, of course, in order for a currency to serve in a reserve role, considerable confidence must exist around the world in the stability and efficacy of the political system that underpins the currency as well as the institutions and financial system that facilitate it.

Needless to say, the United States receives rather mixed reviews with respect

to its handling of these responsibilities. We must be given high marks for providing an open and competitive system of financial markets, relatively free of controls and restrictions, and for the political and institutional stability that underwrites confidence in the dollar and the U.S. financial system. While we are by no means pure when it comes to protectionist and restrictive trade policies, compared to other countries, our goods markets are relatively open.

I would not say, however, that the United States has done an especially good job promoting the kind of monetary and fiscal discipline that is desirable for a reserve currency. The rise in inflation and interest rates in the 1970s and the economic dislocation associated with reducing the inflation rate in the 1980s introduced considerable instability in the world financial system; while the blame for these problems cannot be solely attributed to U.S. policies, U.S. monetary policy certainly contributed importantly to them. In the 1980s, the emergence of record U.S. budget and current-account deficits are similarly contributing to worldwide external imbalances, the adjustment of which has only begun.

The responsibilities to the world monetary system that are associated with reserve-currency status—such as noninflationary monetary policy, fiscal discipline, and so on—generally focus on long-term concerns. These goals therefore frequently conflict with domestic economic policy desires because the latter are usually focused on short-term, often political, goals. The rising inflation and interest rates of the 1970s provide a good example of this conflict. Long-term monetary discipline was repeatedly abandoned for short-term economic and political expediencies to the detriment of our do-

mestic prosperity as well as our international responsibilities.

The question of whether or not the U.S. dollar will continue to be the world reserve currency, whether it will share that role with other currencies, or whether some other currency will come to dominate world financial activities will ultimately be decided by the market. Because reserve-currency status is primarily based on international acceptability and confidence, by nature that status arises from natural market forces.

The status of the dollar as the primary world reserve currency is already diminishing, and my judgment is that we will see that trend continue, much as we saw the influence of the British pound diminish. It is also my view that this is a natural and desirable outcome. Functioning as the world's sole reserve currency carries a certain burden as well as responsibility because while providing, it is hoped, an anchor for the world monetary system, a reserve currency itself—absent a definitional constraint such as the gold standard—has no such anchor. That anchor must be internally provided by appropriate and responsible economic policies, a task at which we have not always been successful. Thus I believe it could be beneficial to both the United States and the world at large if other currencies begin to share the function of reserve currency. As the relative role of the United States in the world economy shrinks, other currencies will naturally emerge and take on more prominence in international finance. The United States continues to have a large and vibrant economy, so it seems likely that the U.S. economy and the dollar will increasingly share the world stage, rather than relinquish it. In my view, it would be best for the United States as well as the world

TABLE 1
WORLD GROSS DOMESTIC PRODUCT

	Billions of 1980 U.S. Dollars			Percentage Share of World Gross Domestic Product		
	1960	1969	1986	1960	1969	1986
World	4,520	7,448	13,468	100.0	100.0	100.0
Developed nations	3,525	5,507	8,989	78.0	73.9	66.7
United States	1,418	2,063	3,157	31.4	27.7	23.4
Developing nations	226	707	2,155	5.0	9.5	16.0
Centrally planned economies	769	1,234	2,324	17.0	16.6	17.3

SOURCES: International Monetary Fund, Organization for Economic Cooperation and Development, and CoreStates Economics.

if the dollar became simply another, albeit important, currency in a world in which many prominent currencies share the function of reserve currency. The U.S. dollar can and should become a planet, traveling as an equal with other currencies, rather than the sun around which all others revolve.

GROWING WORLD
INTERDEPENDENCE

While many of the proclamations about the demise of the U.S. economy are exaggerated, there is no question that the relative U.S. dominance of the world economy has been diminishing. The size of the U.S. trade deficit and the emergence of the United States as a net debtor nation have drawn attention to the declining U.S. role, but this decline is by no means a recent phenomenon—it has generally been occurring for nearly three decades. Table 1 provides some information on world gross domestic product since 1960. (See Table 1.) As can be seen in the table, the relative role of developed nations as a whole has receded while the share of production originating in the developing nations has grown. In par-

ticular, the U.S. share of total world output has declined from about 31 percent in 1960 to about 23 percent in 1986. Within the category of developed countries, the U.S. share of output has fallen from more than 40 percent in 1960 to 35 percent in 1986. While the dollar volume of world exports has increased 16-fold in the past twenty years, the U.S. share of world exports has dropped from 17 percent to less than 11 percent, while U.S. imports have risen from 13 percent to nearly 19 percent of total world imports.

Along with the declining prominence of the United States in the world economy, the interdependence among the economies has become increasingly evident. This is in many ways a natural by-product of specialization and technological change, rather than a result of any particular event. A country is never isolated either from the international implications of its own economic policies or from the effects of others' policies. The technological revolution in information transmission and processing has facilitated an integration of world financial markets such that interest rates and exchange rates reflect emerging information and developments in a matter of seconds. The

integration of world markets has meant that world capital flows have increased dramatically and have become a major determinant of exchange-rate movements.

Finally, the fact that the United States has in the past six years been a net importer of funds from overseas has raised the public awareness of U.S. economic and financial dependence on other countries. Fears that someday foreigners will no longer be willing to lend money to the United States are probably exaggerated. We are large enough, productive enough, and politically stable enough that we will probably be able to attract the funds that are needed. The appropriate concern is, At what interest rate? And at what exchange rate? That is, our dependence on foreign capital increases our interdependence with other countries and increases the extent to which U.S. interest and exchange rates are dependent on economic conditions and policies overseas. Market developments in the recent past demonstrate this vividly. Repeatedly in 1987 and again in the early months of 1988, U.S. interest rates were driven by concerns about the dollar, foreigners' willingness to buy U.S. securities, and economic policies of other industrial countries. The stock market decline in October 1987 itself can to some considerable extent be related to international concerns and exchange-rate policies here and abroad.

It may be a difficult lesson for the postwar generation of Americans, but the United States is no longer the unchallenged economic leader of the free world. Despite the inevitable comparison to Great Britain, there are many differences in our situations, not the least of which is that the United States has never been as dependent as Great Britain on foreign trade or foreign holdings for income. Nevertheless, our dominance has been

successively challenged in the past few decades—by Europe in the 1960s and 1970s, by Japan in the 1970s and 1980s, and most recently by the newly industrialized countries of the Pacific basin. It does not take much imagination to envision the source of tomorrow's challenge. Certainly China and India are potential candidates, and, once they work through their financial problems, Latin American countries such as Brazil will possess the resources potentially to claim an important economic position in the world.

It is, of course, not preordained that one nation will remain forever as the dominant world economic power, nor is it necessary or likely that one single nation will fulfill that role in the future. It ms probable to me that we are moving into an era of more shared economic power, an age of pluralism in which no one country dominates economically or financially but in which that role is shared seeby a number of nations possibly at various stages of development. In that situation, no one country's currency is likely to function solely as a reserve currency, because the currencies of several nations would become equally accepted and recognized. To some extent, we already see this happening as more international transactions are denominated in yen or deutsche marks rather than exclusively in dollars. While not particularly widespread in the United States, there is growing use and recognition around the world of bonds that are denominated in foreign currencies.

WILL AN INTERNATIONAL CURRENCY EMERGE?

A natural extension of this pluralism would be the development of a single, international currency that would be freely accepted by all nations, at least for the purposes of international transactions.

The most likely form of such an international monetary unit would at least initially be some weighted collection of national currencies—a situation where the U.S. dollar would clearly play a role, but one shared by other countries. In a system of integrated world financial markets, such a world currency has growing appeal. If it were generally accepted in international transactions, much of the inefficiencies associated with fluctuating exchange rates could be eliminated.

Of course, an international institution to issue the world currency and maintain member nations' support and cooperation would be required. Such a world central bank is not a new idea. Former Federal Reserve Chairman William McChesney Martin examined the idea at length in 1970 in a speech at the Per Jacobsson Foundation in Basel. As Mr. Martin explained in that speech, many of the functions of a world central bank are already being performed by the various international agencies such as the International Monetary Fund (IMF), the World Bank, and the Organization for Economic Cooperation and Development. The special drawing rights program of the IMF, limited though it is, is a form of world currency, sanctioned by member nations and acceptable in international transactions under certain circumstances. As he pointed out, "Economic cooperation among nations, and especially monetary cooperation, has made enormous strides in the past generation. If we examine what such growing international cooperation means, we shall see that it may be characterized as evolution toward a world central bank."[1] Of the international economic institutions that currently exist,

the IMF is probably the best suited to the task of world central bank and would be most likely to evolve into that role.

To become widely accepted in international transactions, the purchasing power of a world currency would have to be protected. That task would fall to the world central bank, which would have to control the quantity of world currency in existence, just as a national central bank does, in order to assure its value and therefore its general acceptance. The world currency could coexist with national currencies for internal transactions within a country or it could replace existing currencies by the choice of participating countries. If purchasing power were guaranteed and general acceptance occurred, trade flows would be encouraged. In the ideal, financial and trade flows would occur across international boundaries as freely and efficiently as they now occur across states in the Unites States.

There are, of course, enormous impediments to the evolution of a world central bank or a world currency, most of which are political. It would require that member countries increasingly relinquish power to the world central bank in an area of national sovereignty—monetary affairs—that is usually carefully guarded and filled with nationalistic concerns. To be effective, the governors of a world central bank would have to be isolated from political influence, and, given the suppression of national interests that would be required, skepticism is justified. In addition, member nations would have to agree to cooperate and coordinate their economic policies, and, while progress has been made in this area, our record of cooperation even between the major industrial countries is not encouraging. Effectively including the diverse interests and concerns of developing nations and newly industrialized countries under

1. William McChesney Martin, "Toward a World Central Bank?" in *The Per Jacobsson Foundation Lecture and Commentaries* (Basel: University of Basel, 1970), p. 13.

one central bank at present seems politically insurmountable. It is important to note, however, that the development of the European Monetary System with its system of exchange-rate zones is an example of a regional pact that is part of the gradual progress toward world cooperation. In Europe there is increasing talk of the need for a common European currency and a European central bank.

CONCLUSION

I see the diminishing role of the U.S. dollar as a natural part of the process of our sharing both economic and political power with other nations. As that evolution proceeds, many aspects of our international relations will need to change. Arrangements within existing international agencies such as the World Bank and IMF will have to reflect the growing and legitimate roles of other nations. Given that economic power typically mirrors political and military power, I submit that as U.S. economic influence shrinks, U.S. citizens will increasingly come to question the extent of our military responsibility to the free world. Given the budget difficulties of the United States and the growing wealth and economic power of many other nations, I believe it

will become more and more politically acceptable to question whether the United States can afford to assume a disproportionate share of the cost of the military defense of the free world.

As the United States shares its economic, political, and possibly military power with other nations, our interdependence will grow and the need will intensify to coordinate our economic policies nationally. This will entail giving up some national sovereignty and control over economic policy. All nations carefully guard their economic sovereignty, and the United States probably more than any other nation has a national heritage of doing so. Yet as Chairman Martin stated 18 years ago, "We have been witnessing a willingness of nations, by the exercise of sovereign rights, to recognize that the national interest can no longer be pursued in isolation but is dependent on cooperative action in deference to the common good. It has become more and more clear that this involves no loss of sovereignty but rather a pooling of sovereignty. It could even be said that what were once the principle objectives of sovereign powers—the maintenance of economic prosperity and of effective defense—can now only be achieved by the acceptance of cooperative international arrangements."[2]

* * *

QUESTIONS AND ANSWERS

Q (Dario Scuka, Library of Congress, Washington, D.C.): The officials of the federal government do not care about the debt. They feel that we owe it to ourselves when it comes to the domestic debt. When it comes to the foreign debt, or the inflow of foreign capital to our economy, they remark, "Where else can foreign

businesspersons go? They have to come to us." Of course, there will be some adjustment at some time. We have been postponing the adjustment for political reasons for perhaps a couple of years already. We can almost certainly count

2. Ibid., pp. 20-21.

on no changes during the last nine months of the Reagan administration. Therefore, if we do have a basic problem, this nine months may aggravate it slightly, so that the next administration will have an even harder task to arrive at corrective measures.

At the beginning of the current administration, the public debt stood, in round figures, at $740 billion. At the end of 1987, it was almost $2000 billion, an increase of—in terms of the federal government—$1200 billion. Concurrently, and primarily because we had a tax decrease in 1981, which was followed by overreaching by the Federal Reserve in the creation of money, sufficient liquidity was created to be able to spend for the national economic expansion but primarily for more visible, higher imports. Exporters to the United States do not operate very well on credit, except for a few specific large items, so we had to have money available to pay for the growing quantity of imports. Paying for the imports increased our deficit from $40 billion, at the beginning of the decade, to a high of $160 billion last year. Our domestic policies have in effect given the American public the ability to overconsume. If I were just a normal housewife, going to the market and running out of cash, borrowing money from cousins, at some time the borrowing would diminish if not stop altogether. I would very strongly suggest that the corrective measures under any administration, Republican or Democratic, will by necessity result in a lower standard of living for the United States. How can we avoid a drop in the standard of living?

A: I will respond in terms of the foreign debt, because that is most important to the interests of the average citizen. I think we can count on about a trillion dollars of foreign debt—foreign

paper held by foreigners in, for instance, 1990 and 1991. It is true that at some point the increase in foreign debt must be reversed. At the moment, we do not feel the pain of the debt because we have borrowed to pay the interest, too.

———

Q: What are the possible effects of further defaults by the Third World on U.S. banks and the dollar, and is there any chance that the Federal Reserve or perhaps some other government agency might end or at least suspend further foreign loans by U.S. banks to the Third World, perhaps to make it less likely that there will be defaults that would have an adverse effect?

A: At Philadelphia National Bank, we think that lending additional money in order to maintain interest payments is not sound. We ourselves refuse to participate in such lending. We believe that the creditor nations and the debtor nations should come to an agreement whereby, in some way acceptable to them and to the creditor banks, the debt can be managed in a way that debtor nations can afford to service it. Undoubtedly, the new arrangements also mean that only new lending will take place, because these countries do need an inflow of working capital at least, and that it will only take place when it is clearly senior to the old debts—the old debt would become junior debt. When that happens, we will begin to see export financing and import financing, but until that happens the situation remains somewhat precarious. Regarding defaults, I do not expect any country—at least not the major countries—to forget its debt completely. I think there will be cases, however, where a country will say that it cannot afford the interest, and that it is only able to pay part of what is owed.

We will see such cases more frequently as long as the situation remains unsettled.

Q (Kingdon W. Swayne, Bucks County Community College, Newtown, Pennsylvania): As I look at the binge of undersaving and overconsumption that we have had in this country for some time, I wonder if a factor that has permitted us to continue the binge as long as we have is that, at the Bretton Woods Conference in 1944, we rigged the international monetary system to put the dollar in a privileged position.

A: Ultimately, this reserve-currency situation that we are in will be a burden to us. It would have been much better for us if we had the discipline that other countries have with respect to their standard of living. When a country issues a world reserve currency, it can continue borrowing until the day of reckoning comes. But that day comes so much later when a country can borrow in its own currency, and this situation has caused us to live beyond our means to a degree that would not have been possible for another country. If the United States had to borrow in foreign currency, the time would have already arrived that a halt was being called to our borrowing. We are living in a fool's paradise.

Q (Mamoon A. Zaki, Le Moyne-Owen College, Memphis, Tennessee): As long as the world is depending on oil and petroleum as its economic pillar and as long as countries importing oil pay for it with dollars, will the dollar lose its position as the only world reserve currency?

A: Yes, inevitably. In addition, there is nothing dictating that 10 years from now the Saudi Arabians will still be quoting their sales in dollars. It is very possible

that the yen, the mark, or special drawing rights could be the medium of exchange. I am totally convinced that the first transition will be from a single-currency system to a pluralistic one. We will see more and more invoices, even in this country, in foreign currencies. I think that that transition is a healthy development, but my feeling is that it cannot be the ultimate solution. The world economy ultimately needs an institution with the power to impose discipline, and that institution cannot be an institution of an individual country. This institution will have to have more power than the International Monetary Fund. The International Monetary Fund has imposed quite a bit of discipline on borrowing nations but not on creditor nations. We will need a central bank that has equal influence on creditor nations and debtor nations.

Q (John R. Reinard, Cumberland County College, Vineland, New Jersey): It has been noted that the British pound was the world currency and then lost that position and that the American dollar may follow suit. Both countries are very imperialistic and capitalistically based. Having lived in South America for a number of years and witnessed the potential but unrealized strength of a country like Brazil, I would like to hear your comments about which country will have its currency become dominant and what would have to happen in that country. Would it have to seek more democracy, would it have to turn to more capitalism, would it have to seek a higher standard of living for a greater portion of its population?

A: My prediction is that there will not be one country whose currency is dominant; there will be several countries. There will be Japan, there will be Ger-

many, possibly also Taiwan. But Taiwan's reserves are in dollars, so I do not think it will be equal to Japan or Germany. I think that in 1992 the Common Market will be very serious about what it is going to do. If the European market has full movement of labor and capital, not long thereafter a European currency would arise. I do not think that it will be a very strong currency, but along with the yen and the dollar it could be a choice for other countries to put their reserves in. Much further down the line, I would say that if China can shed the impediments that a Communist and socialist regime brings with it, if it can bring to the rest of its economy the combination of socialism and entrepreneurial spirit that it seems to have been able to achieve in agriculture, it will be very, very powerful.

ANNALS, *AAPSS*, **500**, November 1988

Is the United States Losing Technological Influence in the Developing Countries?

By RUSTAM LALKAKA

ABSTRACT: The developing countries, which have over the centuries made their contribution to world scientific ideas, are today in a state of technological dependence and economic deprivation. The United States, which after World War II reached the zenith of prosperity and power, now has a reduced share of the world's research expenditures, patent awards, and trade in high-technology products. Japan, Europe, and the newly industrialized countries have accelerated their pace of technological development. In absolute terms, America is still ahead in the international technology race, judged by its scientific research and education systems, corporation-university synergy, innovation, and employment in small businesses. This article reviews U.S. technological influence from a Third World perspective and concludes that the developing countries are now generally more hospitable to American technology and investment; in turn, America needs their markets and raw materials. Revised forward-looking policies by U.S. government and corporations could well prolong the American Century.

Rustam Lalkaka graduated in metallurgical engineering from Stanford University and worked as research metallurgist with the U.S. Bureau of Mines. On returning to India, he helped establish an engineering consultancy organization and headed its international operations in Düsseldorf. With the United Nations since 1972, he has worked on industrial development and technology transfer in Thailand and Turkey and currently as director of the U.N. Fund for Science and Technology, New York. He has published extensively on technology strategies for the Third World.

NOTE: The views expressed are those of the writer and not necessarily of his organization.

ECONOMIC prosperity and military power go hand in hand and both depend upon an infrastructure of scientific research and technological development. Technology has been the key determinant of total factor productivity and long-term growth. The developing countries are only now recognizing this connection; the industrialized countries, particularly the United States, have known it for a hundred years.

The year 1888 was a great one for U.S. technology. George Eastman had just invented the roll-film camera in Rochester, New York, and Thomas Alva Edison the first commercial phonograph at Menlo Park, New Jersey.[1] William Burroughs and Herman Hollerith were developing their data-processing machines while Nikola Tesla, a Croatian emigrant, invented the electric induction motor. A year before that, Dr. John Pemberton had marketed in Atlanta an "esteemed brain tonic and intellectual beverage," later called Coca-Cola. The next year, 1889, was also good. Mrs. Cockran in Shelbyville, Indiana, produced the first commercial dish-washing machine, and the American Academy of Political and Social Science was established!

Technology has never been apolitical; it is determined by political forces and in turn influences both politics and culture. American popular culture is as pervasive as its industrial products. Both bring with them the message of technological prowess. Indeed, in technology as in all human endeavor, perception is at least as important as reality in the public mind.

The developing countries, it should be recognized, are at very different levels on the development ladder. Their national conditions and aspirations differ widely

and their perceptions of U.S. technological power are different. At the same time, U.S. geopolitical interest differs from country to country and this in turn determines its influence—solicited or hegemonic.

Overall, is U.S. technological influence rising or declining? There are no yardsticks to measure technological leverage, but one can consider some proxies, such as receipts from know-how licensing or number of patent registrations, to make broad assessments. We look first at historical trends and some international indictors. Internal policy factors are then reviewed, taking the case of the steel industry as well as the frontier technologies. The perspective is that of a development practitioner in the United Nations Development Programme, involved in strengthening capacities to apply science and technology for development.

THE HISTORICAL CONTEXT

Science and civilization have pushed and pulled each other across the five millennia of human history. Technical innovation has contributed to military strength, exploration, and social well-being and has in turn been stimulated by a sound social-political structure.

The pharaonic civilization of the Nile, the Hittite of Anatolia, and the Sumerian astride the Tigris and Euphrates rivers were solidly based on artisans' technologies of building mighty edifices, of agriculture and communication. In turn, the torch was passed on to the Greece of Euclidean geometry and Ptolemaic astronomy, to the Rome of military conquest and engineering prowess, and to the Persia of artistic excellence and healing.

On the other side of the globe, China, through an almost uninterrupted span from the fifth century B.C. to the fifteenth

---

1. Kevin Desmond, *A Timetable of Inventions and Discoveries* (New York: M. Evans, 1986).

century A.D., originated the magnetic compass, the stern-post rudder, the breast-strap harness, paper and movable type for printing, massive hydraulic systems, astronomical observations, and the water-wheel clock. A question that naturally arises is, Why did so much technology in China not produce good science? According to Needham, "The answer to all such questions lies, I now believe, primarily in the social, intellectual and economic structures of the different civilizations."[2]

In the Indus River basin, starting with Aryan settlements around Mohenjo-Daro and Harappa, town planning and the decimal system with the numeral zero were developed. Outside the Eurasian land mass, enclaves of civilization emerged among the Incas, Aztecs, and the trading empires of Ghana and Mali. With the coming of Islam, the new spirit of scientific inquiry in the Arab world led to significant advances in physical sciences, food technology, and even the refining of petroleum as early as the ninth century A.D. The prince of Antioch issued a know-how license—covering equipment, experts, and needed supplies—to the doge of Venice in A.D. 1277—and Venetian glass is now famous all over the world.[3]

For centuries, men and ideas moved back and forth along the Silk Road, the routes of the Crusaders, and the sea lanes of European voyages. Then as now, attempts to curtail the free flows of scientific thought and technical invention were hardly successful, and fortunately so, because this sloshing of ideas helped trigger the artistic and scientific glory of the Italian Renaissance, the Spanish and Portuguese explorations, and the ferment of political ideas in Europe and America. It is interesting that at the end of the sixteenth century incomes in Britain were at the same level as those in India. Later came the Industrial Revolution, and Europe began to move rapidly ahead. By 1850-75, Britain had already reached the per capita income that the developing countries on average have today.[4]

"It simply has not been given to any one society," Paul Kennedy points out, "to remain permanently ahead of all the others, because that would imply a freezing of the differential pattern of growth rates, technological advance, and military developments which has existed since time immemorial."[5] Each empire has had its season in the sun, then slowly faded. Each gave rise to a new burst of scientific discovery and military conquest, which, while it lasted, seemed as if it would never end.

During my school days in India, it was claimed that the sun never set on the British empire. History as taught to us started in 1066, and that was that. The well-to-do ate Huntley & Palmer biscuits with their Lipton's tea—grown in India, imported from England—and rode Raleigh bicycles, because Indians were not supposed to have the wit—or the wherewithal—to make these things themselves. But starting in 1947, India together with a procession of other countries became politically independent—although, alas, economic dependence continues. History books were rewritten. Technical education and scientific research were reinforced. In

2. Joseph Needham, *The Grand Titration: Science and Society in East and West* (London: George Allen & Unwin, 1969).

3. Ahmad Al-Hassan and Donald Hill, *Islamic Technology: An Illustrated History* (New York: Cambridge University Press, United Nations Educational, Scientific, and Cultural Organization, 1986).

4. Surendra J. Patel, "1850-1875, The Great Divide in Industrial Development," *Economic and Political Weekly*, 22(19, 20, and 21) (May 1987).

5. Paul Kennedy, *The Rise and Fall of the Great Powers* (New York: Random House, 1987).

a brief forty years, some of these same countries have come to produce not just biscuits and bicycles but jet aircraft.

In the United States, while a sound infrastructure was put in place between the Civil War and World War I, it was really after World War II that the country emerged as the undisputed leader in the economic and technological fields. Its education system, scientific research achievements, agricultural productivity, and near-absolute dominance in most industrial sectors commanded the admiration of all. The American Century had begun.

This fast-forward glimpse of technology is to put events in perspective. While the long waves of supremacy continue to rise and fall, what has indeed changed is the pace at which technological progress is now taking place. Societies with different rates of economic growth have emerged, the balance of technological power has changed and will change again. It is now said, with some hyperbole, that the Mediterranean was the sea of yesterday, the Atlantic of today, and the Pacific of tomorrow. Interest is now focused on what used to be seen from the epicenter of Europe as the Far East and is now from America's perspective the New West with Japan as its hub.

Japan's strategy in the postwar era worked in two directions: Japan utilized its then low labor costs at modern greenfield industrial facilities to gain a market share in international trade. Concurrently, it imported the most advanced technologies, mainly from America, and improved them. In the 1955-75 period, Japan spent around US$10 billion to acquire the best available know-how, and for every dollar spent on that import, it incurred another seven for local research

and development (R&D).[6] With this approach, Japan was able to move rapidly from imitator to innovator, from technology importer to the world's leading exporter of high-technology products.

This strategy has been contagious. Other East Asian countries with a Confucian ethic, the so-called little dragons, are beginning to catch up with their mentor in the export of, for example, ships, automobiles, and computers. Brazil, Mexico, and Thailand are now following this path of export-led growth. China and India, with the potential of good technical labor and vast domestic markets—but the equally vast internal problems of modernization—could become competitors early in the next century. We may soon be talking not only of the newly industrialized countries but also of the big industrializing countries. There is skepticism that this could ever happen, but it may be recalled that only a generation ago, in 1954, Secretary of State John Foster Dulles was reporting to President Eisenhower that "there was little future for Japanese products in the United States . . . Japan should not expect to find a big U.S. market because the Japanese don't make the things we want."[7] History has a way of making even the wise seem fallible in retrospect.

THE SCIENCE-TECHNOLOGY-
RESEARCH SYSTEM

The American research system has been the most productive in the world.

6. F. Neville Woodward, Rustam Lalkaka, and Tai-Soo Chung, *Guidelines for Development of Industrial Technology in Asia and the Pacific* (Bangkok: ESCAP, 1976).

7. Excerpt dated 6 Aug. 1954, quoted from vol. 14 of *Foreign Relations, 1952-54*, records of the Eisenhower administration, by Cyrus S. Eaton, Jr., in a letter to *Fortune*, 15 Apr. 1988.

Both developed and developing countries are studying U.S. programs of federal support and tax incentives for R&D, the corporation-university synergy, the business-incubation modality to nurture small enterprises, the venture-capital sources, the enormous capacity to create employment, Silicon Valley, and the new research consortia such as Sematech.

In basic, fundamental research, the United States has been unequaled, whether measured in terms of scientific papers published—35 percent of world output—or Nobel prizes won—127 U.S. scientists since World War II, compared to 98 Europeans and 5 Japanese. Spending on basic research amounted to some US$15 billion last year. West Germany and Japan are now allocating a larger share of their total R&D budget to fundamental work—22 percent in Germany and 13 percent in Japan versus 12 percent in the United States—in order to catch up. In industrial research, U.S. spending dropped from 1964 to 1978 and picked up again in the last decade.

In total R&D, America spent US$123 billion in 1987, in roughly equal amounts from government and industry. While in absolute R&D expenditures, the United States is still the world leader, its growth rate has declined recently in relation to other industrialized countries. For instance, in America, R&D outlay rose at 1.8 percent annually in the 1969-81 period as against 8 percent in Japan and 4 percent growth for the Organization for Economic Cooperation and Development as a whole.[8] The U.S. share of global R&D expenditures has declined from 40 percent in 1970 to 33 percent in 1983.

When defense and the service sector are removed and industrial R&D is expressed as a percentage of value added in the manufacturing industry, the United States shows a decline: from 2.49 percent in 1967 to 2.21 percent in 1983. In the same period, this ratio has approximately doubled in Japan from 0.84 percent to 1.86 percent and in Germany from 1.28 percent to 2.28 percent.[9]

To put expenditures on R&D in perspective, it should be noted that the developing countries together spend an average of around 0.40 percent of their gross national income of US$2.6 trillion (1985 dollars) on research, that is, only US$10 billion; the more advanced do spend up to 1.0 percent of their gross national product. In contrast, the industrialized countries spend up to 2.5 percent of their US$10 trillion income, that is, over US$250 billion, or 25 times as much as the developing world. The asymmetry in numbers of scientists and engineers engaged in R&D is even greater—4000 per million of population in the industrialized countries and less than 200 in the developing countries.

The view of the developing world is that U.S. corporations are generally not making the needed marketing and research effort to adapt their products to the needs, climate, maintenance regimes, and other conditions of the tropical countries. The U.S. Agency for International Development and various foundations have made significant technical inputs to research efforts in developing countries,

8. Organization for Economic Cooperation and Development, *Selected Science and Technology Indicators, Recent Results 1979-86* (Paris: Organization for Economic Cooperation and Development, 1986).

9. U.S. Congress, Joint Economic Committee, *Technology and Trade: Indications of U.S. Industrial Innovation* (Washington, DC: Congress, 1986); National Science Board, *Science Indicators* (Washington, DC: National Science Board, 1983).

but there are many more opportunities for collaborative research to help tackle specific problems in long-term mutual interests. Centers of research excellence focused on Third World problems—such as the theoretical-physics and biotechnology institutes in Trieste and the chain of international agricultural-research laboratories—could help improve the morale and output of scientists.

PATENTS AS A
MEASURE OF INNOVATION

Patents can be viewed as a useful indicator of the output of the R&D system in a country. In the year 1984, the number of patents granted to nationals at home was 216,000 worldwide. The share held by market-economy countries generally declined—the United States, for instance, from 24.3 percent of the world total in 1975 to 17.7 percent in 1984.[10]

More significant, recent analyses indicate that the quality of patented ideas in Japan may be higher than in the United States. A technique used by Computer Horizons Inc. analyzes the number of times a patent is cited by other patent holders to establish their claims. The analysis shows that "starting as early as 1976, patents awarded to Japanese inventors were cited more frequently than those awarded Americans, and that the gap between Japanese and American patents appears to be growing."[11]

The proportion of patents granted to foreign nationals in the United States has risen sharply, from 27.0 percent of the total in 1970 to 45.0 percent in 1988. At the same time, the proportion of patents

granted abroad to U.S. applicants has declined from 36.9 percent of the worldwide total in 1965 to 31.7 percent in 1983. In this period, Japan's share rose from 3.0 percent of the worldwide total to 12.9 percent.[12] It is possible that the drop in U.S. patent registrations is due partly to a decline in the propensity to patent and to the working of the U.S. patent system itself, but there are indications of a reduction in innovative activity in comparison with that abroad.

Rising research costs and shortened product cycles are increasing the value of proprietary technology and the temptation to imitate it. The proper protection of intellectual property has become a key issue in international trade. Reform of the patent system and appropriate codes for technology transfer are needed urgently in order to ensure protection with equity and, at the same time, provide access by developing countries to the computing and biotechnologies that can help tackle their intractable problems.

THE INTERNATIONAL
FLOWS OF TECHNOLOGY

International flows of technology generally take the forms of direct foreign investment, licensing of know-how, and export of capital goods that embody technology. Informal transfers of technology through the exchange of scientists and conference participation are often very effective, and so also are technical cooperation projects to strengthen human resources through the bilateral and U.N. development systems.[13]

The period of the 1960s was the golden era for U.S. direct foreign investment. U.S. multinationals expanded rapidly

    10. *Trade and Development Report 1987* (Geneva: United Nations Conference on Trade and Development, 1987).

    11. William J. Broad, "Novel Technique Shows Japanese Outpace Americans in Innovation," *New York Times*, 7 Mar. 1988.

    12. *Trade and Development Report 1987.*

    13. *Annual Report of the Administrator* (New York: United Nations Development Programme, 1987).

TABLE 1
**TECHNOLOGY FLOWS FROM THE DEVELOPED MARKET-ECONOMY COUNTRIES
TO THE DEVELOPING COUNTRIES (Billions of U.S. dollars, current prices)**

Technology in the form of:	1962	1972	1982	1985
Capital goods	6.5	20.9	116.9	96.5
Direct foreign investment	1.4	4.4	10.4	7.7
Receipts of royalties and fees	—	0.7	2.0	2.3
Technical assistance	0.7	1.8	5.4	6.0

SOURCE: Based on *Trade and Development Report* (Geneva: United Nations Conference on Trade and Development, 1987).

abroad and accounted for an average of 60 percent of the world's flows of direct foreign investment. Most of this went to Western Europe and to some of the developing countries of Latin America. In the 1970s, with greater financial liquidity in banks due to higher oil revenues, the exports of capital goods to developing countries continued to grow strongly.

Since the beginning of the 1980s, the pace of technology flows to the Third World has remained stagnant. (See Table 1.) Direct investment and capital-goods exports have declined, except in China, which opened its markets in this period. Interest payments and debt amortization by the Third World now exceed new lending. If stagnation is to be overcome and world trade revived, the net transfer of resources to these countries must again become positive.

The bulk of direct foreign investment is now going to the industrialized countries themselves. The United States is absorbing the lion's share and has been transformed from the worlds's largest creditor to the largest debtor within a decade. The U.S. trade deficit is also a cause of real concern. But within this aggregate, the U.S. share of exports of high-tech products has dropped steadily: from a trade balance of over US$26

billion in 1981 to a negative balance in such exports in 1986 for the first time.

Japan, which earlier relied upon forging large market shares in consumer durables through mass production, is moving to a new business strategy: adding further value to high-tech products, and continuing to bring innovations to the market faster than the competitors. This, combined with its proven ability to cut manufacturing costs continuously, has enabled Japan to outpace America in high-tech trade, despite the much stronger yen.

As technological progress creates global interdependence and as corporations operate increasingly on a global scale, aggregate trade statistics of a nation do not properly reflect the performance of individual corporations.[14] Thus exports of U.S.-based corporations, when added to exports of companies abroad that they control, have remained relatively constant through the last two decades; at the same time, imports to the United States also include imports from U.S.-controlled companies. The U.S. economy may be in trouble, but many of its transnational corporations seem to be in fair competitive

14. John R. Munkirs, "Technological Change: Disaggregation and Overseas Production," mimeographed (Springfield, MA: Sangamon State University, 1987).

TABLE 2
TECHNOLOGY KNOW-HOW TRADE OF SELECTED COUNTRIES, 1965-85
(Millions of U.S. dollars)

	United States		United Kingdom		France		Federal Republic of Germany		Japan	
	1965	1985	1965	1984	1965	1984	1965	1985	1965	1983
Receipts	1,534	8,512	138	1,194	169	4,804	75	545	27	1,014
Payments	135	207	131	845	215	2,875	166	995	133	1,176
Balance	1,399	8,305	7	349	−46	1,929	−91	−450	−106	−162

SOURCE: *Transnational Corporations and Technology Transfer: Effects and Policy Issues* (New York: United Nations Center for Transnational Corporations, 1987).

shape and continue to manufacture and export some of the best technology-intensive products.

With respect to the licensing of technology, the United States continues to be the world's foremost exporter of technological know-how. Its earnings in the form of royalties and license fees have grown more than fivefold to US$8.5 billion in the two decades 1965-85 while its investment in foreign know-how remains small. In comparison with other industrialized countries, the U.S. technology trade balance is positive and large. While know-how income in Germany and Japan has risen sharply, both countries continue to be net importers. (See Table 2.)

Actual know-how receipts and the trend over time confirm that the United States remains the main supplier of technology to the developing countries. Indeed, the value of know-how transferred by America to them—US$1546 million in 1985—is almost twice that of all other suppliers combined.

An emerging trend is the exchange of know-how between the developing countries themselves, through government-to-government arrangements as well as through investment by Third World multinationals. Such technical cooperation between developing countries, aided by the U.N. system, shows promise for the future, as the technologies transferred are generally more appropriate to local conditions than those from advanced nations.

Another recent phenomenon is that both developing and developed countries, socialist or market-oriented, are realizing that state control of production has caused enormous losses and that they must create the proper economic environment in order to stimulate innovation and individual entrepreneurship. Given the more hospitable climate for private investment, developing countries would also now be more receptive to U.S. transnational corporations. They would like to see movement on three counts. First, U.S. enterprises should be prepared to take a long-term view of future potential. Second, they must learn to be more sensitive to national aspirations, cultural habits, and local capabilities. Finally, U.S. government policies must provide for reliable long-term relationships.

In turn, the developing countries have to organize, first, to offer stable political and economic conditions for safeguarding foreign investment and intellectual property rights. Second, they must formulate and implement effective monetary and fiscal policies as well as growth-oriented

trade policies. Finally, governments have to rationalize their regulatory measures and create the enabling environment for all-around development.

THE CASE OF THE STEEL INDUSTRY

We turn now to the domestic scene—forces within the United States that are causing the sun to set on some traditional industries and to rise dramatically on the high-tech sector, with significant implications for the Third World.

The American steel industry used to be vibrant and profitable. Its deep forward and backward linkages, potential for employment, and contribution to heavy industry had made it the foundation of the modern U.S. state. The low coke rates in blast furnaces, the high production rates of wide strip mills, and the well-engineered layouts at plants such as Fairless and Burns Harbor were studied by delegations of visiting steel men from all over the world.

India, for instance, has had a long dialogue with the U.S. steel industry. In the early 1900s, J. N. Tata, the pioneer industrialist, dreamed of building the first private steel mill in India. He was rebuffed in Britain. Said the viceroy Lord Lawrence, "I know what private enterprise means! It means robbing the Government!"[15] Another British official promised to eat every pound of steel ever made in Mr. Tata's factory! Finally, it was an American, Julian Kennedy of the consulting engineering firm Kennedy Sahlin & Co. of Pittsburgh, who offered to come to India to help Tata build his steel mill, which today is India's most efficient steel producer.

15. Frank Harris, *J. N. Tata: A Chronicle of His Life* (Glasgow: Blackie & Son, 1958).

In the mid-1950s, three integrated steel mills were being set up by the government of India—one each with German, Soviet, and British assistance. The government was also keen to get America to help build a showpiece at a new site, Bokaro. On the urging of Ambassador John Kenneth Galbraith, the Kennedy administration had a feasibility study prepared by U.S. consultants, but the project was eventually scuttled by a congressional committee because the plant was going to be in the public sector!

In 1950, the United States produced almost half the world's steel and imported only 1 percent of its total needs. In 1985, however, it produced only 11 percent of the world total and imported fully one-fourth of its own consumption. On the other hand, production in the socialist countries and in Brazil, the Republic of Korea, and Mexico has expanded.

Many explanations have been suggested for the decline of U.S. influence in the steel sector. An important factor has been high wage settlements, not accompanied by productivity improvements. In the early 1980s, U.S. hourly rates were around $24 per hour compared with $15 in Japan and $3 in Korea. But labor productivity in the United States was only about half of the 500 tons per man-year in Japan and Korea. Another reason for loss of competitiveness has been lack of vision on the part of U.S. plant managements to adopt advanced, more efficient technologies such as the top-blown oxygen converter, replacing traditional open hearths, and the continuous casting process, instead of conventional primary rolling mills.

In other words, new and improved processes were available globally, but the economic conditions affecting capital formation and investment delayed their use by U.S. industry. Problems were

compounded by the high cost of regulatory compliance with environmental standards. With the quarterly bottom line in mind, investment in the U.S. steel industry went primarily to refit existing plants or into diversified activities unrelated to steel. Its competitors abroad built new steel plants utilizing the most modern technology.

It this context, the real success is that of the state-sponsored Pohang steel works (POSCO) in the Republic of Korea. International experts had warned against building this mill because Korea has practically no raw materials for iron and steel making. But by buying the best at very competitive prices, by sharply reducing construction times, and by deploying a highly trained work force at relatively low wages, POSCO has become the worlds' lowest-cost integrated steel producer. POSCO is now joining U.S. Steel to help modernize its Pittsburgh, California, facility.

While the integrated steel mills have declined, a new breed of mini-mills has vigorously expanded production in the United States. Their share has risen from 3 percent of domestic output in 1965 to over 25 percent today. Based on modern electric arc furnace and continuous casting technology, these mini-mills compete effectively against foreign producers, both at home and abroad.

The steel industry, once a paradigm of U.S. supremacy and until recently of U.S. decline, has in the last year or so demonstrated that it was down but not out. The weak dollar, the closing of obsolete and fresh investment in modern facilities, the reduction of surplus labor, and renegotiated contracts are making the industry competitive again. The same factors are reversing the decline of U.S. technological influence in a variety of manufac-

tures. "Lazarus rises," say the financial magazines.[16]

THE INTERNATIONAL RACE IN ADVANCED TECHNOLOGIES

In traditional industry, technological innovation generally required that the market conditions be right for large investments. In the research-intensive, fast-moving frontier technologies, on the other hand, the real stimulus often comes from small enterprises assisted by venture capital. It is in these partnerships between risk taker and inventor, between business and university research, that the United States has excelled.

In many of the growth areas of computing, biotechnologies applied to health, plants, and livestock, and advanced materials and renewable energies, America continues to lead. This leadership is respected by engineers and businesspersons in the developing countries, who eagerly seek U.S. know-how licenses and joint ventures. An opinion survey of concerned researchers and executives in 1986 rated the U.S. rather high against its competitors (see Table 3). The survey may not be rigorous but the assessments show clear dominance of the United States, with Japan usually second and the USSR far behind.

A more recent survey in 1988 by the *Los Angeles Times* and Booz-Allen & Hamilton of 282 executives from the United States, Japan, and the newly industrialized Asian countries indicated that, in their perception, the United States was clearly ahead of Japan in supercomputers, software, and artificial intelligence. Japan led in robotics, microelectronics, and computer-aided manufacturing. In advanced

16. "Lazarus Rises," *Financial World*, 8 Mar. 1988.

TABLE 3
RATINGS OF ACHIEVEMENT IN SELECTED TECHNOLOGIES

	United States	Japan	Europe	USSR
Computers	9.9	7.3	4.4	1.5
Biotechnology	8.9	5.7	4.9	1.3
New materials	7.7	6.3	6.0	3.8
Optoelectronics	7.8	9.5	5.7	3.6

SOURCE: Gene Bylinsky, "The High Tech Race: Who's Ahead?" *Fortune*, 13 Oct. 1986, pp. 28-37.
NOTE: Ratings were on a scale of 1 to 10, with 10 as the most favorable.

materials, superconductors, lasers, and fiber optics, the United States was out front but Japan was closing the gap.[17] Italy, Germany, and France are carving their own niches in fields such as high-performance machine tools and aircraft, while the Soviet Union is now the leader in space.

Japan's lead in the manufacture of semiconductor memory circuits, particularly advanced and dynamic random-access memory chips, gallium arsenide, and silicon materials and in the export of telecommunications and instruments is due not only to advances in flexible, computer-integrated manufacturing but also to improved social organization and innovative management. These have enabled it to combine high quality with competitive costs.

The competition will become more fierce in the supercomputer field, in concurrent processing applied to artificial intelligence, and in expert systems. Here China, India, and Brazil, with the advantage of latecomers and with intellectual capacities for software development, could become serious players. India's computer industry, which until recently was engaged primarily in screwdriver assembly of imported components, now has an array of foreign technical and financial collaborations: Control Data Corporation will produce mainframes with the government's Electronics Corporation of India, Digital Electronics Corporation with Hinditron, and AT&T with Wipro. Texas Instruments, Nixdorf, Olivetti, Norsk Data, and others also have tie-ins, in the belief that Indian brain power will be a force in the international software market.

Developing countries at sound technical levels have no option but to invest in fields such as microelectronics because these technologies enter into practically all areas of economic activity. A start could be made at the less complex end of the market, selectively and incrementally, even on a partial basis through the manufacture of components. The future will require strategic alliances for research and production with companies in the developed world. But for the least developed countries in Africa and Asia, the advanced technologies could cause considerable hardship, in the intermediate term, by minimizing the use of their abundant low-cost labor or by creating substitutes for traditional commodities or otherwise shifting the pattern of international specialization.

17. "The Technology Race: The Competition Spanning the Pacific," *Los Angeles Times*, 21 Feb. 1988.

Molecular biology is undoubtedly the area of greatest potential benefit to the developing countries in coming years. The products now emerging regularly from U.S. genetic-engineering companies can make a real impact on agriculture, food processing, and human and animal health. Following upon the green revolution, this biorevolution also raises serious concerns for the developing countries.[18] Will these advanced techniques be affordable by the disadvantaged sections of the farming community or will they exacerbate the income disparities? Will expensive new products create a new dependency, or can Third World laboratories be enabled to acquire and adapt the advanced genetic-engineering methods to their own specific needs and at reasonable costs? Are the far-reaching social and economic repercussions being properly assessed by the planners? Despite these concerns, countries as diverse as Cuba, Thailand, Argentina, Mexico, and Algeria have embarked upon major biotechnology programs. India is hosting one leg of the new International Center for Genetic Engineering and Biotechnology while the second is located in Trieste, Italy.

In the emerging bio-industries, as in other sophisticated fields, the U.S. private sector, as leader, and the Third World, as major beneficiary, need to establish a continuous dialogue whereby the interests of one side to safeguard its intellectual property and its strategic concerns and the interests of the other to adapt and apply the techniques effectively can both be protected. In his discussion with us at the First Beijing International Conference on Technology Strategies, in October 1983, Zhou Zhiyang, then China's premier, urged industrialized countries to "actively and far-sightedly transfer technology to developing countries on preferential terms," adding that only when developing countries have advanced technologies and thus developed economies will the industrialized countries have access to the large market and supplies of raw materials they need.[19]

AMERICAN COMPETITIVENESS IN THE TECHNOLOGY FIELD

Developing countries have been important export markets for America while some have become significant competitors through targeted government policies to create comparative advantage.[20] U.S. exports to developing countries and U.S. imports in 1986 have been around one-third of total trade—a drop since the levels in 1981 but nevertheless a significant proportion. The drop has been due to low growth and high debt in the developing countries as well as to overall declines in U.S. productivity and competitiveness.

Several recent studies have suggested prescriptions to overcome the obstacles to U.S. competitiveness in the industrial technology field.[21] The obstacles include macroeconomic policies that diminish growth, regulatory bodies that add costs, large expenditures on military preparedness, and systems of education and research.

19. Rustam Lalkaka and Wu Mingyu, *Managing Science Policy and Technology Acquisition: Strategies for China and a Changing World* (Dublin: Tycooly International, 1984), p. 263.

20. John Sewell, *Growth, Exports and Jobs in a Changing Economy: Agenda 1988* (New Brunswick, NJ: Transaction Books, 1988).

21. See, for instance, Ralph Landau and Nathan Rosenberg, *The Positive Sum Strategy: Harnessing Technology for Economic Growth* (Washington, DC: National Academy Press, 1986); Sewell, *Agenda 88.*

18. See Christopher Freeman, "The Challenge of New Technologies" in *Interdependence & Cooperation in Tomorrow's World* (Paris: Organization for Economic Cooperation and Development, 1987).

A factor contributing to America's industrial decline could well be massive expenditures on defense. They consume 6.7 percent of the country's gross national product and 32.0 percent of its R&D expenditures. In contrast, Germany spends only 3.1 percent of its gross national product and deploys less than 6.0 percent of R&D on defense; Japan, even less.[22] These countries, with much lower defense commitments, are able to focus their research and industry on commercial products. For instance, West Germany produces numerically controlled machine tools for small engineering shops rather than for military industries, while Japan's US$500 million Fifth Generation Project is developing artificial-intelligence software for smart industrial robots and household appliances, not for strategic defense.

Military outlays do not necessarily promote industrial competitiveness. While such research has helped sophisticated aircraft and electronics-based equipment production, it has not given other significant commercial spin-offs. Military procurement places emphasis on custom-made high-reliability products, on a costplus basis, often without competitive bidding. This runs counter to the scale economies of mass production and short product-development cycles needed in a highly competitive, rapidly changing global market.

Further, policies that place restrictions on export of high-tech items, some with potential dual use, and on publication of research results are known to inhibit commercial activity.[23] They prevent U.S. participation in an expanding market, reduce employment, inhibit the free exchange of ideas, and reduce income flows from royalties needed to research the next generation of products.

U.S. industrial competitiveness is also affected by the diversion of needed scientists and engineers to the military-industrial firm. The gap has been filled by an influx of foreign scientists.

While earlier the brain drain was of concern primarily to some developing countries, today even Europe is worried at the loss of its human talent. Nearly half the graduate physics and mathematics students in U.S. universities are foreign and, since 1981, more foreigners than Americans have received doctoral degrees in engineering. It is not surprising, then, that a large proportion of the research personnel in Silicon Valley are from countries such as China and India. This growing dependency is now beginning to cause concern in the United States itself.[24]

Foreign professionals come to the United States because of the openness of its society and the enormous career opportunities it offers. The education system, however, is not fully geared to raising American productivity, improving manufacturing processes, or transforming management practices. In recent lectures, the president of Harvard University, Derek Bok, has asked, "If universities are so vital to post-industrial society and ours are so superior, why are we running such huge trade deficits? Why do we find ourselves losing huge markets to Japan even in high-tech industries?" His answer is that American higher education is the main cause of the nation's faltering economic and industrial performance.[25]

Another important factor is the inability of U.S. corporate R&D to stick tenaciously to an emerging scientific field

22. Steven L. Canby, "The Pentagon Needs Less High Tech," *New York Times,* 6 Mar. 1988.

23. Jay Stowsky, "Competing with the Pentagon," *World Policy Journal,* Fall 1986.

24. Rustam Lalkaka, "TOKTEN: A Ten Year Brain-Gain," *Darshan,* 4(12) (Dec. 1987).

25. Leonard Silk, "Proposals to Keep the U.S. on Top," *New York Times,* 1 Apr. 1988.

over the long haul and to explore broad areas of knowledge in a sustained manner, building patiently and meticulously as one technical advance merges into another. Traditionally, American corporations are required to show short-term results rather than to pursue longer-term goals with uncertain pay-backs.

In the cases of the transistor, the robot, the photovoltaic cell, television, and the laser, inventions made primarily in the United States and the United Kingdom were rapidly commercialized in Japan. The race for high-temperature superconductive materials is now on, and the breakthrough by an American company, IBM, in December 1985 at its Zurich laboratory has ricocheted all over the world, with escalating results. A few large U.S. corporations and many start-up companies are active in this promising field, abetted by government. But Japanese companies have reportedly filed 2000 patents toward converting superconductivity advances into practical applications in computing, medical diagnostics, optics, and transportation. The champion in this race could take a good share of this market that by the year 2000 could be as large as US$20 billion.[26]

"The underlying predicament," Robert Reich points out, "is not that the Japanese are exploiting our discoveries but that we can't turn basic inventions into new products nearly as fast or as well as they can. Rather than guard our technological breakthroughs, we should learn how better to make use of breakthroughs wherever they occur around the globe."[27] The Americans are making components and assemblies abroad for the domestic

market, and Japan is producing automobiles in America for export back to Japan. Research, education, business, and trade have now become so thoroughly intermixed and interdependent that it is no longer possible to speak in terms of technonationalism; the world has to be seen from a technoglobalist's point of view.

The same conclusions are reached by the National Academy of Engineering and the National Research Council: "The benefits of international co-operation in engineering and technology are likely to outweigh risks in many situations, given thoughtful and symmetrical implementation of programmes. Technological protectionism is not a sustainable path as a general course, since technology inevitably diffuses."[28]

Eleven centuries ago, the renowned Arab scientist Al-Kindi wrote, "It is fitting then for us not be ashamed to acknowledge the truth and to assimilate it from whatever source it comes to us." The same approach was adopted as one of the five oaths taken by the Meiji emperor in Japan at the end of the last century: "Knowledge will be sought and acquired from any source with all means at our disposal, for the greatness and security of Japan."[29]

THE VIEW FROM THE SOUTH

For America to regain technological influence in the Third World, its govern-

---

26. David Gumpert and Stanley Rich, "Commercializing Superconductors," *New York Times*, 27 Mar. 1988.

27. Robert B. Reich, "The Rise of Techno-Nationalism," *Atlantic Monthly*, May 1987, p. 63.

28. "Strengthening U.S. Engineering through International Cooperation: Some Recommendations for Action" (Report of the Committee on International Co-operation in Engineering, National Academy of Engineering and National Research Council, 1987).

29. Abdus Salam, *Science, High Technology and Development, Development and South-South Co-operation* (Ljubljana, Yugoslavia: Research Centre for Co-operation with Developing Countries, 1987), pp. 14, 16.

ment and corporations will have to formulate specific new policies properly to address the profound changes now taking place in the developing countries themselves. Military leaders are giving way to democratic movements, and rigid state control is yielding to more liberal market-oriented policies. At the same time, religious fundamentalism is on the rise; so also are daunting problems of debt management, population growth, rapid urbanization, environmental degradation, and massive unemployment.

Despite enormous opportunities for America to refurbish its technological image with the developing world, there is a growing perception abroad that the United States is not willing to play the role befitting a superpower in global issues of science and technology. U.S. contributions through the World Bank and its bilateral programs of technical assistance have undoubtedly helped many developing countries. So have American foundations and voluntary organizations. At the same time, small developing countries with inadequate infrastructures often feel uncomfortable in dealing with a mighty power. A mouse dancing with an elephant, however well-intentioned the latter, is likely to get trampled. For these reasons, bilateral U.S. aid programs can be usefully complemented through multilateral activities. A case in point is the U.N. Financing System for Science and Technology, which was initiated at a world conference in Vienna in 1979 by consensus of the developing and industrialized countries. But the United States has not participated in it to date, and thus opportunities are being missed for strengthening North-South cooperation that would be mutually advantageous.

On global matters, again, the world community has turned in emergencies to the United Nations—for instance, to the International Atomic Energy Agency after Chernobyl, to the World Health Organization and the United Nations Development Programme with respect to acquired immune deficiency syndrome, to the United Nations Environment Programme on acid rain, and to the United Nations Educational, Scientific, and Cultural Organization on biosphere research approaches. But if the U.N. system is allowed to become any weaker, it may not be around when its services are again needed in the overall interests of the United States, of the developing countries, and of the world.

Under programs such as the United Nations Development Programme's Transfer of Knowledge through Expatriate Nationals, America could also assist Third World professionals now settled abroad in helping their countries of origin. The work of these expert volunteers could be facilitated at practically no cost to the U.S. organizations where they now work.

The bulk of technologies needed by developing countries from the United States are for food sufficiency and renewable energy in sub-Saharan Africa, for health and shelter in Asia and Africa, and for problems of urbanization and unemployment in Latin America. In special circumstances, the frontier technologies of, for example, computing and remote sensing may well be the most appropriate. The sharing of this know-how on equitable terms is not likely to create threats to trade and employment in the United States nor to its strategic interests.

When it comes to reform of the international patent system, the formulation of a code for transnational corporations to do business, or the need for fairer technology-transfer arrangements, the developing countries expect from America a leader-

ship role that is responsive to their aspirations.

CONCLUSION

Is the United States losing technological influence abroad? One is reminded of the economist who, when asked how his wife was doing, replied, "Compared to what?" Compared to U.S. power at its zenith in the 1970s, the answer is yes, American influence has diminished in relation to that of Japan, Europe, and the Pacific basin, mainly because the latter three have managed higher growth rates over smaller initial bases. China, Brazil, and India could pose a challenge in the coming millennium, provided they can continue in a stable manner on the path of economic reform. The unified European market of 1992 will be a formidable competitor, and so might a revitalized socialist block.

It is difficult for America's politicians and its media to recognize the reality of a multipolar world, specially when the decline is gradual and relative. Paul Kennedy puts it another way:

It may be argued that the geographical extent, population and national resources of the United States suggest that it ought to possess perhaps 16 to 18 per cent of the world's wealth and power, but because of historical and technical circumstances favourable to it, that share rose to 40 per cent or more by 1945; and what we are witnessing at the moment is the early decades of the ebbing away from that extraordinarily high figure to a more "natural" share.[30]

That being said, the United States remains today, in absolute terms, the world leader. Its projected gross national product in the year 2000 will still be larger than that of Japan and the newly industrialized Asian countries combined. Its economic resilience and democratic institutions, its geographical size and military strength, the technological innovation of its small enterprises, and the management excellence at many large corporations are keeping America at the leading edge. Wise government policies and forward-looking business strategies, both not necessarily oxymorons, could well prolong the American Century.

* * *

QUESTIONS AND ANSWERS

Q (Dario Scuka, Library of Congress, Washington, D.C.): Technology, in these modern times, is dependent on energy. I am inclined to believe that energy in general, and petroleum in particular, are a human patrimony in the current world situation. Petroleum is the most internationally traded commodity. In addition, it is dispersed around the globe very unevenly. Where it is most needed, it is not present, and where it is in ample supply, sometimes it is not exploited properly. Would you please comment on technology transfer in the petroleum and natural-gas industry?

A: There is absolutely no question that energy is the multiplier of human muscle and brainpower in order to create modern goods and services. My office at the United Nations deals primarily with renewable energy. There is no question, again, that in the future we will have to turn increasingly from depletable fossil fuels to some of the renewable ones—new energy sources, such as biomass and solar, tidal, and wind power, among others. Tragically, because of the recent softening of oil prices, the focus of atten-

30. Kennedy, *Rise and Fall of the Great Powers.*

tion has shifted away from the very serious energy problems that the world is bound to experience. As night follows day, the price of oil will rise once more and we will again be in a very serious energy crisis. But new technologies are becoming available, and if the requisite research money and effort were invested, together with effective technology-transfer strategies and sound government polices, then, I believe, we could be better prepared for the next energy crunch, which may arrive by the end of this millennium.

Q (Kingdon W. Swayne, Bucks County Community College, Newtown, Pennsylvania): Given that the number of people creating and otherwise interested in intellectual property is increasing around the world, are the structures in place to achieve adequate safeguarding of new intellectual property?

A: The United Nations Conference on Trade and Development has, for over a decade, been trying to reform the patent system and formulate a code of conduct for the transfer of technology. It has not yet been able to come to any final resolution because, clearly, the interests of the technology haves and have-nots are at loggerheads. The U.N. Center for Transnational Corporations is completing negotiations on a code of conduct for transnational corporations, which, again, touches upon transfer of technology. Existing structures for protecting intellectual property need to be continuously reviewed and strengthened. I believe that there is a clear realization in the developing countries that equitable prices must be paid for technology. Also, history shows us that the flows of technology cannot be prevented forever. The flow of the kind of technology that comes with

blueprints and manuals cannot be stopped in this day of instant communication. One can be prudent and careful, but such flows cannot be fully prevented. What is important, however, is that with blueprints and drawings alone one cannot build a computer or a sophisticated product. It is with experience, depth of knowledge, which can only come through an industrial culture, which can only come through intensive training, that technology can be replicated or new products created. The protection of intellectual property is really a serious problem, and solutions are still to be found. I would urge that a certain openness and equity in the flows of technology and protection of property rights can only help in this highly interdependent world.

Q (Richard D. Lambert, American Academy of Political and Social Science, Philadelphia, Pennsylvania): Many Americans believe that the transfer of technology—through the Marshall Plan, through multinational corporations, through industrial espionage—has contributed to the loss of the technological superiority that the United States had at one time. Would you please address this view of America's decline and fall in this period?

A: Nations do rise and fall technologically, economically, and militarily. These trends can of course be influenced by such factors as the Marshall Plan or policies of multinational corporations. Rather, the rates of economic and technological growth are the determining factors. Wise government policies would prevent further erosion of U.S. technological supremacy.

Q: The growth in technology in the industrial countries so far outstrips any

growth in the developing countries, and the gap is becoming wider and wider. Do you see any hope for narrowing the gap?

A: In the United Nations dialogue 15 years ago, there used to be talk of the technology gap. It was assumed that the differences in technology between nations were somehow bridgeable. I think we have given up that particular notion. There is no way the technological chasm can be bridged. For instance, the developing countries spend less than 5 percent of the world's total research and development expenditures and therefore control, say, 5 percent of the world's technology. The technologies that are needed to solve the problems in Africa, Latin America, and elsewhere, the problems of poverty, are all now available; nothing more may need to be invented. The problem is that this know-how cannot be accessed, it cannot be bought, because the resources are not available or because the technical skills to apply them are lacking. We need a different kind of vision to be able to mobilize those technologies.

Another way of looking at this situation is that it would be impossible today for most developing countries to reach the per capita incomes, the affluent living, that the industrialized West has achieved. They therefore have to think in terms of alternative life-styles, alternative ways of doing things. They do not need to imitate the kinds of life-style that degrade the environment, require high consumption of raw materials and energy, and so on. Furthermore, these countries, along with the rest of the world, will not be able to afford those styles of life in the next century. So it is no longer relevant to talk about bridging the gap. With some vision and good luck, a few countries every 10 years or so join the ranks of the industrialized, but there is no question that the gap will not close for most of the others.

ANNALS, *AAPSS*, **500**, November 1988

Is the United States Losing Ground in Central and South America?

By JAIME BENÍTEZ

ABSTRACT: The Spanish-American War made possible an important reorientation of the traditions of Spain, Latin America, and the United States. With the conclusion of the empire, Spain could forget its martial past, the nations of Latin America were obliged to find their own course, and the United States became engaged anew in European affairs. Over time, Latin America's early admiration for the democratic United States gave way to fear and concern for the violence to which they have been or are potentially subject. The present military involvement of the United States in the Central American nations is best seen in the light of this evolution. A crucial problem that is shared by both Latin America and the United States today is the traffic in drugs. If treated as an opportunity for positive cooperation and change, even for the restructuring of important aspects of our societies, this dire problem may serve to bring the two Americas together in mutual and genuine respect.

Trained in law at Georgetown and in the humanities at Chicago, Jaime Benítez has been chancellor of the University of Puerto Rico (1942-66) and president of the UPR System (1966-71). He was a member of Puerto Rico's Constitutional Convention and president of the Commission on the Puerto Rico Bill of Rights. Emeritus professor of the University of Puerto Rico and distinguished professor at American University, Don Jaime lectures on Ortega y Gasset and continues to exercise great influence on the Puerto Rican educational and political institutions he has been instrumental in shaping.

FOURSCORE and ten years ago your forefathers brought forth upon the Caribbean the "splendid little war" of 1898, as Secretary of State John Milton Hay called it. It was, indeed, a brief encounter.

Congress declared war on Spain on 25 April 1898 to secure Cuba's independence. Queen María Cristina's government sued for peace on 23 July and offered to grant independence to Cuba. Two days later, General Nelson Miles and his army landed in southern Puerto Rico. The fighting was prolonged, and the armistice was delayed until 12 August. By then the Spanish government had agreed to cede all of Puerto Rico as well as the Philippines.

General Miles protested when he was ordered to stop fighting on 12 August as he was only halfway to San Juan. Colonel Theodore Roosevelt's note to Senator Lodge before leading his Rough Riders to Cuba—"Give my love to Nannie and prolong the war until we take Puerto Rico"—was honored even if not communicated to President William McKinley.

The "splendid little war" changed the course of history for all parties involved. To this day, Spanish historians identify it as "*El Desastre.*" But that disaster opened the way for a new generation of writers and leaders, bent upon reassessing the dreams, achievements, and failures of the old empire. They resolved to close forever the sepulcher of the Cid Campeador, to forget the heroes of the past and throw away the keys to ancient glories. The way was opened for a complete reorientation of the future.

The Spanish writers, philosophers, and poets of the Generation of 1898 initiated a new vision in all fields of endeavors: education, science, world outlook, politics. For a while it seemed as if Spain had indeed regained a leadership role in the world of art, of literature, of education, and of democracy. Then came the Civil War of 1936, with its dismal blackout of almost half a century. Fortunately, for the last 13 years, we have been witnessing a highly promising although difficult reorientation of democracy in Spain.

The paths of history followed by Cuba, the Philippine Islands, and Puerto Rico were changed most radically by the war of 1898. The present differences between the last three colonies of Spain provide ample opportunity for meditation on the ups and downs of historical trends. Cuba, the Philippines, and Puerto Rico are as far apart from each other as they can possibly be, each in its separate way struggling to find its own true course.

For the United States, 1898 was its first involvement in European conflicts since its wars with England. It was manifest destiny at its best and at its worst. It was a prelude to the creation of the Republic of Panama out of Colombia and the beginning of the big-stick policy that achieved sea communication between the Atlantic and the Pacific oceans through the Panama Canal.

It must be remembered that manifest destiny began with the wars between the United States and Mexico and the acquisition of almost half of what became the Continental United States. As Alan Riding states in his book *Distant Neighbors*:

Probably nowhere in the world do two countries as different as Mexico and the United States live side by side. . . . Probably nowhere in the world do two neighbors understand each other so little. . . . Over the past 150 years, Mexico has come to know and feel American power: In the nineteenth century, it lost half of its territory to its northern neighbor; in the twentieth century, it has become economically dependent on the United States. In contrast, the United States until recently barely looked south. Mexico's stability was

taken for granted, its flourishing economy welcomed.... Today, things are different. The failure of Mexico's postwar economic model has thrust the country into its most serious crisis since the 1910 Revolution.[1]

As the spiritual leader of the second version of manifest destiny, President Theodore Roosevelt assisted both Russia and Japan in settling the terms of their war of 1905. The Norwegian Parliament awarded President Roosevelt the Nobel Prize for Peace in 1906. Woodrow Wilson, who prevailed over him and over President Taft in the elections of 1912, was to become, five years later, "the savior of Europe." Even though defeated by the Senate in his endeavor to have the United States join the League of Nations, which he created at enormous cost, Woodrow Wilson stands in retrospect as one of the great American presidents, one who struggled without rest for a nobler world. Today the United States has the highest responsibility for peaceful democratic leadership in the world that it has helped to change into "the global village."

LATIN AMERICAN VIEWS OF THE UNITED STATES

Turning now to our present inquiry of whether the United States is losing ground in Central and South America, I must answer, yes, but that this may not necessarily be so in the years ahead.

Paradoxically, the "splendid little war" changed, decisively and negatively, the emotional assessment of the United States in Latin America. Before 1898, Latin American leaders and writers were very much in favor of Cuban independence and against imperial Spain. The United States was often referred to as an exemplary nation, united, democratic, enter-

prising, successful. After 1898, the United States became for Latin America a dangerous white, Anglo-Saxon, Protestant, evil empire. Why?

There are several reasons. First, absolute power offends absolutely. Second, the military humiliation of Spain turned it once again into the beloved mother country. Third, President Theodore Roosevelt lost no time in showing that, for the United States, force may become *prima ratio* instead of *ultima ratio*. Force would be available, if necessary, to add a Rooseveltian corollary to the Monroe Doctrine.

The greatest Latin American poet of all times, Rubén Darío, wrote his "Ode to Theodore Roosevelt" immediately after the president managed to carve Panama out of Colombia:

You are the United States,
the forthcoming invader
of that trusting part of America that still has
    Indian blood,
that still speaks Spanish and still prays to
    Jesus, our Lord.

You are proud, you are strong . . .
educated and able, you believe in action and
    you reject Tolstoy
. . . .
You lack nothing, with one exception: God![2]

In the same vein, in 1900, in his book *Ariel*, José Enrique Rodó, the leading writer and educator from Uruguay, summarized the problems of the New World as a permanent hemispheric struggle between two Shakespearian characters from *The Tempest*: Caliban, the savage and deformed colossus of the North, and Ariel, the dreaming, airy spirit of Latin America. According to Rodó, Ariel is destined both to prevail and to set the

1. Alan Riding, *Distant Neighbors: A Portrait of the Mexicans* (New York: Knopf, 1984), p. 1.

2. From Rubén Darío, *Cantos de vida y esperanza*, in *Poesias completas*, ed. Alfonso Mendez Plancarte (Madrid: Aguilar, 1961), pp. 720-21. English translation by Jaime Benítez.

values, goals, and achievements of future generations in Latin America.

Where does Central America stand today vis-à-vis the United States? It faces a most serious economic crisis. It owes more money than it can pay. Its currencies are out of control. Furthermore, Central America is living through three quite different military presences of the United States: one in Nicaragua, another in Honduras, a third in Panama.

In all three places, there was much to complain about before the interventions. The interventions, however, have not been particularly helpful to the United States' image nor to that of the groups it has befriended. Thus it is particularly revealing that Adolfo Calero, the contra leader, at the moment of reconciliation in Sepoá turned against the Reagan approach, invoking instead the common loyalty he and President Ortega owe jointly to national unity. In Panama, General Noriega has managed to profit from the United States' intervention. Even Del Valle, the president that General Noriega deposed, has pleaded with President Reagan to keep his soldiers out. The same negative reaction developed in El Salvador, where President Reagan has supported President José Napoleón Duarte most actively. But the electorate turned against Duarte in the legislative elections held last March. Finally, the United States' intervention in Guatemala against President Jacobo Arbenz Guzmán in the 1950s is still resented in that most densely populated Central American republic.

Costa Rica is the only one of these republics where the United States is not losing ground at present. It represents a very different political reality and organization. It is the most stable, most democratic, and least populated of the five Central American republics. Costa Rica abolished its army in 1949, has never suffered intervention at the hands of the United States, and exercises a position of leadership in the general concern for peaceful development and growth throughout the region.

Last year, the Norwegian Parliament awarded the Nobel Prize for Peace to the president of Costa Rica, Oscar Arias Sánchez, for his program for peace in Central America. Arias was the third president from the New World to be thus honored. First was Theodore Roosevelt in 1906, and second was Woodrow Wilson in 1919.

There is another problem of critical dimensions, which involves Colombia, Panama, and the United States once again: drugs. Some of the Mafia leaders in this nefarious trade try to justify themselves at home by claiming they are aiming at the Achilles' heel of the colossus of the North. But they are crippling not the colossus but the children and the families targeted by such infamous arrows. The United States and Latin America must develop a joint, effective approach against the present bilateral, criminal relationship of North American demands for and Central American supplies of cocaine and marijuana. Can the battle against drugs be won? I believe so and will offer an approach.

MUTUAL UNDERSTANDING

So far, I have spoken of events, political leaders, and governments. From that limited perspective, it seems obvious that the United States is losing ground and will lose more if it continues on its present course. But there are other, more meaningful, responsible paths available for which the times are ripe.

The most decisive reality within which Central America operates pertains to the

different levels at which the citizenry live in the cities and in the countryside. As Professor Robert S. Leiken summarizes in his book *Central America: Anatomy of Conflict*:

One travels to Central America through time as well as space. . . . A short step from the Central American capitals, and one encounters the middle ages, with its wooden plows and draft animals and seasonal rhythms. Medievalism casts a long shadow on the Central American present.

Nonetheless in the past two decades, the region has known rapid economic growth, new political ideologies and the revolution in telecommunications. The Central American campesino lives at once in the middle ages and in the "global village." The contradiction between the old and the new is one of the central components of the Central American crisis.[3]

The distance between the *campesino* and the city dweller has existed in Latin America for over four centuries. It is part of a cultural background that we Latin Americans inherited from Spain along with many positive and lasting contributions, such as the Spanish language, the Catholic religion, the structure of the family, pride in being oneself and in being faithful to one's commitments. But as far as support for governments of the people, by the people, and for the people, the Hispanic political heritage has been counterproductive. Part and parcel of that inheritance were also the legitimacy of social hierarchies, the division of society into leaders and followers, the priority of personal loyalties over political principles, the essential differences between men and women, the intrinsic worth of every individual, and the acceptance by the under-

privileged of their earthly lot, because final and lasting justice will come in the hereafter.

In his book *The Modernization of Puerto Rico*, Professor Henry Wells discusses at length the almost centennial clash between Spanish and U.S. social and political values in Puerto Rico.[4] Wells is amply and approvingly quoted by Lawrence E. Harrison in his book *Underdevelopment Is a State of Mind: The Latin American Case*.[5] Harrison holds that overcoming mutual misgivings and fears springing from conflicting cultural perspectives is a prerequisite to fruitful relationships between North, Central, and South America.

The operational indifference with which the ruling classes in Latin America glance over the plight of their *campesinos* must come to an end. Professional, economic, and political elites must realize that that cleavage between the city and the rural community constitutes their greatest social injustice. They must take a leading role in overcoming this particular social segregation. Furthermore, we Latin Americans have to overcome the Ariel-Caliban syndrome. The United States may be blamed for many but not for all the ills and evils our communities suffer. Contrary to our frequent obsession, the United States pays much less attention to South America than it pays to many other regions of the world, Israel, for instance. It is much more concerned, often mistakenly so, with Europe, Asia, and certainly with what President Reagan

3. Robert S. Leiken, "Overview: Can the Cycle Be Broken?" in *Central America: Anatomy of Conflict*, ed. Robert S. Leiken (New York: Pergamon, 1984), pp. 3-4.

4. Henry Wells, *The Modernization of Puerto Rico: A Political Study of Changing Values and Institutions* (Cambridge, MA: Harvard University Press, 1969).

5. Lawrence E. Harrison, *Underdevelopment Is a State of Mind: The Latin American Case* (Boston: Center for International Affairs, Harvard University, and University Press of America, 1985).

calls the evil empire of Soviet Russia and with its satellites.

The United States faces an equally difficult task in endeavoring to bridge the gulf of misunderstanding that cuts across and divides the New World. In order to be true to the best self of the United States, its representatives must overcome their monolingual education. They must incorporate into their approaches not only the language but also the ethnology, the cultural and psychological infrastructure, the sensibilities of their next-door neighbors, and vice versa. All sides would profit from cultural osmosis.

If we manage to exorcise from our minds the devils and the evil empires that cloud our thinking and assess with critical realism and goodwill the potential for cooperation, I believe that mutually beneficial programs could be developed.

NORTH-SOUTH PARTNERSHIP

I have already mentioned what may be the worst health problem the United States suffers: drugs. It is the bilateral irresponsibility of supply and demand. It needs to be controlled at both ends.

The United States faces such a no-win situation in combating this new plague that many opinion makers are suggesting giving up the fight. They recommend legalization instead. Such a solution seems suicidal to me. Cocaine and opium are not variations of alcohol. They are addictive and deadly.

I would much rather go all the way in working out an earnest partnership, between north, central, and south, to curtail production, distribution, and consumption of drugs in America. I think it can be done.

It would be a second Alliance for Progress, with one big difference. This time the United States would be the junior partner. Latin Americans would be fully in charge of one side of the battle: putting an end to production of drugs. See who wins first. Drug eradication would be costly and would require important shifts in employment, and the United States would have to foot the bill, but it would be worth it. For the first time in history, the United States would be dependent on the South for assistance, support, and help. Properly handled, it would tap the best and noblest qualities of our peoples for cooperation. I would anticipate the most generous reaction toward joint North, Central, and South American efforts to safeguard the health and future of children who would otherwise be subjected to the most dangerous and, if you will, destructive nuisance of modern society.

One final word. We in Puerto Rico are also victims of this tragic trade. Thirty years ago, Puerto Rico was immune to this calamity. We do not produce cocaine or marijuana or opium or any other drug, but today drugs come to Puerto Rico by sea and by air. The government and the community are fighting the invasion, but there must be a wider, all-inclusive, effective program to eliminate this scourge from our midst.

A joint and successful battle against drugs may lay the foundations for broader cooperation and mutual trust in other fields. It should help in the pursuit of other tasks that call for further understanding and appreciation of these three Americas. All three would gain in a common struggle for a better America.

* * *

QUESTIONS AND ANSWERS

Q: I would like to suggest a Marshall Plan or something like the Lomé Convention for Central America. I have in mind that it would be administered by the Organization of American States, to eliminate any taint of Yankee imperialism. Also, the United States could turn over all disputes and conflicts in this hemisphere to the Organization of American States; in the course of research, I have found that we have signed treaties agreeing to do that. Do you think Puerto Rico and some of the countries of Central America would be receptive to these strategies and would perhaps give some support to the idea of getting them through Congress?

A: I am certain they would be; I am certain that Puerto Rico would be. With respect to the Marshall Plan, the Alliance for Progress, in a sense, was an effort to duplicate the Marshall Plan. Latin America, however, was not prepared, as Europe had been, to receive such an assistance. Unfortunately, too, the United States was to a large extent motivated by trying to defeat Fidel Castro, and Latin Americans were less conscious of their responsibility for the success of the Alliance for Progress. Even so, something significant was started and achieved, but certainly a new approach would be welcome, and I think the ideas that you have mentioned would be very good.

Q (Dario Scuka, Library of Congress, Washington, D.C.): The U.S. government seems to have been overtly rather generous to Honduras for quite a few years. Unfortunately, the generosity was concentrated in the military area. Would you provide your perspective concerning the most recent anti-American demonstration by students and some workers there?

A: One thing that people in the United States oftentimes neglect is that this giant, their country, must communicate spiritually, emotionally with a Latin America that does not continue to think that its position must be one of receiving assistance. It is indispensable that the best aspect of the United States come out in accepting and incorporating and developing mutual tasks so that the Latin Americans discover that they are respected and not treated only, or predominantly, as poor people who receive alms. As a colleague of mine has said, the problem with the United States is that contrary to Oscar Wilde's famous definition of a gentleman as one who only offends deliberately, the United States often offends without trying to and often while endeavoring to help.

Q (James W. Skillen, Association for Public Justice, Washington, D.C.): Given the likelihood of the United States' world economic decline and other developments, the tendency of the United States in the coming decade and beyond will be to turn inward or to become preoccupied with what it sees as its own dilemma, making its interest in and understanding of Latin American or other countries less likely particularly if it begins to see that the debt crisis in Latin America is part of a problem that is a danger to it. Can you give me some signs of hope that U.S. concern with and interest in understanding Latin America in a new way would lead to some greater cooperative efforts?

A: Let me say this. Listening to the current presidential debates in the United

States, I was very heartened when I heard Dukakis speaking Spanish. He spoke Spanish perfectly well, and I think that his fluency will be one of his great assets if he is elected president. It will be the first time that an American president has spoken Spanish. Not only speaking Spanish but having a basic sensibility toward this other psychology and approaches is very important. The awful thing about the United States is that its history or its goals do not call it to be a world leader. This role was thrust upon it by many other factors. One of its problems as a world leader is that it is a monolingual society. For a society to understand other societies and to communicate with them, it has to be bi- or multilingual. I hope that the United States will evolve along these lines; if it does, it will achieve a much better understanding with Latin America. Concerning the economic aspect, I think that the United States has enormous potentials. I was in Washington as a student in 1929, at the time of the Great Depression. For a while then it was felt that there was no hope. I remember hearing President Hoover say that the best government was the least government, and so forth and so on. It took a tremendous revolution in American life, such as President Roosevelt's brain trusts, to change the approach of the United States, and it recuperated from the depression and became the great power in the world. While the United States does indeed have failings and there are possibilities for other countries to replace the United States in economic leadership, all countries, including Japan, know deep in their hearts that the United States, for a number of reasons, has become the unquestioned prime leader and will continue to be so if there is going to be leadership in the years ahead. The hope is that its leadership will be pluralistic.

––––––––

Q (Roderick McDonald, Rider College, Lawrenceville, New Jersey): The United States has heretofore resented and worked against certain strategies of development in the Caribbean and Latin America. I have in mind in particular the cases of Cuba, Jamaica, and Nicaragua. Please assess the relative advocacy for various alternatives for development in Latin America and the Caribbean.

A: Concerning the question of Nicaragua and even the danger of Cuba, I think that the whole situation has been blown out of proportion. The United States has attributed to these little situations an importance that they fundamentally lack, but the basic difficulty is that unless the problem of human destitution is dealt with by the countries that are involved, eventually we will have to have revolutions everyplace. The solution is to aid development, keeping in mind the important factor of diplomacy. Moreover, the United States could have been much more help in the whole Central American problem a long time ago if it had decided to back the Contadora countries instead of trying to substitute them. It is also very important for the United States to let Latin American regions be aware of the possibilities for settling their problems and to let them have the responsibility for doing so.

ANNALS, *AAPSS*, **500**, November 1988

Yesterday's Arms Control Will Not Prevent Nuclear War

By ROBERT H. KUPPERMAN and DEBRA VAN OPSTAL

ABSTRACT: Even as prospects for direct U.S.-Soviet confrontation have decreased, the potential for international collision almost everywhere else is on the rise. Although arms control remains an important long-term issue in superpower relations, the United States and Soviet Union face a more imminent danger of unwanted nuclear escalation through the actions of unstable, unpredictable, and well-armed states in the Third World. This suggests that a better U.S. policy balance must be struck between central strategic threats, to which U.S. resources and attention have been devoted for forty years, and regional conflicts, for which there is a notable lack of contingency planning and a growing record of U.S. failure.

Robert H. Kupperman is senior adviser at the Center for Strategic and International Studies, where he is also executive director for science and technology. He is the author of numerous publications on terrorism, crisis management, and strategic policy and arms control.

Debra Van Opstal is a fellow in science and technology at the Center for Strategic and International Studies. She is an author of Combating Terrorism *and a forthcoming publication on low-intensity conflict,* Meeting the Mavericks.

KEEPING the world safe from nuclear oblivion has been a major preoccupation of policymakers, legislators, generals, and scholars since the dawn of the atomic era. Policy recommendations cover practically every dimension of the bilateral relationship between the United States and the USSR, from cultural, educational, and diplomatic exchanges to crisis-management understandings to never ending debates on how big a nuclear stick is needed to cow one's opponent. Today, our hopes have fastened on arms control—the intermediate-range nuclear forces agreement and the Strategic Arms Reduction Talks—as a way to foster political stability between the superpowers.

The problems with all of these approaches, as Henry Kissinger has noted, is that "the superpowers are conducting international affairs as if they were the principal relevant factors when, in fact, over the next decade new power centers will emerge that will make the relative position of the two superpowers less significant."[1] Indeed, we may one day look back on the cold-war era—a time in which the only major global threat was that the United States and the Soviet Union would annihilate each other—as a relatively simple and stable period. We no longer enjoy the luxury of an exclusively bipolar world. The nuclear perils that lie ahead are no longer limited to the actions of the superpowers.

We today face the grim future of a world of many poles of power—a more independent Europe and Japan, a more mature and capable China, and a host of well-armed regional mini-powers who are actively striving for local predominance. The entire international system is marked by growing uncertainty simply

1. Henry Kissinger, "Next Powers to Play in Pacific Area," *Los Angeles Times*, 24 Jan. 1988.

because of the proliferation of independent actors and advanced weapons systems.

The mysteries of the atom are neither as difficult to master nor as secret as we once hoped. There appear to be few barriers and a great many incentives to the acquisition of chemical, biological, or radiological weapons of mass destruction and sophisticated delivery systems. Given the likely spread of these kinds of capabilities, superpower promises of world peace through a balance of terror are beginning to appear singularly unconvincing.

Although U.S. policymakers remain focused on the threats of an era past, the loci of instability are shifting beyond Europe into Third World regions. It is here that the rules of superpower prudence are ill defined. Here, third-party actors are setting events into motion over which neither superpower may have direct control but in which both may have compelling interests. It is in Third World arenas that the United States and the Soviet Union run a real risk of being drawn into unnecessary and unwanted confrontation.

This is not to imply that the Soviet threat has mysteriously evaporated. It does imply, however, that a better policy balance must be struck between long-term threats and immediate risks. It does suggest that the United States is badly in need of a new global vision that recognizes where the future risks to U.S. security lie and, more important, how we might avoid them.

THE RISKS OF ARMS REDUCTIONS

As long as there remain thousands of nuclear warheads in the superpower arsenals, there is no intellectual escape from the problem of American-Soviet rela-

tions. The threat may be distant, but its finality commands our attention. The prospect of reducing that threat—through a carefully crafted arms-control process—has a great deal of intuitive economic appeal.

Arms control can be a positive vehicle to foster greater stability through mutual interdependence and trust between the superpowers, but it is no panacea. Indeed, the current emphasis on foolproof verification schemes is misplaced; no arms-control scheme is certifiably risk free. The danger in focusing on treaty minutiae is that we ignore the larger instabilities that can be created by the process itself.

Some instabilities are largely self-generated—the product of a conceptual contradiction between mutual vulnerability and individual self-protection. On the one hand, the effective policy of mutual assured destruction (MAD) is designed to guarantee not only that we have the ability to retaliate if struck first but that we remain deliberately vulnerable to Soviet retaliation. In a MAD world, the basis of stability rests on the mutual conviction that striking first would be utter suicide.

The dilemma arises in considering what to do should deterrence fail. The prospect of "nuking the other side back into the Stone Age" offers marginal satisfaction if one's own society lies in ruins. Each side would naturally prefer to protect itself by denying the other an ability to inflict damage. One way to accomplish this goal is defensively, as with, for example, the Strategic Defense Initiative. Another would be to attempt to overwhelm one's opponent offensively. In practice, the United States pursues both avenues of approach, in direct contrast to its declared retaliatory policy.

On the offensive side, U.S. joint staff targeters currently list tens of thousands of aiming points in the USSR that are designed to thwart any possibility of Soviet retaliation and destroy the USSR as an industrial and military power. Virtually any Soviet asset of even marginal military interest has been locked into a computerized attack plan.

Ironically, we do not now possess a nuclear arsenal of sufficient size to meet these targeting demands. But the basic inconsistency between an ever expanding list of targets and a policy of nuclear-arms reduction is patent. Arms-control options increase the strain on targeting goals as weapons are reduced or as U.S. strategic forces, based at home, are slotted to perform additional interdictive and damage-limiting tasks, such as the functions of the intermediate nuclear forces eliminated under the proposed intermediate-range nuclear forces agreement.

This, in itself, creates tension between the policy and operational camps. If the need to achieve our targeting goals becomes paramount, then we may yield to an incentive to achieve them by striking first at a time of crisis. The lesson here is that the United States must rationalize its defense policies across the board or face the consequences of its own failure.

A second instability in the arms-control process is externally generated: the more successful the reduction effort, the more unstable the nuclear balance. At very small force levels, even a small divergence from the agreed-upon levels, such as might occur in cheating, could create a decisive difference in the balance of power and terror at a time of crisis.

Let us say, for the sake of simplicity, that the United States and the Soviet Union agreed to pare their strategic arsenals to 100 missiles apiece; at this level, each side believes it could survive an attack and still inflict meaningful damage on the other. If we assume that

the Soviets secretly add only 40 missiles to their arsenals—a level that might be impossible to detect—then the entire balance of power has shifted. With 10 warheads on each of these missiles, the Soviets would possess the potential to eliminate our entire missile force on a first strike.

While marginal cheating in a world of very small nuclear forces would have a major impact, any discrepancies would be almost impossible to verify. One might suspect, but could never be absolutely sure whether or not the other side was cheating. The costs of mistaken trust would be so high that both sides might well adopt an offensive launch-on-warning strategy.

It is here that ballistic-missile defenses might make a difference by coping with the margin of error that creates an advantage for the other side. But all technological systems leak or fail. We ought not rely on technology alone as the quick fix or panacea to restore a perceptual or political balance.

Moreover, missile defenses by themselves alter the balance-of-terror calculus. To the extent that they provide an additional element of uncertainty about the costs of striking first, they tend to be stabilizing. But they are destabilizing to the extent that they may prevent adequate retaliation by the other side, thereby undermining the core of MAD.

The bottom line is that these instabilities do not favor radical arms reductions as a way to prevent nuclear holocaust. Although we may not be happy with the concept of thousands of nuclear warheads creating a balance of terror, the fact remains that it is a very stable balance. While there is ample room to reduce the numbers of nuclear weapons on both sides, the vision of a denuclearized world is largely utopian. Neither side will or can afford to reduce the number of nuclear weapons below the level at which they can guarantee absolute carnage with absolute certainty.

The assurance of mutual destruction creates very predictable boundaries that neither side will willingly cross. Predictability, in turn, has created a great deal of stability. The prospects of a surprise Soviet nuclear strike against the United States or a Soviet invasion of Europe have never been lower. Unfortunately, the only way to keep those risks at a negligible level is to maintain a robust nuclear deterrent.

THE EMERGING GLOBAL ORDER

Even as the prospects for direct U.S.-Soviet confrontation have decreased, the potential for international collision—political, economic, or military—almost everywhere else is on the rise. Future U.S. leaders will confront a vastly different global environment: a world of competing power centers rather than two superpower blocs; a world in which small powers have the ability to inflict unacceptable damage on great ones; a world of many small fault lines instead of one large European one.

With the breakdown of an exclusively bipolar order, neither superpower will have an unchallenged prerogative to dictate the course of events either by suasion or by implicit or direct coercion. In this respect, the United States may have more in common with the Soviet Union now than at any time in the past forty years. Both have difficulty controlling their allies. Both are wary of committing forces to marginal areas, having backed away in defeat at the hands of guerrilla warriors in Vietnam, Lebanon, and Afghanistan. Both are increasingly preoccupied and constrained by internal problems.

The breakdown of superpower hegemony is being hastened by the prolifcration of high-technology conventional weaponry—primarily missile and aircraft—as well as unconventional chemical, biological, or nuclear capabilities in the Third World. Many of the traditional imbalances of power between the great and lesser states are narrowing. Indeed, future conflicts in the Third World will increasingly be fought with weapons that were once thought of as exclusive to the great powers.

In particular, the spread of missile technologies is likely to shrink the already low number of areas in which the United States can operate without risk. Missile technologies have been employed over the past decade with dramatic and sometimes unexpected results. Examples include the downing of two American A-6 aircraft by Syrian surface-to-air missiles, the downing of an American F-111 by Libyan missile defenses, and the devastating impact of Stinger missiles against Soviet aircraft in Afghanistan.

Anti-ship missiles have also proliferated over the past decade. With over-the-horizon ranges of 50 kilometers or more, these missiles render large naval targets vulnerable. Missiles for export like the Otomat or the French Exocet—successfully used by Iraq against the frigate *Stark* in the Persian Gulf reflagging operation—may give smaller states an unparalleled capability to thwart bigger ones.

The Persian Gulf now also provides a testing ground for the nonnuclear cruise missile. Although discounted as a threat only a few years ago, the use of Chinese-supplied Silkworms by Iran offers yet another platform for attack.

Missiles are being developed and distributed not only by the superpowers and their allies but by developing countries as well. Nearly every class of missile is now being produced by six Third World countries. The technologies they are capable of exporting are not second rate as in previous years. Brazil's Barracuda is thought to be comparable to France's Exocet. The Trishul missile, under development by India, is believed to be a state-of-the-art short-range, surface-to-air missile.

An even more dangerous long-range technological advancement is in the area of ballistic missiles. Ironically, even while the superpowers are in the process of agreeing to destroy intermediate- and short-range ballistic missiles, the technology is the subject of intense interest in countries such as Brazil, India, Israel, Pakistan, North Korea, South Korea, Libya, Iraq, Egypt, and Argentina.

A recent Congressional Research Service study concludes that "U.S. armed forces and those of our allies will in the future be confronted by hostile military forces increasingly armed with ballistic missiles. The inexorable advance of technology in the world argues that it will be impossible to prevent more countries from developing a ballistic missile capability."[2]

Some analysts see the development of ballistic missiles as a major new step in the development of modern Third World forces of mass destruction. It may be inevitable, since the prohibition of the use of such weapons seems to be eroding, that one or more developing countries will fit chemical, biological, or nuclear warheads to ballistic missiles.

In the nuclear arena, only India, Israel, and China have achieved the necessary technology, but it is only a mater of time before nuclear balances become factors to be reckoned with. For the nearer term, chemical and biological substitutes are being acquired.

2. Congressional Research Service, *Ballistic Missile Proliferation Potential in the Third World* (Washington, DC: Library of Congress, 1986), p. 3.

In the chemical-warfare arena, estimates range from 15 to 30 countries that either possess or are actively working to possess chemical weapons.[3] Here it is not so much a matter of technological prowess as availability. The internationalization of the chemical industry—petrochemicals, fertilizers, insecticides—has put chemical arsenals within the reach of Third World militaries and virtually out of reach of any meaningful control regimes.

In the same way, the revolution in biotechnologies has dramatically lowered the threshold for future use. Indeed, it has been suggested that toxins could be produced by a university-level technician operating in a laboratory of only moderate sophistication. To underline the point, French police, in a raid on a terrorist safehouse in 1984, found typewritten sheets on bacterial pathology and flasks of botulinal cultures in the bathtub.[4]

Until recently, maverick states and their terrorist protégés lacked the technical and tactical wherewithal to inflict meaningful damage on the United States. This calculus will be changing as regional actors acquire more sophisticated arsenals through purchases or indigenous production of front-line equipment.

If recent history is any guide, we should recognize that regional powers are determined to acquire and exploit a range of highly destructive weapons against U.S. lives and interests. Although the maintenance of an adequate deterrent in the central theaters remains a critical

element of security, our credibility as a nation may hinge equally on our performance in meeting or extinguishing the far more likely and more frequent challenges from the Third World.

THE CHALLENGE OF U.S. RESPONSE

The net result is that second-rate powers are becoming first-rate threats. They are quite capable of drawing the United States into imbroglios not of its own making and into unwanted confrontation with the Soviet Union.

The ground rules under which the United States has operated since World War II are eroding. For much of the past three decades, the primary concern has been with the Soviet menace. New threats to U.S. security, however, are more closely related to the embedded regional antagonisms of well-armed Third World states. The United States may no longer be strong enough to enforce its will in these areas as and when it chooses, but neither is it strong enough to ignore the mounting danger in the Third World.

Three factors will increase the complexity of coping with Third World challengers: the lack of U.S. credibility in coping with regional problems; the paucity of our planning process in anticipating new threats; and the dearth of unconventional options to respond to conventional threats.

Loss of credibility

There is a latent tension in the American ethos regarding the projection of power to accomplish U.S. foreign-policy objectives. Americans tend to support firm and quick demonstrations of military prowess but fear becoming bogged down in conflicts overseas. The public may equate inaction with governmental impotence, but it is loath to commit forces

3. Brad Roberts, *Chemical and Biological Weapons: New Technologies and the Prospect for Negotiations* (Washington, DC: Woodrow Wilson International Center for Scholars, forthcoming), p. 15.

4. Joseph Douglass and Neil Livingstone, *America the Vulnerable: The Threat of Chemical and Biological Warfare* (Lexington, MA: Lexington Books, 1987), p. 146.

practically anywhere outside Europe or North Asia.

Uncertainty about what to do with America's military power permeates the entire society. In part, this is the legacy of Vietnam; virtually every debate over real or potential U.S. intervention is seen through the painful haze of that experience. In addition, the long nuclear peace has created its own mythology: weapons are built to demonstrate the potential for power, not its actuality.

The issue today is not whether U.S. power will deter regional opponents. Rather, it is whether their capabilities will deter us. Traditionally, the United States has been able to support its policy interests by bringing to bear a threat—even if only symbolic—of overwhelming force against regional adversaries. In recent years, however, that potential has not deterred many states from challenging our interests.

The U.S. choice of response to future challenges, if indeed we do respond, will inevitably be affected by the growth of Third World arsenals. The days in which one battleship could face down an entire Third World navy have disappeared. To cross Libya's Line of Death in the Gulf of Sidra, the United States was forced to deploy three carrier battle groups, the same amount of firepower military planners have allocated to deterring the Soviet navy on the northern flank of the North Atlantic Treaty Organization (NATO). At that level of force, regional operations become a burdensome undertaking. The amount of time and money required, as well as the cost to other options of diverting global forces to a regional task, may well exacerbate the credibility issue.

In mounting the Gulf of Sidra operation, U.S. planners had to overinsure against the possibility that Libya might be able to inflict casualties on American sailors or ships. The prime reason for amassing so much firepower was political and cultural, rather than military. For the United States, virtually any loss in personnel or material can create the perception of U.S. impotence and policy paralysis. The loss of 200 marines in Lebanon was a catastrophe that ultimately broke American policy in the Middle East. By contrast, countries like Iran or Iraq appear willing to sacrifice national and human assets on a wholesale basis.

The point is that a regional adversary does not have to defeat the United States in a high-intensity conflict to achieve a political victory. It need only strike a first, possibly decisive, blow—as in the Beirut marine-barracks bombing orchestrated by Syria—to send shock waves through the American leadership and public.

The graceless exit must not be permitted to become an American hallmark. With regard to specific regional challenges, a U.S. retreat may or may not make a great deal of strategic difference, but the image of failure created will inevitably have far more profound repercussions.

Others are learning that America's will can be broken either by the right kinds of unconventional attacks or by sheer persistence. That record of failure—and how to achieve it—is being readily absorbed abroad. For the Soviet Union, U.S. credibility remains the fundamental basis of deterrence. To the extent that conventional or unconventional successes by Third World states are taken as signs of U.S. military incompetence or loss of will, America's unreadiness to meet these challenges threatens to undermine the foundations of superpower stability as well.

Lack of planning

Framing a common agenda to deal with regional concerns is fraught with

internal pitfalls, largely self-generated. On the one hand, Americans react to the problem of state-sponsored terrorism with near hysteria. On the other hand, we simply assume that we possess the military and economic superiority to force a third-rate challenger to capitulate.

These internal contradictions reflect a deeper reality. The fact is that the United States has not thought through the problems of regional conflicts and, more important, how to avoid them. Our choice of battlegrounds often appears to be ad hoc, rooted in expedience rather than policy advancement.

In the Persian Gulf, for example, U.S. military deployments have been largely reactive—striking only when struck first—without any clearly delineated strategic objective or deterrent value. In Panama, U.S. economic and military pressure failed to dislodge General Noriega but has so far succeeded in crippling the Panamanian economy.

These kinds of incidents reflect less an innate weakness than the lack of a clear understanding of how power can be translated into influence under the new ground rules. For the Third World arena, the United States has few contingency plans or well-defined policies to cope with, much less understand, the challenges that lie ahead. To a large extent, this is directly attributable to the paucity of our own planning process. Outside of NATO and northern Asia, there are no options books that analyze in advance the complexities and consequences of applying various levels of power.

It should be clear by now that merely inserting American forces into an area, in the absence of a specific and feasible mission, is no substitute for policy. Indeed, the search for the quick military fix not only diverts resources and attention away from more promising avenues of response but risks drawing the United States into quagmires that are politically costly, strategically useless, or worse.

While it is impossible to anticipate the course of events or crises with any precision, it is nonetheless essential to try to minimize the degree of U.S. improvisation. Advance preparations should include extensive crisis simulations to explore the range of contingencies and options, lists of experts that can be consulted on the validity of the options book developed, and a better intelligence readout on regional politics and the personalities and propensities of our adversaries.

More important, the United States ought to be focusing more resources and attention on preventing crises from occurring at all. A great deal of resources are consumed in attempting to influence a crises; far less is required to anticipate and shape the course of events early on. For the Third World arena, this implies that the United States must begin to develop policy instruments that can sustain a longer-term, possibly lower-profile, presence in order to shape rather than merely react to the emerging order.

Unconventional capabilities

Another important element of the equation is the U.S. capability to cope with unconventional threats. A number of today's security problems are being played out in the unconventional arena. While many of those may have no direct linkage to the Soviet Union, they inject an element of unpredictability and hence instability into the conduct of global affairs.

Terrorism, for example, has become deeply embedded in the new international order. The United States holds little sway over nations such as Iran, Libya, Syria, Cuba, Bulgaria, or North Korea that

succor, train, and supply terrorist groups. For these states, terrorism represents a unique policy tool.[5] They have learned over time that the United States can be bested with virtual impunity by the use of such tactics as the seizure of the American embassy and diplomatic personnel in Tehran, the bombing of the American embassy and marine compound in Beirut, and attacks on NATO facilities and American servicemen across Europe.

The high-leverage, low-cost elements in such attacks provide them with an impact they are not yet able to duplicate on a conventional battlefield. For the United States, the fact that national intelligence services are providing the wherewithal and planning means that we can no longer gauge what the political or technical limitations of terrorist operations will be.

Similarly, drug smuggling poses a serious threat to our nations' socioeconomic health. With a black market valued at over $200 billion per year in the United States alone, the drug kingpins in South America and elsewhere have a vested interest, the financial wherewithal, and, increasingly, the military capabilities to protect their investment. Because their power and financial bases often rival the governments of the states in which they operate, U.S. diplomatic pressures have not made significant inroads toward resolving the production problem. Indeed, there is evidence that some Colombian officials may be ready to call retreat. The new attorney general has noted, "If one day Colombia's new government considers it wise, convenient, and positive to talk with drug traffickers to find a formula

of peace, which, after all, is the state's first obligation, the prosecutor general's office would have no objection."[6]

The United States has been hard put to devise a workable set of responses against these types of threats. Where diplomatic means have proven ineffective, Congress and the executive branch have been wont to fall back on U.S. military prowess. For the emerging spectrum of unconventional threats, however, this approach promises to yield diminishing returns. The most basic requisites for conventional operations are often lacking: knowledge of who the enemy is, where he is, or even how to impose penalties on him. In the unconventional arena, the enemy is diffuse, such as Colombian peasant coca growers; difficult to identify, such as anonymous terrorists; or difficult to gain access to, such as those under the protection of state sponsors or drug overlords.

The question must be raised, therefore, as to whether the United States will require a covert capability to respond to unconventional threats. Americans tend to be uncomfortable with covert or unconventional operations such as kidnapping, governmental decapitation, or assassination. Such techniques are viewed as ethically repugnant and a misuse of American power. To the extent possible, the United States has relied on the force of domestic and international law or conventional forces to deal with these problems, but there are clear limitations to the effectiveness of the former and escalatory risks associated with the latter.

Although the United States has made great strides in reaching international extraditional agreements to prosecute within our own system of justice terrorists accused of murdering Americans, the

---

5. See Edward Marks and Debra Van Opstal, eds., *Combatting Terrorism: A Matter of Leverage* (Washington, DC: Center for Strategic and International Studies, 1986).

6. Morton Kondracke, "Double Dealing," *New Republic*, 11 Apr. 1988, p. 18.

reliability of such agreements is invariably tempered by political realities. Some countries are not willing to risk the possibility of terrorist retaliation. In the *Achille Lauro* case, for example, not one but two of our allies, Italy and Egypt, granted safe passage to the mastermind of the operation, who today remains at large.

Moreover, when terrorists are operating at the behest of a state sponsor, prosecuting a few armed ruffians does little to deter future attacks. Even when the evidence demonstrates the complicity of hostile states, as in the La Belle disco bombing in West Germany, there is not always a straightforward military solution. In the instance cited, the United States selected Libya as a target of retaliation simply because the potential for outside repercussions was fairly low, while evidence that pointed to Syrian involvement with the terrorists was ignored for good reason. Any retaliation against Soviet client states—which are, not coincidentally, the chief international sponsors of terrorism—or even against Iran, with its proximity to the Soviet Union, might risk a wider confrontation. High-profile conventional military responses are not only questionable on policy grounds— for example, there is doubt as to whether such responses provide a real deterrent against future attacks—but are, in themselves, escalation prone.

Covert operations, as unpalatable as they may be, offer a way out of the inaction-escalation paradox. In the emerging multipolar environment, unconventional threats are likely to increase as Third World opponents exploit ways to challenge the United States. In the absence of a broader set of unconventional options, they are likely to do so with an increased measure of success.

COPING WITH FUTURE CHALLENGES

If one accepts the notion that the viability of U.S. security is currently affected far more by regional turbulence and unconventional threats than by Soviet expansion, then the way in which U.S. leaders define policy must inevitably alter. Our perception of threats outside Europe must begin to shift from the notion that we are troubleshooting at the margins of security to the realization that the ability to meet future regional challenges is itself one of the central objectives of America's security.

We are now at a foreign-policy watershed, perhaps as profound as the development of the containment strategy in the 1940s. In a more diffuse international environment, the demarcation between friends and enemies may become far less distinct. The continuing evolution of competing great-power blocs and regionally dominant competitors implies that greater flexibility in the management of alliances may be necessary. Many recent policy failures in the Third World have emerged from the erroneous belief that a shared vision of world order would continue to permeate our relations with formal allies.

In many ways, the world of the 1990s and beyond will more closely resemble the century before World War I. Erstwhile adversaries may become friends of convenience, while formerly staunch allies may come to be less supportive. The United States must resign itself with good grace to less collective cooperation with our allies in Third World regions.

By the same token, the United States may find it useful, on occasion, to collaborate with the Soviet Union in defusing regional trouble spots. Such collaboration would not be unprecedented. In 1985, for

example, the Soviet Union pressured Syria to intervene in the hijacking of Trans World Airlines flight 847 in Beirut, thereby obviating the need for a U.S. military response to free the hostages.

In the emerging international environment, U.S. leaders must develop the political alacrity to form ad hoc bilateral or multilateral arrangements, depending on individual circumstances. They must begin to relearn a form of diplomacy that is less entangled with formal alliance structures and more fluid in its ability to achieve policy goals.

Second, the United States must rethink its own security commitments. In an age of diminished resources, the financial wherewithal to prepare for every contingency is decreasing, even as the sources of threat are multiplying. Although U.S. interests remain global in scope, our ability to defend them will increasingly be defined by our economic means to do so.

The loss of the financial cushion must propel America's future leaders to define with considerable clarity where the threats to our interests lie and the most cost-effective means to meet them. In the absence of such a framework, budget reductions in themselves will end up shaping the parameters of American security policy.

Too, we must begin to understand and accept our own limitations. The public has been led to believe that the United States has an obligation to do something—or at least to have a statement or position ready—in response to any situation that might occur anywhere in the world. This has led to the corollary perception that the inability of U.S. leaders to employ moral or coercive suasion must imply that someone has bungled the incident. Although the United States has

never been omnipotent, our ability to influence events on the cheap is on the wane. When our vital interests are not at stake, not doing anything must be recognized as a realistic policy option rather than a symbol of ineptitude.

Finally, we must begin to develop rules of the road to avoid superpower confrontation in third areas. It is inevitable that U.S.-Soviet interests will collide; it is not axiomatic that escalation to nuclear confrontation will result.

Currently, the procedures for defusing threats outside central strategic theaters are dangerously ambiguous. In a series of crisis simulations run at the Center for Strategic and International Studies, we found that the former high-level decision makers tended to rely on nuclear signaling devices to warn the Soviet Union that vital U.S. interests were at stake.[7] The nuclear alerting process, successfully used during the 1973 Yom Kippur War, was the tactic of choice in each of the four simulations we conducted. In manipulating defense-condition levels, however, the simulated National Security Council transformed regional conflicts into exercises of global brinkmanship. The former government decision makers who participated in these simulations merely assumed that raising the nuclear ante would inevitably persuade the Soviets to back down. Balance-of-power issues were never implicitly or explicitly considered, primarily because the decision makers never foresaw global nuclear confrontation as a likely outcome of a signaling maneuver. More important, they never anticipated the likelihood that the Soviet team might

7. See Andrew Goldberg et al., *Leaders and Crisis* (Washington, DC: Center for Strategic and International Studies, 1987).

not blink, with the result that Soviet and American nuclear forces stood eyeball-to-eyeball in each of the exercises.

There is a compelling need for a broad range of positive crisis-management tools and procedures for the more frequent regional challenges we are likely to face. The Nuclear Risk Reduction Centers are a constructive step in the right direction.

But, beyond the risks of accident or miscalculation, the superpower crisis-management agenda should be directly focused on regional imbroglios. It is there that the relationships between projection of power and the potential for superpower entanglement are unpredictable and unstable.

* * *

QUESTIONS AND ANSWERS

Q: I think it would be very useful if you could elaborate on the role that the Soviet Union and the United States could play as collaborators in attempting to contain terrorism. It is in our mutual interest at least to cooperate where terrorism occurs, particularly in the event that a terrorist should obtain a nuclear weapon. It appears that the Soviet Union and the United States would benefit from collaborating to ensure that a terrorist does not move from the Warsaw Pact to the East or to the West or vice versa.

A (Kupperman): A great deal of terrorism worldwide was the product of the Soviet Union eight or ten years ago. The USSR has since backed away from it almost completely. Some of its client states, such as Syria, have been actively involved in terrorism. But the Soviets have also helped us. For instance, in the case of Trans World Airlines flight 847 in 1985, we went to the Soviets for help, and they went to the Syrians to convince the Syrians to help us.

There are many informal approaches at this point in time. It is clear that we are in active discussions with the Soviets. The point is that many of our client states or previous client states are not fully controllable, and we at least need to warn other countries of impending trouble.

While the progress is not 100 percent, it is certainly a lot better than it has been.

———

Q (James W. Skillen, Association for Public Justice, Washington, D.C.): Could you comment on the possibility of growing isolationism, at least in the mentality of American people? It seems that American isolationism will be encouraged by our economic problems, problems with our Latin American neighbors, and the ability to reach consensus at home on a broad defense strategy with respect to certain dangers.

A (Kupperman): I think that the tendency toward being isolationist will be a very serious one. We will not want to intervene. Even if we intend to intervene, one of the things that we must do is understand what our interests are. It is not clear that we have ever analyzed our interests carefully. Whether we become isolationist or not will depend upon the degree of clarity and the ability to communicate to the American public and to Congress. I think that the next president, whether it is Bush or Dukakis, will have a very short honeymoon and that isolationism will be one of the biggest things on his agenda.

———

Q (Alan W. Heston, American Academy of Political and Social Science, Philadelphia, Pennsylvania): How does the amount of nuclear strength that the United States and the Soviet Union want affect the U.S. defense budget or the priorities in the defense of the United States?

A (Kupperman): I think that the defense budget will decrease unless there is some clear and present danger that everyone can understand. The issue is going to be internal reallocation within the defense budget, and there is not much room because a lot of the defense budget is paid out for annuities, salaries, and so on. I think that the three military services and the joint-acquisition mechanisms within the Defense Department will fight fiercely over the budget with respect to Third World problems because they will not want to lose their toys. Many other programs will clamor to be included in the budget. We have a so-called war against drugs, which, incidentally, we are not winning. If the grave projections about the epidemic of acquired immune deficiency syndrome materialize, we will have problems of national-security proportions simply because of the costs that are involved, and the budget will be affected because the money must come from somewhere.

———————

Q (Arnold E. Smolens, Princeton Bank, New Jersey): Hans-Dietrich Genscher, the foreign minister of the Federal Republic of Germany, has said his country's official policy is freedom, independence, and nonalignment for the Third World. Do you think there is any chance that the United States would give support to that policy and try to get the other major powers to agree to it, as a means of extrication from those Third World conflicts that could in the end lead to a collision with Soviet Russia?

A (Kupperman): No.

———————

Q (Harrison B. Wilson, Commonwealth of Virginia): What clear policy does the United States have with respect to protecting its interests vis-à-vis the Third World?

A (Kupperman): At this point in time, and a little sad to say, I do not see a policy at all. Whoever becomes the next president will have to pay a lot of attention to this area. The policy not only will have to be based upon economic self-interest and national-security concerns and basing rights, but will also have to have some moral basis.

———————

Q (John C. Shea, West Chester State University, Pennsylvania): First, if you were making American policy, would you continue the presence of the American naval forces in the Persian Gulf or would you put them there in the first place? Do you think they are helpful in preventing the kind of low-intensity threat you have talked about? Second, we have three separate military services without any kind of joint military command. How can the military be integrated?

A (Kupperman): Concerning an integrated military, I think a lot of progress has been made in terms of joint acquisitions. There has been a tremendous amount of effort toward integration, but there are still many problems. As to the Persian Gulf, I think we have to stay there for a while. I am not sure the policy was a good idea to begin with, but there is no way to escape from it at the moment.

———————

Q (Raymond J. Donovan, Baltimore, Maryland): Will we ever have a foreign policy if we have a Congress that has the Boland amendment and son of the Boland amendment and grandson of the Boland amendment and so forth and changes its policy toward the contras with every poll of the American public? It seems to me that one of our problems is that we do not any longer have a foreign policy run by the executive in a consistent way.

A (Kupperman): The problem is that a president must tell Congress very soon after he takes office what he will pursue and how hard. The policy cannot be formulated on an ad hoc basis, and it ought not be formulated by zealots, which has happened in the Reagan administration.

————

Q (Kingdon W. Swayne, Bucks County Community College, Newtown, Pennsylvania): What moral questions should be addressed by U.S. policy vis-à-vis the rest of the world?

A (Kupperman): One obvious question is apartheid. Another matter that disturbs me greatly is the exploitation of Third World assets. We must think about what to give back in return and how to give it back. I think we must support a lot of nonmilitary activities in the Third World.

ANNALS, *AAPSS*, **500**, November 1988

The Price for Effective
Verification in an Era of
Expanding Arms Control

By PATRICIA BLISS McFATE and SIDNEY N. GRAYBEAL

ABSTRACT: Arms control has become an increasingly important aspect of U.S. security and foreign policy; at the same time, verification has emerged as the major consideration in judging arms-control agreements. Although the concept of military significance has been used as the criterion for determining effective verification of arms-control agreements over several presidential administrations, the demand for stringent and comprehensive verification regimes has increased in the past seven years to the point where implementing the regimes for the intermediate-range nuclear forces (INF) and Strategic Arms Reduction Talks (START) agreements will be costly, albeit beneficial because the agreements will contribute to bilateral relations and international security. The verification regime being put into place for the INF Treaty is the most rigorous and comprehensive ever negotiated. Verification of the START agreement will be far more extensive and expensive due to its broader scope and the fact that it reduces rather than eliminates classes of weapons. This article analyzes the verification criteria, costs, and benefits associated with current bilateral arms-control endeavors.

Patricia Bliss McFate, president of the American-Scandinavian Foundation, has served as deputy chairman, National Endowment for the Humanities; vice provost, University of Pennsylvania; and professor, School of Engineering and Applied Science, University of Pennsylvania. She is a fellow of the New York Academy of Sciences.

Sidney N. Graybeal, vice-president of System Planning Corporation, was a member of the delegation of the first Strategic Arms Limitation Talks and the first U.S. commissioner of the Standing Consultative Commission. He has worked on and written about verification and compliance issues for over thirty years.

ARMS control can and should contribute to national security. In today's world, however, there must be assurances that all parties to an agreement are complying with its provisions; thus verification has become an essential part of the arms-control process. Verification has taken a wide swing in popularity in the last eight years. It has been used to prove that agreements with the Soviet Union are neither possible nor in the interest of the United States and, more recently, to prove that agreements are both possible and desirable. Along the way, the Reagan administration's semantic and technological stumbling blocks to arms control have delayed new agreements and undermined existing ones. Moreover, the administration has raised verification requirements to unreasonably high levels, calling for excessive verification regimes. Recent concerns about verification—some real, others manufactured—and the apparent inability to resolve real and purported noncompliance issues could jeopardize the whole arms-control process.

Because verification is an important aspect of arms control and because it takes on added importance in bilateral agreements with the Soviet Union, the benefits of agreements that contribute to strategic stability outweigh the costs of verification even at excessive levels. If, however, verification requirements were brought down to reasonable levels, the benefits would outweigh the costs by far.

Arms-control agreements should be judged primarily on their military and political significance. In recent years, however, verification has become the central factor in evaluating the utility and effectiveness of past, present, and future arms-control agreements and the whole arms-control process. The meaning of the term also has varied from speaker to speaker, and its scope has expanded beyond the bounds of standard definition.

What is now referred to as the verification process goes beyond monitoring and evaluation into areas of designing verification regimes and formulating responses to noncompliance. The process includes the determination of compliance with existing agreements, policy decisions about what constitutes adequate or effective verification, the design and negotiation of regimes to meet security requirements, the implementation of verification provisions of completed agreements, and the determination of appropriate responses to ambiguous situations or clear noncompliance with specific provisions of the agreements. This view of verification as an all-encompassing process should be taken into account in assessing its price.

VERIFICATION CRITERIA

Considerable attention has focused on what constitutes "adequate"—the term used during the Nixon, Ford, and Carter administrations—or "effective"—the Reagan administration's term—verification. Although many would argue that the distinction between these terms is solely in the eyes of the beholder, the latter term seems to place emphasis on the production of a desired effect and suggests the use of more demanding standards. In many respects, the positions taken by the Reagan administration on verification requirements reflect this change in nomenclature. The approach to the verification of the Intermediate-Range Nuclear Forces (INF) Treaty and the resulting provisions of that treaty have produced the most extensive and rigorous regime ever successfully negotiated. In our view, it is probably more

than what is required for effective verification if the criterion of military significance is applied in evaluating the regime.

In fact, both the Carter and the Reagan administrations have utilized this criterion. In testimony given before the Senate in January 1988, Ambassador Paul Nitze described the INF verification regime as "effective," meaning that "if the other side moves beyond the limits of the Treaty in any militarily significant way, we would be able to detect such a violation in time to respond effectively and thereby to deny the other side the benefit of violation."[1]

This is essentially the same definition used by former Secretary of Defense Harold Brown during the hearings on the Strategic Arms Limitation Talks (SALT) II, when he explained that "any Soviet cheating which would pose a significant military risk or affect the strategic balance would be detected by our intelligence in time to respond effectively."[2]

The concept of effective verification is related to the nature and quantity of military forces considered necessary for maintaining stable deterrence and to the scope and nature of the agreement. For example, those who subscribe to a minimum-deterrence theory and consider present strategic forces excessive are unlikely to see the need for rigorous verification regimes. On the other hand, those who are concerned about the ability of present strategic forces to provide an adequate deterrent will press for stringent verification provisions. The latter group clearly dominated the design of the INF veri-

fication regime, and will attempt to determine the scope of the verification provisions as specified in the Strategic Arms Reduction Talks (START).

Similarly, the nature and scope of an agreement will also be a factor in an assessment of the effectiveness of the verification programs. The greater the size and survivability of the remaining strategic forces, the less will be the concern over possible cheating or circumvention. Significant reductions will cause a more careful evaluation of the effectiveness of the regime. In our view, START reductions of 50 percent of U.S. and Soviet strategic offensive arms will not upset the strategic balance or require extreme provisions to assure effective verification if judged on the basis of military significance; however, reductions on the order of 75 percent or greater could begin to generate some serious concerns about possible violations or circumventions affecting U.S. security interests.

Because arms-control agreements are essentially political instruments, any violations, real or perceived, take on major political significance. The Reagan administration's several reports to Congress on Soviet noncompliance with arms-control agreements, the press associated with these reports, and the frequent references made to them by senior officials and several members of Congress attest to their political significance regardless of their military importance. Official analyses of the potential military significance of these real and purported noncompliance issues are rare, suggesting that none of the issues meets the criterion of military significance.

This criterion is compatible with a verification regime that relies primarily on national technical means of verification, essentially unilateral intelligence cap-

1. U.S. Congress, Senate, Committee on Foreign Relations, *The INF Treaty*, 14 Apr. 1988, p. 41.

2. U.S. Congress, Senate, Committee on Foreign Relations, *The SALT II Treaty*, Hearings, pt. 2, 16-19 July 1979, pp. 239-40.

abilities, complemented by cooperative measures; but it stops short of the highly intrusive and potentially destabilizing short-notice, challenge inspections of suspect sites, the anywhere, anytime on-site inspections. The politically significant criterion, on the other hand, demands extensive, extremely stringent, and highly intrusive verification provisions.

COSTS OF VERIFICATION

There are significant costs associated with the verification process. These costs can be analyzed by looking at the verification considerations associated with the recently completed INF Treaty. It should be kept in mind that a START agreement is likely to require a significantly more rigorous regime in order to meet an effective verification level even in the context of military significance.

The verification provisions of the INF Treaty provide a useful precedent for a START agreement and for looking at the costs of verification; considerable additional verification costs will be incurred in implementing a START agreement.

National technical means—the intelligence collection and analysis capabilities—will continue to be the foundation for monitoring arms-control agreements and the key element in achieving effective verification. With or without any arms-control agreements, the United States requires extensive knowledge about Soviet military capabilities and intentions. Arms-control verification costs involve the incremental collection-system capabilities and analytical resources required to monitor agreements.

Two senators have recently expressed concern on this subject. Senator David Boren, chairman of the Senate Intelligence Committee, said that the committee had requested more funds than currently

planned for modernization of "technological systems," a term generally understood to include satellite surveillance, and he stated, "What we have now is insufficient if there were to be a START agreement."[3] Senator Malcolm Wallop has complained that "the confidence level [for verification of the INF Treaty] may be only 3 or 4" on a scale of 1 to 10 because the United States cannot inspect "suspect sites" beyond those specified in the treaty. Senator Wallop believes that the United States will need to spend $7 billion to $15 billion on new spy satellites to be sure that the Soviets do not "squirrel away several dozen [missiles] in Siberia."[4]

Senator Boren's committee adopted by unanimous vote the report *The INF Treaty: Monitoring and Verification Capabilities* on 21 March 1988. The committee concluded that "by a combination of National Technical Means and on-site inspection, the intelligence community will be able to monitor the drawdown and elimination of declared Soviet missiles, launchers and associated equipment with great certainty." The committee noted that the on-site inspections are applicable only to declared facilities, however, and that therefore "the burden of detecting banned activities at undeclared sites, where they are most likely to occur, will fall on National Technical Means of verification." In the report, the committee warned that "the extensive on-site inspection and portal monitoring that may be required by a START agreement, including suspect site inspections, could have a far more significant impact on U.S. counter-intelligence and security interests than

3. Susan F. Rasky, "U.S. Ability to Monitor Strategic Pact Is Doubted," *New York Times,* 17 Feb. 1988.

4. Hedrick Smith, "The Right against Reagan," *New York Times Magazine,* 17 Jan. 1988.

those agreed to in the INF Treaty." In this regard, it was noted, however, that "our own counterintelligence concerns about potential Soviet exploitation of on-site inspection rights may again outweigh the need for more intrusive and direct verification in future negotiations."[5]

INF and START verification requirements are affecting all executive-branch departments and agencies involved in national-security affairs. For example, the Department of Energy has created an Office of Arms Control, and the Federal Bureau of Investigation will require increased resources to monitor Soviet inspectors in the United States, including the Soviet inspection team stationed in Magna, Utah, for 13 years.

On 6 April 1988, Rowland Evans and Robert Novak reported that President Reagan intends to approve "a $6 billion to $12 billion satellite program to detect Soviet treaty cheating." According to Evans and Novak, key senators had warned the president that, without the program, "the new START pact he hopes to sign in Moscow will be dead on arrival in the Senate."[6]

Specific intelligence budget figures are classified, but it is clear that the Senate Intelligence Committee is recommending significant additional expenditures for improving national technical means in order to provide the capabilities for monitoring future arms-control agreements. These expenditures are worthwhile both for enhancing arms-control monitoring capabilities and for improving overall intelligence capabilities. Without access to classified data on both the collection

systems and the intelligence requirements, it is not possible to judge whether such expenditures may be adequate or excessive for security purposes and verification requirements.

The INF Treaty requires the United States and the Soviet Union to eliminate all intermediate-range missiles—which have a range between 1000 and 5500 kilometers—all shorter-range missiles—which have a range between 500 and 1000 kilometers—associated launchers, equipment, support facilities, and operating bases worldwide within a three-year period. This will involve the elimination, either by prescribed destruction procedures or by firing, of 1752 Soviet missiles and 867 U.S. missiles. The treaty also bans flight testing and production of these missiles as well as production of their launchers.

Even with the elimination of whole classes of missiles and their supporting equipment and facilities, along with bans on flight testing and production, the treaty and associated documents constitute the most stringent and comprehensive scheme of verification in the history of arms control. The treaty includes

—a detailed exchange of data, updated periodically, on the location of missile support facilities, the number of missiles and launchers at those facilities, and technical parameters of those systems;
—continuing notification of the movement of missiles and launchers between declared facilities;
—an initial baseline inspection to verify the number of missiles and launchers at all facilities declared in the data exchange;
—an elimination inspection to verify the destruction of missiles and launchers;

5. U.S. Congress, Senate, Select Committee on Intelligence, *The INF Treaty: Monitoring and Verification Capabilities,* 21 Mar. 1988, pp. 11-12, 16, 5.

6. "The Indigo-Lacrosse Satellite Gets the Nod," *Washington Post,* 6 Apr. 1988.

—close-out inspections to verify that the treaty-prohibited activities have ceased at each of the declared facilities;

—short-notice on-site inspections for 13 years at declared and formerly declared facilities;

—the right to monitor the Soviet final-assembly facility for SS-25 intercontinental ballistic missiles (ICBMs) at Votkinsk around the clock for 13 years to ensure it is not being used for SS-20 assembly;

—noninterference with national technical means;

—enhancement of national technical means—specifically, six times a year, the Soviets must, on six hours' notice, open the roofs of those SS-25 garages that are not subject to on-site inspection in order to show that no SS-20s are concealed within, and they must display the SS-25 launchers in the open; and

—the establishment of a Special Verification Commission, which can be convened at the request of either side to resolve problems relating to compliance with the treaty.

Some people are concerned about the accuracy of the SS-20 missile inventory numbers provided in the initial exchange of data and the ability of the Soviets to utilize in an effective military manner alleged excess missiles—it is reported that the Defense Intelligence Agency has estimated this number to be at least 165. A classified report by the Arms Control and Disarmament Agency sent on 8 March 1988 to the Senate Foreign Relations Committee stated that the U.S. intelligence community can effectively verify Soviet compliance with the INF Treaty without knowing the exact size of the Soviet arsenal, and it added that even

without knowing exactly how many missiles and launchers exist, the treaty's verification measures pose significant risks for the Soviets of U.S. detection and impose "considerable complexity on the Soviets should they seek to acquire a militarily useful force." The report also stated that "the ban on flight testing of INF systems will make it difficult over time" for the Soviets to ensure that any remaining missiles are "operationally useful."[7] On the other hand, Senator Jesse Helms has said that the INF verification procedures are "as full of holes as Swiss cheese."[8]

Senator Sam Nunn is questioning whether the INF Treaty also applies to future weapons built with new technologies. Although this issue was generated by Anti-Ballistic Missile (ABM) Treaty reinterpretation on the part of the administration, it is germane to INF and START agreements and will raise additional verification concerns.

COSTS OF IMPLEMENTATION

In order to examine the price for effective verification more deeply, we will look at the five main functional areas of verification in the INF Treaty, which will also be included in a START verification regime: (1) data exchanges, (2) notifications, (3) on-site inspections (OSIs), (4) resolution of questions relating to compliance, and (5) monitoring activities.

Data exchanges

The Memorandum of Understanding (MOU) includes detailed information on

7. R. Jeffrey Smith, "INF Pact Verifiable, ACDA Says," *Washington Post,* 10 Mar. 1988.
8. Helen Dewar, "Democrats Defend White House Candor as Shultz Testifies on INF Treaty," *Washington Post,* 15 Mar. 1988.

the characteristics and numbers of deployed and nondeployed missiles, their launchers and support equipment and structures, and their geographic locations in the United States, the USSR, the countries of the North Atlantic Treaty Organization, and the Warsaw Pact countries. These data must be updated within 30 days after entry into force of the treaty and at the end of each six-month interval thereafter; the updates must include identification of all changes during the six-month interval. The MOU contains 26 sites in the United States and Western Europe and 133 sites in the USSR and Eastern Europe subject to on-site inspection. These data exchanges will take place through the Nuclear Risk Reduction Centers. Keeping track of these U.S. and Soviet data and assuring they are complete and timely will require an extensive management-information system.

Notifications

The INF Treaty calls for elaborate notifications involving:

—the elimination of missiles, launchers, support structures and equipment, deployment areas, operating bases, and support facilities;

—the location of the elimination sites;

—scheduled dates and locations for missile launches for their elimination, including types of missiles;

—the transit of missiles or launchers including points, dates, and times of departure and arrival, modes of transportation, and specific time and location every four days while en route; and

—the date and location of launches of permitted research and development booster systems.

Like the data exchanges, implementing these notifications will require a capable management-information system. In addition, there will have to be numerous directives issued, detailed guidance provided, and periodic checking to assure that the required notifications are complete, accurate, and timely on the U.S. side; considerable monitoring of the accuracy and timeliness of Soviet notifications will be needed as well. All of these notifications are also to be provided through the Nuclear Risk Reduction Centers.

On-site inspections

Articles X and XI of the treaty along with the Protocols on Elimination and Inspection provide for various types of OSIs, including the right to conduct inspections of all declared facilities to verify the data base provided in the MOU over a 13-year period, verification by OSI of the elimination of missile systems and their support equipment and facilities within a 3-year period, and the continuous portal perimeter monitoring of one declared fixed assembly facility in each country for 13 years. The two protocols provide detailed instructions as to the required notifications, timing, and scope of the inspections and detailed data on what is to be inspected and how, including the equipment permitted the inspectors. They also include information on precisely how missiles and their launchers are to be eliminated, on the activities of the inspectors and their hosts in conducting and reporting the inspections, and on the privileges and immunities of the inspectors. The last item is not a small matter; essentially the inspectors will have diplomatic status.

To implement these extensive OSIs of declared facilities as specified in the INF

Treaty and associated documents, the U.S. government has established the On-Site Inspection Agency (OSIA) within the Department of Defense, headed by Brigadier General Roland Lajoie. Secretary of Defense Frank Carlucci told the Senate Armed Services Committee during ratification hearings that the OSIA will spend between $180 million and $200 million this year to begin carrying out the extensive verification provisions. The Defense Department has budgeted $198,350,000 for fiscal year 1988 and $148,200,000 for fiscal year 1989 for INF support costs, primarily for the OSIA and the elimination of missiles and associated equipment and facilities. It is reported that the OSIA will employ about 400 people who will staff a Red Team to inspect Soviet facilities and a Blue Team to escort Soviet inspectors in the United States. There will be 20 inspection teams of 10 members each, 2 of whom will be interpreters. According to press reports, the red inspection team will monitor Soviet activities and also be responsible for collecting military and industrial intelligence during inspections.

The short-notice OSIs of declared facilities over the 13-year period will contribute to confidence in the agreement, making cheating more difficult and costly, and they will provide a useful deterrent to militarily significant cheating. These inspections will pose some security risks but not nearly to the extent posed by the START inspections as contained in the recent Joint U.S.-Soviet Summit Statement, specifically, "the right to implement, in accordance with agreed-upon procedures, short-notice inspections at locations where either side considers covert deployment, production, storage or repair of strategic offensive arms could be occurring." This essentially permits short-notice challenge inspections—anywhere and anytime—of suspect sites in a START verification regime; such inspections of suspect sites were omitted from the INF Treaty.

The potential security implications of the INF on-site inspections of declared facilities and activities merit some attention. For example, there are often sensitive programs or activities being conducted in or near the declared facility that will be subject to short-notice inspections. The Soviet inspectors must be able to determine that there are no treaty-limited items present, but at the same time they must not acquire information on sensitive programs or activities. Such inspections can have an adverse and potentially costly impact on American industries and can raise difficult security and legal questions. If a facility must shut down during an inspection, who bears the costs? There is frequently the potential loss of proprietary information; how is this determined and who is responsible? In addition, some facilities are also involved in very sensitive so-called black programs, in which security considerations are of paramount concern; such programs may need to be removed from a facility subject to Soviet inspection—who bears the cost of the move or the potential loss of such future business by that company? On 29 February 1988, Senator Orin Hatch proposed legislation—the Arms Control Competitive and Economic Adjustment Commission Act—that would set up a five-member commission to hear complaints from defense firms that claim that they have lost potential contracts due to the presence of Soviet inspectors at their plants. The commission would have the ability to order that monetary awards be made to contractors.

Compliance questions

The INF Treaty calls for the establishment of a Special Verification Commission to resolve compliance questions and agree upon measures to improve the viability and effectiveness of the treaty. The ABM Treaty of 1972 established a Standing Consultative Commission, which was also involved in SALT II implementation and compliance issues. The functions and operations of these two bodies are essentially the same. In our view, the Standing Consultative Commission has proven to be an effective forum for implementing bilateral strategic arms-control agreements and for resolving most compliance issues; thus we do not see the need for establishing a new separate body for the INF Treaty. We believe that it would be more cost-effective and efficient to combine the Special Verification Commission and the Standing Consultative Commission into a single body responsible for handling implementation and compliance issues for the ABM Treaty, the INF Treaty, a START agreement, and any other future bilateral agreements with the Soviet Union.

Monitoring activities

Monitoring Soviet activities to determine compliance with the provisions of an agreement is an intelligence collection and analysis function performed by the intelligence community, which issues periodic classified monitoring reports on existing agreements. As noted earlier, the United States requires extensive knowledge about Soviet military capabilities and intentions with or without any arms-control agreements. The detailed monitoring requirements associated with the INF Treaty will place a significant additional burden on U.S. collection and analytical resources; the scope and nature of this burden will depend in large part on whether the military or the political criterion is applied in assessing effective verification. In general, when complete weapon systems are eliminated or banned, the monitoring requirements are less taxing on the resources of the intelligence community. Because a START agreement will not eliminate or ban categories of weapon systems, accounting for permitted systems and determining many of their characteristics—such as throw weight, number of reentry vehicles, nuclear versus nonnuclear payloads, range capabilities, and the like—will require both a major augmentation and a dedication of scarce intelligence collection and analytical resources.

There is also a little-noticed but resource-demanding monitoring task necessary for assuring American compliance with all the provisions of an agreement. This responsibility was assigned to the Department of Defense after the SALT I agreement in 1972 and is currently the responsibility of the Office of Under Secretary of Defense for Acquisition. It requires the establishment of a program to ensure continuing U.S. compliance, including procedures for determining the application of the agreement's provisions to weapons, weapon systems, and related supporting activities, the development and issuance of detailed guidance and instructions for implementing the program to all involved in governmental and contractor activities, and the providing of advice upon request. This overall monitoring task will require significant resources in view of the extensive elimination procedures, various OSIs, and numerous notifications contained in the INF Treaty. Similar monitoring tasks for a START

agreement will likely be an order of magnitude greater.

There is considerable controversy regarding the costs of implementing the INF Treaty versus the savings from eliminating two classes of nuclear weapons. The savings have been estimated to be anywhere from a few million dollars to $1 billion each year. Joseph E. Kelly, associate director of the General Accounting Office, in a letter to Senator Helms dated 24 March 1988, stated that the "Department of Defense has estimated that, as a result of the treaty, costs of $219 million in fiscal year 1988 and $240 million in fiscal year 1989 could be avoided for the Pershing II and GLCM programs."[9] In a letter dated 10 March to the Senate Committee on Foreign Relations, the acting director of the Congressional Budget Office, James L. Blum, wrote that "net savings could be as high as $1 billion per year although there may be a transition period during which the treaty costs slightly more than it saves."[10] According to the *Washington Times,* a government official familiar with the treaty's requirements said that "it will cost the United States about $2 billion annually for the next six years to beef up its intelligence-gathering systems to monitor Soviet compliance."[11]

POLITICAL COSTS

Most of the verification attention associated with the INF Treaty has been focused on the elaborate and rigorous provisions for OSIs, cooperative measures, and notifications. As we have noted, implementation of these complex and detailed provisions will require careful attention and considerable resources. During periods in which there are constructive and cooperative working relations between the United States and the Soviet Union, both sides want to see the arms-control process advance in a mutually advantageous manner; in these periods, it is possible to implement provisions with a minimum of friction and controversy. The potential for mischief making by either party, however, is inherent in the implementation of the provisions should the climate return to a cold-war environment. For example, what would happen if, intentionally or by innocent oversight or neglect, an OSI team requesting a short-notice challenge inspection was not taken to the designated facility within the prescribed time or not allowed into certain parts of the facility? What if a required notification is not received on time or at all? What if the resident inspectors are denied certain privileges they consider inherent in their diplomatic status? There are literally hundreds of such opportunities for mischief making, which in an adversarial climate could be blown up into an expansive and controversial noncompliance record; this record, in turn, could be used to undermine the whole arms-control process and jeopardize U.S.-Soviet relations.

There may be two other little-noticed costs associated with the INF and START agreements. Conventional wisdom says that arms-control agreements save money; it is possible, therefore, that the implementing costs associated with the extensive OSI procedures may erode public support for future agreements. There is also a suspicion on the part of some people that the intelligence community may be using INF and START verifica-

9. "INF Treaty: Cost of Weapon Systems to Be Destroyed and Possible Savings" (Fact sheet, General Accounting Office, Mar. 1988), p. 2.

10. *INF Treaty,* p. 348.

11. Warren Strobel, "INF Treaty Would Bring Savings, Otherwise Differing Studies Agree," *Washington Times,* 29 Mar. 1988.

tion requirements to obtain funding for additional intelligence collection and analysis capabilities.

POTENTIAL FUTURE
AGREEMENTS

There are numerous potential bilateral and multilateral arms-control agreements on the horizon, each of which will entail verification costs. We will only mention two of these: START, to which we have referred throughout this article, and prospective agreements related to conventional arms control in Europe.

START

The nature and the scope of a START agreement were agreed upon in the December 1987 Joint U.S.-Soviet Summit Statement. Each side will be limited to 1600 strategic nuclear delivery vehicles with a total of 6000 warheads. A maximum of 4900 warheads may be on ICBMs and sea-launched ballistic missiles (SLBMs), with no more than 1540 warheads on 154 heavy ICBMs within this limit. These limits will result in a 50 percent reduction in Soviet aggregate ICBM and SLBM throw weight. The Summit Statement also includes the framework for START verification, which builds upon the provisions of the INF Treaty and, at the minimum, will include

- —weapon-systems data base and data exchanges;
- —baseline inspections;
- —elimination inspections;
- —continuous portal monitoring of critical production and support facilities;
- —short-notice on-site inspection of declared and suspect sites;
- —provisions prohibiting concealment or other activities that impede verifi-

cation by national technical means; and
- —cooperative measures to enhance national technical means.

A START agreement will pose serious verification problems. Both rail- and road-mobile ICBMs are difficult to detect and count; rail-mobile missiles in particular can be disguised as ordinary rail cars in the USSR. Sea-launched cruise missiles (SLCMs) present an extremely difficult—if not impossible—monitoring task if the agreement only limits nuclear-armed SLCMs because these are externally indistinguishable from conventionally armed SLCMs. In addition, SLCMs can be deployed on almost any surface ship or submarine. Deployed nuclear-armed air-launched cruise missiles (ALCMs) will be limited, and verification will be accompanied by what are called counting rules, that is, specifications of an agreed number of ALCMs per heavy bomber. ALCMs also pose the problem of differentiation between those nuclear-armed and those non-nuclear-armed. Verifying the range of both SLCMs and ALCMs will be a difficult task, particularly if telemetry is not available. Ballistic-missile warhead limits will also involve counting rules, the accuracy of which must be verified. START may include limits on ballistic-missile throw weight, which will pose additional verification requirements. In our view, it should be possible to formulate verification procedures for land- and rail-mobile ICBMs and throw-weight limits compatible with the criterion of military significance; however, monitoring nuclear-armed SLCMs and ALCMs with no limits on their conventional counterparts will create the most difficult START verification problems even with cooperative measures and OSI procedures.

It is clear from this framework and for the many reasons mentioned earlier that a START verification regime will be far more extensive than that for the INF Treaty, and that the price for effective verification will be considerably greater in both dollars and human resources.

Conventional arms reductions in Europe

With the signing of the INF Treaty, considerable attention is being devoted to the possibility of conventional arms-control reductions in Europe, sometimes referred to as the Conventional Stability Talks. Many people in the arms-control community worry that verification may be so difficult as to make conventional arms control impossible to achieve. We do not share this view. We believe that conventional arms control should focus on armaments, and not on manpower as has been the case in the Vienna negotiations on Mutual and Balanced Force Reductions in Europe, and that any verification regime should be based on the concept of military significance appropriate for the European area. We recognize that there will be major verification challenges due in large measure to the great number of weapons to be accounted for, their geographical extent, their relatively small size, and the importance of knowing both their location and their state of readiness.

Effective verification will be difficult to achieve and probably very costly, but certainly not impossible. In addition to some of the useful verification precedents in the INF Treaty, there are other pertinent factors. For example, the Stockholm Conference on Confidence- and Security-Building Measures and Disarmament in Europe reached an agreement in September 1986 requiring notifications by all parties of major military exercises, that is, exercises and troop concentrations at or over 13,000. Three on-site challenge inspections of certain military activities are permitted per year. To date, there have been nine inspections: five by the West and four by the East. The location of the most recent inspection conducted by the United States was the German Democratic Republic on 10-12 April 1988; the USSR conducted an inspection in Norway on 13-15 March 1988. According to Admiral William J. Crowe, chairman of the Joint Chiefs of Staff, "Those inspections have been very successful."[12] Formidable work lies ahead in formulating and achieving meaningful conventional arms-control agreements; verification will be a dominant consideration, but it should not be the stumbling block in the process.

BENEFITS OF VERIFICATION

Although we have focused on the price of verification, one should not overlook the potential benefits of an effective regime that is implemented in a positive and constructive manner. To mention a few key benefits, effective arms-control verification regimes

—build confidence in the agreements and thus enhance their viability;
—provide an early warning system concerning the erosion of the agreement;
—reduce the opportunities and incentives to cheat;
—strengthen the arms-control process;
—remove uncertainties from the military balance;
—contribute to improved bilateral relations; and

12. Thomas K. Longstreth, "The Future of Conventional Arms Control in Europe," *F.A.S. Public Interest Report,* Feb. 1988, p. 6.

—open up the Soviet Union—and also acquire some positive intelligence that contributes to U.S. security.

The contribution of arms-control agreements and the arms-control process to U.S. security and world stability should dominate any evaluation. Verification costs and benefits, while important, are second-order considerations compared to the substantive content of the agreement.

SUMMARY

Effective verification will continue to be essential for the attainment and viability of arms-control agreements and for the maintenance of the arms-control process. There is, however, considerable controversy over what constitutes effective verification and the price to be paid for it. Application of the test of military significance in judging the effectiveness of verification regimes is consistent with U.S. security and will avoid unrealistic verification requirements and exorbitant costs.

The INF Treaty contains the most extensive and rigorous verification provisions ever negotiated for any arms-control agreement, and its implementation will be costly in both dollars and personnel. In our view, the provisions are probably excessive for protecting U.S. security but necessary to obtain ratification in the current environment. In addition, they will provide a useful precedent for a more complex and militarily significant START agreement, which will contain a markedly more demanding verification regime with commensurate increases in the resources required for its implementation. In the ratification hearings for the INF Treaty, verification will be a key issue; it is likely that much of the debate will be focused on the precedence for a START agreement.

Verification has become the criterion for judging arms-control agreements. In fact, in today's environment, the verification tail seems to be wagging the arms-control dog. Some are beginning to question if the United States may not be generating unnecessary verification procedures and costs to the long-term detriment of arms control. In our view, verification costs are becoming excessive in terms of what is truly required to protect U.S. security, particularly as we ensure strategic stability by making our strategic forces increasingly more invulnerable. Even with these excessive costs, however, we believe that the overall benefits resulting from the confidence that all parties are complying with arms-control agreements outweigh current and likely future verification costs. We reach this conclusion based on our belief that arms control has contributed and will continue to contribute to maintaining national security, to improving relations between the United States and the USSR, and to creating a stable environment marked by constructive international relations.

* * *

QUESTIONS AND ANSWERS

Q (Robert Dodge, Washington and Jefferson College, Washington, Pennsylvania): Concerning your conclusion about too much emphasis on verification and its costs, would it not be advisable not to push ahead with START so quickly but

to wait until there has been a reasonable interval of time to implement the verification process under the INF agreement?

A (Graybeal): You are absolutely correct. The complexities of the INF verification regime are really only the tip of the iceberg; there is much more complexity involved here. The United States would be very smart to take some time and learn from the INF experience, learn from the mistakes, learn from the accomplishments before beginning work on the details of a START verification regime. Signing an agreement on an overall, broad structure for START, such as on force levels, will not jeopardize U.S. security, but if we try to rush through a verification regime for START, with the additional complexities, we would be asking for trouble. We should take nine months to a year to learn from the INF experience and carefully structure the START verification, because a START agreement would be military, whereas the INF agreement is 80 percent to 90 percent political and only 10 percent military.

Q (Robert J. Courtney, LaSalle University, Philadelphia, Pennsylvania): Given that verification is vital, what happens if there is a violation? And what is meant by a country's "effective response"?

A (Graybeal): If a country does not comply, the question is, What can be done? There is no international court for noncompliance; there is no penalty. So far there has been only one clear case of noncompliance with respect to the ABM Treaty, but there are a lot of other ambiguities that need to be clarified.

When we talk about responding effectively, in the context of military significance as defined by Paul Nitze and Harold Brown, we mean that, from a military-significance standpoint, the intel-

ligence community will determine any Soviet activities of sufficient magnitude to jeopardize U.S. security and that it will so determine in time for the United States to respond. The response could be pulling out of the agreement, redeploying forces, or starting new programs. The Reagan administration uses the term "proportional response." We are not sure what that means; we have not seen any proportional response.

There is a third area that should be looked at. If the United States is not sure that the verification regime in an agreement is sufficient to protect U.S. security interests, even in terms of a militarily significant criterion, then why do we not build into the agreement some research and development hedges? These would be specific programs designed to compensate for any possible Soviet cheating in different areas. When Congress ratified such an agreement, it would ratify an agreement with clear and known verification uncertainties but also one with specific Defense Department programs, military research development programs, to assure that security is protected, even if the Soviets should violate the agreement or cheat. Such hedges are normally known as a safeguard, and having them is not new. They were part of the Limited Test Ban Treaty of 1963. One of them was that we would spend $250 million a year for several years to protect our readiness to test in case the Soviets broke the agreement.

Q (Dario Scuka, Library of Congress, Washington, D.C.): Our government has charged abuses of or noncompliance with the ABM Treaty for quite a few years. If we have charged noncompliance, it seems that we have had verification capability all along to that extent. We are now at a

more critical period in which effectively a whole family of nuclear weapons are being eliminated. Our need for verification has increased proportionally—we must have it.

Again, from a logical and intellectual perspective, there is no such thing as complete, total verification. I would also argue that one should look for adequate verification, but we should not ask Senator Helms what is adequate. You have quoted several sources that are less than bias free.

Finally, do you think that a paper similar to yours has already been prepared or is being prepared in Moscow?

A (Graybeal): Concerning Senator Helms, we have tried to provide an objective view from both sides of the coin. We hope it is evident, however, that we believe arms control is in our interest and that we should continue to pursue it. But this is not necessarily a universal position.

Regarding the ABM Treaty, there is a clear-cut case of noncompliance: the Krasnoyarsk radar, which is a large phased-array radar not located on the periphery of the USSR and facing outward as called for by the treaty. The Krasnoyarsk radar, in our view, is not a militarily significant item, but it has to be corrected. To leave a festering wound of that nature would undermine the whole process.

On the question of perfect verification, I know of no one, even the strongest proponents of military force and opponents of arms control, who has said there can be perfect or foolproof verification. Secretary Shultz has testified on the INF agreement that there is no such thing as 100 percent verification; I would add that, from our research, there is no such thing as a perfect agreement. An agreement cannot be drafted that will not raise ambiguities, so a consulting body is needed

to implement it. In addition, criteria must be developed for judging a verification regime. We are in the process of designing a regime for START. Many people are arguing that that regime is going to be inadequate unless we have the ability to account for every single additional Soviet missile. They are applying political criteria. Other people are applying very liberal criteria, namely, that one submarine with about 160 warheads is adequate deterrent for the Soviets, so there is no need to worry about a few hundred of their missiles. Part of our concern is that the verification for declared facilities is so rigorous. The United States is spending millions of dollars to be sure that the Soviets do not build one extra missile when the baseline can be off by several hundred. Assets are being misappropriated. There is a disproportionate emphasis on verification compared to the whole arms-control process and what it can and should contribute to U.S. security.

———

Q (Marvin E. Wolfgang, American Academy of Political and Social Science, Philadelphia, Pennsylvania): First, what are the major parameters involved in an algorithm of costs of verification? Second, is it unreasonable for the United States to ask the countries of the North Atlantic Treaty Organization (NATO), and perhaps even Japan, to contribute toward those costs?

A (Graybeal): Many interrelated factors must be taken into account in assessing the cost of verification. First, there are the national technical means, which are necessary for U.S. security. There are certain incremental costs, and a lot of these are designed to be sure that the Soviets are complying with a specific provision even though that provision may not be militarily significant. In other

words, the intelligence community provides a fairly accurate assessment of Soviet capabilities and usually also a good assessment of their intentions, which it needs for planning. After national technical means and incremental costs—the fundamentals—cooperative measures are added. Cooperative measures could be the exchange of data or the opening of certain facilities for on-site inspection. The data exchanges are not costly, except in labor, resources, and management-information systems. But inspections are costly. To begin inspections under INF, 400 people will be needed to staff the On-Site Inspection Agency, which will have 20 teams. Each team will require two Russian-speaking interpreters, and this stipulation carries a resource cost. There will be costs in finding the interpreters, and in finding them in a very short time. For example, they might have to be pulled from other parts of the government, thereby creating losses that will have to be compensated for.

With a START agreement, there will be a larger number of facilities, and if each requires inspections, costs will include an increased number of teams, the logistics of moving them around, interpreters for each of them, and many other indirect intangible factors. When there are calls for more and better verification, also to be considered are those sorts of costs. Some have even made the statement that the verification cost of future arms-control agreements may be so great that we cannot afford arms control. The cost of arms control is beginning to be a serious concern. Ironically, a beautiful way to kill arms control is through more and better verification and the attendant costs.

Concerning your second question, sharing verification costs is almost impossible in a bilateral relationship. While in terms

of defense of NATO, I agree that the burden should be shared, verification is different. There are two basic problems with arms-control verification in burden sharing, or in having the allies contribute. First, the relevant agreements are essentially bilateral. Second, the United States has its own national technical means, some of which are extremely sensitive. Some of them we share with our allies, a lot of them we do not. The problem here is the difficulty in sharing information. We do provide detailed information to the allies, but it would be difficult, in my view, to have 15 nations sit down and decide whether something is an ambiguity or noncompliance issue or not. Even in arrangements involving several parties, there are advantages in having the key players be the Soviet Union and the United States. The likelihood of conventional arms control is going to require changes, however. Conventional arms-control agreements in Europe will involve our allies in a multilateral way, and it will be absolutely essential to have a mechanism for both sharing information with them and having them share the burden and cost of this information.

———

Q (James W. Skillen, Association for Public Justice, Washington, D.C.): If overemphasis on verification becomes counterproductive, is there a way to demonstrate politically its significance and its worth elsewhere? Are some of the verification means translatable to other kinds of weapons systems and to other parts of the world?

A (Graybeal): Let me begin my answer with a reminder about the role that arms control plays. Arms control is not an end in and of itself. There are national objectives and there are military programs to accomplish those objectives; then one de-

termines how arms control fits into that. The second point is that the great concern ever since 1958 has been nuclear weapons. The nuclear threat has dominated the thinking in the arms-control area. The likelihood of a nuclear war between the Soviets and the United States is very low. I agree that the focus needs to shift away from verification, but putting this cap on the nuclear genie is essential to stability because everybody is worried that nuclear arms will escalate out of control. In terms of application elsewhere in the world, the techniques and assets that are being developed for verification also improve intelligence-collection capabilities. These capabilities could be applied to crisis management. Very few aspects of on-site inspection or special cooperative measures, though, have application to Nicaragua or other areas. The likelihood of that spillover is very small.

Q (Kingdon W. Swayne, Bucks County Community College, Newtown, Pennsylvania): For the past 25 years, the main battle lines were between those who saw nuclear weapons as instruments of national security through deterrence and those who saw nuclear weapons as instruments of national security through domination, through relative superior war-fighting capability. Now that the emphasis in Washington has shifted to arms-control agreements, where is the balance between the deterrence school and the war-fighting school? In addition, may some of the sniping that is going on through the verification issue become the straw man raised by the nuclear-superiority crowd?

A (Graybeal): I cannot give you much insight into strategy in Washington because it is a moving target. It is clear that deterrence has been the basic U.S. strategy and that it will continue to be. The

question is what mechanism should be used to deter war. There are some major shifts taking place between the nuclear and the nonnuclear forces. Technology is moving so fast now a lot of military objectives can actually be accomplished with nonnuclear weapons. Some people worry a little bit about that because the world is being made safer for conventional war.

I do not know to what extent the verification-of-deterrence argument will still be based on a deterrence philosophy with respect to the Soviets, but the strategy must be adjusted to take care of the Third World. My personal view is that we cannot be the policemen of the world. In addition, we should pull back and assess our interests and be a little less aggressive in moving forces into regions of the world before we are quite clear of what the outcome may be.

Q (Swayne): Is there comparable discussion taking place in the USSR with respect to the costs of verification?

A (Graybeal): There seems to be a concern for cost on the part of the Soviets, but I do not believe costs drive any major Soviet considerations. The Soviets choose the least expensive, most reliable, proven systems, so cost is not a driving factor in that sense, but they are facing so many economic problems that I think cost is going to come to the forefront in structuring their forces and in moving into the conventional arms area. Verification cost would probably not be a significant factor for them. They have satellites, they have a better espionage system, they have agents, and I do not see that they will cut back on that area. Furthermore, I do not think that the Soviets' verification requirements are anywhere near as great as those of the United States. The Soviets also have an advantage in that the United States is an open society, with many

sources of information available to them—for example, congressional records. They have a tremendous sense of what the United States can do. Likewise, it is difficult for the United States to cheat. It is hard to imagine a U.S. plan to build 400 clandestine MX missiles in a plant out in the country that would not be leaked out. So there is a built-in protection mechanism the Soviets have with respect to our open society that we do not have with respect to Soviet society.

ANNALS, *AAPSS*, **500**, November 1988

The United States and the International Control of AIDS

By JAMES F. McTIGUE

ABSTRACT: Before the end of 1988, 300,000 cases of acquired immune deficiency syndrome (AIDS) are expected to have been reported worldwide since 1981. Three epidemiological patterns have emerged. One, in the Americas and Europe, is where transmission is primarily among homosexual men and intravenous drug users. In Africa, the virus primarily is spread heterosexually. A third pattern, in Asia, the Middle East, and Eastern Europe, is manifested by low prevalence but transmission through homosexual and heterosexual contact and contaminated needles. AIDS cases will increase in number dramatically over the next three years, with devastating social and economic consequences. Health-care systems and economic resources in large cities in the United States will be severely strained. African countries will lose many educated and economic leaders. Many Third World countries will have lower productivity and economic output. A global strategy is emerging to understand and control the spread of AIDS. To provide the commitment and leadership necessary to control AIDS in the rest of the world, the United States must first demonstrate a stronger moral conviction and societal will to control the disease in this country.

James F. McTigue is currently research director at the National Center for Social Policy & Practice, Washington, D.C. He was the chief scientist officer of the U.S. Public Health Service from 1982 to 1987. In that capacity, he was the principal scientific writer and epidemiologist for the Surgeon General's Report on AIDS. His current research interests include ethical dilemmas raised by acquired immune deficiency syndrome (AIDS), access to care for people with AIDS, and the psychosocial aspects of AIDS.

F EW diseases in modern times have been called pandemics, occurring over wide geographic areas of the world and affecting an exceptionally high proportion of the population. Acquired immune deficiency syndrome (AIDS) is a pandemic. It has been compared to bubonic plague, and the people with AIDS are treated as outcasts, like lepers of old. AIDS is in all parts of the world, affects many people, and is socially and politically explosive. AIDS poses an unparalleled challenge to the world's public health authorities and to political leaders seeking to reduce the spread of the disease and to provide care for the people with AIDS.

Since AIDS was first identified in 1981, over 85,000 cases of it have been reported worldwide by approximately 140 countries[1] (see Table 1), but because of incomplete surveillance and reporting, the exact number of cases is probably closer to 150,000 cases in 160 countries.[2] Another 150,000 cases are expected during 1988, bringing the estimated number struck by the disease worldwide to be over 300,000 by the end of the year. Over the next five years, the world could add anywhere from 500,000 to 3 million new cases.[3]

Three distinct epidemiological patterns have emerged throughout the world. The first pattern occurs in the United States, most of the other American countries, and Europe, where the transmission of the human immunodeficiency virus (HIV) has occurred predominantly among homosexual men and intravenous drug users. A second pattern occurs in Africa, where the infection primarily spreads heterosex-

ually. In some African cities, up to 30 percent of the 20-to-40-year-old age group and 90 percent of the female prostitutes are infected. A third pattern occurs in Asia, the Middle East, Eastern Europe, and some rural areas of South America, where the virus has more recently emerged. This latter pattern is manifested by a very low prevalence of infection even among persons with multiple sex partners. There are both homosexual transmission and heterosexual transmission as well as recent indication of spread into the intravenous-drug-abusing communities.[4]

The incidence of AIDS in Asia has been lower than elsewhere. Asia accounted for only 1 percent of the almost 90,000 cases of AIDS reported to the World Health Organization (WHO).[5] Many of the cases reported from Asia have been in foreigners or in Asians who acquired the infection elsewhere and returned home. Health officials have been monitoring prostitutes and venereal-disease clinics to detect early infections.

Rather than sex or prostitution as the primary entry point of the disease into Asia, however, intravenous drug abusers are playing the main amplification role. In Bangkok, no infections among intravenous drug abusers were reported in 1985 or 1986, and only 1 percent of the intravenous drug abusers tested in 1987 were HIV positive. But in the first three months of 1988, the number of intravenous drug abusers testing positive for infection with the AIDS virus jumped to 16 percent. This explosive increase closely parallels similar outbreaks in the communities of intravenous drug abusers in Edinburgh, Scotland, and in Milan, Italy.[6]

The disease has established significant beachheads in Europe and Latin Amer-

1. *Weekly Epidemiological Record,* 1 Apr. 1988.

2. Jonathan M. Mann, Presentation to International Conference on AIDS Prevention, London, Jan. 1988.

3. Peter Piot et al., "AIDS: An International Perspective," *Science,* Feb. 1988, pp. 239, 583.

4. Ibid.

5. Jonathan M. Mann, Presentation to the President's AIDS Commission, Washington, DC, 18 April 1988.

6. Ibid.

TABLE 1
AIDS CASES REPORTED TO THE WORLD HEALTH ORGANIZATION
AS OF 31 MARCH 1988

Continent	Number of Cases	Number of Countries Reporting		
		Total	Zero Cases	One or More Cases
Africa	10,995	51	8	43
Americas	62,536	44	2	42
Asia	231	36	15	21
Europe	10,677	28	1	27
Oceania	834	14	10	4
Total	85,273	173	36	137

SOURCE: *Weekly Epidemiological Record*, 1 Apr. 1988, pp. 102, 103.

ica, each region reporting more than 8000 cases by the end of 1987.[7] The disease is especially rampant in Central Africa, where between 5 and 30 percent of young adults in the major urban areas are infected. Americans now account for about two-thirds of the reported worldwide cases.[8] At the present rate of growth, the United States will add at least 90,000 new cases per year within the next three years, and the U.S. Public Health Service estimates that by 1991 more than 270,000 people in the United States will have contracted the disease.[9]

Between 1 and 1.5 million persons in the United States are believed to be infected with the AIDS virus, and it is conservatively estimated that more than 0.5 million of these have signs of illness.[10]

(See Table 2.) Approximately 30 percent of these AIDS-virus carriers will develop AIDS within the next five years. An ongoing prospective study of a cohort of homosexual males in San Francisco who have been followed for six years indicates that 80 percent of these men developed signs of immune-system damage.[11]

Little doubt now exists about how this disease spreads. AIDS is transmitted by sexual contact and the exchange of infected blood. Among homosexual and bisexual men, rectal intercourse is the primary means of transmission. The virus enters through the ready pathway of the hemorrhoidal tissue in the lining of the rectum.

AIDS IN THE UNITED STATES

Since AIDS was first reported in the United States, it has been confined pri-

7. Piot et al., "AIDS: An International Perspective."

8. *Weekly Epidemiological Record*, 1 April 1988.

9. David D. Ho, Roger J. Pomerantz, and Joan C. Kaplan, "Pathogenesis of Infection with Human Immunodeficiency Virus," *New England Journal of Medicine*, 317(5):278 (1988).

10. Thomas C. Quinn et al., "Seroprevalence of HIV," *Science*, Nov. 1986, pp. 234, 955.

11. Harold W. Jaffe, "AIDS Syndrome in a Cohort of Homosexual Men: Six Year Follow-up Study," *Annals of Internal Medicine*, 103:2 (Aug. 1985).

TABLE 2
PROPORTION OF EACH RISK GROUP ESTIMATED TO BE INFECTED

	Size of Risk Group	Percentage Infected	Number Infected
Homosexual men	2.5 million	20-25%	500,000 to 625,000
Bisexual men	2.5 million to 7.5 million	5%	125,000 to 375,000
Regular intravenous drug users (at least weekly)	900,000	25%	225,000
Occasional intravenous drug users	200,000	5%	10,000
Hemophilia A (severe)	12,400	70%	8,700
Hemophilia B	3,100	35%	1,100
Heterosexuals	142 million	0.021%	30,000
Others	Not available	Not available	45,000 to 127,000
Total			945,000 to 1.4 million

SOURCE: Centers for Disease Control, Atlanta, GA, 1988.

marily to homosexual and bisexual men; they account for approximately 75 percent of the cases to date. (See Table 3.) Intravenous drug abusers make up about 16 percent of the total cases reported. In the winter and early spring of 1988, there was a definite shift in this country. For the first time since the epidemic began, the number of new AIDS patients in major cities who were intravenous drug users exceeded the number who were homosexual or bisexual men. In New York City, from January to March 1988, the number of intravenous drug users reported with AIDS surpassed the number of homosexual and bisexual men for the first time.[12]

12. Stephen C. Joseph, "AIDS in New York City" (Study released by New York City Department of Health, 16 Apr. 1988).

AIDS IN AFRICA

The available data suggest that the AIDS virus has long festered at low levels in various areas of Africa. The social upheavals and migration to the cities during the late 1970s allowed the virus to spread dramatically within urban areas of Central Africa.[13] The migration of large numbers of people from the rural areas of Africa, where there were strong tribal and familial restraints, into the urban settings brought about disruptions in traditional life-styles and invited high-risk behavior and exposure to HIV. The

13. Nzila Nzilambi, Keven M. DeCock, and Joseph B. McCormick, "The Prevalence of Infection with Human Immunodeficiency Virus over a 10-Year Period in Rural Zaire," *New England Journal of Medicine,* Feb. 1988.

TABLE 3
REPORTED AIDS CASES BY RISK GROUP (Percentage)

Homosexual and bisexual men	74*
Intravenous drug users	16
Hemophilia-affected people	1
Heterosexuals	4
People infected by blood transfusions	2
Others	3
Total	100

SOURCE: Centers for Disease Control, Atlanta, GA, 1988.
*Includes 8 percent homosexual and bisexual intravenous drug users.

life-style of many urban Africans, minus the previous tribal taboos, often involved multiple sexual partners, prostitution, and widespread venereal disease. The prevalence of gonorrhea is 10 percent in Kampala, Uganda. Venereal diseases, which compromise the integrity of the tissues of the vagina and the penis, contribute to the transmission of AIDS.

Throughout Africa, prostitutes are believed to be a major reason for the spread of the disease. A study completed last year in the Congo's capital, Brazzaville, found that 34 percent of the prostitutes tested had the virus and that 64 percent of the prostitutes in Pointe-Noir, also in the Congo, tested positive for the HIV infection.[14]

Transfusions of blood are the second most common source of AIDS transmission in Africa behind heterosexual sex. A study has found that nearly 1 in 15 Central African children who received blood transfusions in the treatment of malaria-related anemia may have become infected with the AIDS virus. More than 1000 children in Central Africa may have received transfusions with HIV-infected blood in the past five years.[15] Some hospitals have only recently initiated screening of blood for transfusions.

The cost of HIV testing of the blood supply can be an additional economic burden. It therefore has a relatively low priority for many Third World countries struggling with other expensive programs to control malaria, river blindness, malnutrition, and childhood diarrhea. It is estimated that in all of sub-Saharan Africa there are 1 million blood donations per year. The cost to test each blood donation is $1.00, for a cost of $1 million per year to provide a safe blood supply.[16]

ECONOMIC AND SOCIAL
IMPACT OF AIDS IN
THE UNITED STATES

The pragmatic imperatives and political impact yet to be realized in the United States will be the inability of the health-care system to care for the number of AIDS cases in certain areas of the coun-

14. James Brooke, "New Surge of AIDS in Congo May Be an Omen for Africa," *New York Times,* 22 Jan. 1988.

15. Thomas C. Quinn et al., "The Association between Malaria, Blood Transfusions, and HIV Seropositivity in a Pediatric Population in Kinshasa, Zaire," *Journal of the American Medical Association,* 22 Jan. 1988, p. 545.

16. Anthony F. H. Britten, "Making Blood Transfusions Safer," *World Health Magazine,* Mar. 1988.

try. In some cities, ambulances already divert patients from one hospital to another. Even heart-attack and stroke victims sometimes linger in emergency rooms or corridors for days waiting for a bed. The cities with a high prevalence of AIDS will be unable to meet the coming demand physically or fiscally. By 1991, one-half of the hospital beds in New York City will be occupied by AIDS patients. Underscoring this dire estimate is a recent report from the Greater New York Hospital Association, which showed a record 1531 AIDS patients in March 1988. This is an increase of 41 percent over the same period of 1987.

If this trend continues, the city's case-load will reach 4241 in 1991, far exceeding the New York State projection of 3000.[17] This means that there will be a need for the addition of 1500 to 2000 hospital beds in New York City by 1991—the equivalent of about three medium-sized hospitals. A new report from the New York State health commissioner has estimated that AIDS treatment would require 3382 new hospital beds statewide by 1991 and 2800 more nurses, 2000 more aides, and 700 more technicians and technologists.[18]

In Miami, the health-care system was unprepared for the more than 1400 cases to date. A local physicians' referral service reports that only five physicians accept AIDS patients. Indigent AIDS patients seen at Dade County's Jackson Memorial Hospital face a three-month appointment backlog to see an AIDS specialist and an even longer wait to receive treatment.[19]

The average cost of caring for a patient with AIDS in the United States, from infection to death, ranges between $80,000 and $140,000. Much of the bill is either paid by the public sector through Medicaid, which presently covers an estimated 54 percent of the costs, or not paid at all and absorbed by the hospitals as uncompensated charity care. (See Table 4.) The cost of the care is passed on to the taxpayers, in the case of the public hospitals, or to the insurance company policy holders, by means of increased premiums. The total cost of AIDS in terms of lost output and earnings due to premature morbidity and mortality is estimated to be $541,000 to $623,000 per patient.[20]

At the present rate of growth in the number of people with AIDS, one can predict that, in the U.S. cities with the largest number of cases, even the prestigious teaching hospitals will have difficulty attracting interns and residents. The brighter students will opt for small cities and rural areas where they will not be inundated caring for patients with one disease. Urban areas will have to pay astronomical salaries to health-care workers willing to care for people with AIDS. By the early 1990s, AIDS patients will far outnumber the available physicians, nurses, and other health-care providers, and the federal government may have to intervene to meet local crises or assist with assignment of federal health workers.

ECONOMIC DEVASTATION AND COST IN THE THIRD WORLD

Throughout the Third World, the developing countries are economically devastated by the burden that AIDS has placed

17. Greater New York Hospital Association, "AIDS Patients in Public and Private Hospitals" (Report, Apr. 1988).

18. David Axelrod, "Manpower Estimates" (Report, New York State Health Department, Apr. 1988).

19. Bruce Lambert, "Confronting AIDS with a Sense of Realism," *New York Times,* 17 Feb. 1988.

20. David E. Bloom and Geoffrey Carliner, "The Economic Impact of AIDS in the United States," *Science,* Feb. 1988, pp. 239, 604.

TABLE 4
SOURCES OF FUNDING FOR AIDS (Percentage)

Medicaid	54
Medicare	2
Private insurance	17
Uncompensated care	27
Total	100

SOURCE: Dennis P. Andrulis et al., "The Provision and Financing of Medical Treatment for AIDS Patients in U.S. Public and Private Teaching Hospitals," *Journal of the American Medical Association*, 11 Sept. 1987, p. 1343.

on their economies and their already scarce health-care budgets.

With about 5 percent of the Congo's 2 million people already infected with the AIDS virus, health authorities predict that up to 100,000 Congolese will die of AIDS in the next decade. To put that in proper perspective, a similar rate of infection in the United States would mean 12 million Americans would die in the next 10 years.[21]

The situation in the Congo is about the same as in the other seven African countries of what has come to be called Africa's AIDS belt: Zaire, Zambia, Tanzania, Burundi, Rwanda, Uganda, and the Central African Republic. Surveys in the capitals of these countries have revealed over a 5 percent rate of AIDS-virus infection among urban adults.

Most infectious diseases in developing Third World countries are fatal mainly to the very young, as reflected by high infant mortality, and to the elderly. AIDS is different; it affects the sexually active age groups, who are also the wage earners, food producers, and mothers of children. These are the people who normally support the children and the elderly parents and grandparents. Increased deaths among the wage- and food-producing age groups will increase the dependency

ratio, such that each worker will have even more dependents to support. Per capita incomes, family incomes, and gross national products will decline. Nutritional status will worsen. Expenditures for medical care, the poverty rates, and the disease rates will inevitably rise.

AIDS is reaching into Africa's middle class and killing the men who were that continent's investment for the future, resulting in devastating political and economic consequences from AIDS in these countries. Many of the victims are the educated, political, and economic elite of the countries. They were the long-hoped-for future politicians and economic leaders of Africa.

The Development Institute at Britain's Norwich University has predicted that the disease will also spread from Africa's urban areas into the rural farming communities, where there will be shortages of workers in farming and agricultural production, particularly with crops like maize that require labor-intensive farming.[22]

Another set of projections, by Harvard University's Institute for International Development, shows that the overall economic costs of AIDS-related deaths for Zaire alone could reach some $350 million

21. Brooke, "New Surge of AIDS in Congo."

22. Sholto Cross, Quoted by Paul Lewis, "W.H.O. Joins Third World AIDS Campaign," *New York Times*, 27 Mar. 1988.

a year by 1995, or about 8 percent of Zaire's total 1984 economic output.[23] In Pointe-Noir, in the Congo, a city of 200,000 people, the annual budget of the only public hospital is around $200,000, or about the amount of money spent to care for three Americans with AIDS.[24]

AIDS ACTIVITIES ELSEWHERE

Several countries are taking drastic measures against AIDS. Cuba has undertaken a campaign to test 7.0 million men and women over the age of 15 for the disease. To date, the testing of over 1.5 million Cubans has turned up only 174 carriers and 27 cases of AIDS, according to the Cuban minister of health. These individuals are sent to a sanatorium, which has been in operation since 1985. According to unofficial accounts, it may house between 300 and 400 patients under clean and humane conditions. The patients work, are paid a salary, receive visits, and participate in sports.[25]

Bulgaria and the Soviet Union are proponents of internationally recognized AIDS-test certificates, similar to smallpox and yellow fever certificates, to govern international travel and immigration.

Denmark uses very explicit information in the form of pictures, cartoons, and videos to show exactly what safe sex means.

The Dutch have extensive programs to reach intravenous drug addicts. About 75 percent of Amsterdam's addicts take part in methadone treatment. They also report positive results from a controversial program to exchange free sterile needles and syringes with drug addicts. The propor-

tion of addicts sharing needles has decreased from 75 percent in 1985 to 25 percent in 1987, when 700,000 needles were distributed.[26]

MULTINATIONAL STRATEGY OF THE UNITED STATES

Although the prevention and control of AIDS is ultimately the responsibility of the individual, voluntary, political, and resource commitments and cooperation are necessary at the local, state, national, and international levels. Since the disease was first recognized in the early 1980s, the U.S. Public Health Service, through its Centers for Disease Control, the National Institutes of Health, and the surgeon general, has provided leadership at the national level. Working closely with the state health authorities, cooperative efforts are now under way in this country. Because of unfortunate and misleading information, AIDS was known in many parts of the world as the "American immunodeficiency syndrome." This connotation and misinformation were particularly detrimental to international cooperation and information sharing and were not conducive to the support of bilateral U.S. efforts to assist other countries. This was particularly true in Africa. The strategy that emerged was for the United States to join in multinational research, scientific information sharing, and control efforts. WHO was the obvious international focus for developing global programs. With support from the United States, the WHO Global Program on AIDS (GPA) was established in February 1987 as the central organization to fight AIDS. Since that time, the GPA has collaborated with 136 countries. Its goals are to

23. Lewis, "W.H.O. Joins Third World AIDS Campaign."

24. Brooke, "New Surge of AIDS in Congo."

25. Ernesto F. Betancourt, "Cuba's Callous War on AIDS," *New York Times,* 11 Feb. 1988.

26. Hans Moerkerk, Presentation to World AIDS Summit, London, Nov. 1987.

—prevent AIDS-virus transmission;
—care for AIDS-virus-infected people; and
—unify national and international efforts against AIDS.

The GPA provides periodic and up-to-date technical-scientific meetings and consultations on research and policy issues. Consensus statements have been developed, including criteria for screening, safety of blood and blood products, and guidelines on AIDS prevention and control programs. Bilateral assistance was pledged for operations to control AIDS in Uganda, Tanzania, Rwanda, Kenya, Zaire, Senegal, and Ethiopia.

In 1987, the GPA made $18.9 million available for national control programs and $24 million for research and information efforts. For 1988, the GPA plans to spend $66.2 million. The GPA has received support from 15 countries: Australia, Belgium, Canada, Denmark, Finland, France, Italy, Japan, the Netherlands, Norway, Sweden, Switzerland, the United Kingdom, the United States, and the USSR. Of all GPA funds, 75 percent goes to national program support. The GPA currently has a staff of over sixty professional and support personnel.[27]

WHO recently created the Global Commission on Aids to bring together eminent experts from a wide variety of disciplines to review and advise WHO on the GPA's activities.

RECOMMENDATIONS

Aside from the dubious distinction of having the majority of cases reported in the world, the United States has a special responsibility to provide international leadership in the control of AIDS. The world community bestows this responsibility on the United States because of its preeminence in immunology and virology research and its recognized ability to apply public-health principles to combat communicable diseases. Just 10 years ago, the United States provided the leadership for WHO's successful smallpox-eradication program. Already, the National Institutes of Health and the Centers for Disease Control are providing technical assistance through WHO to control the AIDS epidemic. They have the epidemiological, clinical, and laboratory research capacity that no other country possesses.

Dr. Jonathan Mann, who heads WHO's AIDS Program, acquired much of his public-health experience in Africa while on loan from the U.S. Public Health Service. He is providing admirable expertise and leadership.

Knowledgeable and culturally aware world leaders have agreed through WHO to undertake the following measures:

—to coordinate worldwide epidemiological data;
—to develop education programs that emphasize AIDS prevention, especially education and information to prevent sexual transmission;
—to curb intravenous drug abuse, treating those addicted and discouraging lethal practices of needle and syringe sharing;
—to provide training and equipment to make blood and blood products safe through screening and testing;
—to develop educational programs to prevent mother-to-child spread;
—to provide counseling for HIV-infected individuals;
—to provide compassionate care and treatment for those individuals infected with AIDS; and

27. World Health Organization, Press release, 1 Dec. 1987.

—to encourage world governments to provide increased financial, medical, and social support.

Without a vaccine or drug treatment to cure this disease, explicit and directed education is the best and only resource available today to prevent further spread. The disagreements within U.S. society, among our religious and political communities, on how candid and explicit educational materials should be and on the role of condoms in reducing the risk have handicapped our educational programs. Moral differences have also presented barriers in communities where there is resistance to sex education on the grounds that it promotes promiscuity and illicit sex practices. As a result, at international AIDS conferences, the United States is often put on the defensive because its response to AIDS in terms of education has fallen short of what many other Western nations have accomplished.

CLOSING

AIDS is the most difficult medical problem facing the world today. It is a difficult area for the world's leaders, who are also politicians, because the wisdom of present policies to control the disease will not be validated for five or more years.

Many of these politicians are treating AIDS as a temporary problem that will disappear if ignored. It will not, and world leaders must overcome their own fears of dealing with contagion and of using awkward oratorical language. They must withstand those forces that call for policies predicated on overreaction and ignorance that threaten to isolate and victimize the sick. World leaders must develop policies based on considered knowledge about this disease. Such knowledge was not available to previous genera-

tions, imprisoned in ignorance during the past pandemics of the black plague, leprosy, cholera, and the invisible menace of yellow fever.

The world has an opportunity to utilize the vast biomedical and scientific knowledge of the United States and other countries regarding this world epidemic, which was not available during those past pandemics. History is replete with sad and sobering glimpses of the social price of ignorance and fear of misunderstood contagion. The lessons learned must be considered with the facts about this new pandemic, so that understanding based on biomedical and behavioral achievements can minimize the social costs. It would be an egregious error to have invested so heavily in the scientific elucidation of AIDS and the insights of recent years into HIV epidemiology and immunology and then not to use them to meet this present world crisis.

The scientific efforts to control this disease are as international as the disease. The fruits of international research to describe the virus, to develop treatment drugs and vaccines, and to design effective preventive education programs should be made available to the entire world.

There is a new sense of realism and activism to control the disease and prepare for the care of people with AIDS in the United States. Health-policy analysts see a shift to do things that should have happened two years ago. In the perceived absence of federal leadership, state and local governments and voluntary organizations have started planning care-giving and preventive programs.

As a nation and a society, the United States has not dealt directly, explicitly, or forcibly enough with the difficult issues of changing sexual behavior and controlling drug addiction. By far the biggest problem is the inability to take effective

action to curb the spread of the disease among drug addicts, their sex partners, and their babies.

In summary, AIDS spreads through sexual behavior and the exchange of blood. It spreads by way of specific and known high-risk behaviors that are avoidable and controllable and preventable.

The United States has the scientific knowledge, the vast biotechnologies, and the resources necessary to provide leadership to the world in controlling the spread of this disease. It now must gain the moral conviction and will to control the disease within its own borders. Only then can it as a nation, as a society, and as a people be able to give a commitment to provide the leadership necessary to control AIDS in the rest of the world.

* * *

QUESTIONS AND ANSWERS

Q (Marvin E. Wolfgang, American Academy of Political and Social Science, Philadelphia, Pennsylvania): You have given us statistics about the number of cases of AIDS in the United States and worldwide that can be expected by the end of this year and over the next five years. How good, how valid, would you say these predictions are?

A: In 1986 the epidemiological model used by the Centers for Disease Control yielded the projection of 270,000 cases by 1991. A recent review of the model and the projection indicated that we have reached about 80 percent of the projected number of cases, so the model itself is estimated to be accurate within plus or minus 10 percent over a five-year period. The model for the projections for Africa are as good as the data that are available, and we are less optimistic that the projections for some of the African countries are very accurate. If anything, they are lower than the actual numbers that may occur.

_____

Q (James W. Skillen, Association for Public Justice, Washington, D.C.): I am entirely sympathetic to your urge for research and education, but I want to play the devil's advocate and ask the toughest question that I know regarding the kind of proposal you are making. Will education make any difference in the spread of AIDS? For instance, surely there is no one that is not aware that drinking and driving may lead to death and yet people continue to do it. Education does not seem to be a factor in that case. Surely the knowledge that drug abuse can be a very dangerous and life-destroying process is not foreign to young people, but they do it anyway. All the education in the world does not seem to prevent those who want to live dangerously from doing so. On the other hand, is it not the case that education concerning frightening situations moves like wildfire anyway? In other words, why bother with education—will it not happen anyway? Should the concentration instead be on research, care, or finding solutions? I ask the question so that I can answer it when people ask me.

A: I do not think there is an easy answer. Education in the gay community in this country has proven to be useful. There is a leveling-off of the HIV positivity rate in the gay community. The gay community did a tremendous job in educating people about the dangers of

HIV and about safe sex. The general public in this country knows an awful lot about AIDS. For the people who read newspapers and watch television it is hard not to have been exposed to some information on the dangers. The adolescents in this country are a particular problem because adolescents are high-risk takers anyway; they feel they are immortal. The educational materials that are aimed at adolescents can have an impact as far as safe sex and the dangers of AIDS are concerned. In the past, adolescents were warned about pregnancy and venereal disease, but AIDS is deadly, so education about AIDS should have more of an impact. Unfortunately, we do not know yet how to reach a lot of these adolescents.

The drug-abuse community is a particular problem. It is very difficult to reach drug abusers. Based on international experience, however, particularly out of Amsterdam and Great Britain, we can say that there are ways of reaching them. I think we will have to be very innovative. Getting intravenous drug abusers into treatment, where they can be monitored and where they can become educated, is essential. We have a long way to go in this country before we reach the point where we have under treatment all those who want to come into treatment. There are programs in Amsterdam, for example, where needles and syringes are provided free to intravenous drug users. In this country that is still too controversial. A voluntary organization in New York City had proposed having drug abusers bring in their old needles and exchanging them for new ones; at the same time they would have contact with drug-treatment possibilities. Needles would not just be given away on the street; there would also be education. Due to protest, however, this program has not been able to get off the ground. The problem of drug abuse, from production to consumption, is one that the United States as well as other countries must face more directly and not sweep under the rug. How we deal with the drug problem will very much affect the spread of the AIDS virus. We could say that the resources are not worth it, but I think we still have to experiment with some programs in intravenous drug abuse.

Q (Wolfgang): Would decriminalization of hard drugs in this country have a significant impact on the reduction of AIDS?

A: My opinion is that decriminalization would not affect intravenous drug abuse in this country to the extent that some of the proponents say it would. I think there are other things that we can try first, for example, the provision of clean needles and bringing people under treatment. I do not think we have tried these approaches to the extent that we should in this country. A lot of the programs have failed in trying to control drug abuse. We have never really had a war on drugs. We have not really begun to deal with the drug issue, and legalization is something even further down the road. It is too simplistic right now to say that legalization will solve the drug problem.

Q (Jaime Benítez, University of Puerto Rico, Rio Piedras): Has the medical profession concluded that AIDS is incurable?

A: Nobody is willing to say that HIV infection is 100 percent fatal because we have not had enough experience with it. The most conservative estimates are that somebody who is infected with the virus has a 30 percent chance of developing AIDS within 5 years. A less conservative

estimate is that 50 percent would contract the disease and die within 6 years. In a study in San Francisco, 80 percent of the subjects, who have been followed for 7 years, show immune-system damage. Extrapolating that finding for a period of 10, 11, or 12 years, some projections are that AIDS will prove to be almost 100 percent fatal, with some surviving as a mystery.

Q (Benítez): Is there a vaccine to provide immunity against AIDS?

A: There is a great deal of research on vaccine development at the National Institutes of Health, the Pasteur Institute, and elsewhere, including a number of private companies. Predictions are that no vaccine will be developed before the end of the century.

Q (Benítez): Basically, as of today, the judgment is that there is no cure for the disease and the only thing to do is to avoid contracting it, is that right?

A: Yes. That is why education is our only resource at the present time.

Q (Samuel Lipman, *New Criterion,* New York City): I find the moral dimension unaccountably missing from the discussion of AIDS in general. One of the most frightening and perhaps the most enlightening of the points you made was that the spread of AIDS in Africa occurred because of movement from the tribal areas to the cities and the breakdown of tribal religions and taboos. The lessons of Africa are also lessons for us. It is no secret to anyone, especially anyone who tries to raise a child, that in the United States we live in a culture where the most promiscuous sexuality is not only pandemic but is actually encouraged by all of the media. Can we possibly have an educational campaign that does not stress the moral dimension? And can we attack the problem via a moral crusade as well as an educational and scientific crusade?

A: The educational programs in this country have been structured to try to treat each community individually. Each community is to develop its own program of, for example, sex education in the schools. This approach, I think, follows what the courts have done relative to pornography in this country in terms of local authority and autonomy. It is very difficult in this country to gain consensus across a broad spectrum of moral, religious, and political viewpoints in order to have one set of criteria for the prevention of the spread of AIDS.

Q (Lipman): I agree that achieving consensus in any large and pluralistic society is immensely difficult, but this is a war. Is there not a moral dimension that must be harnessed if we are to combat AIDS successfully? It seems that you avoid using the word "moral."

A: I would not avoid the use of the word "moral" personally. Problems of AIDS, drug abuse, and promiscuity in the United States all have moral undercurrents to them. We live in a pluralistic society and we will not achieve agreement, but these differences also provide an opportunity for us as a nation to start addressing some of the deep problems that we are experiencing. I think, from a personal point of view, that the drug-abuse problem in this country certainly reflects the fracturing of some of the moral systems and traditional family values that this country was based upon. Those are some of the issues where this country needs some leadership.

Q (Mamoon A. Zaki, Le Moyne-Owen College, Memphis, Tennessee): If

we have an emergency threatening our national interest in the United States, the president and the power elite will take certain measures regardless of public opinion. Do you think that the power elite sooner or later will come to the conclusion that, notwithstanding the civil rights of AIDS patients, they should be quarantined or sent to a sanatorium, following the model of Cuba and other countries? In other words, the leadership will have come to the conclusion that the national interest is at stake economi-

cally, socially, morally, and maybe even militarily.

A: Quarantine is not acceptable! The fact that the president of the United States has mentioned AIDS only twice and that the presidential contenders are avoiding the issue of AIDS is indicative of the political pariah that AIDS is. I do not see that the country will address AIDS before the presidential election. Local governments are addressing the issue, however, and some admirable leadership has been provided at that level.

ANNALS, *AAPSS*, **500**, November 1988

American Music's Place at Home and in the World

By SAMUEL LIPMAN

ABSTRACT: Despite major nineteenth-century achievement in the other arts, American musical life, for decades dependent on Europe, lagged behind. Matters improved from the 1920s on, as major native composers achieved recognition. Our musical independence was helped by World War II and the arrival of European refugees to live and work here. But by the early 1950s, control of American musical life moved back to Europe, and with it went much of our self-confidence. Today, as for many years past, American musical life—especially on the level of our top orchestras—is determined by European artistic personalities and by commercial decisions taken abroad. Our problem is not to reject foreign figures when they are beneficial and willing to work here on a permanent basis, but to create an American classical music, in the tradition of great Western classical music, that we can call our own.

Samuel Lipman is an author, musician, and the music critic for Commentary. *He has been publisher of* The New Criterion *since 1982. He has a graduate degree in political science, and for many years has been a concert pianist. He has also been a member of the artistic faculty of the Waterloo Music Festival since 1976 and has been the festival's artistic director since 1986. Among his books are* Music after Modernism *(1979) and* The House of Music *(1984).*

TO begin, I would like to express my views on the ideas of American empire and dominance. Even if the word "empire" is used objectively, to mean an absolute and lengthy sway exercised, in the manner of nineteenth-century empires, over subject states and peoples, I would not agree that history has seen an American empire. Still less can I agree that an American empire has existed if "empire" is intended—as I am afraid it is today—to connote an arrogant usurpation of power for malign purposes. What I have just said is political, but so is the formulation of this issue of *The Annals*.

Similarly, with respect to whether the United States is losing world dominance in the realm of the arts, of culture, I feel that the word "dominance" is misplaced. "Dominance" is a nasty word these days; it is not too much to say that it is a fighting word. Even when "dominance" is taken at its least ideological, and perhaps even more when it is associated with losing, it conjures up images of the outmoded application of Darwin and Mendel to society. When used ideologically, "dominance" serves as a first cousin to that academic buzzword "hegemony." I do not wish to bring these connotations to a discussion of culture.

Finally, I find that the consideration of all culture in this international context seems too much to grapple with. I want to concentrate, therefore, on the world of music, a world in which I have direct experience. I must confess that I am not very interested in the temporary albeit influential shifts in taste associated with the worldwide circulation of an ephemeral popular culture; therefore, when I speak about music, I have in mind classical music, a music written to belong to a great tradition and at the same time to form it.

MUSIC HISTORY

What, then, is the situation of American music in the world today? Before the present can be described, some history is necessary. This history, and after it a description of our current situation, will present a situation more complicated and subtle than the tired catch phrases to which I have already objected can possibly encompass.

It is well known that the earliest years of our founding were occupied with questions of political organization, commercial prosperity, and, most of all, national survival. As time passed, the first arts to develop in the new republic were literary, and the success and influence abroad of a long line of nineteenth-century American authors, including Washington Irving, Nathaniel Hawthorne, Edgar Allan Poe, Herman Melville, Walt Whitman, and Mark Twain, are too well known to require comment. Even in the increasingly French-dominated nineteenth-century world of the visual arts, there were consequential and original American painters with important European reputations, including Winslow Homer (1836-1910) and Thomas Eakins (1844-1916)—not to mention the expatriates James McNeill Whistler (1834-1903), Mary Cassatt (1845-1926), and John Singer Sargent (1856-1925). Somewhat later, in architecture, Louis Sullivan (1856-1924) and Frank Lloyd Wright (1869-1959) emerged as constitutive figures, in the world as well as in America.

Concerning the body of music we have until recently qualified by the word "classical" and which we now, at the behest of no less an authority than the 1980 *New Grove Dictionary of Music and Musicians,* must modify with the word "art," the situation is quite different. Why Amer-

ican music lagged behind the other arts remains obscure, and indeed this condition did not indicate any lack of early interest. From the first decades of the nineteenth century, there had been great enthusiasm on these shores for classical-music performance. From at least the time of Jenny Lind's great tour of the United States from 1850 to 1852 under the promotional aegis of no less a judge of public taste than P. T. Barnum, the United States was the most profitable venue in the world for international celebrity musicians. Similarly, American symphony orchestras had appeared on the scene even before the founding of the New York Philharmonic in 1842, and by the 1890s, they were impressing foreign observers as being among the world's best. Furthermore, as the contemporary writings of the now underhonored and underremembered critic James Gibbons Huneker clearly show, New York musical life at century's end, very much including American singers and the Metropolitan Opera, was rich and rewarding, even for the many European artists coming to settle on this side of the Atlantic.

The American musical problem, I hardly need stress, was in composition. Here, with the possible exceptions of the European-educated John Knowles Paine (1839-1906), Edward MacDowell (1860-1908), and Charles Martin Loeffler (1861-1935), there were no American classical composers of the last century whose work today sounds in any way fresh and distinctive. Dvořák's three-year stay in New York remains more important for his Symphony *From the New World* (1893) than for any long-term influence on American composition.

The first American composer to speak with a unique voice within the tradition of classical music, of course, was the self-educated Charles Ives (1874-1954). It is significant that his works, though mostly written before World War I, generally lay unperformed and thus unknown for years after their composition and had to wait for the composer's discovery in the early 1930s by the Russian émigré conductor Nicolas Slonimsky. The German-trained and greatly gifted Charles Tomlinson Griffes (1884-1920), the other major American composer of the period between the Civil War and World War I, composed in a style characterized by a deep sympathy with French and Russian music.

From the 1920s on, our classical music began to find its own voice, building upon European tradition but also claiming a distinctively American quality. A major part of this new American identity, without doubt, came from the exploding rhythmic freedom and excitement of black jazz, with the possibility these strengths provided conventionally trained musicians of breaking free from the romanticist but hypertrophied worlds of German academicism and French impressionism. It must also be stressed that it is with jazz—and with its predecessor art, ragtime—that we first find a true influence of an authentic American music on the composition of classical music in Europe.

The first widely performed composers of this new American breed were born in the years between 1893 and 1910, and they reached maturity in the 1920s, 1930s, and 1940s. Their names, with all the variety they connote, provide an honor roll to which we fail today to pay sufficient attention. I will mention them here, if only to jog our musical memories: Douglas Moore, Walter Piston, Virgil Thomson, Howard Hanson, Roger Sessions, Henry Cowell, Roy Harris, Elliott Carter, Samuel Barber, and William Schuman. I am happy to say that Thomson, Copland,

Carter, and Schuman are alive today, and the last two are still composing large-scale works.

Though all these composers, with the exception of Schuman, studied in Europe, they remained deeply American in their music as much as in their choice of permanent residence. Between them, they represent the major facets of the twentieth-century American experience in classical music. In particular, with the music of Copland, the world first heard the multi-form voice of the city and the wide-open spaces of the West; in the later music of Elliott Carter, the world has learned the ultimate limits of musically authentic compositional discipline and complexity; in the music of Henry Cowell, the world learned what the reclusive and ignored Ives had earlier proved only to himself—that Americans are inventors and visionaries in music as much as they are in mechanics. Altogether, by the 1930s, American contemporary music was recognized the world over as a coequal partner with activity in Europe and as a significant and original achievement in its own right.

It hardly takes a sociological bent to notice that this newfound American strength in classical music first appeared on the domestic and world scene in the interwar years, a time of American demographic vitality and concomitant European exhaustion. Two much discussed phenomena must serve here to describe the increasing power of American art in this period. The first was the German composer Ernst Krenek's initially successful jazz opera *Jonny spielt auf,* performed by the Leipzig Opera in 1927 and by the Metropolitan Opera in 1929. The succinct plot synopsis contained in *The Concise Oxford Dictionary of Opera* tells us what we need to know of the influence of American demotic music at this period: "Jonny (bar.), a jazz-band leader, steals a violin from Daniello (bar.) and becomes so immensely successful that his performance from the North Pole sets the world dancing the Charleston."

The second emblematic phenomenon was Arturo Toscanini's musical canonization in 1938 of Barber's achingly yearning *Adagio for Strings,* in origin the slow movement from the composer's 1936 String Quartet opus 11. Merely to mention the role this quintessentially Italian conductor played in the discovery of one of the core works of the American sound is to raise another aspect of the American role in world music during this period. Our country, it cannot be repeated too often, was the safe harbor during World War II and the years immediately preceding it for what must now rank as the golden age of European musical performance, as well as for some of the most important composers of the twentieth century, among them Béla Bartók, Paul Hindemith, Arnold Schoenberg, and Igor Stravinsky. But whereas the composers' stay in this country hardly constituted the most important parts of their creative lives, the performers who graced our shores achieved as residents here the summits of their careers, rather than in the Europe whence they came.

Such was certainly the case with the conductors Toscanini, Bruno Walter, Fritz Reiner, Artur Rodzinski, and George Szell, the pianists Vladimir Horowitz, Arthur Rubinstein, and Artur Schnabel, the harpsichordist Wanda Landowska, the violinists Joseph Szigeti and Nathan Milstein, and the Budapest String Quartet. When to these great performers are added those who had arrived earlier from Europe to live and in many cases to teach—among them conductors Serge Koussevitzky, Leopold Stokowski, and Pierre Monteux—it becomes clear that by war's end, the United States had

become the center, this side of the Soviet Union, of the Western musical universe. To remark on this American preeminence is perhaps only to note the obvious: America was the only country during World War II that was able to wage war while still enjoying something very close to peace.

A WANING AMERICAN POSITION

There was, however, much more to the state of our national musical life than the presence of the great Europeans. Let us take the success of Leonard Bernstein as an indication of what was going on. By 1945, he had rocketed to fame both as conductor—it must be remembered that he first came to national attention by filling in at a radio concert of the New York Philharmonic for the *echt*-European conductor Bruno Walter—and as the composer of the proudly American ballet *Fancy Free*. Taken as a whole, Bernstein's stardom marked not just our perceived coming of musical age but also the beginnings of what seemed to be our coming independence.

But real peace did arrive in 1945, and with it the American position in world music inexorably began to wane. Not only did those who were already old upon their arrival here cease to work; some still active, as in the case of Hindemith and Schnabel, to name only two, returned to Europe to resume their Hitler-shattered careers. Perhaps more important, American music students, both in composition and in performance, used the generous scholarship aid made widely available here in conjunction with favorable foreign-exchange rates to go to Europe to study.

By the early 1950s, therefore, the action in contemporary music composition, and in vocal and instrumental performance as well, had moved back to the mother countries the largest part of our tradition. Sadly, the wildly successful post-World War II popular musics, unlike the much less profitable jazz of earlier years, have proved unable to fructify a living classical music tradition. Whether the new meccas were to be Vienna and London in classical and romantic pianism, or Paris and Darmstadt in serial composition, the operative models for Americans ceased to be, as they had been during the war, Europeans resident in America and participant in American life. The models had now become Europeans, as in the cases of Messiaen and Stockhausen, transmitting their art from the geographical and cultural environment of their homelands. In this respect, it is significant that Copland, certainly our most successful Americanist, has never been successful in Europe. While Carter is, in all his complexity, an intellectual cult figure in London, he, too, has made no impact on a wider musical public. Closer to the present, the much-hyped American New Romanticism of the last few years has been based upon the models of European styles and aesthetics, rather than upon anything of our own origin.

Nor was this primacy of European influence confined purely to artistic matters. Classical-music recording in Europe, brought almost to a standstill by the war, revived almost immediately. When to the availability of cheaply produced European master tapes was added the American introduction of the long-playing record by CBS in 1948—continuing a history of American innovations in recording technology—the stage was set for a flood of foreign artists, not just in American record stores but also on American stages.

The important point is that with the recrudescence of traditional patterns of looking to Europe for musical inspiration and satisfaction went a loss of American

musical self-confidence. As always in such matters, it is difficult to separate cause and effect. What is clear is that this change in the originating world role of American music emerged fully formed at the same time as what progressives everywhere see as the palmiest days of the supposed American imperium, and years before even the most tentative prophecies of our decline had started to emerge from the dovecotes of radical politics. This clarity ought to provide a much-needed warning for the quasi-Marxist believers in a direct and simple relation between the economic base and the cultural superstructure.

As I go on to bring the historical record up to the present, I think it will be obvious that this post-1945 world still obtains today, and that as I now describe the events of the last four decades, my function as a historian will for all intents and purposes be replaced by that of a reporter.

What, then, has been happening over these many years in American classical music, viewed at one and the same time as a national and as a world phenomenon? Let me suggest an overarching generalization: musical decisions of the greatest significance for our musical life have originated, and now originate, in Europe. As corollaries to this broad statement, I want to suggest the following: our viable concert and operatic repertory in this period has been, and remains, European; our best composers of the past are little heard; the leading models for our aspirant operatic composers, even when they sail under the colors of an American-developed minimalism, have in fact gained much, if not most, of their currency from their validation by European opinion; the leading artists and ideas of performance before our public have been, and remain, European; most of our successful American performing artists are so because of

the imprimatur of European audiences; all major label decisions regarding recordings of American music and American performers are made by companies owned and directed abroad; last, and perhaps really least, American writing about music has become, since World War II, increasingly influenced by foreign models and writers.

So far as our concert and operatic repertory is concerned, a quick glance at the offerings of performing institutions large and small will immediately proclaim the obvious. The core of the repertory is of eighteenth- and nineteenth-century European origin. The sway of the three Bs— Bach, Beethoven, and Brahms—and kindred masters is more total than it has been within living memory. What exploration in the repertory does take place does so looking at past centuries rather than our own. In an effort to invigorate concert life, for example, one of New York's most prestigious concert presenters has just launched a massive ten-year presentation of every one of the many hundreds of pieces written by Franz Schubert; this presentation will include his complete juvenilia, as well as many other works hitherto thought to be of insufficient interest to be performable. Similarly, we are now just at the beginning of a major and widespread campaign to present the endlessly prolific and facile baroque composer Georg Philipp Telemann (1681-1767) as a master on the level of J. S. Bach. In general, the most attention-getting development in music programming now, as it has been for the past two decades and more, is the authentic-performance and original-instrument movement; this conception is devoted to creating unfamiliar new versions of familiar works by familiar composers.

As has been true now for years, when American music is programmed, the performances are more often than not pre-

mieres of works that are not intended to be played ever again. Classic works of the golden age of American composition in the 1930s and 1940s, with the exception of one or two works by Copland, are rarely played; when they are, the creaking sound of duty is loud in the land. The entire generation of composers, whether Americanists or European-influenced cerebralists, who flowered in the 1950s now seems entirely ignored. Of the avant-gardists of this period, only the very provocative John Cage, remarkable more for his silences than for his sounds, remains an object of contemporary notice.

It is indeed arguable that the present enthusiasm for the new, putatively popular compositions of Philip Glass, Steve Reich, and John Adams marks an exception to this rule of desuetude for our native music. It is certainly true that American opera houses are now rushing to present the *tableaux morts* of Glass and the popcorn orientalism of Adams; it is also true that our press is full of the triumphs of Glass's operas on German operatic stages, and of homilies to the effect that if we Americans would only have total state support of culture, we, too, could have Glass opera houses. For the moment there is as yet no sign that this new music has made any headway either with traditional performers or with traditional audiences; it is significant that the Philadelphia Orchestra has only recently severed its association with the American conductor Dennis Russell Davies, on the grounds, it is widely rumored, of his commitment to new American music—in particular, the music of Glass and his colleagues.

In any case, it is clear that the hopes for an American opera that reached their climax in the great New York City Opera seasons of the late 1950s have vanished, leaving in their wake no impact at all on the standard operatic repertory. The re-sult is deleterious in two ways: American audiences know nothing of the significant works of our operatic past, and American singers and conductors are trained and build careers in works that, as we become ever further distant from the great tides of European immigration, grow ever more distant from their immediate experience and comprehension.

While there is a great deal of hoopla now about American conductors, the brute facts remain the same: of our greatest orchestras—New York, Boston, Philadelphia, Chicago, and Cleveland—not one is in the hands of an American music director. In the case of the estimable second tier of our orchestras—Los Angeles, Pittsburgh, St. Louis, San Francisco, Washington, Cincinnati, and Seattle—only St. Louis and Seattle have, in Leonard Slatkin and Gerard Schwarz, American-trained conductors whose careers have been made here rather than abroad. Elsewhere in this second tier, while Los Angeles, Pittsburgh, and San Francisco do have American music directors—respectively, André Previn, Lorin Maazel, and Herbert Blomstedt—these leaders all made important careers in Europe before being asked to assume executive duties in this country. There is nothing new about all of this: when the music directorship of the Boston Symphony became vacant in 1949 upon the retirement of Serge Koussevitzky, the already highly successful—and popular in Boston—Leonard Bernstein was rejected in favor of the French Charles Münch. Bernstein was not to be asked to direct the fortunes of an American orchestra until the New York Philharmonic engaged him in 1958—but that happy and singular event occurred only after he had made a huge success a year earlier with the Broadway musical *West Side Story*.

Whatever the activity American conductors may now be enjoying in Europe,

such welcome news does not involve a commensurate acceptance of American music. It is significant that an April article in the *New York Times* about the European activities of our conductors does not mention one American composer, not even the supposedly triumphant minimalists. On the contrary, the Juilliard-trained and very gifted James Conlon, now in his fifth season at the Rotterdam Philharmonic, is quoted as saying:

The music I'm interested in was born on another continent. I found that I was fascinated by European life—the history, the art, the culture—and that it was actually more germane to the works that I lived with and loved than living in America full time.[1]

It should be added, too, that by far the greatest influence on the rapidly burgeoning revision of approaches to the performance of baroque, classical, and early romantic music has always been European. There are, for example, no American counterparts to the recent successes here and internationally of the recordings of the English conductors Roger Norrington, John Eliot Gardiner, and Christopher Hogwood and the English conductor-harpsichordist Trevor Pinnock.

In the instrumental world, the story is much the same. Van Cliburn's great career, for many years now seemingly at a sad end, was owed entirely to his victory in the 1958 Tchaikovsky competition in Moscow. Prior to winning in the USSR, Cliburn's career had languished in this country, and it was only his recognition by Soviet musicians and by an embrace from Nikita Khrushchev that served to make this attractive Texan an acceptable American musical hero. At the present

time, the American-born and -trained pianist Murray Perahia owes much of his acclaim here to his earlier success in the highly influential London musical world. Furthermore, no reigning star of the violin in this country today is American by birth, and there is no American style whatsoever in string playing, as for some years after World War II was said to exist in the piano.

The present plight of the recording of American performers and American music on major labels is truly remarkable. Major attention has recently been focused on the recent purchase of RCA by the Bertelsmann group in Germany and of CBS by Sony in Japan. As a result of these developments, no major American label is owned by Americans; all the labels that have come to represent, through rich backlists and the current recording of great performing institutions and soloists, greatness in classical music—London, Angel, Deutsche Grammophon, and Philips, in addition to RCA and CBS—are based offshore in both financing and control. As a result, it is increasingly said that only massive government subsidies can secure needed recordings of American music, both new and old.

We will surely be told that this deplorable situation is a result of current American economic weakness, but the present situation is not new. As long ago as the early 1950s, RCA and CBS, in ceasing to press the best products of the English-based EMI catalog for American distribution, ceded a primary role in our record market to Angel Records, EMI's American subsidiary, and to London Records, the American subsidiary of English Decca. With this important sector of the market thus removed from American auspices, the stage was set for the abandonment of large-scale RCA and CBS domestic record-

1. Heidi Waleson, "Why Europe Charms Maestros," *New York Times,* 17 Apr. 1988.

ing, which had gathered strength in the 1970s and has now become terminal in the 1980s.

While I am talking about developments in what I might call the music trades, I should mention some disturbing recent developments in the piano business. The American-owned and -based firm of Steinway & Sons, for more than a century the proud and almost universally acknowledged maker of the world's best grand pianos, has now been challenged in the concert field itself by Yamaha, the Japanese motorcycle, electronic, and musical-instrument conglomerate. This development, coming as it does in the wake of a twenty-year-old shift in artist allegiance from American-made to European-made Steinways, suggests a further weakening of American musical life.

Finally in this recital of our parlous situation vis-à-vis the rest of the world, I must mention the state of writing about music. I do not have in mind the problems of music criticism, now increasingly unable to differentiate between the requirements of writing for a possibly nonexistent intelligent general public and the need to earn compliments from the ever more intrusive watchdogs of academic musicology. Instead, I am referring to the current disappearance of serious magazines addressed to the sophisticated concert audience. As a recent article by Michael Kimmelman in the *New York Times* documented, our music magazines are in grave and probably terminal financial trouble.[2] The latest news is that the seriously intentioned *Opus* magazine, founded by refugees from the gutting of *High Fidelity,* has now been sold—and is being combined with the lackluster *Musical America,* a publication under common ownership with none other than

2. *New York Times,* 20 Dec. 1987.

High Fidelity. The result is that now, as for many years, there is no American competition for the highly inclusive and professionally gotten-up English publication *Gramophone,* as always the very center of the old-boy network of London music publicity and reviewing. The dire implications for the formation of musical reputations in this country remain clear. The situation has in fact not changed since Münch rather than Bernstein replaced Koussevitzky in Boston almost forty years ago; today, for example, we have the pleasure of witnessing the present boomlets for the English conductor Simon Rattle and the Finnish Esa-Pekka Salonen, talented young men perhaps without major repertories but certainly not without countries.

CONCLUSION

As I come to the end of this article, I am painfully conscious that I have talked about little but the past and present power of Europe in our American life. I am aware that American performers, as I have mentioned earlier, are employable abroad and even, on occasion, successful. But with the exception of Leonard Bernstein—and then only the conductor, not the composer—no American classical musician occupies anything like a commanding position at the center of European musical life; I have already suggested, I believe, that no American musician occupies such a position in American musical life. I should add—but this is another subject entirely—that it is especially disheartening that this imbalance occurs at a time when music in Europe, whether performance or composition, is so lacking in originality and creative distinction.

I have tried to show that this unhappy condition of American classical music has not changed in its essential outlines

since World War II and that this condition can hardly be correlated with the fluctuations of American political and economic strength. I have sketched this picture of the state of American music in reaction to the stimulus of a formulation that strongly suggested that a mythical American musical empire was losing its dominance abroad. If I have sometimes seemed angry, it has been because the pressure to confess to a supposed political and economic guilt is now so prevalent in American society. It is clear to me that, musically speaking, our empire has never existed and that we are now not even masters in our own house. It may well be true that what is true for classical music also holds true for the world role of the other components of our high culture, which I have not felt able to address; such a determination, however, must be left to others.

I would be very unhappy if the lesson to be drawn from what I have said about music were to be one of nationalistic retaliation and exclusion. There is no point in denying ourselves the contributions of great artists and thinkers, wherever they are to be found; it is vastly in our interest to encourage their continued appearance, and especially their residence and teaching, here. The great treasures of the Western musical tradition, after all, are a major component of the imperishable corpus of civilization; they belong to all the nations of the West and indeed to all the world. As Americans, we, no less than the peoples of the countries that gave birth to this art, are the inheritors of a glorious tradition; as Goethe wrote in the first part of *Faust,* that which we have inherited from our fathers we must earn in order to make our own. We cannot accomplish this necessary task of intellectual repossession by succumbing to what, so far from being imperialist arrogance, is in fact a colonial mentality, a slavish following of trends and careers selected elsewhere. The problem is not the need to relinquish our pride, but to create music.

* * *

QUESTIONS AND ANSWERS

COMMENT (Dario Scuka, Library of Congress, Washington, D.C.): The theme of pride runs through this paper and very correctly so. Pride suggests influence. There are two kinds of influence, solicited and unsolicited. In the case of the former, the receiving party appreciates the influence and can learn to live with it. The case of the latter suggests a situation that could evoke the word "dominance." In the world today, including the artistic arena, the United States is considered dominant and not necessarily benevolent. In contrast, none of the European performers and composers of classical music can be considered dominant because we accept them freely—they have not been imposed on us.

A: I do not think the model of solicited or unsolicited influence operates in the transmission of high culture. Rather, art conquers, on the level of the individual artwork, on its own. I have had the experience, as I am sure everyone has, of listening to an artwork, looking at an artwork without the desire, at the beginning, to like it. Then something happens and one has no choice, because the artwork makes its demand. European music has never been foisted upon the United States; there has never been an evil motive in the triumph of European

music in the United States. We asked for it, we found it beautiful, we wanted it. The problem arises when in a general discussion of the relation between nations, one aspect of that relation is viewed as American dominance and it is expected that everything then follows from that dominance. What I have tried to do is to show that in one of the most important and permanent components of civilization, American dominance does not exist and that, so far from this dominance existing, we have major problems of our own existence in this area. What I have tried to do was to erode this notion that there is a direct relationship between the economic base and the cultural superstructure, to destroy the easy connection that culture follows from the barrel of a gun.

Q (Mamoon A. Zaki, Le Moyne-Owen College, Memphis, Tennessee): Classical music reached a very high level of accomplishment in the nineteenth century. Since the decline of the middle class after World War II, have music and the other arts also declined?

A: First, I do not believe that Beethoven, for instance, is a middle-class phenomenon. I would doubt if either Mozart or Haydn was a middle-class phenomenon. Second, I disagree that classical music reached its summit in the nineteenth century. I have devoted fifty years to classical music and I would hate to think that it has been all downhill. But let me put the question more widely. Is there something in mass democratic society, on the one hand, and mass totalitarian society, on the other, that is inimical to the

formation of culture? That is a difficult question. Ortega y Gasset took a position quite clearly that it was hopeless. Such a position has been associated, not always fairly, with political conservatism and social conservatism. I have to say that it is a very disquieting situation. As far as the sciences are concerned, it seems to me that we have a lot of evidence that the continuous creation of great science can occur in mass societies. I do not see a split between the creation of a scientific culture and the creation of a humanistic culture. I feel that it is the same people who do both, who can do either. At this time, we are witnessing the creation of a scientific culture rather than a great humanistic culture, but I do not see that it is necessary that we not have a humanistic culture. The same position I take on classical music I suppose I have to take on the creation of humanistic culture. My faith is that a democratic society is, in the long run, capable of creating a humanistic culture. The portents are not very happy at the moment. And this brings us rather close to the AIDS discussion because the problem for me concerning AIDS is whether a moral system can be developed that will enable society to survive this threat. The same problem underlies the creation of culture. Can a humanistic culture be created in democratic society to triumph over the anarchic and anomic and even nihilistic possibilities that are contained in mass society and that lie there as promiscuous sexual behavior lies at the very heart of the human being? That is really the central problem; that is what brings high culture, science, politics, and economics all together.

ANNALS, *AAPSS*, **500**, November 1988

News of the Culture or
News of the Universe?

By GEORGE ROCHBERG

ABSTRACT: There is widespread and justified concern over the steady decline of culture in America—and in the West generally. In this article I examine the societal forces I believe to be largely responsible for this disquieting tendency. Among them I identify the loss of psychic and intellectual immunity to Bad Art; the century-long slide into vulgarity, tawdriness, and sleaziness, which have helped turn America into the Land of Entertainment; the loss of standards and criteria of taste and judgment in both the production of art and its critical evaluation; the loss—especially in America—of innocence brought on by the corrosion of human values; and, finally, the rise of sentimentality and the consequent triumph of kitsch, which has come to be accepted as an illusory substitute for genuine seriousness and sentiment. In this context I juxtapose what I call "news of the culture" with "news of the universe."

George Rochberg has composed a large body of musical works, which include six symphonies and seven string quartets. He taught composition at the University of Pennsylvania from 1960 to 1983, having served as chairman of its Department of Music from 1960 to 1968. In 1983 he retired as Emeritus Annenberg Professor of the Humanities. He is the author of a collection of essays, The Aesthetics of Survival *(1984).*

M Y subject is the state of American culture viewed within the larger context of Western culture.

My method will be to weave a concatenation of voices together with the strands of five major themes that characterize for me the present, all-pervasive cultural and societal atmosphere blanketing America and the West, an atmosphere that has produced in the arts particularly—but not limited to the arts—qualities and characteristics fascinating and appealing to some but repellent and disturbing to others.

These voices—aside from my own, which will come in the form of entries from my journal—are those of composers, poets, painters, sculptors, writers, critics, and journalists who have said something I feel illuminates some aspect of the cultural scene and, in most cases, resonates with my own view of things. By letting these voices speak in their own way I hope the picture I have in mind will begin to emerge and take shape around the following major themes:

    —the loss of psychic and intellectual immunity to Bad Art, best characterized by calling it cultural AIDS;
    —the century-long slide into vulgarity, tawdriness, and sleaziness—qualities that have turned America into what I think of at times as the Land of Entertainment, other times as the Disneyland of Culture;
    —the detritus of modernism and postmodernism compounded of the loss of standards and criteria of taste and judgment, the constant revision and redefinition of what constitutes art, and the resulting pluralism and ambiguities of relativism;
    —the loss of innocence accompanied by the corrosion and corruption of human values; and

—the loss of seriousness and the rise of sentimentality and kitsch in its place.

I begin with the opening lines of Robinson Jeffers's poem, "Shine, Perishing Republic," which he wrote sometime between 1917 or 1918 and 1925:

While this America settles
    in the mould of its vulgarity,
    heavily thickening to empire,
And protest, only a bubble
    in the molten mass, pops and
    sighs out, and the mass hardens,

I sadly smiling remember
    that the flower fades to make
    fruit, the fruit rots to make earth.
Out of the mother; and through
    the spring exultances, ripe-
    ness and decadence; and home to the
    mother.

You make haste on decay:
    not blameworthy; life is good,
    be it stubbornly long or suddenly
A mortal splendor:
    meteors are not needed less than moun-
    tains: shine, perishing republic.[1]

In his introduction to the volume of poetry that established his reputation as a major American poet, *Roan Stallion, Tamar and Other Poems,* from which I have just quoted, Jeffers recounts a crucial experience in his inner life as poet. He refers to "a bitter meditation" that took place while walking in the woods not far from his home in Carmel, California. He was, as he says, "still quite young at 27" and still uncertain about the value of his work and the direction it should take. His "bitter meditation" was on the problem

1. Copyright 1925 and renewed 1953 by Robinson Jeffers. Reprinted from Robinson Jeffers, *Roan Stallion, Tamar and Other Poems* (New York: Modern Library Edition, 1935), p. 97, by permission of Random House, Inc.

of modernism, which was then still in its heroic stage—urgent, expanding, gathering energy in all directions, and unrelentingly on the march. The year was 1914.

I shall let Jeffers speak:

This originality, without which a writer of verses is only a verse-writer, is there any way to attain it? The more advanced contemporary poets were attaining it by going farther and farther along the way that perhaps Mallarmé's aging dream had shown them, divorcing poetry from reason and ideas, bringing it nearer to music, finally to astonish the world with what would look like pure nonsense and would be pure poetry. No doubt those lucky writers were imitating each other, instead of imitating Shelley and Milton as I had done. . . . But now, as I smelled the wild honey . . . and meditated the direction of modern poetry, my discouragement blackened. It seemed to me that Mallarmé and his followers, renouncing intelligibility in order to concentrate the music of poetry, had turned off the road into a narrowing lane. Their successors could only make further renunciations; ideas had gone, now meter had gone, imagery would have to go; then recognizable emotions would have to go; perhaps at last even words might have to go or give up their meaning, nothing be left but musical syllables. Every advance required the elimination of some aspect of reality, and what could it profit me to know the direction of modern poetry if I did not like the direction? It was too much like putting out your eyes to cultivate the sense of hearing, or cutting off the right hand to develop the left. These austerities were not for me; originality by amputation was too painful for me. . . . I laid down the bundle of sticks and stood sadly by our bridgehead. The sea-fog was coming up the ravine, fingering through the pines, the air smelled of the sea and pine-resin and yerba buena, my girl and my dog were with me. . . . And I was standing there like a poor God-forsaken man-of-letters, making my final decision not to become a "modern." I did not want to become slight and fantastic, abstract and unintelligible.[2]

2. Ibid., pp. viii-x.

In the light of what happened in Europe and America as the century unfolded, Jeffers's statement is wholly astonishing. His decision not to become modern and his prescient, almost clairvoyant insights into America's settling "in the mould of its vulgarity" and "heavily thickening to empire" are all of a piece. As early as 1914, he foresaw the rising tide of developments that have not only taken place but have, in the process, changed a world and value system, the one Jeffers had been born into and lived by, into something we have every reason to question and doubt today.

With the advance of "the American Century," as Henry Luce called it, have come the changes and troubles besetting art and culture and the rapid rise of all forms of mass media and popular entertainment fully vindicating Jeffers's insights. It is doubtful Jeffers knew what was happening in Vienna around the same time he was meditating his fate as poet. Had he known, I am convinced he would have been even more determined not to become modern, not to become, as he said, "slight and fantastic, abstract and unintelligible."

April 1982

"'When the age laid hands upon itself, he [Karl Kraus] was the hands,' Brecht said. Few insights can stand beside this, and certainly not the comment of his friend Adolf Loos. 'Kraus,' he declares, 'stands on the frontier of a new age.' Alas by no means, for he stands on the threshold of the last judgment." (Walter Benjamin)

Modernism began as a series of acts of purification and of justice in the minds of its apocalyptic perpetrators. Purification led, as it must, to destruction; justice to calling down theological hell-fire on the cultural crimes of humanity. Modernism started out to expose

hypocrisy, falsehood, the dead word of the past, ornamentality. . . .

We are only now beginning to appreciate the ferocity with which the modern movement started. It was as if suddenly in one place—Vienna—a whole generation made up its mind to effect a new creation, a new Genesis; wipe the slate clean; erase every vestige of what has been.

Modernism is apocalyptic. As apocalypse it is prophetic.

In an essay in the June 1987 issue of *Harper's Magazine,* Alberto Moravia, the Italian novelist, writes on what he calls "the terrorist aesthetic," linking terror to power, both political as well as artistic. Terror, an invention of the bourgeoisie of the time of the French Revolution,

does not admit that there are such things as stable values. It is connected with the idea of progress; but, one should note, a progress that has nothing to do with the concept of improvement, but only with that of movement in time . . . it matters little if this progress is downward instead of upward, toward decadence instead of toward renewal. . . . If nothing stands still, then everything—opinions, styles, information, fortunes, success, groups, society—falls victim to continuous change. Snobbery comes to stand as the fickle and arbitrary surrogate of good taste, which is based no longer on the canon of the beautiful but on that of fashion, of whatever is in vogue. . . . The shout of "down with tradition" summarizes terror in the artistic field. . . . The avant-garde is terroristic because it believes not in values but in time. . . . Terrorism . . . is always the exalter of fictitious values and disparager of real values, and its purpose is always the enhancement of power. . . . The critical debate, the respectful appraisal, the strenuous analysis are of no purpose to the avant-garde, because it is impatient for certain styles to crumble away and certain others to be established in their place. The movements of enduring value

through time (precisely because it is a question of art, of something that is by its nature outside of time) are extremely slow and quite imperceptible. Hastening these movements to the point of absurdity (in Europe, during the first postwar era, almost every day one was a witness to the birth of new "movements" and new "currents") has always brought about the end of the avant-garde. In this way, the terroristic and bourgeois idea of time as a creator of value comes to be identified with the idea of modernity.[3]

January 1, 1984

Before the 20th century (which is ebbing away), there was a wide and general understanding of the difference between the potential and the actual. Now we are in the midst of a swamp of words that have taken the place of reality. The culture subsists more on the substitution of the verbal for reality than on a grasp of reality itself. . . . With the substitution of the verbal for the real has come too a visible depreciation of how things are . . . judged and explains why non-real things or things of little or no value are taken seriously and can even be . . . evaluated better than or higher than the genuine article. . . . When language no longer reflects reality, it becomes a tool of propagandists . . . and a means not only for deluding others but oneself as well.

In its winter 1988 quarterly issue, the Museum of Modern Art published a lead interview with Vito Acconci, an American sculptor, on the occasion of an exhibition called "Vito Acconci: Public Places." Acconci's responses to the interviewer capture unwittingly the essence of our degenerating culture:

I'm thinking in terms of public space, which would mean there's no "art viewer"; this is a

3. Alberto Moravia, "The Terrorist Aesthetic," *Harper's Magazine,* 274(1645):37-39, 42-44 (June 1987).

place that a person happens to pass by. In a public space, I don't think you are justified in attacking a viewer, whereas a person who enters a museum or gallery is thinking, "I am an art viewer." By extension, "I am submitting to the art's terms." By extension, then, "I agree to be victimized by the art."

Acconci, who might qualify as one of the last vestiges of avant-gardism as defined by Moravia, is interested in opposing the traditions of public monuments and modern public sculpture that are found in parks and other public places. To accomplish this, he sees his work as

much more in the tradition of architecture, park-like stuff. I guess for me and a lot in my generation, we're certainly not thinking of monuments. We're thinking more of a monument brought down to earth, cut down to size. There's a statue on a pedestal: person is here, statue is up there. It's bigger than you are, it's made of stone. It's going to last longer than you are, so all you can do is genuflect, all you can do is bow down. What I'd like to do is topple that monument and make it a place to gather and question rather than nod your head.

I don't think I could forget about that sculptural tradition—to forget about it would be foolhardy since it does exist. I'm not going to just ignore it. Ideally, I'd like my stuff to come to terms with that tradition and try to analyze it, subvert it, knock it down. I don't think my work does that enough.

I'd love public art to start a revolution.

This revolution Acconci would like public art to start is, in the words of Christopher Lyon, the interviewer, "almost a Greek idea, the creation of a place for public debate." To this Acconci adds, "In America we once had a tradition of the town square. Now it's become a shopping mall. We need to reproduce that place of discussion."[4]

4. Christopher Lyon, "The Public Art of Vito Acconci," *Museum of Modern Art Members Quarterly,* Winter 1988, pp. 1, 6.

August 26, 1985

Curious cross-referencing . . . in yesterday's New York Times:

1) A survey by John Rockwell of new music at Aspen under [Paul] Fromm's auspices
2) Doctorow's essay in book review section on "The Passion of Our Calling"
3) S. Freedman's piece in Arts and Leisure section on whether "tranquil times" can produce great art
4) James Atlas' piece in Magazine section on the demise of the New York intellectual.

Essentially they are all dancing around the same point (or points). Doctorow does it best because he's a writer and understands the true nature of the problem. Atlas is perceptive, but it is the perception of a critic, however astute; so it lacks the bite of Doctorow. Rockwell and Freedman are merely reporting on the state of things, and except for the slightest hint on Rockwell's part, not committing themselves to any stand.

The chief conclusion of all four pieces seems to be that nothing of great moment is happening in our culture. The scale of interests and achievements is small—and even diminishing. Our writers, painters, composers are not moved by great ideas or passions; neither do they possess large-scale means with which to attempt to say large-scale things. . . . There's too much comfort, too much success in the marketplace. There is no rage at injustice. There is no moral revulsion. Tepidness has spread itself over the land. All the old definitions of art have undergone revision so that no distinction holds any longer between high art and popular culture. In fact, some people (Atlas is good on this) see no difference between Stravinsky and The Talking Heads; and in order to discuss who is (or what makes) a great artist today you must include Chuck Berry along with Proust in the discussion— otherwise, it's worthless. What's interesting, what works is good, therefore art. (Questions like "interesting to whom" and "for how long" are not asked. Nor is there any hint of the

presence of criteria in what makes something "work"—beyond the fact of its momentary appeal.) It's a picture of the great morass spawned by declining Western culture and the confusions born out of the demise of heroic modernism and the onset of post-modernism. To my way of thinking it's the onslaught of cultural AIDS, born out of self-indulgence and lack of morality. If I understood her at all, this is exactly what Suzi Gablik was getting at in her little book on the failure of modernism. The depths of the penetration into the body cultural was made very clear when, some weeks before going to Germany, I talked with Ann d'Harnencourt (who is the director of the Philadelphia Art Museum) at M. F.'s about Gablik's book. d'Harnencourt was immediately stand-offish and, without saying so directly, denied any merit to Gablik's views. But if you take Gablik on painting, John Gardner on writing, Doctorow on the same and add them all up, you get the same basic condemnation of our culture, the same decrying of easy success at the expense of the creation of real art. What they are saying is we live in gutless, passionless times, we've lost all immunity to the production of Bad Art; worse, that Bad Art that "works" in the immediate sense of being innovative and sensationalist is now touted as "good"—the proof being that it makes money and earns the support and accolades of those who form the infra-structure of the art world and its culture today precisely because it *does* make money. Obviously, nothing is as overtly crass as all that; i.e., dealers and museum directors, publishers and critics must invent a whole vocabulary of rationalizations [New Speak] which, by setting up new "definitions" and new "standards" of what makes for "good" art, removes them personally from being directly tainted by the brush of crass materialism. . . . The shifting sands of expediency—how can one hold to a point of view, a moral stance, a sense of what is ultimately right in idea and execution if all one cares about is riding the waves of what is currently fashionable, momentarily successful? Rudderless, aimless wanderings in a deepening night of terror and confusion. Doris Lessing's "degenerative disease"—by which she meant Western individualism—is prophetic. Beyond

imagining. She hit the mark absolutely. Another term, more poetic, metaphoric for AIDS. Insidious, invidious, mysterious . . . and terrifying. Because no one will acknowledge that AIDS—whether of the physiological or cultural variety—is self-induced and self-incubated. . . . Hence the instinctive terror. As in all things human: first the physical sign, then slowly, gradually the spiritual sign manifest themselves. And all too typically human, because we live more in relation to the external than the internal, the recognition and acknowledgment of the spiritual sign will come when it is too late to do anything about it.

———

Into the moral and cultural morass that critics have dubbed "postmodernism"—Gablik calls postmodernism "the somewhat weasel word now being used to describe the garbled situation of art in the '80's"[5]—steps a new, major figure, that of the German painter Anselm Kiefer. According to the critic Theodore F. Wolff, "Seen next to Kiefer's accomplishments, the work of" such artists as Julian Schnabel, Enzo Cucchi, David Salle, and Francesco Clemente "appears skin-deep and overblown, and their promises that they would propel the art of the late 20th century toward and into the 21st seem unlikely to be fulfilled."[6]

Born in 1945, Kiefer seems to have taken it upon himself to do penance through his art for the heinous crimes of the Nazis. He goes still further in his art's moral reevaluation of traditional German culture and German idealism by subjecting the "spiritual heroes" and "ways of wisdom" of pre-Nazi Germany to pointed irony and pungent sardonicism. He is morally outraged at what Germany perpe-

5. Suzi Gablik, *Has Modernism Failed?* (New York: Thames and Hudson, 1984), p. 73.

6. *Christian Science Monitor,* 21 Mar. 1988, p. 23.

trated upon Europe and the Jews—but mostly, I feel, at what Germany perpetrated upon itself. In 1978 Kiefer said:

When I cite Richard Wagner, then I do not mean the composer of this or that opera. For me, it is more important that Wagner changed, if you will, from a revolutionary into a reactionary. I also mean the phenomenon—Wagner. The way in which he was used in the Third Reich. . .[7]

Kiefer's scorching moral revulsion is echoed on a more general plane by the German writer Günter Grass: "What are they [the Germans] looking for? God? The absolute number? The meaning behind meaning? Insurance against nothingness? They want at last to know themselves. . . . Who are we? Where are we from? What makes us Germans? And what in God's name is Germany?"[8]

What I find remarkable about Kiefer is his passion not to forget the past, however painful the memories of former events and baneful or delusory the attitudes of mind may be to the one who must remember. Instinctively he knows that to forget the past is to erase meaning from the present and rob past, present, and future of any continuity, any relation to each other. All this he manages to convey through his canvases, which arise as consummate art expression out of an impressive diversity of imagery and an all-inclusive vocabulary of twentieth-century techniques of painting that communicate what he feels in his soul.

Kiefer's dream of the artist transcending the chaos and destruction of history is symbolized in canvas after canvas by one

7. Cited in the brochure for the Anselm Kiefer Exhibition, Philadelphia Museum of Art, Philadelphia, 1988.
8. *Headbirths, or, The Germans Are Dying Out* (1980), cited in brochure for the Anselm Kiefer Exhibition.

of his primary images: an artist's palette with wings. By means of his winged palette he wants desperately to rise above history and its physical chaos, to resurrect himself, and perhaps even Germany, through his art. In one of his most gripping canvases, *Icarus-March Sand,* we see the palette looming large over a strangely troubled landscape, one wing full out and still intact, but the feathers of the other on fire and falling to earth in flames. Is Kiefer saying that art cannot escape the burning truth of reality any more than the mythical Icarus could escape the fire of the sun? It seems so to me. I think Kiefer is also asking the question, If art cannot transcend history, how can it hope to change anything?

———

Something of this same awareness and questioning haunts a letter I received recently from Yinam Leef, a young Israeli composer. In his letter from Jerusalem dated 15 March 1988 he writes:

In a time like this, everything becomes very fragile: our democracy is very fragile (some people claim, and I tend to agree with them, that actually we live in a military society and a totalitarian regime, with our parliamentarian system acting as a fig leaf to cover up our shame); our safety is put into question, and we become very vulnerable. The whole cultural makeup of society becomes very fragile, and things like art, music and the media become either completely meaningless, or tools for solidifying one's basic hypocrisy. You know, when in Philadelphia, one of the issues was always "who is really my audience." I couldn't stand to think that I was creating in a kind of vacuum. . . . Well, I am very sad to say that the kind of vacuum that exists here is more frightening and sits more heavily on me than I could even dream. I feel that artists should relate to reality and their society, and should have the ability to voice their opinions and try to change something.

The same motif of the helplessness of the artist in the face of the brutal reality of enormous events, of his or her sense of art's ineffectiveness in altering their nature, in bringing about a change in their direction tolls in this passage from a letter of Rainer Maria Rilke, the great German poet of the first half of this century, to a friend in June 1915. In despair and shock at the outbreak of World War I, Rilke is distressed

that such confusion, not-knowing-which-way-to-turn, the whole sad man-made complication of this provoked fate, that exactly this incurably bad condition of things was necessary to force out evidences of whole-hearted courage, devotion and bigness ... while we, the arts, the theater, called nothing forth in these very same people, brought nothing to rise and flower, were unable to change anyone. What is our metier but purely and largely and freely to set forth opportunities for change,—did we do this so badly, so half-way, so little convinced and convincing? That has been the question, that has been the suffering for almost a year, and the problem is to do it more forcefully, more unrelentingly. How?![9]

What then, if any, is the purpose of art, its function in society? How can we reconcile ourselves to a situation where art is unable to offer any hope, to either the artist or society, of self- or societal transformation? Is it merely a mirage, a rainbow on the far horizon arcing across the sky, beautiful to contemplate but having no power to affect reality? Is it an Icarus-like endeavor doomed to failure, to fall to earth because it cannot bear the fires of reality? Is there no way out?

9. George Rochberg, *The Aesthetics of Survival* (Ann Arbor: University of Michigan Press, 1984), p. 219.

March 29, 1985

Down to the Academy today to hear the St. Matthew Passion. Wonderfully beautiful music; and sobering—because ... it makes no effort to impress, to astonish. . . . We hear Bach's deepest feelings and reflections, offered unself-consciously, about one of the most incredible stories of our culture. . . .

It would be a near miracle if someone today could capture again in his own way the soberness of Bach.

February 17, 1985

We watched the Marx Brothers on our VCR last night. "Animal Crackers." Not as zany as I would have liked but thoroughly delightful. What comes across so easily, practically "sings" out, is the genuineness of play and humor—all mixed up with music. . . . The overall effect is one of intelligence, however "corny" Groucho's puns and play-on-words, Chico's "Italian" character, slightly off-key (suggestive of the "hood" but not really evil in any sense), Harpo's endlessly expressive and corny schtick (his knee gag, his long coat full of idiotic props)—and Zeppo, played straight and serious. A thoroughly lovable gang played off against "Mrs. Rittenhouse" (Margaret Dumont, high-class dignity personified).

Probably 60 years since this early film which exhibits good will, good faith, unself-conscious horseplay, wit—yes, and innocence itself. In short, emblematic of a spirit which pervaded American entertainment in the teens and twenties. So unlike what passes for "entertainment" today. Heavy-handed, self-conscious—so that even Mel Brooks and Woody Allen have to go to unbelievable lengths and extremes to be "funny"—although each succeeds admirably at times (Brooks in "The Producers" and "To Be or Not to Be," Allen in "Sleeper" and "Bananas"). But Brooks and Allen are exceptions. What we get now are "soap-opera" elevated to ... so-called "prime time," shows like "Dallas" and "Dynasty," where tacky sex, corporate chicanery, moving

mannequins, male and female, read lines in the deadest way possible, where "plots" are totally fabricated to bring out "media" issues. . . . The overall sense of this sleazy fare is bad will, bad faith, bad intent—knowing and sophisticated. . . . As the Marx Brothers (and Chaplin and Buster Keaton and Harold Lloyd) are emblematic of the age of American "innocence," so are the dreckish things purveyed today (solely to make money) emblematic of the age of "experience" holding America in its thrall today. You remember the Marx Brothers with a smile on your lips. You "remember" today's garbage with utter distaste and disgust. From innocence to corruption, from the Golden Age to the Iron Age—all in one life-time.

One of Milan Kundera's obsessions is kitsch, a term he has defined in innumerable ways and in innumerable places, including his novel *The Unbearable Lightness of Being*. Kundera, the expatriate Czech writer now living in Paris, is obsessed with kitsch because it represents to him the triumph of sentimentality in Western culture. If one follows the logic of his thought, every nation in the West today has its own version of kitsch, all of them sharing the common property of sentimentality about ideology, customs, mores, and traditions, which bind people in national, political, or cultural entities together. According to Kundera, kitsch has literally overwhelmed the West, and in place of reality kitsch has supplanted that reality with what he calls "the beautifying lie."

In recent years, on receiving the Jerusalem Prize for Literature, he spoke eloquently on this most favorite topic of his:

Some eighty years after Flaubert imagined his Emma Bovary, during the Thirties of our own century, another great novelist, the Viennese Hermann Broch, would write: "The modern novel struggles heroically against the tide of kitsch, but it ends up overwhelmed by kitsch." The word, *Kitsch,* born in Germany in the middle of the last century, describes the attitude of those who want to please the greatest number, and at any cost. In order to please, it is necessary to confirm what everyone wants to hear, to put oneself at the service of received ideas. Kitsch is the translation of the stupidity of received ideas into the language of beauty and feeling. It moves us to tears for ourselves, for the banality of what we think and feel.

Today, fifty years later, Broch's remark is becoming truer still. Given the imperative necessity to please and thereby to gain the attention of the greatest number, the aesthetic of the mass media is inevitably that of kitsch, and as the mass media come to embrace and to infiltrate more and more of our life, kitsch becomes our everyday aesthetic and moral code. Up until recent times, modernism meant a nonconformist revolt against received ideas and kitsch.

Today, modernity is fused with the enormous vitality of the mass media, and to be modern means a strenuous effort to be up-to-date, to conform, to conform even more thoroughly than anyone else. Modernity has put on kitsch's clothing.[10]

May 7, 1985

A long time ago I wrote about what I called "moral presence." Moral in the sense I mean it is *the true,* that which is incontrovertibly the hidden reality of all that is, the essence and *suchness* of all things. Moral presence is hard won in human art—though it is there before us in every flower, in every animal (the gentle

10. *Mishkanot sha'anna'im* (newsletter published by Mishkanot sha'anna'im, Jerusalem, Israel). A slightly different version of these same remarks, presumably edited by Milan Kundera for inclusion as pt. 7, "Jerusalem Address: The Novel and Europe," appears in Kundera's *Art of the Novel* (New York: Grove Press, 1988), pp. 163-64.

and the ferocious), in every tree and blade of grass. It literally saturates the universe. Human consciousness is too distracted to be aware of it. That's why . . . the Buddhists speak of quieting the mind. Only by the effort of inner seeing and inner hearing does moral presence bloom into consciousness. It is almost impossible to discover in this age; though it *is* there in a Bartok and occasionally flashes through a Schoenberg, but rarely—in fact almost never—in my contemporaries. They are too distracted with superfluities and superficialities.

April 28, 1983

"High-tech" music is very canny, i.e., ultra-knowing and sophisticated. As sound, it tends to be "brilliant," full of spit and polish, flashy as hell, lots of fancy-footwork, if not to say also lots of fireworks and uses of the orchestra . . . as a machine which operates at high levels of physical power and ingenuity. . . . But what is gained in treating the orchestra as a gleaming, 1000 horse-power piece of chrome-plated steel machinery is gained at the expense of radical simplicity, seriousness, nobility and gravity of demeanor, genuine emotional power. It results in a series of mere cosmetic effects—one more "brilliant" than the other. And mostly vacuity and hollowness of musical meaning. . . . The sheer concentration on texture and color ends up by the 80's in complete extrusion of any possible solid values so that everything becomes surface—glistening, shining, polished—and superficiality of gesture and manner—in fact, *all* gesture and manner. . . . "High-tech," I suppose, had to be when you consider there is a kind of talent in the world today that finds only the surface of things available to it: such talent can't go below the surface, it dies there. But on the surface of things it dances and prances, prates and pirouettes; it trades simplicity for fake complexity; . . . it loves the trivial, the obvious, the sure-fire, or goes in for a kind of fake seriousness—which is to say it is full of pretension and gaseous material.

June 13, 1985

S. called this a.m. to talk about his reaction to the *Hammerklavier* Sonata. He found it repellent, couldn't relate to it as a human musical expression. It was evidence [to him] of an uncaring, unloving attitude on Beethoven's part despite its brilliance of composition. He feels similarly about the *Missa Solemnis* and The Grand Fugue and attributes them to Beethoven's will rather than heart. At the same time he said he loves the later quartets and considers them consummate expression of musical gestures and ideas. Along the way he compared the *Hammerklavier* Sonata and its world of "non-human" gestures to Shakespeare's *King Lear*. We must have talked for almost an hour during which time I tried to point out that the only way one could grasp the essence of the *Hammerklavier* Sonata (and The Grand Fugue and *Missa Solemnis)* was to recognize that it lay beyond the ordinary limits of human culture; and particularly, that despite the fact of Beethoven's being an historical personality, such a work lies outside of history itself and refuses any of the constraints of the normal historical perspectives. In short, the *Hammerklavier*, though written in the early 19th century, has nothing to do with what we call "the 19th century" but rather is concrete evidence that Beethoven had entered the cosmic realm and plugged into those incredible forces which are the source of human and animal life, solar and stellar life. In that realm beyond the ordinary human ken (but which nevertheless is its source and continually feeds it) what possible need did a man like Beethoven have for what we refer to as "human feelings," the tight, circumscribed circle of the human ego and its petty, warring round of dominance/subjugation . . . that pea-sized perspective on the universe and the ferocious forces that make up the world in which we exist so painfully and blindly?

June 15, 1985

Heard some 15th century music on the car radio and suddenly realized that such music,

like most music since that remote time, only brings us "news of the times," "news of the culture." Whereas Beethoven brings us "news of the universe" (to borrow a phrase from [the poet] Robert Bly). Stretching a point, I suppose it's possible to say that "news of the universe" was conveyed through religion in the 15th century and that music had not yet evolved a sufficient language to be able to break through the confines of culture. One can even suggest that were it not for a Beethoven a music which conveyed "news of the universe" would never have emerged from the 19th century either. . . . In this sense, Beethoven is, though inheritor of Haydn and Mozart, an anomaly. One faces the problem of trying to understand how it was and why it was he was compelled to develop his powers to the level of bringing the world "news of the universe." Far from an answer—indeed, if one is even possible—we have to consider Beethoven's deafness which relieved him, though its onset initially caused him great mental and psychological suffering, of petty distractions and the banal, inane, ceaseless chatter of the world around him. This is no small thing when you come to recognize how much of life and energy is frittered away in small talk, in exchanging "opinion" on the current issues of the day and working oneself up over personal affronts and grievances which occupy so much time and attention in the average human life. These are the great concerns of most human beings who sleep-walk their way through existence. These and overriding concerns with career, money, appearance of things, keeping busy to avoid self-reflection and self-control. In a world where the individual has been given license by society to pursue personal gratification at all costs—to oneself and others—"news of the universe" has no particular value or meaning. . . . In other words, by displacing his center of existence from outward concerns to his inner life Beethoven's physical misfortune helped turn his work into a great spiritual victory—nor was he unaware of it. It turns out then that what S. objects to in Beethoven's *Hammerklavier* is that he breaks away from giving us "news of the times" to giving us "news of the

universe.". . . Who of us, even artists, can achieve that level of self-sacrifice (of "career," of "success," of the blandishments and pleasures of the quotidian life) where one's work exists for the sole purpose of reaching higher levels of existence—and break with "culture"? . . . He gave us "news" which shattered illusions, that cultural atmosphere without which most of us cannot live. Man lives in illusions as much as he lives in oxygen; and would die without them, regardless of their character and quality (according to the "mental structure" which prevails). Beethoven shed the protective tissue of human illusions; and if we are to follow him, we must shed it too. Whatever truths may emerge from this shedding, whether they set us "free" or only make us sadder, hopefully wiser, it is the only road to reality.

The news of our time, of our culture is not good. I once had a dream of bright, shiny, new ruins. That, as I see it, is the picture of our culture. We dream collectively of coming to wholeness again, perhaps individually of attaining to that "four-fold vision" without which William Blake felt nothing would be set right again. If we can achieve wholeness or can attain to something approaching Blake's "four-fold vision," perhaps then art and artists will once again be able to bring us news of the universe.

There is a bitter paradox in all this that, ironically, only a character like William Butler Yeats's "Crazy Jane"—touched by Plato's poetic "divine madness"—can utter:

For nothing can be sole or whole
That has not been rent.[11]

11. From "Crazy Jane Talks with the Bishop," *The Collected Poems of W. B. Yeats* (New York: Macmillan, 1964), p. 255. Reprinted by permission of A. P. Watt Ltd. on behalf of Anne Yeats and Michael Yeats.

Report of the Board of Directors to the Members of the American Academy of Political and Social Science for the Year 1987

MEMBERSHIP AND SUBSCRIPTIONS
AS OF DECEMBER 31

Year	Number
1977	14,202
1978	12,816
1979	10,884
1980	10,059
1981	9,874
1982	9,536
1983	8,904
1984	6,564
1985	5,704
1986	5,606
1987	5,151

PUBLICATIONS
NUMBER OF VOLUMES OF *THE ANNALS* PRINTED (6 PER YEAR)

1977	91,367
1978	85,605
1979	71,513
1980	65,153
1981	69,313
1982	74,211
1983	68,236
1984	52,154
1985	52,800
1986	53,201
1987	43,629

FINANCES
SIZE OF SECURITIES PORTFOLIO
MARKET VALUE AS OF DECEMBER 31

1977	451,545
1978	385,795
1979	377,915
1980	368,926
1981	351,886
1982	390,119
1983	485,809
1984	384,312
1985	369,389
1986	373,320
1987	387,997

NUMBER OF VOLUMES OF *THE ANNALS* SOLD (IN ADDITION TO MEMBERSHIPS AND SUBSCRIPTIONS)

1977	6,296
1978	8,124
1979	5,907
1980	8,751
1981	5,884
1982	7,562
1983	5,877
1984	5,230
1985	5,910
1986	5,119
1987	5,314

STATEMENT OF INCOME AND RETAINED EARNING FOR THE YEAR ENDED DECEMBER 31, 1987

Income
Royalty—Sage Publications	$110,000
Sales of review books	516
Royalties and reprint permissions	3,059
Annual meeting revenue	6,323
Miscellaneous	10,495
Total Income	130,393

Operating Expenses
Salaries	72,626
Payroll taxes	5,788
Pension expense	17,629
Employee benefits	3,596
Annual meeting expense	23
Depreciation	4,148
Insurance	21,812
Postage	2,745
Repairs and maintenance	13,713

Supplies	5,576
Telephone	3,053
Utilities	7,423
Total Operating Expenses	163,466
Loss from Operations	(33,073)
Other Income (Expenses)	
Investment income (net)	18,039
Gains (loss) on sale of investments	45,417
Grant administration overhead	22,005
Total Other Income (Expense)	85,461
Net Income (Loss)	52,388
Retained Earnings–January 1	294,024
Retained Earnings–December 31	$346,412

Report of the Board of Directors

During 1987, the six volumes of THE ANNALS dealt with the following subjects:

January   *International Affairs in Africa*, edited by Gerald J. Bender, Director, School of International Relations, University of Southern California, Los Angeles.

March   *Foreign Language Instruction: A National Agenda*, edited by Richard D. Lambert, Professor of Sociology, University of Pennsylvania, Philadelphia.

May   *The Fulbright Experience and Academic Exchanges*, edited by Nathan Glazer, Professor of Education and Sociology, Graduate School of Education, Harvard University, Cambridge, Massachusetts.

July   *Unemployment: A Global Challenge*, edited by Bertram Gross, Visiting Professor of Peace and Conflict Studies, University of California, Berkeley, and Alfred Pfaller, Head, Research Group on International Economics and Development, Friedrich Ebert Foundation, Bonn, West Germany.

September   *The Informal Economy*, edited by Louis A. Ferman, Professor of Social Work and Research Director, Institute of Labor and Industrial Relations, University of Michigan, Ann Arbor; Stuart Henry, Visiting Associate Professor of Sociology, Eastern Michigan University, Ypsilanti; and Michele Hoyman, Associate Professor of Political Science and Fellow, Center for Metropolitan Studies, University of Missouri, St. Louis.

November   *Policies to Prevent Crime: Neighborhood, Family, and Employment Strategies*, edited by Lynn A. Curtis, President, Milton S. Eisenhower Foundation, Washington, D.C.

The publication program for 1988 includes the following volumes:

January   *Telescience: Scientific Communication in the Information Age*, edited by Murray Aborn, Senior Scientist, National Science Foundation, Washington, D.C.

March   *State Constitutions in a Federal System*, edited by John Kincaid, Director of Research, U.S. Advisory Commission on Intergovernmental Relations, Washington, D.C.

May   *Anti-Americanism: Origins and Context*, edited by Thomas Perry Thornton, Adjunct Professor, School of Advanced International Studies, Johns Hopkins University, Washington, D.C.

July   *The Private Security Industry: Issues and Trends*, edited by Ira A. Lipman, Chairman and President, Guardsmark, Inc.

September   *Congress and the Presidency: Invitation to Struggle*, edited by Roger H. Davidson, Professor, University of Maryland, College Park.

November   *Whither the American Empire: Expansion or Contraction?* edited by Marvin E. Wolfgang, President, American Academy of Political and Social Science, and Professor of Sociology and Law, University of Pennsylvania, Philadelphia.

During 1987, the Book Department published over 240 reviews. The majority of these were written by professors, but reviewers also included university presidents, members of private and university-sponsored organizations, government and public officials, and business professionals. Over 600 books were listed in the Other Books section.

Fifty-four requests were granted to reprint material from THE ANNALS. These went to professors and other authors for use in books in preparation and to nonprofit organizations for educational purposes.

MEETINGS

The ninetieth annual meeting was postponed from 1987 to 1988.

OFFICERS AND STAFF

The Board reelected the following officers: Marvin E. Wolfgang, President; Richard D. Lambert, Vice-President; Randall M. Whaley, Secretary; Elmer B. Staats, Treasurer; Henry W. Sawyer, III, Counsel. Reappointed were; Richard D. Lambert, Editor, and Alan W. Heston, Associate Editor.

OFFICERS AND STAFF

The Board reelected the following officers: Marvin E. Wolfgang, President; Richard D. Lambert, Vice-President; Randall M. Whaley, Secretary; Elmer B. Staats, Treasurer; Henry W. Sawyer, III, Counsel. Reappointed were; Richard D. Lambert, Editor, and Alan W. Heston, Associate Editor.

Respectfully submitted,

THE BOARD OF DIRECTORS

Elmer B. Staats
Marvin E. Wolfgang
Lee Benson
Richard D. Lambert
Thomas L. Hughes
Randall M. Whaley
Lloyd N. Cutler
Henry W. Sawyer, III
William T. Coleman, Jr.
Anthony J. Scirica
Frederick Heldring

Philadelphia, Pennsylvania
20 November 1987

Book Department

INTERNATIONAL RELATIONS AND POLITICS

CALLEO, DAVID. *Beyond American Hegemony: The Future of the Western Alliance.* Pp. 336. New York: Basic Books, 1987. $20.95.

The premise of many recent books and articles on the United States is the decline of its hegemony. Ironically, these writings are pouring in when the United States is experiencing the longest peacetime expansion of the economy and when employment has been rising since the last recession ended in 1982. Meanwhile, Europe is limping behind the United States with high unemployment and low growth.

Why is there so much discussion about U.S. economic problems when by historical standards the economy seems to be healthy? Samuel Brittan, the distinguished economic commentator of *Financial Times*, has provided one answer. In the *Financial Times* of 18 May 1987, he wrote that American political and business leaders, like their British counterparts before, are afflicted with hypochondria. A few months later, in the *Financial Times* of 14 September 1987, in another indictment of public and private officials, he wrote, "There is no longer any novelty in saying that a country, like a patient, does itself no good, if it keeps on taking its economic temperature. We now have an even worse form of hypochondria: taking the temperature with a cracked thermometer." According to Brittan, the magnitude of the U.S. balance-of-payments problems is exaggerated because of the so-called black hole. The "black hole" refers to the fact that when all the official figures of the surpluses and deficits of countries are added up, there is a discrepancy of $50 to $100 billion. The balance of payments of the world should be zero by definition. Although Calleo does not exaggerate U.S. economic problems, his book can be considered as another account of the thesis that the United States is in decline.

Calleo argues that the Atlantic alliance has been the foundation of the international system since World War II. Militarily, it has been nothing but an American nuclear protectorate for Europe; as such it is no longer viable. The reasons are the relative decline of the United States, the successful policy of the United States in bringing power and prosperity to Europe as well as the Third World, the political importance and the rise of some Third World states individually or collectively—for example, the Organization of Petroleum Exporting Countries—and nuclear parity between the Soviet Union and the United States. This is a pluralistic world that has no room for a hegemonic power. The era of "Pax Americana"—Calleo likes this

130

term—has come to an end. Calleo advocates a graceful exit for the United States. The defense of Europe should be left to the Europeans, especially in the form of a Franco-German alliance. Calleo illustrates how a joint nuclear defense of Europe could be a credible deterrence against a Soviet first strike. He argues that Europeans resent American leadership of and hegemony over the alliance, but they are not willing to pay for their own defense as long as the United States is doing it for them.

Calleo thinks that U.S. leaders are willing to tolerate this state of affairs because "in a world that has changed drastically, American leadership remains enthralled by hegemony and duopoly." Calleo believes that this faith in the role of a hegemon as the guarantor of world stability is unwarranted. He argues that the instability of the period before and after World War I and one of the causes of the war was Britain's refusal to accommodate the rising Germany. In brief, it is not the lack of a hegemon on the international scene that causes instability and war, but the presence of a declining hegemon that wants to preserve the status quo.

Calleo's achievement in presenting his case is impressive. He has a great deal to say about the history of the North Atlantic Treaty Organization (NATO), why Europe—especially France and Britain—wanted to use its protection to maintain empires, the United States' balance-of-payments problems, and the foreign policies of France and Germany and their military capabilities.

One can make the case that the U.S. public, at some future date, would not be willing to pay for European defenses. Enough publications and speeches constantly remind the Americans of their burden in defending Europe, Calleo's work being one of the best. The case can be made stronger when the burden of each country's share of NATO's expenditure is understood by the taxpayers. Hence the unviability of NATO can be asserted without invoking the decline-of-America thesis. Calleo's whole argument hinges on the premise that the United States cannot afford the defense of Europe and its other global commitments.

The economic problems of the United States and its declining hegemony are simply not obvious to me. Maybe by the time this review is published, Calleo's point will have become all too obvious. In that case, his argument is flawless.

A. REZA VAHABZADEH
University of Pennsylvania
Philadelphia

MODELSKI, GEORGE. *Long Cycles in World Politics.* Pp. 254. Seattle: University of Washington Press, 1987. $30.00.

Why does a global era under a dominant world power end, what will take its place, and who will lead it? The end of an era also raises questions about the existence of these cycles in the past. Is there a grand pattern to international politics?

Many historians and political scientists have been asking these questions as the end of American world leadership becomes apparent. Paul Kennedy's popular *Rise and Fall of the Great Powers* is the best-known work on the subject.

George Modelski's *Long Cycles in World Politics* may be an even better work, although the jargon of systems analysis and Parsonian sociology therein may disaffect some readers. Do not let it. Modelski's book is a powerful exposition of macropolitics and, as such, holds that managing the problems of the future must rely on understanding the inexorable, phased, long cycles of the past. The world, says Modelski, is not anarchic. The long cycles' "principal impulse is to animate the global political system along a path that includes both a repetitive beat and an upward thrust."

He begins in 1494, when the global system first formed. Global warfare is the first phase of long cycles. The preference for order is high but the availability of order is low. A world power emerges in the next phase. Historically, first Portugal, then the Netherlands, then Britain for two phases, and finally the United States assumed the role. In this phase the

preference for order is high, as is its availability. The next phase witnesses the delegitimation of the world power. The functions that the world power had performed—agenda formation, mobilization, decision making, administration, and innovation—the world power has difficulty performing. The principal reason is that while the availability of order is high, the general global preference is low. A challenger emerges in the next phase as both the preference for order and the availability of it decline. Challengers or the challenged with attributes of insularity, cohesion, economic leadership, and the proper organization for a global reach pass the test of major warfare to begin the next long cycle.

Modelski sees the phases of long cycles performing functions similar to Talcott Parsons's fourfold model. He devotes a chapter each to the relationships between long cycles and the rise of the nation-state, the rise of the party systems, and "the processes of dependency creation and reversal." He also sees long cycles as provoking a learning process.

He warns that the end of the present cycle of American world leadership holds great dangers for war, and he explores substitutes for global war as the crucible for the next long cycle. It is all thought-provoking material.

My criticism is sparse. Treating long cycles as independent variables risks their reification, as if they act as if alive. Modelski knows this trap. But when one uses language such as "with the passing of the Portuguese era, the global system thus faced two problems," the global system and long cycles can become too historically powerful.

NICHOLAS O. BERRY
Ursinus College
Collegeville
Pennsylvania

WALT, STEPHEN M. *The Origins of Alliances.* Pp. x, 321. Ithaca, NY: Cornell University Press, 1987. $32.50.

A worthy addition to the excellent works published in the series Cornell Studies in Security Affairs, this book is a major contribution to the theory of international politics. Stephen Walt has managed to combine a detailed empirical study of Middle East alliance shifts since World War II with a set of general hypotheses about the causes, effects, and results to be expected of alliances in superpower relations. He postulates a revision of the traditional balance-of-power theory; more in harmony with the historical record would be his conclusion that sovereign states form alliances primarily to balance threats.

Especially intriguing is his use of statistical hypothesis testing and reasoning from a mix of subjective and hard numerical data to support his conclusions. The best examples of this feature of the book are the two appended tables. Appendix 1 categorizes the 36 Middle East alliances from 1955 to 1979 on the nominal variable of balance/bandwagon and the ordinal variable of ideological solidarity (high, moderate, low, nil). The appendix supports his hypothesis that ideological similarity may influence alliance formation somewhat but not too much in situations of crisis. Appendix 2 details the U.S. alliance network and the Soviet alliance system on the interval variables of population, gross national product, size of armed forces, and defense spending, giving rather overwhelming support to his conclusion that, insofar as its position in the world is concerned, the United States enjoys a far more favorable prospect than does the Soviet Union.

The organization of the book follows a logical pattern. Beginning with two chapters on alliance formation and traditional balance-of-power theory, it continues with two factual summaries of Middle Eastern history from the Baghdad Pact of 1955 to the Six Day War of 1967 and thence to the Camp David accords of 1978, which led to the Egyptian-Israeli peace treaty of 1979. Walt then applies his findings in three theoretical chapters on the significant causes of alliances: power balancing versus threat balancing, ideological solidarity, and the efficacy of economic or military aid and penetration as instruments of superpower influence over client states. In his last chapter, with admirable audacity, he

instructs the policymakers in the United States as to the lessons they should draw from his results.

Those lessons are worth listing here. The United States can count on the continued support of the world's most important countries; marginal increases or decreases in its military strength will have little effect on the loyalty of its allies; misplaced belligerence by the United States will do more to frighten our allies than to guarantee their loyalty; the United States should avoid efforts to rally the Third World under the anti-Communist banner—the developing nations are relatively indifferent to that cause; the United States should avoid knee-jerk opposition to leftist Third World forces and its belief in Marxist solidarity, a myth proved wrong by examples from Tito to Pol Pot; it should reject the simple idea that Soviet arms recipients are reliable agents of the Kremlin, as well as the idea that U.S. aid recipients are reliable agents of Washington. Finally, the United States should concentrate more attention on its domestic society: a robust and productive economy is exactly the force that creates U.S. power and prestige in the world.

OLIVER BENSON

University of Oklahoma
Norman

AFRICA, ASIA, AND LATIN AMERICA

EVRON, YAIR. *War and Intervention in Lebanon: The Israeli-Syrian Deterrence Dialogue.* Pp. x, 246. Baltimore, MD: Johns Hopkins University Press, 1987. $39.50.

One aspect of the Lebanese civil war has been the continuing intense interest in the course of events there shown by regional powers and by the superpowers. Syria and Israel have intervened in the conflict to suit their own interests. On several occasions they have come close to war, only to pull back because they have devised a tacit system of deterrence over the years, a system made more explicit by occasional public pronouncements, by military maneuvers, and by diplomatic efforts through third parties, primarily the United States.

Writing for both a general and a specialized audience, Yair Evron, a political scientist at Tel Aviv University, begins his book by alluding to the familiar system of deterrence practiced by the nuclear powers. Evron argues that because nuclear deterrence has never been tested, regional modes of deterrence—and their thresholds—may be of some theoretical interest to students of international relations. What better case study than the Israeli-Syrian standoff over Lebanon, which each power has invaded and partially occupied but which has not yet become the cause of a major war between them?

Evron pursues this broad question chronologically, beginning with a brief chapter on Lebanon's history, followed by a chapter comparing Syrian and Israeli interests and policies in that country. Then comes the principal part of the book, tracing the twists and turns of the two regional powers from 1977 to 1985. A final summary chapter links Evron's findings to theoretical questions of interest to students of international relations.

Although some readers might differ with the account of Lebanese history contained in the first chapter, the balance of the book is supported by a great deal of evidence, which Evron gathered through interviews and access to Israeli official thinking—some of the interviews are anonymous—plus sources in the public domain, official and scholarly. Writing primarily from an Israeli viewpoint—because much official Syrian thinking is generally inaccessible—Evron argues that Israel, although long suspicious of the U.S. policy after 1976 of encouraging a Syrian presence in Lebanon that might help to end the civil war, and seeing a strategic threat from a Syrian presence in south Lebanon in particular, made the mistake of applying an unusually sensitive deterrence threshold to the Palestine Liberation Organization and its Lebanese allies after 1981. The 1982 invasion of Lebanon, and its disastrous consequences for Israel, showed the limits of deterrence: al-

though the PLO was defeated, some of its forces have now returned; as for Syria, it has been able to build a new air-defense system over Lebanese airspace and to reclaim political preeminence in that country. Without being explicit, Evron shows more sympathy with the policies of the Labor Party from 1975 to 1977, when the Israeli-Syrian deterrence was first established, than he does with the policies of Likud from 1977 to 1984, when deterrence was redefined and the two countries nearly engaged in a full-scale war.

As a historian of the Middle East, I find Evron's theoretical discussion fascinating but am disturbed by the frequent use of terms such as "collateral damage"—a euphemism for civilian casualties and property destruction—"strategic assets," "tolerance thresholds," "interfaces," "punishing modes," and "perceptions." These terms, particularly the latter, are now casually thrown about in policy discourse. Although Evron duly mentions the immense suffering of the Lebanese and Palestinian peoples and the casualties sustained by Syria and Israel, he is concerned primarily with the theoretical implications of deterrence and with future prospects. He closes his book by observing that

strategic stability may develop out of the continued experience of successful deterrence. This, coupled with the diminution of political grievances, is a precondition for conflict management. . . . Deterrence theory should therefore be seen as an essential building block in a wider theory of conflict management and strategic stability (p. 224).

Will this hope be fulfilled?

                                KARL K. BARBIR

Siena College
Loudonville
New York

HALL, EDWARD T. and MILDRED REED HALL. *Hidden Differences: Doing Business with the Japanese.* Pp. xx, 172. New York: Doubleday, 1987. $16.95.

This book provides extraordinary reading on Japanese culture for academics and practi-

tioners for the following reasons: (1) the framework is simple, broad, and understandable and is a usable guide for recalling content; (2) the book is excellently written, easy to read, and as enjoyable as listening to advice from a guru on the subject; and (3) the reading list that is provided is indispensable.

A major, underlying concept in the book is the importance and pervasiveness of culture in all facets of Japanese life, private and public. Because "communication is culture," as Hall and Hall claim, Japan's culture is characterized as a "high-context" communication system, which means that "most of the information is already in the person, while very little is in coded, explicit, transmitted parts of the message." Hall and Hall also show that Japan is a high-information-flow society; individuals on average are very well read and informed on diverse subjects. In Western cultures, communication messages are "low context," that is, information must be made explicit through procedures and formal ways of getting messages understood. High-context cultures are compared to twins who grew up together and communicate more economically; low-context cultures are compared to two lawyers in a courtroom trial. In high-context cultures—such as the Japanese, Arab, and Mediterranean—individuals are more open to interruptions, are in tune with what goes on around them, are spatially involved with each other, share information continuously, and are more sensitive to body language. What is said, how it is said, and what is not said are all important. In low-context cultures, on the other hand, as in the United States and Europe, information is compartmentalized, does not flow freely, is controlled, and requires rules, procedures, and formal channels to be communicated.

The implications for Westerners in communicating and doing business in high-context cultures such as the Japanese are significant. On page 33, and throughout the book, Hall and Hall advise Western businesspersons on effectively communicating and negotiating in Japan's culture. In general terms, two tenets offered are to "proceed slowly, taking every action possible to maintain course and stay on

an even keel; and [to] seek the advice of a skillful, subtle interpreter of the culture."

Hall and Hall provide in part 2, "The Japanese," an excellent overview that links Japan's history to current cultural behavior and values. We are reminded of the two dominating roles in historical Japan: the role of the feudal lord and of the agricultural village that sustained him. Out of these roles evolved current cultural emphases on leisurely and task-oriented teamwork, which grew out of planting, cultivating, and harvesting rice; consensus decision making; and equality among coworkers and members of families. From these roles, Japanese may appear to Westerners as paradoxically egalitarian and rigidly hierarchical. The historical context explains the paradox, however.

Other important cultural characteristics are discussed in this section, such as Japan's group-oriented and family-centered culture, the role of harmony, dependency, order and rank, closeness, and cooperation. Relative to these cultural characteristics, Hall and Hall suggest effective ways for reading and responding to unspoken cues. In addition, a "vocabulary of human relationships" is provided on page 54.

In part 3, "Japanese Business," Hall and Hall provide a detailed understanding of Japanese corporate philosophy, for example, the role of the team and the Japanese work ethic, loyalty, responsibility, and the role of quality-control circles. They also fully describe the Japanese organization in terms of, for example, its structure, leadership, marketing, planning, and human resource practices.

Part 4 provides helpful advice for starting a business and doing business in Japan. Like the book, it successfully combines a how-to-do-it approach with interesting descriptions of cultural themes that influence business. In a step-by-step approach, Hall and Hall discuss common American expectations, the need for a long-term plan, the initial visit to Japan—which they advise to keep simple—a checklist for starting up in Japan, how to communicate and negotiate, how to save face and allow Japanese to do so, how to manage a Japanese staff, and how to sell, market, and distribute.

In short, Hall and Hall have provided a very readable, comprehensive, interesting, and usable road map for successfully understanding, starting, and maintaining a business in Japan. All this in 192 pages is, indeed, commendable.

JOSEPH WEISS

Bentley College
Waltham
Massachusetts

MARCUS, HAROLD. *Haile Sellassie I: The Formative Years, 1892-1936.* Pp. xvii, 242. Berkeley: University of California Press, 1987. No price.

DEJENE, ALEMNEH. *Peasants, Agrarian Socialism, and Rural Development in Ethiopia.* Pp. xiii, 162. Boulder, CO: Westview Press, 1987. Paperbound, no price.

In an oft-quoted sentence, Edward Gibbon declared more than two centuries ago that "encompassed on all sides by the enemies of their religion, the Aethiopians slept near a thousand years, forgetful of the world by whom they were forgotten." Harold Marcus's study, the first of the two books under review, recounts the first half of the life of Emperor Haile Selassie, the monarch who did more than any other to awaken the Ethiopians from their thousand-year slumber, engineering, almost single-handedly, Ethiopia's "entry into the world." The first of a projected three-volume biography of the Ethiopian monarch, this work exhibits all those qualities of erudition, lucidity, and insight that have made Marcus a leading historian of the Horn of Africa.

In eight brief but packed chapters, Marcus tells a remarkable story—the story of how a relatively inexperienced youth, orphaned at age 14, rose to become Ethiopia's preeminent sovereign, with absolute powers at home and global influence abroad. Haile Selassie was scarcely self-made, though. On the contrary, he was born to privilege, a member of a race of warriors—the Amharas—whose elite had built itself a feudal utopia on the back of conquered,

degraded subject peoples. Haile Selassie's father was the mighty Ras (Duke) Makonnen, Emperor Menelek's cousin and lord of the dominions of Hararghe, a rich province in what, after Menelek's conquest, had just become eastern Ethiopia.

Why did the ruling aristocracy anoint Haile Selassie crown prince and regent, thereby paving the way to his accession to the imperial throne, over the heads of senior, more experienced royal candidates? Marcus gives an astounding answer: "[Haile Selassie] was named only because the leadership believed that Zawditu, who would establish policy, needed a weak executive officer." His adversaries, in other words, underestimated the ambition, cunning, and tenacity of the wily, diminutive *ras*, to their subsequent regret.

From the time he became regent to his imperial accession in 1930, Taffari—as was his given name—was the supreme ruler of Ethiopia in all but name. Easily manipulating the hapless, simple-natured Empress Zauditu, Taffari bribed, banished, or jailed all rivals; built up a new cadre of loyalists, the Young Ethiopians, who filled the growing bureaucracy of the state; kept the traditionally autonomous and powerful Ethiopian Orthodox Church under a firm leash; patronized American and European advisers; and gathered the empire's growing wealth into his hands. Even the empress's husband, the strong Ras Gugsa, could do nothing to escape Taffari's long hand. After trumped-up charges manipulated from behind the scenes by Taffari, the unfortunate Gugsa was banished to distant Gojjam, where he had to languish under house arrest in a lonely, dungeonlike palace throughout Taffari's tenure as regent.

What was the secret to the emperor's improbable success? The words "cunning" and "tenacity" jump out from every page of Marcus's description of Haile Selassie's ascent to power. To these he might have added "disarming, specious humility." Though a book review is not the place for vignette telling, a slice of my life as a footnote to Haile Selassie's would serve to illustrate the point. As Islamic magistrate of the town of Qallaafo on the Shabeelle river basin, my father was among the notables and elders that received Jan Hoy (His August Majesty) when he came to the Ogaden in 1956-57 to show the flag to the "wild Somali tribes" on the fringes of the empire. The notables' children, too—including myself—were presented to Jan Hoy to be consecrated in hopes of eventual assimilation with the empire's other children of diverse nationalities. What struck me most—and remains vivid to this day—was the gentle, meek face of that petite man whose sense of dignity and importance was betrayed only by the luminous piercing eyes and a full-gray beard that sat on a Mephistophelian jaw. Though we were 12- and 13-year-olds, we stood above him to a boy, and Jan Hoy required prostration from neither us nor our elders, as he demanded of his disciplined highland subjects. The scene of the Somali elders stooping over him and staring him in the eye and the trembling dukes, generals, and other imperial dignitaries who bowed and prostrated whenever he turned cut a striking contrast. Jan Hoy knew that the surest way to provoke an insurrection in his Muslim, egalitarian, Somali subjects was to require them to prostrate. That discriminating judgment to treat every situation according to the etiquette of its environment was a telling example of Haile Selassie's political genius.

In view of Marcus's manifest achievement, it may seem churlish to complain, yet the work stirs a number of technical and historiographic currents that should not pass without comment. Stylistically, Marcus's prose suffers from overerudition. He writes as if he has a compulsive urge to support every homely fact with a contemporaneous remark, often by some petty European hanger-on or other at the Ethiopian court, a remark that the indefatigable Marcus inevitably dug out from some obscure archive. He tells us, for example, that in 1908 Menelek "posted his confidant, Dej. Balcha," to the governorship of Harar and attributes the revelation of this "remarkable fact" to French sources. No ghost needs to come from French archives to tell us this. The result is that pages on end consist of nothing but a string of quotations. This is a pity, for Marcus's prose, authoritative in its own right,

is far superior to the archival mishmash that he allows to mar his pages. On the other hand, when archival or journalistic information is deployed to augment Marcus's prose, the result can be electrifying: this, for example, describing Haile Selassie's first European tour in 1924 as he was courted by the French, British, and Italian governments in a racist Europe that had yet to learn to cope with black power:

The *Manchester Guardian* commented that during one of Tafari's outings in France, "his hosts gave the black monarch what no northern rival for his favours could attempt, a kiss from little [six-year-old] Marcelle Colin. . . . A kiss for a Negro king is more than all the wealth of England can afford.

More intriguing is Marcus's shifting historiographic stance. The study of Ethiopian history in the past three decades, non-Ethiopianists will appreciate knowing, has been split along a center-periphery dichotomy. The centralists, consisting in the main of expatriate scholars and their students at Addis Ababa University, have tended to chronicle and interpret the Ethiopian past from the perspective of the central Ethiopian government with a sympathetic eye to the interests and concerns of the highland Christian, imperial establishment. Theirs may be characterized as the highland or imperial school of Ethiopian history, and their writings have been marked by a decided lack of expressed sympathy for the plight of the empire's disinherited and downtrodden—the peripheral peoples. The peripheral or lowland school, on the other hand, has looked at events from the standpoint of the fringe peoples, conquered, exploited, and excluded from state benefits.

Up until recently, Marcus, to judge by his writings, could justly be described as a confirmed centralist. In another, memorable biography—that of Emperor Menelek—for example, Marcus writes about the highland Christian conquest of the lowland Muslim south and east with an approving tone that seems to regard the event as a glorious process, redounding to the good of both conqueror and conquered. By contrast, in the book under review, Marcus ambiguously speaks of the relationship between victim and victor in the conquered lands as that of "the colonized and colonizer"—an observation the centralists will find anathema. He even rehabilitates the fallen prince, Lij Yasu, here characterizing him, in a judicious mix of blame and praise, as "undoubtedly bright, even visionary, but politically unrealistic"—whereas he offers no kind sentiment for him in the earlier work. Where is Marcus coming from? Is he about to have a conversion experience to the lowland school of Ethiopian history?

It is also a matter for regret that he does not give us the benefit of his informed reflection as to Prince Yasu's manifest self-destruction. What caused the prince of a chauvinistic, anti-Islamic Christian aristocracy to flirt so openly with Islam, thereby ensuring his doom? Prince Yasu's father, King Michael, was the former Ras Ali, the muslim duke who was forcibly converted to Christianity by Emperor Yohannes under the threat of the expropriation of his patrimony. Did Prince Yasu harbor hidden sympathies for the Islamic heritage of his Muslim forebears—a closet Muslim all along? How else to explain his egregious political blunders?

Another point, finally, on which Marcus is curiously silent is Prince Yasu's fate as Haile Selassie's prisoner. The prince, who languished in prison throughout Haile Selassie's regency and preinvasion reign, died mysteriously in incarceration just before Haile Selassie boarded the exile train to Djibouti. Did Haile Selassie order his execution to eliminate any risk of his restoration by the Italians as a puppet monarch in Haile Selassie's absence? Perhaps it is a matter of retributive justice, characteristically Ethiopian, that Haile Selassie, too, came to die mysteriously in prison in 1975, after his overthrow by a revolutionary military junta. Is Marcus silent on Yasu's death because he is too reluctant to soil the subject of his biography, his "political icon," with bloody hands?

Still, Marcus has written a major work, one that is likely to remain the standard biography of Haile Selassie's early life for some time to come. We can only look forward with pleasant eagerness to the promised se-

quels dealing, respectively, with the emperor's golden and silver years.

If Marcus contributes a valuable book on the Ethiopian past, Alemneh Dejene provides a thoughtful, sobering study on its present—a useful how-to manual on community development in the Arsi province of Ethiopia, the only one or two of Ethiopia's 14 provinces that is not inhabited by a starving populace.

The work, Dejene tells us, is based on a comprehensive field survey and his own participant observation. His aim? To examine "the perspective of peasant farmers . . . focusing on conditions that constrain agricultural productivity as well as the potential to increase it." His approach? Interviews with 150 farmers, "randomly selected rural heads of households from 30 peasant associations." His discovery? Something that Mikhail Gorbachev has been hinting at lately, to wit, that farmers—even those who hold just tiny plots—do not like their land to be turned into collectivized state farms. They invest more eir land, take more risks in experimenting with new methods of farming, and produce more when they work for themselves rather than for in ththe government.

Not that Dejene is a die-hard advocate of soulless, private enterprise. On the contrary, the hero of the book is "the service association"—a kind of agrarian socialism in which peasants associate voluntarily to pool land and labor resources for the common good of all. He advises the government to keep its hands off peasant cooperatives and to offer them fair prices for their produce—something the government does not do now. Will the Marxist ideologues in Addis Ababa listen?

Dejene's book—to voice my sole complaint—reads too much like a dissertation, with such section headings as "Nature of the Problem," "Objective of the Study," "Approach of the Study," "Limitation of the Study," and so forth. It is too learned and laced, through and through, with chic social science abstractions. We Third Worlders have apparently copied from the Americans not only cultural consumerism but also their academic jargon and must now define, as

Dejene does here, all of life's activities as "problems"! Next time round he would do well to write in his own natural style and natural voice, whatever these may be, rather than ape the computer language of his academic colleagues at the W.E.B. DuBois Institute for Afro-American Research at Harvard. The book also contains too many typographical errors, which makes one wonder what became of his Westview editors, who are presumably paid for their labor. Still, this is a helpful contribution that makes sensible suggestions toward food self-sufficiency in Ethiopia.

SAID S. SAMATAR

Rutgers University
Newark
New Jersey

MOZAFFARI, MEHDI. *Authority in Islam: From Mohammed to Khomeini.* Pp. xii, 127. Armonk, NY: M. E. Sharpe, 1987. $29.95.

AHMED, ISHTIAQ. *The Concept of an Islamic State: An Analysis of the Ideological Controversy in Pakistan.* Pp. xi, 235. New York: St. Martin's Press, 1987. $32.50.

As Mehdi Mozaffari points out in the introduction to his book, political scientists have paid the least attention to the Iranian revolution of 1979. To assert this truism, however, he does not have to accredit the fundamentally false and impervious assertion that "[Islam] has profoundly political aspects," as if even Gandhi's ahimsa did not connote the same charge. All religions have, and have indeed demonstrated historically, profound political propensities, even Hinduism, which Mozaffari presumes to be somehow apolitical.

Despite its offering some useful and occasionally even valid generalizations that he likes to call "models," Mozaffari is hindered in his analysis by the essential and inherent malfunctions of any single text trying to cover a vast historical continent, "from Mohammed

to Khomeini," by such wobbly bridges as watered-down notions of authority and legitimacy hurriedly borrowed from Weber and others.

The first two chapters of the book center on the Muhammad side of this 14-century-long bridge, the latter two chapters presumably on the Khomeini end of it. This bridge may be an ideal "model" for a political scientist, but the serious student of the political dimension of Islam ought to be aware of the vast lacunae that separate the Sunni, Shiite, and Kharijite "models" from those of Abd al-Wahab, Qaddafi, and Khomeini.

Mozaffari postulates four "approaches" inherent in Islam as it pertains to the question of power: (1) "the philosophical," as represented in such figures as al-Farabi (872-950); "the administrative," as in the works of al-Mawardi (974-1058); "the dogmatic," as in the works of al-Ghazzali (1058-1111); and "the sociological," as best represented in Ibn Khaldun (1332-1406). These authors are taken completely out of their respective epistemological contexts and are discussed in modern political parlance that may or may not be compatible with their traditional universe of discourse.

Mozaffari also examines the early divisions in the Islamic community—the Sunni, Shiite, and Kharijite formations—in terms of their respective themes of authority. This section of the book is basically argued through interpretation of certain Koranic passages pointlessly reproduced in the original Arabic with no English translation.

By chapter 3, Mozaffari has plunged into "contemporary models": the monist, the semi-monist, the dualist, and the fusionist models. Within these models, the specific relations of authority in modern Iran, Turkey, Syria, Iraq, and Saudi Arabia are categorized.

The final chapter of the book addresses the questions of "Islam and secularization" through the watered-down issue of, "Is Islam an obstacle to the building of a nation-state?" There is no convincing continuity of theoretical thrust between the preceding chapters and the concluding remarks in this chapter. In

fact, Mozaffari fails to establish any meaningful and sustained set of arguments as to why the events of the first Islamic century have anything to do with modern events.

The most essential and troubling problem with studies such as this one is their transcendental generalizations and artificial model-building enterprise. More than anything else, all branches of social sciences need detailed studies of specific topics, which should not necessarily be incompatible with attempting theoretical approaches and even possible insights.

Ishtiaq Ahmed's *Concept of an Islamic State* is a relatively more detailed and balanced study of the experiment of Pakistan with the notion of an Islamic state. Most of chapter 2, however, is wasted on a futile attempt to formulate a conceptual basis for "ideology," which ultimately turns out to be a dilettante exercise on Marx, Manheim, and Gramsci without contributing anything significant to the theoretical ambition of the text.

Chapter 3 is equally wasted on some redundant generalizations on the Koran, the sunna of the prophet, the shariah, fiqh, and so on. Political science will make no progress in Islamic studies as long as every minimum of solid primary data easily presentable in a good article is unduly elongated by utterly useless and primitive treatments of certain facts explained generations of scholarship earlier. Such wasteful repetitions should be replaced with accurate and detailed observations of factual data.

Chapter 4 begins to save the book by grounding a systemic account of the role of Islam in the formation of the state of Pakistan. In this chapter, the early Muslim settlements in India, and the ideas of creating a modern secular Pakistani state, following the British colonial experience, are discussed. Such prominent figures of Pakistan independence as Muhammad Iqbal (1876-1938) and Mohammed Ali Jinnah (1876-1948) are examined and their contributions analyzed.

Part 3 consists of four chapters in which Ahmed examines the positions of the ulama and the Tanzim Islam-i Pakistan on the

matter of the Pakistan state. The theocratic, liberal, and socialist tendencies in Pakistani politics are also examined.

Part 4 consists of some careful, however occasionally generalized, conclusions about the concept of an Islamic state through such categories as "legitimacy," "form of government," "law," and the like.

Since Ahmed's study is at least partially founded on a specific case study, the tentative conclusions in chapter 10 are relatively insightful. Here his discussion of Islamic state as a political ideology leads Ahmed to some interesting observations on the possible reciprocities between Islam and democracy.

The section of the bibliography on primary sources contains some very useful citations demanding further studies.

HAMID DABASHI
University of Texas
Austin

PELEG, ILAN. *Begin's Foreign Policy, 1977-1983: Israel's Move to the Right.* Pp. xx, 227. Westport, CT: Greenwood Press, 1987. $35.00.

Ilan Peleg's book is an insightful analysis of the psychological, ideological, and political origins of Israel's foreign policy during the prime ministership of Menachem Begin, and more. It is also a psycho-ideological interpretation of the link between ideology and policy and the gradual drift of Israel's body politic to the right in its foreign policy preferences. The terms "Right" and "Left," it may be worth noting, are useful for describing the political divisions in Israel regarding foreign policy, security issues, and the Arab-Israeli conflict. They are much less useful, perhaps even misleading, for describing attitudes on social and economic questions.

The link between ideology and policy is clearly evident by the organization of the book, which is divided into two parts. The first part describes and analyzes the ideological foundations of the Begin regime. The main argument of the first section is that many of

the apparent contradictions surrounding Begin's policies are resolved if his foreign policy is seen as a continuation of the principles and vision of Vladimir (Ze'ev) Jabotinsky, founder of the revisionist strain of Zionism. Begin and his generation represent a radicalized version of Jabotinsky's revisionism, neorevisionism. This radicalized variant, with its emphasis on force as a supreme political instrument, its call for territorial expansion, and its rejection of the outside world—a "we-they" perspective—reflects the life experiences of Begin and his associates. Neorevisionism views the Arab-Israeli dispute as an extension of the eternal struggle between Jews and the hostile world around them. Given that Arabs harbor the traditional anti-Jewish outlook, a compromise of differences cannot be achieved.

The second part of the book addresses the policies that derive from the neorevisionist belief system by focusing on Menachem Begin's foreign policy during his tenure in office, spanning the years 1977-83. The cornerstone of this policy is Begin's relentless effort to consolidate Israeli control over the occupied territories—the Golan Heights, the West Bank, and the Gaza Strip. The instruments used to achieve that objective and the tactics to deal with foreign opposition to these policies are reviewed in detail. Israel's invasion of Lebanon in 1982 is seen as a logical extension of Begin's foreign policy. The Camp David accords represent for Begin American acquiescence to his goal of Israel's ultimate absorption of the West Bank and the Gaza Strip in return for Israel's unqualified support for U.S. global and regional objectives.

Peleg's book is much more than a case study. By focusing on Begin's policies as giving voice to the emergence of a growing right-wing constituency, he provides a potent analytical framework for comprehending the foreign policy positions of Begin's successors. The book also provides persuasive evidence to show why the Begin phenomenon, with or without Begin, is not an aberration. The centrality of the constituency that brought Begin's Likud coalition to power in 1977 and sustained it in the elections in 1981 and 1984 will affect Israeli politics for the foreseeable

future. It will certainly limit the flexibility and latitude for compromise of any Israeli coalition government in response to new initiatives or opportunities to settle the Arab-Israeli conflict. Peleg's analysis clearly anticipates the reasons behind friction between Israeli Prime Minister Yitzhak Shamir and the efforts of U.S. Secretary of State George Shultz to reach a settlement of the Arab-Israeli conflict based on a variation of the land-for-peace formula that is contained in U.N. Security Council Resolution 242.

LEWIS W. SNIDER

Claremont Graduate School
California

POTTER, DAVID C. *India's Political Administrators, 1919-1983.* Pp. xv, 289. New York: Oxford University Press, Clarendon Press, 1986. No price.

This is an important and interesting comparative study of the Indian Civil Service (ICS) at the beginning of the period of reforms leading to self-rule, the Montague-Chelmsform Act of 1919, and the Indian Administrative Service (IAS) that succeeded the ICS shortly after independence. Interesting, that is, if one skips quickly through the introduction, a dull but thorough review of theoretical literature that seems incumbent on authors to repeat from the dreadful requirements of a dissertation. Do not be put off by this, but read on.

Potter looks first at the tradition of the ICS in three areas. First is the location and movement of ICS officers. This means primarily the location of the posts of ICS officers at the district level, the provincial—later, state—secretariat, and central, or government-of-India, positions. He finds that there is little change at the end of the period from the beginning with the key exception that many IAS officers are posted at a location earlier nonexistent, the government corporation or enterprise, a posting resulting from the vast expansion of the economic interests of the central and state governments. He finds also, not with approval, that IAS officers are

transferred rapidly, as were their ICS predecessors, to the probable detriment of their performance caused by lack of continuity.

He also compares the level of political involvement; he describes both groups as "political administrators." As the period of dyarchy (1921-37) yielded to provincial autonomy (1937-47) and then to independence (since 1947), possibilities for competition and conflict between administrators, who before 1919 ran the show, and elected politicians and ministers increased. With examples gained from research and interviews, Potter demonstrates this well.

He examines also the patterns of recruitment and training; he calls the latter "shaping." He finds that the pattern of the British gentleman prevalent before the rapid opening of the ICS to Indians in the 1920s continued for Indian ICS officers before independence and almost equally did so for IAS trainees after India became free.

Potter also covers the rivalries between services and the jealousy of other all-India groups toward the preeminent position of the IAS, which continues the pattern of the ICS. He refers in passing to the inability of the Civil Service of Pakistan, the Pakistani successor to the ICS, to forestall the creation of a unified administrative service by Bhutto in that country. He wonders if the IAS can survive an eventual challenge in India.

There are some points that are unclear. For example, Potter's description of dyarchy would not pass muster with a political historian and a good copy editor. The latter, perhaps, is what the book needs most simply in order to improve the flow and style. One also wishes Clarendon Press would use the University of Chicago style manual's system on citations and in the bibliography. If the reader is, as I was, interested in locating some of the sources, it will indeed be a difficult search.

Potter's volume is a book that should find a firm place in libraries on South Asia and on comparative public administration.

CRAIG BAXTER

Juniata College
Huntingdon
Pennsylvania

RABUSHKA, ALVIN. *The New China*. Pp. xii, 254. Boulder, CO: Westview Press, 1987. $32.50.

The People's Republic of China (PRC), Taiwan, and Hong Kong, taken together, provide an interesting laboratory for comparing the effectiveness of different economic systems. In this study, Alvin Rabushka analyzes the economic development of these Asian societies since 1949.

While all three economies have grown during this period, the economic performances of Taiwan and Hong Kong have greatly surpassed that of the People's Republic. By 1985, Hong Kong's per capita income was 30 times greater than the PRC's; Taiwan's per capita income was 15 times greater. The key variable, Rabushka concludes, is the economic policies and institutions of the three governments. The evidence shows that an economic policy relying on material incentives and free market principles will greatly outperform a socialist command economy.

The PRC's economic performance can be divided into two periods, Deng Xiaoping's coming to power in 1978 being the point of demarcation. The first period, from 1949 to 1978, was characterized by the collectivization of agriculture, investment in heavy industry, centralized planning, autarky, and reliance on psychological rather than material incentives. Wild oscillations marked this period, including the economic catastrophes of the Great Leap Forward (1957-58) and the decade-long Cultural Revolution. Optimal economic growth was not a hallmark of this epoch.

Since 1978, Deng Xiaoping has instituted a number of economic reforms. Material incentives and some features of a free market system have been introduced in the huge agricultural sector, where output doubled between 1978 and 1985. Deng has trodden more cautiously in the urban industrial sector, but here, too, some features of a market economy have been injected. The PRC has moved away from autarky and has deemphasized centralized planning. Economic growth under Deng's aegis has improved, although there have been problems with inflation and corruption. Recent ideological trumpet blasts against "spiritual pollution" and "bourgeois liberalization" suggest that Deng's reforms still face entrenched bureaucratic opposition.

Taiwan's economy has also been characterized by two discrete periods. From 1949 to 1958, the government undertook a campaign of land reform in agriculture and a program of import substitution in industry. The latter required protectionist measures for the young domestic industries, which distorted the optimal allocation of resources. After 1958, the Taiwanese switched to a policy of export promotion. The protectionist measures were jettisoned and economic growth has boomed.

The Hong Kong economy represents the purest model of a competitive free-enterprise economy among the three societies. Its economic performance has been the best of the three since World War II. In 1997, however, the PRC will obtain full sovereignty over Hong Kong. The PRC promises to respect Hong Kong's unique economic and social structure for fifty years, but Hong Kong is now totally dependent on the goodwill and stability of the PRC. Given the PRC's track record, Hong Kong's economic future is at best cloudy.

Rabushka is guardedly optimistic about the economic prospects of these Pacific Basin societies. Of course, much depends on whether Deng's reforms will be deepened, or even maintained, once he passes from the scene. Will the PRC's system of "socialism with Chinese characteristics," augmented in 1997 with a productive Hong Kong appendage, ultimately see the "Chinese characteristics" swallow the "socialism"? It will be exciting to watch this drama unfold.

SCOTT NICHOLS

Southern Illinois University
Carbondale

SHEPHERD, GEORGE W., Jr. *The Trampled Grass: Tributary States and Self-Reliance in the Indian Ocean Zone of Peace*. Pp. viii, 177. Westport, CT: Greenwood Press, 1987. $39.95.

George Shepherd, the inveterate liberationist, has performed an admirable feat in his latest book. He demonstrates how the pallid savannas of African aspiration, bowed and broken under the heavy heels of superpower geo-economics, can rise up one day to full green dignity and self-reliance. A new autonomy for the Third World will materialize, he believes, from a hopeful concatenation of forces, combining a self-aware weariness of the dominant powers, the assistance of well-meaning liberals and social democrats in the West, and the emergence of enlightened nationalist leadership to replace the discredited comprador elites and their brutish military protectors in the African states. Collective self-reliance will eventually bring about the peace, justice, and prosperity—not the Western individualist-materialist variety, to be sure—that African and other oppressed peoples of the world deserve.

Using Amílcar Cabral's culture-class variant of Fanon, with references to Nyerere, Freire, Galtung, and other Third World liberationist thinkers, Shepherd offers a useful typology of tributary stages, from praetorian-protected comprador exploitation to the regional imperialisms of Israel, South Africa, and Vietnam. These subimperialisms are to him creatures of the superpowers working through collaborationist elites, unlike Kapur, who sees them as relatively autonomous from global power influence. Shepherd skillfully examines the ethnic-class dynamics of South African apartheid, the intricate national rivalries of the African Horn, the contrasts between comprador Kenya and frustrated self-reliant Tanzania, and the vicissitudes of the United Nations' zone-of-peace movement for the Indian Ocean. There is criticism, irritation, irony, but no reason to despair. A new dawn is coming for the earth's wretched, as the dominance system disintegrates and the superpowers themselves weary of the expensive burdens of accepting tribute.

Keeping critical analysis and humane vision in balance, Shepherd manages to persuade his reader more by the force of enthusiasm for what must become than by the probable vectors from what is happening now. He grasps with fervor at straws of hope—Sudan's dissatisfaction with the results of comprador tightrope-walking, Tanzania's ability to obtain international credit without the collateral of economic performance, the superpowers' presumed disillusion over their erstwhile Arabian Sea adventures. He accepts the inevitable peacefulness of progressive regimes and foresees prospects for a new, better Ethiopian revolution, thanks to the exhaustion of the last, thwarted, one. He exaggerates the importance of Seychelles' collaboration with Tanzania in security matters, and he prolongs the complicity of Mauritius far beyond the longevity of the Mauritian government involved in that brief, happy experiment.

As for the United Nations' much-maligned campaign for an Indian Ocean zone of peace, Shepherd believes in the possibility of the autonomous collective security system entailed in that movement. He suggests that Third World collective security could even be enhanced by completing the bilateral Soviet-American naval limitations agreement that President Jimmy Carter initiated in 1977 and broke off a year later. Skeptics might differ. Surely, when Moscow and Washington agree to lower their respective thermostat settings in the Indian Ocean, they are far from turning their interests over to proud Third World parties seeking full self-determination. Many of those latter parties will continue to demand great-power protection, whether for comprador greed or concern for national security, hence sustaining the very great-power presence abhorred by self-reliant logic. It is a nasty thought for zone-of-peace patriots, but the Soviet Union and United States will remain inclined to intervene in the Indian Ocean for the protection of valuable clients and for other ends that they themselves regard as entirely peaceful, whatever the resolution of their excoriated rivalry. If they weaken as global powers, the system that they represent may find other ways to fill the vacuum, for national aggrandizement is no more the name of the global game than it is a synonym for Third World development. Alas, the zone of peace just simply has not started living up to its name.

Moreover, Shepherd's theory, rejecting rigidly ideological assessments of motives and interests, betrays some judicious inconsistencies. His vision of liberation sometimes accepts help from international liberals and social reformers, as in his elaborate program for a South Africa sanctions coalition, and sometimes sees them in league with cosmopolitan elites to keep comprador capitalism from succumbing to true liberation. Likewise, with nationalists, some, like Southern African anti-apartheid leaders, Sudanese reconcilers, and Seychelles' René, seem to promote the evolution of self-reliance; others wallow in the "national narcissism" that only obstructs the transnational communities essential to the good health of a system of self-reliant Third World societies.

The "trampled grass" of Shepherd's title is almost purely African, although Shepherd manifests sensitivity to India's key role in the delicate situation of South Asian security. Despite his inability to write polished prose, Shepherd's optimism becomes contagious in the final chapters, in which paradigm change is based on service to human needs, human rights. His book should be read widely, for in it he shares his insight into how the South African and Namibean imbroglios may one day be resolved and how the example of Tanzania might convert to continentwide fruition. His emphasis on the link between economic privilege and security is exceedingly helpful, particularly in the context of neoconservative theory, such as that of Annie Kriegel, that responds to the preponderant economic determinism of the Left by attributing supreme neorealist weight to military-security influence. As Shepherd shows, the Third World's grass is not only trampled; it is scythed, too, and the new national cultures that must breed transnational community must cultivate that garden in addition to fencing in the global elephants.

PHILIP M. ALLEN

Frostburg State University
Maryland

TROTMAN, DAVID VINCENT. *Crime in Trinidad: Conflict and Control in a Plantation Society, 1838-1900.* Pp. xiii, 345. Knoxville: University of Tennessee Press, 1986. No price.

The principal merit of this book is its subject. The volume constitutes the first study of crime in a nineteenth-century Caribbean society and is concerned with "the organic linkages and relationship between the structural organization of plantation society and the pattern and nature of criminal activity." It seeks to provide therefrom a closer understanding of Trinidad's plantation system, arguing that the nature and pattern of crime was linked to the attempts of the elite to ensure the perpetuation of that system and the subordination of the laboring classes. For Trotman, criminal actions "represented the conflict between, on the one hand, a plantocracy bent on defending and extending a system of production and a way of organizing society and, on the other, a disenfranchised and unorganized working class equally determined to create a new life for itself out of the wreckage of slavery." The plantation system is seen as inherently "criminogenic," with the plantocracy labeling as criminal those activities inimical to their interest, including the cultural activities of the nonwhite Creole population. He finds that crimes against property were more harshly punished than those against the person, because those found guilty of predial larceny were sometimes flogged. Trinidad in the later nineteenth century is seen as a society in which a widespread tendency to violence was honed by the prevalence of cockfighting and other recreations that "contributed to the glorification of violence."

Trotman persistently overstates his case, however. Perhaps the most spectacular instance is the statement that under indenture "the whip was as commonly used as a mechanism for labor persuasion as it had been in the worst days of slavery." Despite the citation of four particular cases, this statement borders on fantasy, apparently the product of an

excess of enthusiasm for depicting the oppressed laborer. Overstatement is also evident in the picture of "open war" between the public and a "belligerent" police force. At times, too, as in discussing the rudimentary health services and the administration of justice, Trotman expects too much of the nineteenth century. He is also much too fond of undocumented assertions, both probable and improbable. We are told, for instance, of "the slow, fragile, but nonetheless persistent development of a sense of caste/class consciousness" among those who had seen the inside of the prisons, but no evidence is adduced to support that picture. Neither does the reader know why Trotman concludes that short prison sentences were deliberately designed to avoid depriving the planters of labor during harvest.

This volume is also marred by a distressing number of factual inaccuracies. The indenture law did not make a nine-hour working day mandatory, except for the small minority who worked indoors; the name of the Colonial Company appears as "Colonial Estates"; and the list could go on. There are, moreover, too many errors of proofreading, and both the index and many of the end notes are unsatisfactory. Trotman discusses with some care the limitations of the available statistics and the dangers involved in using them. Thereafter, however, he does not always avoid the pitfalls he has identified and while he recognizes that Trinidad's population was increasing—by more than 130 percent between 1871 and 1901, the period on which his attention is concentrated—he frequently ignores this fact in assessing the increase or decrease in crime.

In sum, while this pioneering book contains much that is interesting, its weaknesses are such as to require its content to be treated with caution.

K. O. LAURENCE

University of the West Indies
St. Augustine
Trinidad

WIARDA, HOWARD J. *Latin America at the Crossroads: Debt, Development, and the Future.* Pp. xiii, 114. Boulder, CO: Westview Press, 1987. $23.95.

LOWENTHAL, ABRAHAM F. *Partners in Conflict: The United States and Latin America.* Pp. xi, 240. Baltimore, MD: Johns Hopkins University Press, 1987. $19.95.

Two longtime specialists on Latin America address the "peculiar relationship" between the United States and Latin America. Each postulates the decline of so-called American hegemony and offers hopeful suggestions for resolving this loss. The two differ greatly in their styles of analysis, but they arrive at similar conclusions: specific and structured policy responses are essential if the United States is to be perceived as an effective and concerned ally and one that retains salutary influence and credibility in the hemisphere.

Wiarda's essentially two-dimensional discussion begins with the assertion that Latin American national systems have made use of historical experience and incremental and pragmatic responses to problems. He then offers an overview of the present Latin American debt crisis. To a lay readership, the overview is useful because the language is not technical. He cites the many factors that have contributed to the region's present problems of debt, disorganization, and social insecurity. His most useful contribution—not to existing scholarly literature but to lay readers—is his linkage of the outcome of the Latin American crisis to the well-being of the United States and thus of the world. He warns that the collapse of Latin America's national systems may result in severe injury to the other larger areas. This may strike some readers as somewhat apocalyptic, given America's habitual condescending view of Latin America; but it is adequately developed and persuasive. Finally, his conclusions (which are founded on the premise that Latin Americans *must* somehow pay their gigantic debts, in theory if not

wholly in fact) renew the faith of past decades (and past "American" administrations) in international lending institutions.

Lowenthal's work parallels that of Wiarda, but it possesses substantially more depth and authority. Unlike Wiarda, he elects to offer much detail about the "transformation"—that is, developmental change—of Latin America's national systems. This process is described by periods: to the end of World War II, the two decades of the 1950s and 1960s, and since the 1960s. The very rapid economic growth of the second period, with its associated socio-political changes, is described and explained, and the growing crisis of the last period is described in redundant detail. Although there is some generalization about the entire region, specific chapters focus on Mexico, Brazil, and the "Caribbean Basin," which is, peculiarly, described as containing all of the countries fronting on the Caribbean Sea except for Venezuela, Mexico, and Colombia. His conclusions and recommendations go far beyond those of Wiarda. He urges not only a detailed series of economic policy adjustments and reversals but also a broader rethinking of American attitudes toward social, political, cultural, and military policies. Were Lowenthal's recommendations put in place, there would be nothing less than a fundamental overhauling of both policy and supporting bureaucratic structure within the U.S. government.

There are two principal weaknesses in Wiarda's work. First, it is intentionally very short. It forces him to resort to a long series of succinct and virtually ex cathedra statements about Latin America's experience with itself and with its northern neighbor. Second, Wiarda focuses largely on economic problems, to the partial exclusion of political ones. This concentration allows him to evade completely the need to discuss American ideologically inspired blindness toward the Latin American values and attitudes that contribute so forcibly to the region's near self-destruction. Wiarda has previously published works that develop powerfully the ideological bases of national political and economic behavior; in my judgment, this book would have gained in effectiveness and in scholarly integrity had its treatment

of the ideological theme been more ample and direct.

Lowenthal's work is conceived with a notably different purpose. It is both didactic and analytical. Although he has not footnoted his book, as a voucher of his intent, there is a 35-page bibliography. His policy recommendations are stated extensively and almost redundantly. One cannot quarrel with their content nor with their intent, but they are—like Wiarda's—too focused on American shortcomings and report to only a modest degree on Latin America's equally great need for self-examination and reform. Further, the work is uneven in both concept and treatment. One must admit that Mexico and Brazil are indeed major states of the developing world and of the hemisphere, but they are scarcely alone in that role although an inexperienced reader might so assume. Finally, the peculiar treatment of the so-called Caribbean Basin allows Lowenthal to shortchange the entire region in an unfortunate manner. In the concluding chapter, the reader recognizes Lowenthal's determination to argue the bankruptcy and gratuitously flagellant nature of American policy toward Nicaragua and toward Central America as a whole. The discussion preceding this chapter fails, however, in my judgment, to lay the groundwork that would place that policy in the context he intends.

A final note seems in order. Wiarda's position has led to a large number of books in recent years. Lowenthal's activities have led to few. The book of Lowenthal's reviewed here is a serious, if conceptually skewed, contribution, reflecting scholarly care and matured judgment. Others of Wiarda's publications have reflected first-rate competence, but a nearly annual book means running the risk of disappointing the reader.

PHILIP B. TAYLOR, Jr.
University of Houston
Texas

EUROPE

KOLCHIN, PETER. *Unfree Labor: American Slavery and Russian Serfdom.* Pp. xiv,

515. Cambridge, MA: Harvard University Press, 1987. $25.00.

The author of this comparative study has attempted a most difficult task: examining the differences and similarities of the two institutions named in the subtitle. He succeeds well, considering that he had to look at the very different historical, cultural, social, and political circumstances under which each institution developed and was abolished.

Indeed, this monumental task occupied him for over 15 years; it is reflected in the fact that over 20 percent of the book—over 100 pages—are devoted to footnotes and citations of U.S., Russian, and Soviet sources.

Kolchin's ability to utilize extensive Russian sources is notable, considering how difficult it is to gain access to archives in the USSR. This difficulty applies even to pre-Soviet documents and even under U.S.-Soviet agreement for scholarly exchanges. Indeed, many U.S. researchers, after arriving in the USSR and expecting to be able to use its archives, have given up in frustration from bone-wearying red tape and delays.

As a result of Kolchin's massive research effort, his book examines thoroughly such aspects of bonded labor in the United States and czarist Russia as the economics and management of that labor, communal ideas and mores, and protest, resistance, and economic conditions that ultimately forced the demise of slavery and serfdom.

Then, too, the study is highly interactive: it looks at master-slave and *pomeshchiki*—serf relations from the view of the dominated as well as from, as is customary, the view of the masters.

Precisely because the book is so thorough and laden with detailed footnotes, however, it will have limited appeal to general readers; indeed, even specialists in Russian and Soviet affairs will find the reading very demanding. By the same token, though, the book will serve as an indispensable basic reference on the comparison of the two institutions that were major societal steps in the evolution of U.S. and Soviet systems.

Moreover, precisely because Kolchin's work can serve as a basic reference, it can play a key role against unfounded generalizations that have been made lightly in the past about convergence between U.S. and Soviet systems; such generalizations have disregarded fundamental differences, despite superficial similarities, between such institutions as slavery and serfdom and their demise.

It is true, for example, that in such institutions, both the United States and Russia had a similar economic form of unfree labor. Also, both slaves and serfs were politically disenfranchised. Yet after being emancipated in 1861, the descendants of U.S. slaves, after a long and tortuous path, achieved political freedom and influence; indeed, by developing big voting blocs in key states, they can affect, and have done so in recent years, the shape of federal, state, and local governments. They now have the potential for reaching the top U.S. post in the very near future. By contrast, the descendants of the serfs, while arguably having improved their standard of living, have become part of the political disenfranchisement of all Russian and non-Russian peoples, both under the autocratic czars and, after 1917, under the commissars. The 99.9 percent votes garnered by "the Bloc of Party and non-Party candidates" in Soviet elections to date only demonstrate *pro forma* political participation of Soviet peoples, with little effect on Politburo decision making, particularly when compared with the effect in the United States of black voting on elections in, say, the former solid South.

To confirm these judgments about these fundamental differences, one need only recall the experience of U.S. blacks who went to the USSR in the 1920s and 1930s. Attracted initially by Soviet slogans of equality and political power sharing, most soon became disenchanted—except for the likes of Paul Robeson or Angela Davis—and appreciated the political evolution in the United States.

The Kolchin book, in making its comparison, serves as an effective reminder of—and sheds light on—how the abolition of the two economically similar institutions of slavery and serfdom through the 1860s led to different political resolutions. In the United States, the descendants of slaves have obtained a chance, through the civil rights movement, to influence

and change political, and thereby economic, development significantly. In the USSR, it is still an open question as to whether the descendants of the serfs will, even under Gorbachev's *perestroika* and *demokratizatsiya*, achieve a comparable opportunity.

JOHN R. THOMAS

Washington, D.C.

THURLOW, RICHARD. *Fascism in Britain: A History, 1918-1985.* Pp. xvii, 317. New York: Basil Blackwell, 1987. $29.95.

This is a scholarly account of British fascism from its beginnings until very recent times. To date, it is undoubtedly the best and most comprehensive treatment, based as it is on cabinet documents and the invaluable archives of the Board of Deputies of British Jews. It is particularly strong on the minor extremist right-wing groups that emerged in the 1920s and 1930s. One of these, the Nordic League, had managed, until Thurlow investigated it, to screen its activities from historians. Both MI5 and an intelligence agent of the Board of Deputies had penetrated it by 1939, however, and they were aware of its obsession with a world Jewish conspiracy, which it had purveyed to other similar societies, some of them secret like itself, such as the Imperial Fascist League, the National Socialist League, the White Knights of Britain, the Britons Society, the National Socialist Workers Party, the Militant Christian Patriots, and the Right Club. Archibald Maule Ramsey, a Conservative member of Parliament, was at the center of this anti-Semitic network. The White Knights of Britain, or Hooded Man, a British version of the Ku Klux Klan, was led by Commander E. H. Cole, who described the House of Commons as "a house of bastardised Jews."

It is the great merit of this work that it retains its sense of balance about this constellation of fantasy. Richard Thurlow keeps a strict sense of proportion in reminding us of how tiny the fascist groups were in relation to the British public and this in spite of their

grandiose ambitions and ideas. He skillfully dissects the ideological corpus of the movement, which included extreme jingoism, radical imperialism, pro- and anti-Germanism, pseudobiological racism, socioeconomic anti-Semitism, virulent anti-Marxism, and antidemocratic socialism. Proponents of all these elements were united in their view that the British political system had failed the nation. Sir Oswald Mosley, incomparably the most important figure in this story, turned against the Labour Party because of his disappointment with its unimaginative economic policy and set himself up as a potential totalitarian dictator.

It is in his account and assessment of Mosley that Thurlow may be most criticized. Perhaps because it has been recounted many times before, he says little about Mosley's transition from Labour to fascism through his New Party. Moreover, he criticizes MI5 and Churchill for interning so many members of the British Union of Fascists on the grounds that there was no evidence in existence in 1940 that could prove their treasonable activities. "The vast majority of British Fascists," he writes, "like Mosley, were patriots not potential traitors." One could defend Laval and Quisling in similar terms. Fascism made treason and patriotism different sides of the same coin.

FRANK BEALEY

Aberdeen University
Scotland

ZINOVIEV, ALEXANDER. *Le Gorbatchévisme, ou les pouvoirs d'une illusion.* Translated by Wladimir Berelowitch. Lausanne: Éditions L'âge d'homme; Montreal: Guérin littérature, 1987. No price.

Alexander Zinoviev has published a feuilleton against Gorbachevism and Western Gorbachev mania, just in time to be read with Mikhail Gorbachev's *Perestroika*.

Zinoviev was, up to the time of the publication of his first anti-Soviet tracts, a professor of philosophy at the University of Leningrad, after a stint as a fighter pilot in World War II.

He is best known in the West for *The Yawning Heights* a dystopian satire on the Soviet Union.

In the book under review, Zinoviev first addresses the question of why the West is making so much of *glasnost, perestroika,* Mr. Gorbachev's relative youth, and his well-dressed wife. One would not expect that if the pope or the president were any younger it would cause the Church to become Communist or the United States to abandon free enterprise, but people expect great things from Gorbachev. Zinoviev reminds us that change is unlikely to come from within the Soviet leadership. Gorbachev was already being groomed as a successor to Chernenko before his death, and as would any other candidate for the position he had to pass through all the ossified echelons of the *nomenklatura.* Though Gorbachev may have the same intentions as Stalin to revolutionize the socialist system, he can only have the capacities of action of Brezhnev, for the time of revolution is past in the USSR.

Zinoviev, a dissident living in Switzerland, is still a dialectic materialist. Even though he rejects communism, his ideas reflect its idea of historical determinism. He believes with strong certainty in the evolution of society through the struggle of dialectal materialism, but instead of the evolution leading toward the shining heights of communism, it leads into a cesspool. He explains that Andropov, the former head of the KGB, could succeed Brezhnev, but Beria, Stalin's secret police boss, could not because one can never take power in the Soviet Union, only be admitted to it.

He speaks about the West's self-blinding to the faults of the Soviet Union, because of the Soviet's capacity to mimic its enemies—in this case, Europe and America—and because of the West's ideological bias. Zinoviev uses ideology in Marx's sense of the word, as a system of perception of reality that is distorted by the values of a given society, unlike the way in which Marxists use the word to mean any way of thinking, including their ideologies. Thus mutual cooperation and peaceful coexistence are unlikely.

Zinoviev makes one ask who exactly is on whose side. He says that many émigrés serve the state's interest abroad as much as party apparatchiks do at home and that the reforms and artistic renaissances are as stage-managed as ever. He coined the word "shamizdat" for the publications and criticisms of corruption and inefficiency that are permitted before any so-called reform campaign. *Glasnost* would be impossible in a system like the Soviet Union because the society is based on secrecy. What passes for *glasnost* is the false front of a new set of Potemkin villages.

MARK BELLIS

Ste.-Foy
Quebec
Canada

Note: This review was originally published in the *Montreal Gazette,* 23 Jan. 1988.

UNITED STATES

BELKNAP, MICHAL R. *Federal Law and Southern Order: Racial Violence and Constitutional Conflict in the Post-Brown South.* Pp. xv, 387. Athens: University of Georgia Press, 1987. $35.00.

In both of its Reconstructions, the American South has been the battlefield for a war of words concerning the nature of American federalism and its relation to states' rights. Particularly in the era immediately after the Supreme Court's *Brown* decision outlawing school segregation, the war was more than verbal. Martyrs for the cause of civil rights were created as the federal government struggled with the challenge of protecting its citizens when local law enforcement abdicated its responsibilities. Michal R. Belknap has given us an extremely useful narrative of the federal government's all-too-gradual efforts to control racial violence in the civil rights period. In the process he clearly demonstrates that federal officials from the Oval Office to the judiciary acceded to the South's view that law enforcement was a purely local matter.

Belknap appropriately begins his story in the lynching era, documenting the nearly total failure of the Southern criminal system to punish these perpetrators. Of the approximately 5150 lynchings committed between 1882 and 1940, legal action resulted in only 40. All the while, "traditional concepts of federalism prevented the national government from suppressing lynching." After *Brown*, while the specific practice of lynching fell into disfavor, the tradition of racial violence as well as the arguments against federal intervention were revived.

Belknap vividly describes both the violence and the argumentation over the role of the federal government in these critical years. In the telling, he shows how the bloodshed of freedom riders and demonstrators and even children in Sunday school slowly prodded the government toward a widening role. Ultimately, the Civil Rights Act of 1968 became a means of effectively controlling racial violence. Belknap shows that only when state authorities created constitutional crises did the federal government act to protect these victims. Only the wave of racial violence between 1963 and 1968 persuaded the government to move beyond the traditional constitutional interpretations of the federal role. By then, Belknap accurately argues, the South, fearing the complete breakdown of law and order, had begun to deal with its own problems. Michal Belknap combines solid documentation with perceptive analysis and powerful narration. The result of his labor is convincing, compelling, and highly recommended.

ANDREW MICHAEL MANIS
Xavier University of Louisiana
New Orleans

FISCHER, ROGER A. *Tippecanoe and Trinkets Too: The Material Culture of American Presidential Campaigns, 1828-1984.* Pp. x, 322. Champaign: University of Illinois Press, 1988. $34.95.

Being a presidential-election year, 1988 is an appropriate time for the publication of a new scholarly study exploring the development of campaign artifacts and their impact on the nation's quadrennial decision-making process.

Roger A. Fischer, a professor of history and American studies at the University of Minnesota at Duluth, wrote *Tippecanoe and Trinkets Too* "to assist two disparate groups: the curators, antiquarians, and collectors who gather and preserve the physical relics of past American presidential campaigns and the academic historians who create the scholarly interpretations of those quadrennial contests." He better meets the needs of his first target audience than those of the second group.

Fischer catalogs a fascinating and vast array of presidential campaign accoutrements from both major and minor parties, ably tracing the technological innovations that made possible new types of political items, such as the ubiquitous celluloid buttons introduced in the 1890s. With 247 illustrations, this work is a treasure trove for political junkies.

Fischer also issues a call for historians to view these items as serious sources for understanding the dynamics and important issues of various presidential campaigns. Yet, in his own homework, he is often too enthralled with the materials themselves—or lack thereof—and loses track of the broader political contexts.

For example, the People's, or Populist, Party, one of the most important third-party movements in U.S. history, rates very little mention here. The Pops may have been deficient in material culture during the 1892 campaign, but their presidential ticket stirred up paroxysms of fear among both Republican and Democratic leaders by garnering 22 electoral votes from six states, leading the Democrats within four years to become a reform party in their own right.

In concluding his study, Fischer writes:

Reducing a complex political appeal to slogans or symbols that fit a banner or bumper sticker may demean both the campaign and our cherished illusions about democracy in action, but scholars who seek to understand the behavior of voters limited in literacy, attention span, and political curiosity would do well not to dismiss altogether the

relevance of such artifacts to their endeavors [p. 304].

While Fischer is essentially correct on both counts, his attempt to reconcile these two points falls short of the mark. Notwithstanding its limitations, however, this is a book that should challenge other political historians to continue the work Fischer has begun.

JOE PATRICK BEAN
Concordia Lutheran College
Austin
Texas

HART, RODERICK P. *The Sound of Leadership: Presidential Communication in the Modern Age.* Pp. xxiii, 277. Chicago: University of Chicago Press, 1987. $39.95. Paperbound, $14.95.

This book is valuable in two important ways. First, it contains great amounts of data—analyses of 9969 "communicative acts" by recent presidents of the United States, beginning with Harry Truman and concluding with the beginning of Ronald Reagan's second term, covering four decades, each event coded in twenty ways, producing 200,000 data points. It includes the analysis of set speeches and material from a variety of other occasions, including ad-libbing from the back platforms of trains, statements at press conferences, and impromptu remarks consisting of no fewer than 150 continuous presidential words that appeared in the public record.

It is straightforward stuff—Hart refers to it as "humble" data—detailing when and where presidents spoke to what kinds of audiences and, in general terms, what they spoke about. Some of the numbers are startling. Gerald Ford spoke in public an average of once every six hours in 1976. Jimmy Carter spoke 1313 times during his single term, Reagan 1360 times during his first. Hart identifies John Kennedy as the first of the "rhetorical presidents"; he made 771 appearances during his three years, more than triple Eisenhower's and double Truman's in the comparable period of their administrations.

All those numbers and that content analysis build a picture of successive presidents becoming more and more talkative, more inclined to speak to predictably friendly audiences, moving further away from genuine political discourse and toward appearing to be nice guys who care.

"It has been argued before, and will be again in this book," Hart says in the beginning, "that such an exclusive concentration on matters rhetorical may bode ill for leadership, if not for Democracy itself."

That judgment illustrates the second great virtue of this volume: it is genuinely provocative. Hart does not perform careful data analysis and push it noncommittally across to the reader; instead, he provides a running commentary, generally normative. Sometimes he even waves his arms and yells, as, for example, in this selection: "When the American people chose Ronald Reagan over Walter Mondale they embraced a certain style of presidential communication as well as a certain brand of politics. . . . But did it enoble them the way only real eloquence can? No, definitely, no!"

The book contains many samples of presidential address; interestingly, only one is cited as genuinely eloquent: Lyndon Johnson on voting rights in March 1965. Most of the remainder exemplify incompetence, banality, or simply the mouth running without the mind being engaged.

Hart is not an empiricist who writes in social science instead of English. This is a personal book—the first person pronoun appears regularly—and a very lively one that has style and contains a mine of information. It also contains an excellent index and an appendix that explains the mechanics of the content analysis.

WILLIAM E. PORTER
University of Michigan
Ann Arbor

KUTTNER, ROBERT. *The Life of the Party: Democratic Prospects in 1988 and Beyond.* Pp. xiii, 265. New York: Viking, 1987. $18.95.

According to Robert Kuttner, the prospects for the Democratic Party's capturing the presidency in the 1988 election hinge upon the ability of the party to recapture many of the working class who voted for Ronald Reagan in 1980 and 1984. The party, of necessity, must also activate the large number of potential Democrats who have not participated in recent elections.

Kuttner rejects the current conventional wisdom of many of the Democratic professionals who believe that the key to future party success is to move to the right ideologically. According to Kuttner, the Democratic candidate must not use the media to position him- or herself around the current public agenda set by the Reagan administration. Moreover, the nominee should not focus a campaign upon foreign policy blunders of the Reagan administration nor upon the so-called social issues. Kuttner's basic thesis is that to be victorious, Democrats must stress the traditional economic populist issues around which the historically successful Democratic presidential coalitions, beginning with Franklin Roosevelt, have been fashioned.

Kuttner suggests an agenda for the post-Reagan era in which an active government addresses the numerous everyday problems of the working class and the poor. The problems of accessible and affordable health care, job security, job retraining for the unemployed, welfare reform, day care, and a coherent industrial policy stressing labor-management cooperation top his public agenda. Moreover, Kuttner argues rather persuasively that even a tax increase necessary to pay for this increased government activity can be recast as a populist issue. Instead of calling for a general tax increase—the mistake of the 1984 Mondale campaign—the Democrats should adopt a tax-the-rich plank in their party platform.

Without a doubt, a successful Democratic presidential nominee in 1988 must be able to mobilize the traditional groups of the New Deal coalition. Whether Kuttner's approach can be accomplished with the current front-runners—as of early 1988—remains to be seen. Nevertheless, Kuttner's insightful analysis of the contemporary political scene coupled

with his policy recommendations provides hope for the future of the Democratic party.

DAVID D. DABELKO

Ohio University
Athens

KWITNY, JONATHAN. *The Crimes of Patriots: A True Tale of Dope, Dirty Money, and the CIA.* Pp. 424. New York: Norton, 1987. $19.95.

In this work, Jonathan Kwitny, an investigative reporter for the *Wall Street Journal,* laboriously traces the rise and fall of the Nugan Bank of Australia. Frank Nugan, cofounder of the bank, was found shot to death in 1980, an apparent suicide or perhaps a murder victim. Nugan's partner, Michael Hand, mysteriously disappeared after the bank's failure in 1980. Kwitny spins his true tale around various events prior to and after Nugan's death and Hand's disappearance.

Relying upon official records of Australian boards of inquiry and interviews with some of the bank's key officials, Kwitny describes how Nugan Hand systematically laundered and moved money throughout the Far East and Middle East, evading currency exchange and tax statutes of Australia and other countries. "Much of the money Nugan Hand received," Kwitny asserts, "consisted of tax cheatings, dope payments, Marcos family money, and, rumored, the hoarded wealth of a few other Third World potentates." During its existence, Nugan Hand bilked many unsuspecting Australian and American citizens, including U.S. servicemen, out of their life savings. Kwitny argues further that Nugan Hand actually was a Central Intelligence Agency (CIA) front organization that received substantial financial and logistical support from the U.S. government. Thus Nugan Hand was merely another mechanism in the U.S. government's covert war against global communism.

To support his main thesis, Kwitny puts forth an indigestible mass of background material—lengthy verbatim excerpts from transcripts of Australian governmental hear-

ings and inquiries, a rambling discourse on supposedly proven U.S. involvement in Southeast Asian drug trafficking, and a recapitulation of well-publicized allegations of a CIA plot to subvert the Australian political system in the mid-1970s. The reader apparently is expected to draw certain conclusions from this evidence and then connect them to the case of Nugan Hand. Although Kwitny presents a credible case in dealing with Nugan Hand's mismanagement of investors' funds, he is less successful in proving that the bank was affiliated with the CIA.

Despite his preface's disclaimer that this book will produce more questions than answers and his appendix's list of 57 "questions whose answers are secret," Kwitny owes his readers a more incisive analysis of the material at his disposal. Most readers will not be impressed by the number of people who refused to return Kwitny's calls or to be interviewed on the record, yet he cites these as proof of his exhaustive research. One is left with the impression that someone rushed this manuscript into print in response to keen public interest in the Iran-contra hearings of 1987.

In conclusion, this book clearly exemplifies one of the major problems inherent in researching and writing in the field of recent or contemporary history: there are simply not enough available primary sources to produce a coherent, definitive work. The general reading public would be better served if authors focused on topics that could be documented by a variety of sources or if they simply waited until the relevant sources were available for research. Consequently, the resulting publications would rely less on rumor, gossip, hearsay, and unsubstantiated evidence, as is the case with *The Crimes of Patriots*, and more on hard facts.

DAVID E. ALSOBROOK
Jimmy Carter Library
Atlanta
Georgia

McLAURIN, MELTON A. *Separate Pasts: Growing up White in the Segregated South*. Pp. ix, 164. Athens: University of Georgia Press, 1987. $13.95.

"Tell about the South. What's it like there? What do they do there? Why do they live there? Why do they live at all. . . ." With these words, Faulkner's Quentin Compson was implored by his Harvard roommate to disclose the bizarre tale of incest and murder that makes up *Absalom, Absalom!*. Faulkner, as Fred Hobson has recently reminded us in his *Tell about the South*, was neither the first nor last white Southerner compelled to explain the South to outsiders.

Not surprisingly, Southern autobiographies have told about the South: William Alexander Percy's *Lanterns on the Levee* (1941), Lillian Smith's *Killers of the Dream* (1949), Ralph McGill's *South and the Southerner* (1963), Willie Morris's *North towards Home* (1965), and Harry Crews's *Childhood* (1978) are among the genre's better known examples; many more could be cited. Some have served as regional apologias while others have been devastatingly critical. No doubt it is with some "anxiety of influence" that Melton A. McLaurin, a professor of Southern history at the University of North Carolina at Wilmington, transgresses disciplinary boundaries to provide his account of growing up in a small North Carolina town during the 1950s.

McLaurin's book is a significant achievement. As a historian, he is fully aware of the past's complexity and understands that remembered experience is, at best, an uncertain guide. To his credit, he does not claim to represent his generation and class; *Separate Pasts* is an intensely personal statement. Nonetheless, McLaurin is carefully attuned to the congruency of a particular place—the not quite rural but not really urban Southern small town—at an especially marginal moment: just prior to the changes brought by the civil rights movement. His book is a rich historical document.

The place is Wade, North Carolina, a crossroads village 12 miles south of Fayetteville, and the time is the early to middle 1950s. McLaurin is a part-time clerk at his grandfather's gas station cum grocery store, a position that brings him into contact with

many of the town's blacks, who depend on remaining in "grandaddy's" good graces, both for credit at the store and for his possible influence in dealing with other whites. Jim Crow culture is portrayed as a combination of paternalism and oppression in which the former potently reinforces the latter. The power of whites to extend or withhold support to individual blacks was, according to McLaurin, the glue that held the system together. McLaurin's account is striking not only for its perceptive, unsentimental portrayal of institutionalized segregation at the community level but also for its revelations about the advantages of such a system to a white teenage boy. The allegation that segregation harmed Southern whites as much as blacks, as some white liberals have claimed, runs counter to his testimony.

In addition to reflecting, often quite movingly, upon his encounters with various blacks and his growing realization of segregation's injustice, McLaurin probes the meaning of his grandfather's life. In *A Southern Renaissance,* Richard King observed that confronting the legacy of their Civil War grandfathers was a major preoccupation of writers, such as Faulkner, of the Renaissance generation. *Separate Pasts* suggests that white Southerners who came of age during the civil rights years might find in their segregationist grandfathers and grandmothers an equally compelling theme.

MORTON SOSNA

Stanford University
California

SUMMERS, MARK W. *The Plundering Generation: Corruption and the Crisis of the Union, 1849-1861.* Pp. xv, 362. New York: Oxford University Press, 1978. $29.95.

Historians have frequently blamed the Civil War on a "blundering generation" that failed to resolve the problems of the 1850s. Now, in an exhaustively researched book, Mark Summers presents us with compelling arguments that the war was also made more

likely by a "plundering generation," whose corrupt political practices brought into question the ideals on which the Republic had been founded. The years following the Civil War have usually been seen as the nadir of American public morality, the era of the robber barons, but Summers convincingly demonstrates that ten years before the war, corruption was already endemic in political life.

The first half of the book is a superb study of the impact on American politics of almost a decade of rapid economic and territorial expansion, mass immigration, and urban growth. During the 1850s, Americans plunged headlong into a quest for wealth with devastating effects. Not all or even most politicians were corrupt, but Summers uses a mass of private correspondence, newspapers, and committee reports to show how thousands of Americans subverted the political process for personal gain and party ends. Using vivid and often hilarious examples, he documents rigged elections, bought newspaper opinions, the abuses of a greatly expanded spoils system, crooked claims and land frauds, misuse of public contracts, and default by public officials besieged by lobbyists with long purses and few scruples. Corruption was equally rife in urban, state, and federal politics and was as common in rural America as among city rowdies. Graft promoted internal improvements and pushed the frontier west. Opposition politicians attacked financial beneficiaries, but they employed the same methods when in power. Corruption might be scandalous and sometimes result in retribution, but it was rarely seen as heralding the decay of the Republic.

During the 1850s, the atmosphere changed. In the second half of his book, Summers charts with subtlety and judgment a growing public alarm about corruption and the manipulation of that alarm by sectional-minded politicians. The Kansas-Nebraska Act was a key stage in this process, with the opponents of the expansion of slavery reacting violently to what they saw as the unscrupulous use of executive patronage to push the bill through Congress. The Republican Party increasingly represented itself as a moral crusade against

the corruption emanating from the slave power. Buchanan's administration played straight into Republican hands by compounding shocking financial scandals with an attempt to bribe Congress into accepting the pro-slavery Lecompton constitution. Although the Republicans had many men of dubious financial morals in their ranks, their presidential candidate was portrayed as a symbol of rustic honesty and a restorer of sound public ethics.

Not surprisingly, defenders of Southern rights had by this time developed their own corruption myth, in which the North became a region of debauchery, where corrupt politicians, brimming with malevolence against the South, manipulated ignorant foreign voters for selfish ends. The North was a lost cause, and the restoration of political integrity necessitated the creation of an independent South.

Summers does not claim too much for his thesis, rightly seeing political corruption not as a cause of the Civil War but as a useful weapon in the armories of politicians confronted by more fundamental issues on which opinions could not be bought.

Both as political and intellectual history, Summers's book is a major study that deserves a wide audience.

LOUIS BILLINGTON
University of Hull
England

TULIS, JEFFRY K. *The Rhetorical Presidency.* Pp. x, 209. Princeton, NJ: Princeton University Press, 1987. $19.95.

This book is a welcome addition to others published in commemoration of the two-hundredth anniversary of the United States Constitution. By "rhetorical," in the book's title, Tulis does not mean to suggest bombast but rather the role and effectiveness of presidential messages and speeches. The volume is well annotated and contains tables and a useful index.

Fittingly, the book is published by the press of the university from which Woodrow

Wilson rose to the governorship of New Jersey and the presidency of the United States. While many presidents are cited, from Washington to Reagan, special attention is given to Wilson as an example of the newer dynamic view of the Constitution and executive leadership.

Tulis holds that the Founders did not anticipate the use of rhetoric and tried to prevent it in the Constitution through a system of representation, independence of the executive, and separation of powers. Presidents of the nineteenth century paid more heed to their constitutional limitations, while those of the twentieth, beginning with Theodore Roosevelt, circumvented Congress on occasion.

Tulis finds that Wilson gained support partly because the public became familiar with popular leadership under Theodore Roosevelt. In view of the animosity between the two men, however, may not Wilson have engaged in rhetoric on his own? The point is made that Wilson, frustrated by Senate opposition when U.S. membership in the League of Nations was at stake, used his rhetorical skill in appealing directly to the people.

Concerning the League of Nations debate, Tulis apparently does not agree that the personal differences between Senator Lodge and Wilson were of crucial importance, nor does he mention French Premier Clemenceau's skepticism concerning the League as a peace organization. Has it been verified that Britain and France would have honored the Senate's reservations if by so doing the United States would have joined the League? More convincingly, Tulis makes the point that Wilson addressed the public one way and the Senate another way. The public was told that the ideal of an international organization was bound to be realized, but the Senate was informed that a moral consciousness was needed if the League were to succeed. Nevertheless, Wilson's rhetoric brought about a "fundamental transformation" in presidential leadership.

Tulis cites the decline in structural argument. Speeches are now written, usually by wordsmiths, or speech writers, for popular

156

THE ANNALS OF THE AMERICAN ACADEMY

consumption. They are almost innocent of "political discourse." The old "deliberation" is wanting. The media direct their attention to the president, not to the Congress. Faith in Reagan's administrative ability, his control of subordinates, has been shaken by the Iran-contra affair, yet he presents the image of a hands-on president when delivering his formal addresses. Implied in this study, as I see it, is the idea that quality and substance in speeches—such as Lincoln's, for example—are more important to posterity than are quantity and style.

This carefully crafted monograph helps to fill an important gap in American political and constitutional history.

ARLOW W. ANDERSEN
University of Wisconsin
Oshkosh

WINKS, ROBIN W. *Cloak & Gown: Scholars in the Secret War, 1939-1961.* Pp. 607. New York: William Morrow, 1987. $22.95.

"Cloak" and "gown" are used to symbolize the symbiotic relationship between intelligence work and scholarly pursuits of students and faculty of a university. Using these symbols, Winks illustrates that there is a parallel structure in the university climate of study, research, and methodology to the structure and climate of research for espionage and counterespionage. The universities served as prime recruiting grounds for intelligence analysts for the Office of Strategic Services during World War II and later for the Central Intelligence Agency.

The training historians, economists, and others receive at universities is applicable to work required of intelligence researchers and analysts. In one case, the university served as a cover-up for intelligence activities by a Yale professor. Joseph Toy Curtiss was a librarian at Yale. He was recruited for intelligence work by Donald Downes. The plan was to send Curtiss to Switzerland. There he would establish himself as a book buyer for a consortium of colleges, but his real purpose was to seek military information for the Allies. Before he could get to Switzerland, however, the military situation had changed and his place of operations was changed to Istanbul. He was successful in telling the Allies which railroads carried chromium from Turkey to Germany. These roads were bombed by the Allies—and rebuilt by the Germans. He also learned from a German general about the plot, which failed, to kill Hitler.

The United States never carried Curtiss on its roster as one of its personnel. The government paid his salary and maybe for some of the books, but the money was laundered through Yale. Wild Bill Donovan of the Office of Strategic Services and others knew of his exploits, but they were never officially recognized by the U.S. government. Curtiss returned to Yale after the war.

Throughout the book, Winks emphasizes the development of methodologies and theories for the study of espionage and counterintelligence. He relates this to the training of historians, or archivists, or economists—and finds they have the requisite skills for espionage and counterintelligence.

Sherman Kent is one operator Winks admires very much. He retells the story of how Kent wanted to prove his theory that 90 percent of intelligence could be found through unclassified documents, newspapers, and available books. Kent recruited five Yale professors to spend five weeks developing U.S. battle lines. These professors were to consider themselves Soviet agents.

When they submitted their results to Kent, he submitted them to a Sovietologist to ensure that the document looked like a Soviet one. Then he submitted it to General Walter Bedell Smith, who in turn told President Truman about it; Truman misconstrued the whole idea and used it to defend his policy of classifying documents. The report was further misused by people of the far Right persuasion to accuse Dean Acheson and the Truman administration of being Communist led and to assert that Yale was home for Communists. Everybody—but Kent and the five Yale professors—missed the point of the original exercise. Kent came to wish that he had never started the project.

At the end of each chapter, Winks evaluates the person or persons he talks about. It is in these evaluations that he defends the need for a centralized intelligence agency to protect our democratic ideals.

He realizes that covert actions raise moral questions. He points out how intelligence officers of the Central Intelligence Agency were angry about the Bay of Pigs fiasco. They blamed the failure for poor execution on President Kennedy. Winks notes that the complaints were about poor intelligence, poor preparation, and poor support, but there was no objection to the operation on moral grounds. Although Winks does not say so directly, one can assume that he favors the collection and analysis of intelligence information in peacetime but would not condone covert actions in peacetime, although he would see them as a necessity in wartime.

The major biographies that Winks relates provide interesting accounts of people who were truly interested in serving their country in wartime and peacetime. Winks brings in so many details and other personalities to explain his main character, however, that I found myself forgetting who the main characters were. If one can overcome this detail, Winks's book is a most interesting one. It also introduces the reader to other books on the subject of intelligence that could provide many hours of enjoyment.

ARTHUR GALLANT

Silver Spring
Maryland

SOCIOLOGY

COLEMAN, JAMES S. and THOMAS HOF-
FER. *Public and Private High Schools: The Impact of Communities.* Pp. xviii, 254. New York: Basic Books, 1987. $21.95.

James Coleman is the grandfather of large-scale empirical work in educational effectiveness. His 1965 Equal Employment Opportunity study launched a new attack on the intransigent problems of educating the disad-

vantaged. His work has had considerable influence on research and policy in the field. This newest study by Coleman and Hoffer again breaks new ground in important ways, though it is marred by some careless interpretation of the empirical results and by the omission of some support material that is relevant to assessing the study.

The big contribution of this book is the systematic documentation of the role of inter-generationally developed norms—a functional community—in successful educational outcomes. Coleman and Hoffer examine the achievement score dropout, and post-high-school activities of three samples of high school students: 19,569 in public schools, 2102 in Catholic schools, and 419 in other private schools. They compare the inputs in the three types of schools, the socioeconomic characteristics of the sample students and their peers, and the outcomes. After controlling for the differences between the school and student characteristics, they conclude that there are not big differences in the success measures between public and non-Catholic private schools—but that there are big differences between public and Catholic schools. The important findings here are the conclusion that Catholic high school students do much better than the non-Catholic private students, and that the reasons for this difference seem to be attributable to the strength of the community values.

The policy recommendations flowing from these findings relate to directing resources to building up the long-term steady community norms. For families in communities that do not have clear intergenerational values, sending children to schools founded on some is the recommendation. For principals and school superintendents, the challenge is the creation of these values in the schools—through strong relationships among students and teachers, with parents, and with the business community. For government policymakers, the objective would be to associate schools with strong institutional entities—with work locations, for example.

The evidence and argument of the book are persuasive. It is disturbing, therefore, to

find a large number of examples of careless treatment of the data. These are a few illustrations. First, Tables 2.1 through 2.4 each have a column labeled "High Performance Private," with very relevant differences between those results and results in other categories. They are not discussed at all in those sections. Second, in interpreting Table 2.9, Coleman and Hoffer state that "vocational program enrollments . . . in other private schools are concentrated in business or office training." The data show they are not—they are concentrated in technical and trade or industrial programs. Third, Coleman and Hoffer repeatedly interpret statistically insignificant variables as if they were significant. In the interpretation of Table 2.13, for example, they describe the nonsignificant positive differences in the coefficients for English and foreign language for "Other Private" as indicating an advantage! Similarly, in the interpretation of Table 3.6, about half the coefficients are not significant, yet important conclusions are drawn from the stability of the coefficients. If half should be read as zero, they may well be less stable.

Two other points of concern should be raised. First, throughout the book, Coleman and Hoffer compare the coefficients of the three samples, recognizing the great differences in the sample sizes. There is a simple test for the significance of the differences among the coefficients, which corrects for sample size. The reader needs the results of that test to interpret the results accurately. Second, the full set of regression results should be given in an appendix. It is very difficult to appraise the interpretation when selected results are the only ones presented.

The insights of the Coleman and Hoffer book are important ones. The literature on educational effectiveness has converged on the general conclusion that nonschool inputs dominate schooling outcomes. This study takes that conclusion one step further by identifying more closely which nonschool input is very influential. Beyond that, Coleman and Hoffer are developing a counterargument to the public-choice theorists who advocate educational vouchers. These theorists interpret the unsatisfactory educational outcomes as the product of an inability to articulate individual self-interest. Coleman and Hoffer are articulating a communitarian theory, where students are inspired to excel in response to strong community norms—and the school is the community. Were I the secretary of education, a state commissioner of education, or a school district superintendent, I would act in directions suggested by this book.

ANITA SUMMERS
University of Pennsylvania
Philadelphia

ETZIONI-HALEVY, EVA. *National Broadcasting under Siege: A Comparative Study of Australia, Britain, Israel and West Germany.* Pp. xii, 228. New York: St. Martin's Press, 1987. $39.95.

National Broadcasting under Siege has the potential of becoming an *Uncle Tom's Cabin* or a *Jungle*, for it exposes important realities generally unknown to the broad publics of the four democratic countries it covers, Australia, Great Britain, West Germany, and Israel. Etzioni-Halevy presents authenticated data showing that in these four countries the governmental broadcasting system is under attack in numerous ways.

The importance of the issues treated in the book was recently characterized in an article in the *Boston Review*:

The electronic communications revolution is a technological megatrend that is reshaping not just America, but our entire planet. Its marvels of instant global communication inundate us with massive quantities of new information and images in alluring new packages, challenging and even overrunning traditional values as it alters lifestyles around the world. It is transforming our allegiances. Yet few recognize its impact; fewer still understand.

Etzioni-Halevy has handled the uncovering extremely well. Every revelation is authenticated by painstaking research with experts, quotations from diverse authorities, and personal observation.

The book opens with a discussion of democracy and the perils and dilemmas presented by numerous power elites wanting to exert their influence on broadcasting. The power of political elites is counteracted by other elites. Etzioni-Halevy says that the powerful broadcasting elite suffers from the threats of other elites, which are necessary for its proper functioning. She points out that such struggles may affect broadcasting independence and may affect elections, citing as an instance the extensive put-on of state broadcasters by Margaret Thatcher in England. She also points out the ambiguities in the laws that set up broadcasting under the state in the four democracies discussed.

Next she takes up external pressures through direct intervention: complaints, suggestions, and threats. Another variation is influencing broadcasts through informal relations and contacts. These methods have been used in all of the four countries investigated. Etzioni-Halevy quotes a contemporary author to validate her point: "Few things corrode democracy faster than private deals among the great quietly eroding away the right to judge for ourselves what is happening."

External pressure is used also in connection with funding the broadcasting system. In all four countries, broadcasting systems are dependent on parliaments and government for funding. Funding has been used as a formidable political instrument. In the four countries, political pressure is exerted by the well-known truth that "if you hold them by the purse strings, heads and minds will follow." Examples of how this method of pressure is carried out are presented.

There are pressures, too, that come from privatization, that is, competition from private broadcasting companies. Privatization brings with it greater popularization of the material that is broadcast and a shrinking of the more serious public broadcasting.

Next, external pressures to affect personnel appointments in public broadcasting are discussed. Etzioni-Halevy notes differences in how the director of public broadcasting is chosen in the four countries, but in all of them politics prevails to some extent.

Next come internal pressures on public broadcasting from the board of directors. These cover intervention and guidance from inside the hierarchy of the broadcasting organization. This influence implies that in all four countries broadcasters can do what they like as long as they do what they are told. Political interference with state broadcasting systems is a well-established custom.

Internal pressure can also be applied through dismissal, demotion, and displacement of the broadcasting staff. These are political devices to which staffers are particularly vulnerable. Management can exert political pressure by displacing a broadcaster from one program to another, for example. These practices have been found in all of the four countries examined.

In her last chapter, "Friction and Conflict," Etzioni-Halevy gives some case studies that illustrate the various points she has made earlier in the book. She offers no specific solutions on how to meet the problems she has so carefully researched and discussed. She concludes that her study has documented a state of siege that threatens to diminish the state of public broadcasting and its role and significance in a democratic society. She feels that her study has also shown that public broadcasting "has not become as insignificant as its optimistic enemies and its pessimistic friends might have wished to believe."

EDWARD L. BERNAYS

Cambridge
Massachusetts

FILDES, VALERIE. *Breasts, Bottles and Babies: A History of Infant Feeding.* Pp. xviii, 462. Edinburgh: Edinburgh University Press, 1986. Distributed by Columbia University Press, New York. $30.00.

Valerie Fildes presents an exhaustive examination of the practices of infant feeding from 1500 to 1800; she concentrates on the British Isles, with some information from North America as well. The book is based on her thesis, written at the University of Surrey,

and its organization betrays these origins: each chapter ends with a thorough summary of the previous discussion. In fact, no significant information would be missed if one simply read these summaries. The full chapters provide amplification and examples but are written in a rather dry prose style.

Although the style is unexciting, the subject matter is interesting, the book has been painstakingly researched and documented, and the conclusions are sound. Fildes has consulted works by experts of the period, including pediatric and midwifery texts, theological works, and popular medical guides. In addition, she has included references from literary sources such as diaries and memoirs, which provide examples of infant feeding as actually carried out. Fildes finds that from 1500 to 1800 there was a change in the literature from a primary concern with the health of the infant to a primary concern with the well-being of the mother. She also notes a shift in that period among the upper classes from the practice of having one's infants wet-nursed by another to the practice of maternal breast-feeding, established by the end of the eighteenth century. The shift to maternal breast-feeding occurred at the same time that medical experts began to recommend that newborns be put to the breast at once, leading to a decline in the neonatal death rate and in maternal mortality from milk fever. At the beginning of the period, experts still believed, with the ancient Greeks, that the colostrum present in the mother's breasts in the first days after childbirth was harmful to the child. Fildes speculates that the shifts in practice "may have been a factor in the improved emotional attitudes towards infants and their welfare noted during the 18th century."

Fildes includes a particularly interesting discussion of wet nurses, who were relied on heavily by the upper classes until the eighteenth century. In Fildes's research, wet-nursing emerges as a common and potentially lucrative occupation for women, a valuable conclusion that I have not seen elsewhere in literature on working women. The book also contains information on practices of mixed and supplementary feeding, substitutes for nursing, and weaning practices. There is food for thought here indeed.

CHARLOTTE L. BEAHAN
Murray State University
Kentucky

GIDDENS, ANTHONY and JONATHAN TURNER, eds. *Social Theory Today*. Pp. vi, 428. Stanford, CA: Stanford University Press, 1987. $37.50.

CASTORIADIS, CORNELIUS. *The Imaginary Institution of Society*. Pp. vii, 418. Trans. K. Blamey. Cambridge: MIT Press, 1987. $35.00.

Giddens and Turner's anthology is another product of the Polity Press enterprise, originated a few years ago and still run by Giddens and some of his students in England. It has published many theoretical works, some of them quite good. In this book, the editors did what Polity does best: inviting young writers to describe and then evaluate various schools of theorizing, in this case, those that still seem to have a following among Anglo-American sociologists. Chapters are given to the classics (Jeffrey Alexander), behaviorism (George Homans), symbolic interactionism (Hans Joas), Parsonianism (Richard Münch), so-called analytical theory (Jonathan Turner), structuralism and post-structuralism (Giddens), ethnomethodology (John Heritage), structuration theory, namely, Giddens's own ideas (Ira Cohen), world-systems theory (Immanuel Wallerstein), class analysis (Ralph Miliband), critical theory (Axel Honneth), and mathematical models (Thomas Wilson). This is an international pool of writers, with six Americans, three Germans, and three Britons, an unusual strategy for such a book given that most of the approaches treated flourish in the United States. Despite an introduction that tries to draw the contributions together, there is precious little cross-fertilization, and many of them are actually parts of longer works Polity will or has published, including Giddens's own chapter. The volume becomes, in a sense, advertising for other Polity titles.

The tone of each chapter varies enormously, with apodictic claims made by Homans, Wallerstein, and Turner and more tentative conclusions drawn by the younger writers. Alexander's meditation on reading classical social thought is among the best, partly because of its length and also because his point is rather congenial to current hermeneutical interests. Homans repeats what he said 25 years ago about his brand of behaviorism, its alleged superiority to every other explanatory mode, and the only current aspect of the chapter is his reference to several German works, none in English yet, that apparently put his ideas to use. Joas concentrates on Mead—hardly surprising given his fine book that Polity published on the father of symbolic interactionism—and does not deal much with later developments in the field. Münch has for some years been trying to revive Parsonianism in Germany and has also published several essays in English. They are hard to read, an unholy mixture of Parsons's bad English translated into academic German, then retranslated into awkward English. As an introduction to current Parsonianism, it does not work. From Turner one hears about his version of analytical theory, by which he means a neo-Comtean desire to find laws of social action with universal validity. The project is quixotic but clearly presented and more courageous than most writers in the field.

The remaining papers do not vary much in style from the preceding ones, in that each tries to prove a point that holds special relevance for the writer, such as Giddens's wish in his chapter to defrock decontructionism. None, however, is truly a trend report on current thought, which is what the naive reader might expect from the title and introduction. There are also an alarming number of references to Giddens's work throughout, which, given his role at Polity Press, raises ethical and scholarly questions.

Castoriadis's book is similar to Giddens and Turner's only in that it deals in social theory, broadly conceived, and its translation into English also originated with Polity. Beyond this it could hardly be more different.

Whereas the other volume is putatively addressed to novitiates with a yen for discovering what is currently of interest to theorists of various types, Castoriadis's unique adventure in ideas is the culmination of a life within the special orbit of French Marxism but motivated by the strongest possible divergence from orthodoxy. Habermas calls the book "the most original, ambitious, and reflective attempt to think through the liberating mediation of history, society, external and internal nature once again as praxis" (*The Philosophical Discourse of Modernity*, p. 327). The work is much too complex to analyze here other than to point out that its unique usage of terms like *legein* and *teukhein*—roughly, "language" and "technology"—and their connection to the social imaginary is unlike anything else in the Marxist canon and deserves study. Though somewhat dated in that the French circumstances that provoked the book took place twenty years ago, for Americans, Castoriadis is a new face, and his psychoanalytic and phenomenological transformation of Marxist categories is worth pursuing.

ALAN SICA

University of Kansas
Lawrence

HACKER, BARTON C. *The Dragon's Tail: Radiation Safety in the Manhattan Project, 1942-1946.* Pp. x, 258. Berkeley: University of California Press, 1987. $25.00.

With so much of today's literature on radiation safety of a polemic nature, it comes as a pleasure to find a book on the subject that is both thoroughly scholarly and professional. This book is the result of an exhaustive research effort funded by the Department of Energy. The research involved interviews with over eighty key participants of the era and drew upon an enormous literature. Still another eighty reviewers were enlisted to review various chapter drafts.

The book documents radiation safety from the first atomic test, Trinity, to the final Bikini

test, Operation Crossroads, in 1946. Its title is taken from the sentiments expressed by a scientist who participated in the early open-air bomb design experiments in the canyons around Los Alamos. He likened the experiments to "tickling the tail of a sleeping dragon."

Hacker says that the dragon stayed dormant: "the weight of the evidence, though less overwhelming than it once seemed, still supports the judgment at the time that neither Trinity nor Crossroads directly harmed anyone."

That there were no fatalities seems to have been, in part, just good fortune. The wartime created an environment in which risks were viewed as a normal part of the effort to win the war. Scientists and workers willingly put themselves at risk in order to move both research and production of the bomb ahead. This does not mean that safety concerns were ignored; just that they did not receive the priority we would accord them today.

Aside from good luck, safety was maintained because those in charge foresaw the dangers and drew from a base of experience with X rays and radium that was forty years old. Despite the unprecedented challenges presented by testing, Hacker concludes that the safety standards drawn up by professional societies prior to the Manhattan Project served the project well. Though surprises did take place, a sufficient, if uncomfortably thin, margin of safety prevailed.

While Hacker succeeds admirably in two of the three stated goals for the book—to document the period authoritatively, and to make the volume understandable to the layperson, yet useful for technical purposes—it is questionable whether the third goal, capturing the reader's interest, can be easily achieved. The writing is dense and requires a dedicated reader. This is unfortunate because the interviews undoubtedly turned up many interesting anecdotes, of which surprisingly few are reproduced. Let us hope that in the succeeding volume, which will trace radiation safety in testing up to the present, Hacker will use a lighter touch in his painstaking exposition on the facts.

JACK BARKENBUS

University of Tennessee
Knoxville

KAHN, ALFRED J. and SHEILA B. KAMERMAN. *Childcare: Facing the Hard Choices.* Pp. xi, 273. Dover, MA: Auburn House, 1987. $26.00.

If your knowledge of the child-care industry, the composition of demand for child-care services, and the federal and state roles in financing and regulating child care has remained unchanged in the last decade, then you know nothing about current conditions. Few industries have undergone so many changes in such a short period. In child care, the changes have been triggered by an exploding demand from working parents coupled with a massive shift in the federal government's role during the Reagan administration. Given that the emotional and cognitive development of our nation's children is at stake, it is striking that so little is known about the extent and consequences of these changes.

In *Childcare*, Alfred Kahn and Sheila Kamerman compile up-to-date facts about the use of child-care services, document the nature of the changes that have taken place during the Reagan era, explain and evaluate numerous state and local initiatives, and assess critically the nature of social-policy choices now facing us. The result is a thoughtful and timely contribution to the field that deserves the attention of public officials and private citizens who are concerned about the quality and quantity of child-care services, as well as of students of social welfare issues involving children.

Massive changes have jolted the nation's child-care service industry in the past decade. Labor force participation rates of mothers of infants and toddlers have doubled in the last 15 years and are 30 percent higher than in

1980. Although day-care center capacity is probably twice what it was 10 years ago, demand appears to have outstripped supply. Virtually all five-year-olds, half of all four-year-olds, and one-quarter of all three-year-olds are enrolled in public or private schools or preschools; for them, however, child-care supply appears adequate, at least for part-day programs.

The Reagan years have drastically altered the federal role, reducing direct expenditures—although increasing funding for Head Start—but dramatically expanding the tax expenditure of the child-care income-tax credit. Total expenditures have thus increased, with middle-income families gaining from subsidies to taxpayers and employers and lower-income families losing as a result of various program cutbacks. There are no longer federal standards associated with programs receiving federal subsidies.

State and local governments have taken up some of the slack in a variety of ways that have been carefully described by Kahn and Kamerman. Indeed, one of the virtues of the book is that it offers a wealth of ideas for state and local officials coping with their new child-care responsibilities. Experimentation has produced a substantial body of knowledge on successful information, resources, and referral services. Kahn and Kamerman look kindly on various voucher systems as a way of expanding demand, assisting low-income working mothers, and perhaps bringing more unlicensed providers into the regulated portion of the market. But local efforts have been limited in scope and will remain so until more resources are made available by higher levels of government.

This book makes a strong case for a more comprehensive approach to child-care policy, centered more at the state than federal level and focused on the development and enforcement of standards and protections in family and center day care, the expansion of public preschools for three- and four-year-olds, and increased support for child care for low-income families. Participants in the policy

debate would do well to give this book a careful reading.

GREG J. DUNCAN
University of Michigan
Ann Arbor

REINARMAN, CRAIG. *American States of Mind: Political Beliefs and Behavior among Private and Public Workers.* Pp. x, 262. New Haven, CT: Yale University Press, 1987. $25.00.

Craig Reinarman's study is an important and often provocative contribution to our understanding of the political consciousness of American workers. *American States of Mind* has two large purposes. The first is to explore in depth the content of the political consciousness of a small set of private and public sector workers. The second purpose is to explain the particular configurations of political belief and behavior that Reinarman discovered among his worker-subjects and to advance our theoretical grasp of the determinants and formation of political consciousness.

Reinarman's study is based upon qualitative research on a group of 12 workers in an anonymous California city during the early 1980s. He conducted in-depth interviews with six private sector workers in a local branch of the United Parcel Service and a like number of public employees in a city welfare office. Reinarman makes no claim for the generalizability of his findings; it is the breadth and depth of understanding of the political consciousness of particular workers achieved through qualitative methods that makes his book so valuable.

Reinarman's attempt to plumb the political consciousness of the 12 workers is centered on their views of the state-market relation, that is, their beliefs about the actual and proper roles of the market and the state in American society. A striking feature of these beliefs is the shared—with but one exception among the 12—and principled conviction of "the

legitimacy of the state in all its basic welfare and regulatory aspects." Reinarman emphasizes above all, however, the profound ambivalence of these workers toward both the market and the state. They tend to grant a legitimate and substantial role to each sphere; on the other hand, they seem torn between the rival logics of market and state, and they are sharply critical, in ideologically disparate ways, of the principles, practices, and outcomes of both. For these workers, neither market nor state accords well with the democratic and populist character of their fundamental political values. These values, it should be noted, do vary between the private and public workers. The political values of the private sector workers tend to be inflected toward the moral code of the market, those of the public employees toward the moral code of the welfare state.

Reinarman's rich and detailed analysis of the 12 workers' views on the state-market relation is his central contribution. His attempt to explain those views and, more generally, to give an account of the determinants and formation of political consciousness seemed to me less successful but nonetheless theoretically significant. Noteworthy in this connection is Reinarman's subtle argument that differences in the lived experience—as well as in the material interests—of those who work in the market and those who work in the public sector lead to rather distinct ideological dispositions.

American States of Mind closes with an important analysis of the disjunction between the political beliefs and the political behavior of the workers Reinarman studies. Here we find more distressing evidence that the electoral and party systems of the United States fail to provide the opportunities that many want to act politically in ways both meaningful and consistent with their beliefs.

I hope that Craig Reinarman's book receives the wide and serious attention that it deserves.

ANDREW CLARK BATTISTA

East Tennessee State University
Johnson City

SAMMONS, JEFFREY T. *Beyond the Ring: The Role of Boxing in American Society.* Pp. xix, 318. Champaign: University of Illinois Press, 1988. $24.95.

Speaking of heavyweight boxers, Budd Schulberg once wrote that "America gets the champion it deserves." This claim underlies Jeffrey Sammons's examination of the uneasy relationship between Americans and the world of boxing, in both its sporting and business dimensions.

Sammons approaches his subject chronologically, rightly concentrating on the heavyweights as symbolic standard-bearers of the sport. Beginning with the half-mythic John L. Sullivan, he centers on the careers, in and out of the ring, of Jack Johnson, Joe Louis, and Muhammad Ali. A fierce and trenchant conclusion treats the very real danger of boxing, both in the ring and in its cumulative physical and mental effects in later life.

Sammons asserts that "boxing *is* history," a microcosm of American society reflecting social trends and developments. This sweeping pronouncement applies best to one of his two major themes, racism. By examining the careers of the flamboyant Johnson, the moderate Louis, and the aggressively idiosyncratic Ali, he offers a useful and coherent look at the multifaceted dimensions of the nation's racial tensions and fears.

Sammons is less successful with his second major theme, the role of organized crime in boxing. He details the sport's descent into the sewer, beginning with Mike Jacobs's management of Louis in the 1930s, and is at his best describing the roles of the odious Frankie Carbo—of Murder, Inc., notoriety—and the wealthy Jim Norris in disgracing the fight game after World War II. But he does not convince the reader that such shenanigans provide a mirror of the larger society.

Indeed, Sammons touches on several interesting topics—the role of women, concepts of manliness, and, above all, the reaction of the dominant middle class to the sport—but none of these are fully developed. He perceives racism and social discrimination, particularly in the 1920s, as being the "potent acids eating

at the core" of boxing, downplaying the ballyhoo and the corruption.

Boxing in America developed from the underside of society. Despite television, multi-million-dollar gates, and the creation of national celebrities, in the underside of society it remains. It is by definition a social phenomenon. Thus Sammons's conclusion argues that boxing reveals the country's ambivalent attitude toward the concepts of progress and individualism, and here he is right on target. But his penchant for overstatement, such as "boxers pursue a sport at once scorned and glorified for its violence by a confused people who have prided themselves on civility and modernity but who cling to atavistic instincts," almost does him in.

Sammons provides an interesting, engaging attempt to fuse sport and the history of the society that spawns and perpetuates it. Problems with focus and scale should not obscure his vital concern with what should be, for historians, the root of the matter: the way we play, even in a vicious and at times lethal sport such as boxing, is of historic importance.

MICHAEL T. ISENBERG
United States Naval Academy
Annapolis
Maryland

WAGNER-PACIFICI, ROBIN E. *The Moro Morality Play: Terrorism as Social Drama.* Pp. xi, 360. Chicago: University of Chicago Press, 1986. $45.00. Paperbound, $14.95.

The Moro Morality Play: Terrorism as Social Drama, its title notwithstanding, is less concerned with terrorism per se than to "reveal the multidimensionality of events and to make us conscious of the assumptions about reality that the representations of these events contain." More specifically, Wagner-Pacifici documents how the spectacular kidnapping on 16 March 1978 of Aldo Moro, former Italian prime minister, by the Red Brigades was interpreted and used toward divergent purposes by a variety of politically contending parties. Not only did these pro-

tagonists—Socialist, Communist, and Christian Democratic parties, Moro's family, Moro himself, the press—struggle to impose their own meanings onto the event, but such interpretations "pronounced *during* an event . . . turn back on the event to actually shape it as it unfolds." Wagner-Pacifici documents these variant interpretations with a particular focus on the rhetorics, mainly dramaturgical, that each employed.

By means of deconstructing the public pronouncements of these contending protagonists, Wagner-Pacifici puts together a compelling case that each interpretation was an attempt to appropriate the kidnapping and its aftermath to the political and self-legitimating ends of the various contenders. In light of the fact the Aldo Moro was the leading figure in the historic compromise that would have for the first time allowed the Italian Communist Party into the ruling coalition, a perhaps unexpected result of these attempts was that "the immediate effect of Moro's kidnapping was the realignment [toward more conventional partitions] of all the familiar components of Italian social and political life." In other words, the variant interpretations of the kidnapping, of the place of the Red Brigades in—or outside of—Italian society, and of the positions regarding the drama staked out by competitors in the wider political arena combined to reproduce and legitimate the lines of demarcation of Italian political life. In this regard, Wagner-Pacifici's assertion that "in modern pluralistic 'society' the absolutist order is fictive, problematic and often illusory" seems a bit like a non sequitur or at least overstated. Even if the unity of Italian society asserted by the media, the Social Democrats, and the Communists in the aftermath of Moro's kidnapping was merely rhetorical in the sense that it was posited for politically self-legitimating ends, the apparent—if transient—success of this rhetorical strategy suggests that this order was nonetheless real.

The Moro Morality Play will be especially welcomed by literary critics and cultural anthropologists accustomed to interest- or power-maximizing theories of political action because it attempts to make a case for understanding

all such action as culturally mediated. Interests and power are not just maximized, they are contested, communicated, and arguably even constituted by means of rhetorical forms, symbols, and culturally reproduced values. Wagner-Pacifici's study makes this point most convincingly. Unfortunately, the models for cultural analysis she employs strike me as less than compelling. She asserts, rather than argues, that "the social world may fruitfully be viewed as a text accessible to hermeneutical analysis." Drawing inspiration most explicitly from Victor Turner's ideas of "social dramas" and more profoundly from Paul Ricoeur's notion of social action as text. Wagner-Pacifici organizes her narrative as though history itself, and not just its rhetorical appropriation, were put into a plot.

I believe there are important logical difficulties in equating text with society, despite the current popularity of this equation in current academic discourse. One of the most important of these difficulties is that it tends to flatten the dialectical relationship between representation and institutions to a single level, the text, making analysis of the role of ideological misrepresentation in social reproduction difficult to conceive.

There are other dangers in making social analysis into a kind of literary criticism. For example, were one to accept the notion of society as text, Wagner-Pacifici's own study would then be reduced to an attempt to reappropriate the kidnapping and eventual killing of Aldo Moro as tragedy—presumably more socially redemptive—in contrast to the melodramatic interpretation imposed—in Wagner-Pacifici's view, inappropriately—by many of the main contending protagonists. By the same token, I suspect that many anthropologists who read The Moro Morality Play will find Wagner-Pacifici's allegiance to dramaturgical analysis especially unconvincing when it leads her to insist that modern societies are dramaturgical as opposed to small-scale societies, which are ritualistic. This idea stems from Wagner-Pacifici's assumption that small-scale societies are solitary, if not monolithic, and that modern societies are not, but more profoundly from her apparent lack of a sense of the ways collective representations and social institutions in both small-scale and complex societies are dialectically linked in the process—systematically ordered—of social reproduction.

Readers more congenial to the application of literary critical techniques to social analysis will no doubt find the foregoing misgivings beside the point. Whatever one's biases in this regard, however, The Moro Morality Play is a most worthy study that I hope is one of the first of many that will attempt to ground political action and historical event dialectically in the context of cultural and social reproduction.

P. STEVEN SANGREN

Cornell University
Ithaca
New York

ECONOMICS

BARR, NICHOLAS. The Economics of the Welfare State. Pp. xiv, 475. Stanford, CA: Stanford University Press, 1987. $39.50.

The subject of the welfare state and the variety of social programs that it generates has received center-stage attention in Western industrial democracies during the past several decades. In this carefully written book, Nicholas Barr provides an in-depth analysis of the raison d'être of the modern welfare state as it performs its income-maintenance functions for the poor, elderly, and unemployed as well as its allocation of education, health-care, and housing benefits. The institutional coverage is primarily British, yet the theoretical analysis transcends political boundaries and thus provides valuable insight across the broad spectrum of Western industrial nations.

Although Barr's approach is basically that of the professional economist, interdisciplinary considerations are also included. A strong point of the book is found in its carefully planned organizational structure, which allows the reader to select a particular pattern of reading based on personal background and degree of interest in distributional and social-

welfare matters. The serious student of the subject has a comprehensive reference source near at hand while the casual reader can follow the equivalent of a road map through specific sections of the book from which the main arguments and conclusions are readily understandable.

Libertarian/conservative, socialist/Marxist, and liberal positions on distribution are presented in an objective and thorough manner. Barr's preference for the liberal position is made known, but this does not detract from the usefulness of the book for readers of different ideological persuasions or, for that matter, with no particular persuasion. Barr argues persuasively that the welfare state can be defended on grounds of efficiency as well as the conventional grounds of distributional equity, resulting in greater welfare for all members of society regardless of income, wealth, or demographic status. The important distinction between goals and methods is made clear, and, in so doing, a credible argument is made that much of the continuing controversy between the libertarian/conservative and liberal positions rests mainly on the weight given to informational problems as they relate to economic efficiency.

The question of the appropriate role for the welfare state in Western society is not about to go away. Barr provides an enlightened perspective on this important issue that, if heeded, could result in a better understanding of the topic and, consequently, in more effective social policies. It is important that, once the efficiency dimension of the welfare state is given its proper recognition, the central issue becomes not so much one of the size of the welfare state as it does the particular equity and efficiency goals that are to be pursued and the methods that are to be utilized for their attainment.

BERNARD P. HERBER

University of Arizona
Tucson

BIERSTEKER, THOMAS J. *Multinationals, the State, and Control of the Nigerian*

Economy. Pp. xvii, 344. Princeton, NJ: Princeton University Press, 1987. $45.00. Paperbound, $12.50.

This exceptionally lucid analysis of the changing relationship between the state and multinational corporations simultaneously examines the specific Nigerian experience and engages in a sustained critique of the theoretical literature on international political economy. Biersteker initially distinguishes six competing schools of thought: conservative neoclassical realists, liberal internationalists, structuralists, "vulgar" and "sophisticated" dependentists, and classical Marxists. He finds that none of these alone provides an adequate ground on which to pursue the question of whether multinationals have or have not constrained the exercise of state power. Each of them, however, offers insights into the character of the modern state, insights that Biersteker pursues with a careful historical account of the Nigerian indigenization program initiated in 1972. Overall, Biersteker's account is especially indebted to the "sophisticated" dependencia position associated with, for example, Cardoso and Evans, but it is equally informed by a rather more conventional sensitivity to the untidy compromises of policy-making and the political process.

Indigenization programs have now become a familiar aspect of contemporary state policy in most parts of the world. They have been treated by many observers as evidence of the way national sovereignty is a good deal more resilient than we were led to believe by those who were so impressed by the spectacular growth of the global reach of multinationals in the 1970s. All too often, however, a simple-minded internationalism has been superseded by a simpleminded statism.

Biersteker's analysis points to a more complex development. To begin with, he examines the Nigerian experience on three levels: on the level of the firm, the economic sector, and the state as a whole. He also distinguishes between the objectives of local capital, foreign capital, and the state, and he draws attention to important differences between policy formulation and policy implemen-

tation. The story he tells is in some ways all too familiar. It is a story of bargaining and compromise, of policies giving rise to contradictions that lead to new policy initiatives. As a story, it is certainly more convincing than the claims of those who treat governments as rational actors trying to maximize national economic and political objectives. It also provides a account of the severe limits within which states like Nigeria are able to respond to powerful multinationals. In the "much longer run," he says, "a combination of extensive technical and managerial training plus a political coalition interested in controlling multinationals could make a difference in the balance of bargaining power"; but "that shift is still a long way off for most developing countries." As to whether Nigerians are now in greater control of enterprises, sectors of their economy, or their national economy as a whole as a consequence of the indigenization program, he concludes that they are, but not by much. States like Nigeria may have learned how to wrest some control away from multinationals, but multinationals have in turn learned how to respond to state policies.

Even so, the very lucidity of Biersteker's discussion of this dialectical learning process only serves to amplify the suspicion that contemporary transformations in global economic processes are more complex—and more threatening—than can be suggested by any analysis that is concerned only with the struggle for control between states and multinationals.

R.B.J. WALKER

University of Victoria
British Columbia
Canada

HUNT, H. ALLAN and TIMOTHY L. HUNT. *Clerical Employment and Technological Change.* Pp. x, 296. Kalamazoo, MI: W. E. Upjohn Institute for Employment Research, 1986. $23.95. Paperbound, $15.95.

H. Allan Hunt and Timothy L. Hunt present a careful analysis of past changes in U.S. clerical employment and critically review forecasts of future changes in this largest of all occupational categories. Their motivating question is, Will the spread of microprocessor technology in the office lead, through displacement, to a dramatic reduction in the number of clerical jobs? Their answer is no, though they do expect clerical employment growth to be much slower than it has been in the past, and they do see evidence of technological displacement of some clerical jobs.

Most of the book is devoted to describing and analyzing changes in the clerical work force using census data from 1950 to 1980 and annual data from the Current Population Survey for 1972 to 1982. Hunt and Hunt have undertaken a painstaking construction of comparable occupation data from the various census years. They are keenly aware of the difficulties inherent in their data, and they forthrightly share these problems with the reader. The data they use are laid out in numerous clearly presented and described tables and charts that will be of great use to others working in this area. Data hounds will love the tables; others may find the reading slow going because of a style that is reminiscent of government publications. The style should not, however, deter the nonspecialist from understanding the value of this work. The conclusions reached are sound, and we are better off for having been led, in great detail, through the process by which they were reached.

The main result from the analysis of past data is that while, in the long run, clerical employment has grown very rapidly, its rate of growth has slowed markedly since 1970. In looking at detailed clerical occupations for the years 1972-82, Hunt and Hunt find some evidence of the negative impact of technological change on employment; slow growth or outright decline in some back-office occupations that are most easily mechanized. Hunt and Hunt also, however, stress the clerical jobs created by computerization. Computer equipment operators constitute the fastest-growing group of clerical workers.

Many readers will find the chapter on forecasts of future clerical employment the

most interesting. Hunt and Hunt critically review projections by the Bureau of Labor Statistics and others. They conclude that those who project large future declines in clerical employment due to office automation are overestimating the productivity growth that will result from automation. Hunt and Hunt expect that overall clerical employment will grow slightly more slowly than will total employment, with office automation creating some jobs, reducing others, and changing the content of most.

ELYCE J. ROTELLA

Indiana University
Bloomington

NOYELLE, THIERRY J. *Beyond Industrial Dualism: Market and Job Segmentation in the New Economy.* Pp. xii, 140. Boulder, CO: Westview Press, 1987. $28.50.

MARSDEN, DAVID. *The End of Economic Man? Custom and Competition in Labour Markets.* Pp. x, 278. New York: St. Martin's Press, 1986. $27.50.

These books have a common subject: changing features of labor markets and, in particular, the degree of competition that exists, that is, the relative importance of promotions within firms versus wider, more open labor markets. Both adopt an interdisciplinary approach in attempting to appeal simultaneously to economists, industrial sociologists and industrial-relations specialists.

Both books emphasize the importance of institutional labor market features as opposed to theoretical analysis, but they differ in style and subject matter. Noyelle's is short and easily readable; it examines American labor markets and presents three lengthy case studies. Marsden's is long and academic in style; it examines European as well as American labor markets and synthesizes a wide range of literature. Neither book is sufficiently rigorous or original as to constitute major contributions to the literature or to warrant recommendation for either the general professional or student reader. Both contain substantial passages

based on loose reasoning and spotty evidence. Moreover, Noyelle and Marsden reach opposite conclusions. Noyelle concludes that there has been a resurgence of labor market competition in recent years and that employers have moved away from earlier patterns of internal promotions. Marsden concludes, on the other hand, that competitive labor markets are fragile and, indeed, that firms are placing a greater emphasis than ever before on internal labor markets.

Both books have additional negative features in common. They appear to have sat on the shelf for a long time prior to publication. Noyelle's data in several places are only as recent as 1984, although more recent data are easily available. Marsden's references, except for one or two cases, are old. The heavy hand of the publisher with an eye to sales is evident in the titles of these books. "The end of economic man" has nothing whatsoever to do with the Marsden book, and the "new economy" refers to nothing new at all but to the long-term rise in service jobs that has been going on for many decades and that has been noted repeatedly.

Noyelle's final chapter is an agglomeration of policy recommendations that do not follow from the preceding material and that favor increased government interventions of many types in labor markets. Although Noyelle points to increased labor market competition and acknowledges some of its advantages for both workers and firms, the powerful incentives that markets provide for private investment in human capital are ignored. Noyelle sees employers in the future investing less in their workers' education and training, and he wants increased government spending to fill the anticipated gap. Marsden's concluding passage is also a non sequitur, pointing to the slow progress of European countries toward integration and convergence.

Marsden similarly fails to appreciate the role of private incentives in investments in education, training, and work experience. Marsden also fails to note the recent trends in many European countries away from restrictive policies that increase costs of firing and hiring labor; these trends place greater reliance

on flexible labor markets. Many countries in the 1980s have eased restrictions on employment termination and have reduced government interventions in labor markets. The benefits of such pro-competitive policies have been formally recognized by the Organization for Economic Cooperation and Development and by the 1987 Venice Economic Summit. Marsden reasons that competitive labor markets are unstable and that they are, like public goods, incapable of being sustained without considerable public and institutional support. Labor market interventions, however, as the European experience shows, tend to undermine, rather than enhance, labor market competition and job opportunities for workers.

ARLENE HOLEN

Council of Economic Advisers
Washington, D.C.

SMITH, TONY. *Thinking like a Communist: State and Legitimacy in the Soviet Union, China, and Cuba.* Pp. 244. New York: Norton, 1987. $16.95.

This is a book not intended for specialists and not written by a specialist on the subject. Its purpose is "to provide a brief, readable account of what it means to think like a communist." It succeeds only in falling between a whole series of stools and in rendering a disservice to both the general reader as well as the specialist, to Marxism and anticommunism.

It is an extraordinarily difficult book to review. It is not about the psychology of radicalism or about the sentiments of legitimacy prevailing in the three Communist states of the title. It has a number of glaring factual errors and anachronisms that reduce its credibility. Smith's own ideological position is unclear. He criticizes every Marxist he reviews, yet he also disagrees not only with Western scholars who see communism as mellowing but with its harshest critics, with the result that his message is ambiguous and confusing.

According to Smith, "The structural properties of the communist belief system" are such that Communist thinking proceeds by a logic of its own, independently of the thinkers themselves. This belief system contains "three basic principles," which are a faith in communism, the interpretation of history as class struggle, and membership in the Leninist party. Here Smith is telling us that what chiefly distinguishes Communists is their belief in communism. If this is not sufficient to insult the intelligence of the reader, then I do not know what is. That communism has to do with the advocacy of equality and hostility toward exploitation seems oddly to have escaped Smith's attention.

The structure of Communist thinking, because this is a "hard" rather than "soft" ideology, is characterized as being "comprehensive, adaptable, and directive," as opposed to eclectic, ambiguous, and tentative. Because eclecticism, ambiguity, and tentativeness are never distinguished here from adaptability, this classification is not very helpful in understanding the difference.

An unbreakable and inevitable link, therefore, connects Marx, Lenin, Stalin, Mao, and Castro. It does so because all of them believe in the same basic things: communism, the party, and economic planning. Communism is totalitarianism from start to finish, it fails to recognize the power of the Communist state itself, and no prospect of reform is in sight. Smith's argument is difficult to accept in view of the progressive deradicalization of Marxism and its well-known loss of potency, the splintering of the Communist movement, and the sharp disagreements among Communists: which Communists' word for it should we take that they are thinking like Communists? Obviously, the logic of the Communist belief system is not so strong as to resist fragmentation—which means there is no such logic.

Smith's account of what it means to think like a Communist is itself like communism: it has to be accepted on faith.

BOHDAN HARASYMIW

University of Calgary
Alberta
Canada

OTHER BOOKS

AHMAD, ZAKARIA HAJI, ed. *Government and Politics of Malaysia*. Pp. xi, 178. New York: Oxford University Press, 1987. $32.50.

ALLEN, PHILIP M. *Security and Nationalism in the Indian Ocean: Lessons from the Latin Quarter Islands*. Pp. xi, 260. Boulder, CO: Westview Press, 1987. Paperbound, $37.50.

ALTER, PETER. *The Reluctant Patron: Science and the State in Britain, 1850-1920*. Pp. 292. New York: St. Martin's Press, 1988. $45.00.

ARMSTRONG-WRIGHT, ALAN and SEBASTEIN THIRIEZ. *Bus Services: Reducing Costs, Raising Standards*. Pp. x, 97. Washington, DC: World Bank, 1987. Paperbound, $6.50.

ARTER, DAVID. *Politics and Policy-Making in Finland*. Pp. xii, 255. New York: St. Martin's Press, 1987. $45.00.

BARNETT, DONALD F. and ROBERT W. CRANDALL. *Up from the Ashes: The Rise of the Steel Minimill in the United States*. Pp. xii, 135. Washington, DC: Brookings Institution, 1986. $26.95. Paperbound, $9.95.

BEAULIEU, LIONEL J., ed. *The Rural South in Crisis: Challenges for the Future*. Pp. xvi, 384. Boulder, CO: Westview Press, 1988. Paperbound, $29.85.

BEHRMAN, JACK N. *The Rise of the Phoenix: The United States in a Restructured World Economy*. Pp. xiii, 104. Boulder, CO: Westview Press, 1987. Paperbound, $12.85.

BELL, DANIEL. *The End of Ideology*. Pp. 501. Cambridge, MA: Harvard University Press, 1988. $25.00. Paperbound, $10.95.

BELLAMY, RICHARD. *Modern Italian Social Theory*. Pp. 215. Stanford, CA: Stanford University Press, 1987. $35.00.

BERG, ROLF and ADAM-DANIEL ROTFIELD. *Building Security in Europe: Confidence-Building Measures and the CSCE*. Edited by Allen Lynch. Pp. iii, 181. Paperbound, $11.85.

BERGER, PETER L. and MICHAEL HSIAO, eds. *In Search of an East Asian Development Model*. Pp. xi, 243. New Brunswick, NJ: Transaction Books, 1988. $29.95. Paperbound, $16.95.

BERKOWITZ, BRUCE D. *American Security: Dilemmas for a Modern Democracy*. Pp. xvi, 282. New Haven, CT: Yale University Press, 1988. Paperbound, $12.95.

BLACK, ERIC. *Our Constitution: The Myth That Binds Us*. Pp. xiii, 173. Boulder, CO: Westview Press, 1988. Paperbound, $10.95.

BLOOMFIELD, BRIAN P. *Modelling the World: The Social Constructions of Systems Analysts*. Pp. xiv, 222. New York: Basil Blackwell, 1986. $49.95.

BREMER, STUART A., ed. *The Globus Model: Computer Simulation of Worldwide Political and Economic Developments*. Pp. xxiii, 940. Boulder, CO: Westview Press, 1987. $98.50.

BRODSKY, G.W. STEPHEN. *Gentlemen of the Blade: A Social and Literary History of the British Army since 1660*. Pp. xxxiii, 224. Westport, CT: Greenwood Press, 1988. $39.95.

BROWN, HAROLD, ed. *The Strategic Defense Initiative: Shield or Snare?* Pp. xii, 297. Boulder, CO: Westview Press, 1987. Paperbound, $24.95.

BROWN, RICHARD HARVEY. *Society as Text: Essays on Rhetoric, Reason, and Reality*. Pp. x, 252. Chicago: University of Chicago Press, 1987. Paperbound, $24.95.

BUECHLER, HANS CHRISTIAN and JUDITH-MARIA BUECHLER, eds. *Migrants in Europe: The Role of Family, Labor, and Politics*. Pp. viii, 319. Westport, CT: Greenwood Press, 1987. $55.00.

BURKE, EDMUND, III, ed. *Global Crises and Social Movements: Artisans, Peasants, Populists, and the World Economy*. Pp. xi, 276. Boulder, CO: Westview Press, 1988. $35.00.

BURROWES, ROBERT D. *The Yemen Arab Republic: The Politics of Development, 1962-1986*. Pp. xvii, 173. Boulder, CO: Westview Press, 1987. $29.95.

BUSSON, TERRY and PHILIP COULTER, eds. *Policy Evaluation for Local Govern-*

ment. Pp. xx, 266. Westport, CT: Greenwood Press, 1987. $39.95.

BYRNE, JOHN and DANIEL RICH, eds. *Planning for Changing Energy Conditions.* Vol. 4. Pp. xiii, 300. New Brunswick, NJ: Transaction Books, 1987. Paperbound, $16.96.

CARLSNAES, WALTER. *Ideology and Foreign Policy.* Pp. xi, 234. New York: Basil Blackwell, 1986. $39.95.

CARTER, ALAN B. *Marx: A Radical Critique.* Pp. xiii, 301. Boulder, CO: Westview Press, 1988. $38.50.

CAUTHEN, KENNETH. *The Passion for Equality.* Pp. x, 193. Totowa, NJ: Rowman & Littlefield, 1987. $29.50.

CITINO, ROBERT M. *The Evolution of Blitzkrieg Tactics: Germany Defends Itself against Poland, 1918-1933.* Pp. xiv, 209. Westport, CT: Greenwood Press, 1987. $32.95.

COKER, CHRISTOPHER, ed. *The United States, Western Europe and Military Intervention Overseas.* Pp. x, 190. New York: St. Martin's Press, 1988. $39.95.

COLE, JOSETTE. *Crossroads: The Politics of Reform and Repression 1976-1986.* Pp. xii, 175. Athens: Ohio University Press, 1988. Paperbound, $15.95.

CONROY, MICHAEL E., ed. *Nicaragua: Profiles of the Revolutionary Public Sector.* Pp. xix, 247. Boulder, CO: Westview Press, 1987. Paperbound, $24.50.

COUSINS, NORMAN. *The Pathology of Power.* Pp. 228. New York: Norton, 1987. $15.95.

CURRIE, DAVID P. *The Constitution of the United States: A Primer for the People.* Pp. ix, 150. Chicago: University of Chicago Press, 1988. Paperbound, $6.95.

DAVIS, CHARLES E. and JAMES P. LESTER, eds. *Dimensions of Hazardous Waste Politics and Policy.* Pp. xvii, 256. Westport, CT: Greenwood Press, 1988. $49.95.

DEWITT, JOHN. *Shifting Responsibilities: Federalism in Economic Development.* Pp. x, 149. Washington, DC: National Governors' Association, 1987. Paperbound, $12.50.

DIN, ALLAN M. *Arms and Artificial Intelligence.* Pp. xiv, 229. New York: Oxford University Press, 1988. $54.00.

DOGAN, MATTEI, ed. *Comparing Pluralist Democracies: Strains on Legitimacy.* Pp. xi, 288. Boulder, CO: Westview Press, 1988. $39.95.

DONNELLY, JACK and RHODA E. HOWARD, eds. *International Handbook of Human Rights.* Pp. x, 495. Westport, CT: Greenwood Press, 1987. $65.00.

EDELMAN, MURRAY. *Constructing the Political Spectacle.* Pp. vi, 137. Chicago: University of Chicago Press, 1988. $19.95. Paperbound, $7.95.

EL GUINDI, FADWA. *The Myth of Ritual.* Pp. xvii, 147. Tucson: University of Arizona Press, 1987. $22.95.

ELLISON, HERBERT J., ed. *Japan and the Pacific Quadrille: The Major Powers in East Asia.* Pp. xii, 252. Boulder, CO: Westview Press, 1987. Paperbound, $33.50.

EVANS, ERNEST. *Wars without Splendor: The U.S. Military and Low-Level Conflict.* Pp. xiv, 160. Westport, CT: Greenwood Press, 1987. $27.95.

FAGEN, RICHARD. *Forging Peace: The Challenge of Central America.* Pp. xi, 161. New York: Basil Blackwell, 1987. Paperbound, $7.95.

FENN, RICHARD K. *The Spirit of Revolt: Anarchism and the Cult of Authority.* Pp. vii, 179. Totowa, NJ: Rowman & Littlefield, 1986. $27.95.

FINER, S. E. *The Man on Horseback: The Role of the Military in Politics.* Pp. 342. Boulder, CO: Westview Press, 1988. $42.50.

FLAMM, KENNETH. *Targeting the Computer: Government Support and International Competition.* Pp. xiii, 266. Washington, DC: Brookings Institution, 1987. $31.95.

FREY, LINDA and MARSHA FREY. *Societies in Upheaval: Insurrections in France, Hungary, and Spain in the Early Eighteenth Century.* Pp. xii, 142. Westport, CT: Greenwood Press, 1987. $29.95.

GALL, GILBERT J. *The Politics of Right to Work: The Labor Federations as Special*

Interests, 1943-1979. Pp. xiii, 244. Westport, CT: Greenwood Press, 1988. $39.95.

GAY, PETER. *Voltaire's Politics: The Poet as Realist.* 2d ed. Pp. xv, 417. New Haven, CT: Yale University Press, 1988. $40.00. Paperbound, $15.95.

GEOGHEGAN, VINCENT. *Utopianism and Marxism.* Pp. 164. New York: Methuen, 1988. Paperbound, $10.95.

GINZBERG, ELI, ed. *Medicine and Society: Clinical Decisions and Societal Values.* Pp. xi, 153. Boulder, CO: Westview Press, 1987. $19.95. Paperbound, $8.00.

GITTINGER, J. PRICE et al., eds. *Food Policy: Integrating Supply, Distribution, and Consumption.* Pp. xiv, 567. Washington, DC: World Bank, 1987. Paperbound, $16.50.

GODFRIED, NATHAN. *Bridging the Gap between Rich and Poor.* Pp. xii, 225. Westport, CT: Greenwood Press, 1987. $37.95.

GOLDMAN, RALPH M. and WILLIAM A. DOUGLAS, eds. *Promoting Democracy: Opportunities and Issues.* Pp. xv, 285. Westport, CT: Praeger, 1988. $39.95.

GORDON, MILTON M. *The Scope of Sociology.* Pp. viii, 252. New York: Oxford University Press, 1988. Paperbound, $9.95.

GOULD, LEWIS L. *Lady Bird Johnson and the Environment.* Pp. xv, 312. Lawrence: University Press of Kansas, 1988. $29.95.

GOUREVITCH, PETER. *Politics in Hard Times: Comparative Responses to International Economic Crises.* Pp. 267. Ithaca, NY: Cornell University Press, 1986. $27.50. Paperbound, $12.95.

GRINTER, LAWRENCE E. and PETER M. DUNN, eds. *The American War in Vietnam: Lessons, Legacies, and Implications for Future Conflicts.* Pp. ix, 165. Westport, CT: Greenwood Press, 1987. $37.95.

GUDMONDSON, LOWELL. *Costa Rica before Coffee: Society and Economy on the Eve of the Export Boom.* Pp. xvi, 204. Baton Rouge: Louisiana State University Press, 1986. $30.00.

GUPTA, R. K. *The Great Encounter: A Study of Indo-American Literary and Cultural Relations.* Pp. viii, 276. Riverdale, MD: Riverdale, 1987. $24.00.

GUTTMAN, DAVID, comp. *European American Elderly: An Annotated Bibliography.* Pp. xv, 122. Westport, CT: Greenwood Press, 1987. $35.00.

HAHN, HARLAN and SHELDON KAMIENIECKI. *Referendum Voting: Social Status and Policy Preferences.* Pp. xii, 170. Westport, CT: Greenwood Press, 1987. $35.00.

HAMILTON, NORA et al. *Crisis in Central America: Regional Dynamics and U.S. Policy in the 1980s.* Pp. x, 272. Boulder, CO: Westview Press, 1988. $32.50. Paperbound, $9.95.

HASTINGS, ELIZABETH HANN and PHILIP K. HASTINGS, eds. *Index to International Public Opinion, 1985-1986.* Pp. xxi, 655. Westport, CT: Greenwood Press, 1988. $175.00.

HAWKINS, ANGUS. *Parliament, Party, and the Art of Politics in Britain, 1855-1859.* Pp. xii, 415. Stanford, CA: Stanford University Press, 1987. $38.50.

HEENAN, LOUISE ERWIN. *Russian Democracy's Fatal Blunder: The Summer Offensive of 1917.* Pp. xv, 188. Westport, CT: Praeger, 1987. $37.95.

HERMAN, DONALD L., ed. *Democracy in Latin America: Colombia and Venezuela.* Pp. xi, 344. Westport, CT: Praeger, 1988. $45.95.

HOWE, FREDERIC C. *The Confessions of a Reformer.* Pp. xxii, 352. Kent, OH: Kent State University Press, 1988. Paperbound, $12.00.

HULA, RICHARD, ed. *Market Based Public Policy.* Pp. xiv, 265. New York: St. Martin's Press, 1988. $35.00.

HYMAN, BARRY and R. CHARLES PETERSON, eds. *Electric Power Systems Planning: A Pacific Northwest Perspective.* Pp. xxv, 325. Seattle: University of Washington Press, 1988. $35.00.

JACKSON, THOMAS H. *The Logic and Limits of Bankruptcy Law.* Pp. viii, 287.

Cambridge, MA: Harvard University Press, 1986. $25.00.

KAPUR, HARISH, Ed. *As China Sees the World: Perceptions of Chinese Scholars.* Pp. vi, 239. New York: St. Martin's Press, 1987. $39.95.

KASPERSON, ROGER E. and JEANNE X. KASPERSON, eds. *Nuclear Risk Analysis in Comparative Perspective.* Pp. xiii, 242. Winchester, MA: Allen & Unwin, 1987. $39.95.

KELLY, RITA MAE and JANE BAYES. *Comparable Worth, Pay Equity, and Public Policy.* Pp. xi, 280. Westport, CT: Greenwood Press, 1988. $49.95.

KELMAN, STEVEN. *Making Public Policy: A Hopeful View of American Government.* Pp. x, 332. New York: Basic Books, 1987. $19.95.

KETTERING, SHARON. *Patrons, Brokers and Clients in Seventeenth-Century France.* Pp. x, 322. New York: Oxford University Press, 1986. $36.00.

KIM, ROY and HILARY CONROY, eds. *New Tides in the Pacific: Pacific Basin Cooperation and the Big Four (Japan, PRC, USA, USSR).* Pp. xiii, 216. Westport, CT: Greenwood Press, 1987. $37.95.

KIM, YOUNG YIN and WILLIAM B. GUDYKUNST. *Cross-Cultural Adaptation: Current Approaches.* Pp. 320. Newbury Park, CA: Sage, 1988. $35.00.

KNOLL, ARTHUR J. and LEWIS H. GANN, eds. *Germans in the Tropics: Essays in German Colonial History.* Pp. xiv, 178. Westport, CT: Greenwood Press, 1987. $39.95.

KUMAR, L. C. *The Soviet Union and European Security.* Pp. ix, 329. New York: Advent, 1987. $25.00.

KUMAR, V. SHIV. *U.S. Interventionism in Latin America: Dominican Crisis and the OAS.* Pp. xv, 215. New York: Advent Books, 1987. $22.50.

LACHS, JOHN. *Mind and Philosophers.* Pp. 244. Champaign: University of Illinois Press, 1987. Paperbound, $15.95.

LANE, JAN-ERIK, ed. *Bureaucracy and Public Choice.* Pp. 314. Newbury Park, CA: Sage, 1987. Paperbound, $17.95.

LINDZEY, GARDNER et al. *Psychology.* 3d ed. Pp. xvii, 734. New York: Worth, 1988. $34.95.

LITTELL, NORMAN M. *My Roosevelt Years.* Pp. xxi, 422. Seattle: University of Washington Press, 1988. $35.00.

LOFFE, OLIMPIAD S. and PETER B. MAGGS. *The Soviet Economic System: A Legal Analysis.* Pp. ix, 326. Boulder, CO: Westview Press, 1987. $45.00.

LOPEZ, GEORGE A. and MICHAEL STOHL, eds. *Liberalization and Redemocratization in Latin America.* Pp. xiv, 270. Westport, CT: Greenwood Press, 1987. $39.95.

LOWENTHAL, LEO. *False Prophets: Studies on Authoritarianism.* Pp. ix, 312. New Brunswick, NJ: Transaction Books, 1987. $24.95.

MARGOLIS, HOWARD. *Patterns, Thinking, and Cognition: A Theory of Judgment.* Pp. xii, 332. Chicago: University of Chicago Press, 1988. Paperbound, $15.95.

McGUIRE, PHILLIP. *He, Too, Spoke for Democracy: Judge Hastie, World War II, and the Black Soldier.* Pp. 176. Westport, CT: Greenwood Press, 1988. $35.95.

McNEIL, LINDA M. *Contradictions of Control.* Pp. xxiv, 234. New York: Methuen, 1987. $25.00.

MOYLAN, TOM. *Demand the Impossible: Science Fiction and the Utopian Imagination.* Pp. viii, 242. New York: Methuen, 1987. $18.95.

MULLER, HARALD, ed. *A European Non-Proliferation Policy: Prospects and Problems.* Pp. xxii, 416. New York: Oxford University Press, 1987. $84.00.

NAJITA, TETSUO. *Visions of Virtue in Tokugawa Japan.* Pp. x, 334. Chicago: University of Chicago Press, 1987. $37.50. Paperbound, $14.95.

NANDY, ASHIS. *Traditions, Tyranny, and Utopias.* Pp. xx, 168. New York: Oxford University Press, 1988. $19.95.

NATHAN, RICHARD P. et al. *Reagan and the States.* Pp. xv, 375. Princeton, NJ: Princeton University Press, 1987. $42.50. Paperbound, $12.95.

NELSON, RONALD R. and PETER SCHWEIZER. *The Soviet Concepts of Peace, Peaceful Coexistence and Detente.* Pp. xvi, 177. Lanham, MD: University Press of America, 1988. Paperbound, $14.50.

O'NEILL, ROBERT, ed. *East Asia, the West and International Security.* Pp. viii, 253. Hamden, CT: Archon, 1988. $29.50.

PASCALL, GILLIAN. *Social Policy: A Feminist Analysis.* Pp. 263. New York: Methuen, 1987. $45.00. Paperbound, $14.95.

PERUSSE, ROLAND I. *The United States and Puerto Rico: Decolonization Options and Prospects.* Pp. xiii, 177. Lanham, MD: University Press of America, 1988. Paperbound, $11.75.

PETER, KARL A. *The Dynamics of Hutterite Society: An Analytical Approach.* Pp. xxiii, 232. Lincoln: University of Nebraska Press, $27.50. Paperbound, $16.95.

RAMIREZ, FRANCISCO O., ed. *Rethinking the Nineteenth Century: Contradictions and Movements.* Pp. xix, 222. Westport, CT: Greenwood Press, 1988. $39.95.

RESNICK, STEPHEN A. and RICHARD D. WOLFF. *Knowledge and Class: A Marxian Critique of Political Economy.* Pp. vii, 352. Chicago: University of Chicago Press, 1987. $32.50.

RESSLER, EVERETT M. et al. *Unaccompanied Children: Care and Protection in Wars, Natural Disasters, and Refugee Movements.* Pp. x. 421. New York: Oxford University Press, 1987. $49.95. Paperbound, $18.95.

ROSEFIELDE, STEVEN. *False Science: Understanding the Soviet Arms Buildup.* Pp. xxxvi, 463. New Brunswick, NJ: Transaction Books, 1987. $39.95.

ROSEN, STANLEY. *Hermeneutics as Politics.* Pp. 213. New York: Oxford University Press, 1987. $24.95.

ROSENBAUM, HERBERT D. and ELIZABETH BARTELME, eds. *Franklin D. Roosevelt: The Man, the Myth, the Era, 1882-1945.* Pp. xv, 441. Westport, CT: Greenwood Press, 1987. $49.95.

ROSSITER, CLINTON. *The American Presidency.* Pp. xxix, 266. Baltimore, MD:

Johns Hopkins University Press, 1987. Paperbound, $9.95.

ROTHCHILD, DONALD and NAOMI CHAZAN, eds. *The Precarious Balance: State and Society in Africa.* Pp. x, 357. Boulder, CO: Westview Press, 1988. $32.50.

ROUQUIE, ALAIN. *The Military and the State in Latin America.* Pp. ix, 468. Berkeley: University of California Press, 1988. $37.50.

SAKSENA, K. P. *Cooperation in Development: Problems and Prospects for India and ASEAN.* Pp. 220. Newbury Park, CA: Sage, 1987. $22.50.

SCHALL, JAMES V. *Reason, Revelation, and the Foundations of Political Philosophy.* Pp. 254. Baton Rouge: Louisiana State University Press, 1987. $27.50.

SCHOTT, KERRY. *Policy, Power and Order: The Persistence of Economic Problems in Capitalist States.* Pp. ix, 206. New Haven, CT: Yale University Press, 1988. Paperbound, $10.95.

SENDER, JOHN and SHEILA SMITH. *The Development of Capitalism in Africa.* Pp. xi, 177. New York: Methuen, 1987. Paperbound, $16.95.

SHARABI, HISHAM, ed. *The Next Arab Decade: Alternative Futures.* Pp. xii, 347. Boulder, CO: Westview Press, 1988. $39.95.

SHEERAN, PATRICK J. *Women, Society, the State, and Abortion: A Structuralist Analysis.* Pp. xiv, 168. Westport, CT: Praeger, 1987. $32.95.

SPEARE, ALDEN et al. *Urbanization and Development: The Rural-Urban Transition in Taiwan.* Pp. xxii, 217. Boulder, CO: Westview Press, 1988. Paperbound, $25.00.

STANSELL, CHRISTINE. *City of Women: Sex and Class in New York 1789-1860.* Pp. xiv, 301. Champaign: University of Illinois Press, 1987. Paperbound, $9.95.

STEPHENSON, WILLIAM. *The Play Theory of Mass Communication.* Pp. xxii, 225. New Brunswick, NJ: Transaction Books, 1988. Paperbound, $16.95.

STETSON, DOROTHY McBRIDE. *Women's Rights in France.* Pp. xvi, 239. Westport, CT: Greenwood Press, 1987. $32.95.

STOHL, MICHAEL, ed. *The Politics of Terrorism*. 3d ed. Pp. xviii, 622. New York: Marcel Dekker, 1988. $45.00.

STUART, DOUGLAS T., ed. *Politics and Security in the Southern Region of the Atlantic Alliance*. Pp. ix, 209. Baltimore, MD: Johns Hopkins University Press, 1988. $29.50.

SUGAI, WAYNE H. *Nuclear Power and Ratepayer Protest*. Pp. xi, 475. Boulder, CO: Westview Press, 1987. Paperbound, $33.50.

THUROW, SARAH BAUMGARTNER, ed. *To Secure the Blessings of Liberty: First Principles of the Constitution*. Pp. xi, 331. Lanham, MD: University Press of America, 1988. Paperbound, $16.75.

TIPTON, FRANK B. and ROBERT ALDRICH. *An Economic and Social History of Europe, 1890-1939*. Pp. vii, 323. Baltimore, MD: Johns Hopkins University Press, 1987. $30.00. Paperbound, $9.95.

TIPTON, FRANK B. and ROBERT ALDRICH. *An Economic and Social History of Europe from 1939 to the Present*. Pp. vii, 297. Baltimore, MD: Johns Hopkins University Press, 1987. $32.50. Paperbound, $12.95.

TOPITSCH, ERNST. *Stalin's War: A Radical New Theory of the Origins of the Second World War*. Pp. 152. New York: St. Martin's Press, 1987. $19.95.

VAN VLIET—, WILLEM et al., eds. *Housing and Neighborhoods: Theoretical and Empirical Contributions*. Pp. xii, 319. Westport, CT: Greenwood Press, 1987. $49.95.

VOLCANSEK, MARY L. and JACQUELINE LUCIENNE LAFON. *Judicial Selection: The Cross-Evolution of French and American Practices*. Pp. 168. Westport, CT: Greenwood Press, 1987. $35.00.

WACHTEL, DAVID. *Cultural Policy and Socialist France*. Pp. xvi, 114. Westport, CT: Greenwood Press, 1987. $29.95.

WALBY, SYLVIA. *Patriarchy at Work*. Pp. vii, 292. Minneapolis: University of Minnesota Press, 1987. Paperbound, $16.95.

WEINBERG, LEONARD and WILLIAM LEE EUBANK. *The Rise and Fall of Italian Terrorism*. Pp. xii, 155. Boulder, CO: Westview Press, 1987. Paperbound, $25.00.

WINANT, HOWARD and MICHAEL OMI. *Racial Formation in the United States: From the 1960s to the 1980s*. Pp. xiv, 201. New York: Methuen, 1987. Paperbound, $10.95.

WORCESTER, DON. *The Texas Longhorn: Relic of the Past, Asset for the Future*. Pp. 97. College Station: Texas A&M University Press, 1987. $12.95.

YANARELLA, ERNEST J. and WILLIAM C. GREEN, eds. *The Unfulfilled Promise of Synthetic Fuels*. Pp. xxii, 225. Westport, CT: Greenwood Press, 1987. $39.95.

YOUNG, MICHAEL. *American Dictionary of Campaigns and Elections*. Pp. xi, 246. Lanham, MD: Madison, 1987. $24.95.

ZAPANTIS, ANDREW L. *Hitler's Balkan Campaign and the New Invasion of the USSR*. Pp. vi, 250. Boulder, CO: Eastern European Monographs, 1987. Distributed by Columbia University Press, New York. $25.00.

INDEX

177

NEW from Sage

Handbook of Sociology
edited by NEIL J. SMELSER,
University of California, Berkeley

The **Handbook of Sociology** ushers in a new age of sociological thought and practice.
This long awaited volume synthesizes the field. It provides an original and comprehensive look at this vital discipline— that has not had a new handbook in 25 years...years
in which sociology as a field of study and practice has undergone significant change.
Eminent scholars representing both micro and macro perspectives combine their
expertise to address the diversity, growth, and new developments that characterize the
field of sociology today.

Smelser, one of the leading sociologists of our time, introduces the **Handbook** with a
reflective and insightful essay on the historical developments within the field, the status
of sociology as a discipline, and the future of the profession. The first set of essays offers
definitive statements on theoretical and methodological principles (Wallace, Alexander, Smelser, Rossi, and Berk). Inequality, institutional and organizational settings, and
social process and change are each examined at length by experts in such subfields as
work and labor (Granovetter and Tilly, and Miller), race and ethnicity (See and Wilson),
aging (Riley, Foner, and Waring), environments and organizations (Aldrich and
Marsden), family (Huber and Spitze), medical (Cockerham), world economy (Evans
and Stephens) and more! Offering incomparable depth and breadth, the **Handbook of
Sociology** effectively synthesizes the complex and controversial issues that surround
the discipline of sociology.

*"I have had occasion to read carefully through almost every one of these chapters.
Reflecting Professor Smelser's tasteful coordination, they are a remarkable collection
of ideas and reflection. Never in recent years have I felt so excited by the insights and
potential of work in such diverse areas of our discipline. If you were to buy only one
book this year, you just found it — a powerful review, critique and reconceptualization
of the state-of-the-art; more, an exhilarating look into the future."*
Professor Ronald S. Burt, Columbia University

1988 (Summer) / 832 pages / $89.95 (c)

SAGE PUBLICATIONS, INC.
2111 West Hillcrest Drive,
Newbury Park, California 91320

SAGE PUBLICATIONS, INC.
275 South Beverly Drive,
Beverly Hills, California 90212

SAGE PUBLICATIONS LTD
28 Banner Street,
London EC1Y 8QE, England

SAGE PUBLICATIONS INDIA PVT LTD
M-32 Market, Greater Kailash I,
New Delhi 110 048 India

NEW from Sage

Falling From The Faith
Causes and Consequences of Religious Apostasy
Edited by DAVID G. BROMLEY, *Virginia Commonwealth University*

The place of religion in the social order is undergoing an historic restructuring. Although much has been written about religious affiliation, **Falling From the Faith** is one of the first books to assemble current research by leading scholars about disaffiliation -- the breaking of religious ties. Contributors discuss religious apostasy from mainline churches as well as from alternative religious groups, concentrating on the causes of disaffiliation, the social process involved, and the social and psychological consequences for both individuals and churches.

This well-written overview strikes a balance between quantitative and qualitative research. It calls attention to the diversity of work, the patterning of findings, and issues which require further exploration in this area. **Falling From the Faith** will serve as an indispensable text for courses in religion, and especially as a useful tool for sociologists interested in the study of religion in today's society.

Sage Focus Editions, Volume 95
1988 (Summer) / 272 pages / $35.00 (c) / $16.95 (p)

Cults, Converts & Charisma
The Sociology of New Religious Movements
by Thomas Robbins, *Independent Scholar*

Recent decades have seen a dramatic increase in the number and vitality of new religious movements. In turn, this has given rise to a number of significant questions: How prevalent are new religious movements? To what extent do new religious movements lead to social conflict? Do new religious movements actively attract members from more established religions? In this wide-ranging survey, Robbins analyzes the growth of such movements in the United States and Western Europe, the dynamics of conversion to and defection from movements, patterns of organization and institutionalization, and social controversies over cults.

Written in an engaging style, this insightful volume will be an invaluable resource for all students and researchers of social movements, the sociology of religion, and in religious studies.

1988 (Summer) / 258 pages / $39.95 (c) / $16.50 (p)

SAGE PUBLICATIONS, INC.
275 South Beverly Drive,
Beverly Hills, California 90212

SAGE PUBLICATIONS, INC.
2111 West Hillcrest Drive,
Newbury Park, California 91320

SAGE PUBLICATIONS LTD
28 Banner Street,
London EC1Y 8QE, England

SAGE PUBLICATIONS INDIA PVT LTD
M-32 Market, Greater Kailash I,
New Delhi 110 048 India

NEW from Sage

WOMEN, THE COURTS, AND EQUALITY

edited by LAURA L. CRITES, *Chaminade University of Honolulu*
& WINIFRED L. HEPPERLE, *Director of the Office of Court Services,*
Alameda County, California

Almost ten years ago Crites and Hepperle edited a book that examined the extent of judicial commitment to freeing women from a subordinate role in American society. They concluded that there was sufficient evidence to show that judges were influenced by traditional beliefs regarding the role and nature of women and that these beliefs affected their decisions regarding women.

Women, The Courts, and Equality addresses the same subject in light of developments and events of the last decade in the women's movement. Today more women are employed in a greater variety of jobs because of the equal employment opportunity and affirmative action laws that have passed. Feminist-supported legislation has improved the rights, opportunities, and treatment of women in many areas, including spouse abuse and rape victim testimony. There is also a greater awareness of how prevalent victimization and discrimination against women has been in the U.S. In spite of these gains there have also been setbacks: the defeat of the Equal Rights Amendment, the negative effect of conservatism, the abortion controversy, and reduced emphasis on enforcement of equal opportunity laws.

"In a recent study conducted by the New York Task Force on Women in the Courts it was found that women litigants, attorneys, and court employees are denied equal justice, equal treatment, and equal opportunity—the result of problems rooted in a web of prejudice, circumstance, privilege, custom, misinformation and indifference. This gender bias in our courts is unacceptable . . . this book by Laura Crites and Winifred Hepperle should enlighten the bar, the judiciary, and the general public, thus bringing the problem of gender bias in the courts that much closer to resolution."
—Chief Judge Sol Wachtler,
New York State Court of Appeals

Sage Yearbooks in Women's Policy Studies, Volume 11
1987 (Autumn) / 258 pages / $29.95 (c) / $14.95 (p)

SAGE PUBLICATIONS, INC.
2111 West Hillcrest Drive,
Newbury Park, California 91320

SAGE PUBLICATIONS, INC.
275 South Beverly Drive,
Beverly Hills, California 90212

SAGE PUBLICATIONS LTD
28 Banner Street,
London EC1Y 8QE, England

SAGE PUBLICATIONS INDIA PVT LTD
M-32 Market, Greater Kailash I,
New Delhi 110 048 India

WITHDRAWN